CABINETS
AND
BUILT-INS

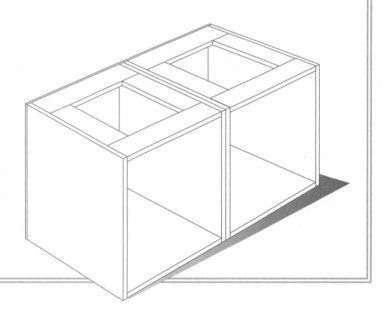

CABINETS
AND
BUILT-INS

A PRACTICAL GUIDE TO BUILDING
PROFESSIONAL-QUALITY CABINETRY

PAUL LEVINE

RODALE PRESS, EMMAUS, PENNSYLVANIA

OUR MISSION

We publish books that empower people's lives.

RODALE BOOKS

The author and editors who compiled this book have tried to make all of the contents as accurate and as correct as possible. Plans, illustrations, photographs, and text have all been carefully checked and cross-checked. However, due to the variability of local conditions, construction materials, personal skill, and so on, neither the author nor Rodale Press assumes any responsibility for any injuries suffered or for damages or other losses incurred that result from the material presented herein. All instructions and plans should be carefully studied and clearly understood before beginning construction.

**Library of Congress
Cataloging-in-Publication Data**

Levine, Paul
   Cabinets and built-ins : a practical guide to building professional-quality cabinetry / Paul Levine
        p.   cm.
   Includes index.
   ISBN 0–87596–590–3   hardcover
   1. Cabinetwork.   I. Title.
TT197.L467   1994
684.1'6—dc20   94–19247
                                    CIP

**Distributed in the book trade
by St. Martin's Press**

2   4   6   8   10   9   7   5   3   1   hardcover

**CABINETS AND BUILT-INS
EDITORIAL AND DESIGN STAFF**

Editor: KENNETH S. BURTON, JR.

Contributing Editor: ROBERT A. YODER

Interior and Cover Designer: FRANK M. MILLONI

Interior Illustrators: MARIO FERRO,
   GLENN HUGHES, AND FRANK ROHRBACH

Interior Photographer: PAUL LEVINE,
   except photos on pages 86 and 268 by
   MITCH MANDEL

Cover Photographer: PAUL LEVINE

Cover Illustrators: LEN EPSTEIN (front),
   GLENN HUGHES (back)

Copy Editor: SARAH DUNN

Administrative Assistant: SUSAN NICKOL

Production Coordinator: JODI SCHAFFER

Indexer: LAURA OGAR

RODALE BOOKS

Executive Editor, Home and Garden:
   MARGARET LYDIC BALITAS

Managing Editor, Woodworking and DIY Books:
   KEVIN IRELAND

Copy Manager, Home and Garden:
   DOLORES PLIKAITIS

Art Director, Home and Garden:
   MICHAEL MANDARANO

Office Manager, Home and Garden:
   KAREN EARL-BRAYMER

Editor-in-Chief: WILLIAM GOTTLIEB

On the cover: A close-up of the
   Cherry Window Seat and Shelves, page 216.

If you have any questions or comments
concerning this book, please write to:
   Rodale Press, Inc.
   Book Readers' Service
   33 East Minor Street
   Emmaus, PA 18098

For Samantha and Jordana,
the lights of my eyes.

CONTENTS

PART 1 TECHNIQUES

PART 2 PROJECTS

ACKNOWLEDGMENTS

To me, reading a book is like having a personal conversation with the author. It's very easy to forget that there was ever anyone else involved. This simply isn't true. It takes a small army of people to put a book together.

Whenever you see my face in a photo, you can bet that my lovely wife, Janet, was on the other end of the camera. While she is not a woodworker, she has plodded through endless piles of sawdust to help me capture on film how I do what I do. Thanks, "podna."

This is my third book on woodworking. I have been very fortunate to meet and work with many wonderful people in the process. The people at Rodale Press are no exception to this.

First among these people is Ken Burton. Ken's patience and endless good humor have made this a much lighter task. Thanks also to Rob Yoder for breaking down my custom profiles into shapes able to be produced with off-the-shelf router bits so my moldings can be made without a shaper.

This book was written on a computer and transferred between my home and Rodale's offices over the phone lines. Thanks to Bob Moran, everything made it through intact with nothing lost into the ether.

Whenever I teach a woodworking class, I always end up learning at least as much from my students as I teach to them. For those who have read my books and shared their thoughts with me, the same is true, and I thank you.

I have taken great care—and received enormous help—in presenting the projects you will find in this book. Every detail has been gone over to make sure that you will have correct drawings and lists of materials to work with. If you find any fault, I apologize in advance.

I hope that you will enjoy using this book.

INTRODUCTION

This is a book about cabinetmaking for the small wood shop. I wrote it for the woodworker who wants to make cabinets for his own home, or for the craftsman running a small, custom shop. I've made my living running this type of operation for more than 20 years.

In this time, I've developed a simple system of putting together cabinets that is practically foolproof. It anticipates mistakes and allows for their easy repair. And, instead of requiring a shop full of expensive machinery, it relies principally on two tools: the table saw and the router. (However, access to a jointer, planer, and drill press will make life easier.)

The system revolves around two joints: a tongue-and-groove joint for assembling cases and a loose tenon joint for putting together door and face frames. The real beauty of this system lies in its versatility. Using these two joinery techniques, you can build practically any kind of cabinet you'd like. This is a little different from the approach many other cabinetmakers take.

Within the world of commercial cabinetmaking, there are two main systems of putting cabinets together: the European—or frameless—system and the traditional—or face frame—system. A different mind-set accompanies each.

With frameless cabinets, the cabinet (or case) is the key feature. Everything from the doors to the drawers is attached directly to the cases. With a face-framed cabinet, the face frame is the central element, and the rest of the pieces (including the case) are attached to it. In industry, these mind-sets are practically exclusive. Frameless manufacturers don't make face frames, and vice versa.

For the small shop, however, there is no reason to be locked into one method or the other. In fact, it is better to become versed in both. That way, you'll have a wider selection of techniques open to you as you sit down to design a set of cabinets. My system allows this kind of flexibility. The simple techniques I use work equally well whether you're building a sleek, Euro-design kitchen or a rich, traditional bathroom vanity.

The book is divided into two sections. The first details the techniques that make up my system. Here, you'll find explicit instructions for everything from cutting the case joinery to hanging doors. Beyond the basics of cabinetmaking, I've included chapters on many of the special techniques I've developed for creating truly unique designs, including custom door panels and handmade pulls.

The second part of the book includes plans for 14 projects I've built using my system. These range from a simple pine storage unit to an elegant cherry kitchen. Some of the plans are for entire projects. You can build these as drawn or modify them to suit your needs.

In the other plans, like those for the kitchens, I only included details of individual cabinets. Since most built-in cabinets are designed to fit specific places, it is unlikely you'd be able to duplicate any of the kitchens in the photos. So the plans show how to build a typical cabinet. You can take that cabinet and design others similar to it to fill your space. By mixing and matching parts of the three kitchen projects, you'll find plans for all the different cabinets I typically include in a kitchen design.

With each project I build, I am continually looking for ways to improve the way I work. Please feel free to experiment with the ideas I've presented. Be sure to let me know if you come up with a better way.

Paul Levine

PART 1
TECHNIQUES

Building Cabinets from the Ground Up

1 MATERIALS

Wood and other components of fine cabinetry

Most of the projects made and methods described in this book involve hardwood and hardwood plywood. The combination of these two materials yields beautiful cabinetwork of lasting quality.

Hardwood is a natural material. There are many species of hardwood and, even within each species, no two boards are ever exactly alike. This irregularity gives hardwood its beauty, but it also makes it a demanding—and somewhat unpredictable—material to work with.

Plywood is a processed product made up of thin layers of wood called *veneers*. These wood plies give plywood many of solid wood's characteristics—strength, relatively low weight, and beauty. But plywood is much more predictable than solid hardwood and is less likely to be affected by changes in humidity. These factors make plywood and hardwood perfect companions for cabinetry.

In addition to these forest products, there are other materials used for the projects in this book. These include granite, limestone, and plastic laminate. While I have a strong bias in favor of natural materials, some man-made goods—like laminate—work well in certain situations.

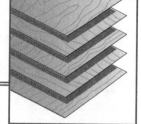

SUPPLIERS

One of the most important concepts of cabinetmaking is to start off with good materials. You may pay more for them, but the time and effort they save you will more than offset the higher price. One of the hardest parts of beginning cabinetmaking may be finding suppliers for the quality materials you need.

Your local lumberyard or home center is probably not the best place to start. The lumber and plywood they sell is generally construction-grade material. Even if you find a larger lumberyard that carries birch plywood or hardwood, it will probably be more expensive than is available elsewhere.

Instead, seek out suppliers in your area who deal specifically in the materials you need. These may include plywood dealers, specialty hardware stores, and lumberyards that cater to local cabinetmakers. Check the Yellow Pages under lumber and hardware. More often than not, you'll end up with the materials you want at a reasonable price. Before you start calling around, let's take a look at the different materials used in cabinetmaking so you'll know what questions to ask.

UNDERSTANDING WOOD

Hardwoods come from deciduous trees. *Softwoods* come from conifers. The terms are more for classification than they are for description: Hardwood is *usually* harder than softwood. Take, for example, a piece of balsa and a piece of southern pine. By definition, balsa is a hardwood, yet you can easily push a finish nail into it. In contrast, you'll have a tough time driving the same nail into the southern pine—a softwood—with a hammer.

So, despite the distinction, there is a good deal of overlap in the relative hardness of both hardwoods and softwoods. The two types of wood also share other characteristics.

Chief among these is wood's tendency to expand and contract with changes in moisture content. If the air surrounding a piece of wood has a lot of moisture in it, as during a humid summer day, the wood will absorb some of that moisture and expand. When the air is dry as it is in a heated house during the winter, the wood will lose moisture and shrink. This wouldn't be all that big a problem if this expansion and contraction were the same in all directions—but it's not. A board moves (expands and contracts) the most across its width, tangent to the tree's annual growth rings, as shown in *Figure 1-1*. It will move less perpendicular to the annual rings. And it moves hardly at all lengthwise.

The problem this poses becomes evident when the movement is restricted. This happens when a piece is joined to another so that it can't expand and contract, as shown in *Figure 1-2*, or when a panel is contained too tightly within a frame. Almost all of traditional cabinetmaking revolves around solving the problems of wood movement.

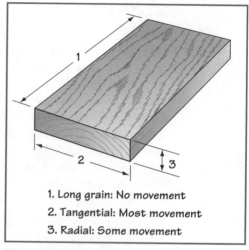

1. Long grain: No movement
2. Tangential: Most movement
3. Radial: Some movement

Figure 1-1. How wood moves

Along with the shared problems come common strengths. Wood is relatively light and strong. In fact, pound for pound, it's as strong as steel—and in some ways it's even better. If you ever see the aftermath of a fire in a building where both wood and steel beams were used, you'll see what I mean. The steel beams will be twisted and bent out of shape, while the wood ones are still intact and structurally sound, although charred.

If you want a better understanding of the material, here are two good books that can help you out: *Wood Handbook: Wood as an Engineering Material* by the Forest Products Laboratory, and *Understanding Wood* by R. Bruce Hoadley.

Hardwood

Furniture makers have long prized hardwoods for qualities such as color, beautiful grain patterns, and durability. When you are planning a project, look for a species of wood that has the right blend of these characteristics. Butternut, for example, can be very beautiful, but it is also very soft. If you use it in a piece of furniture

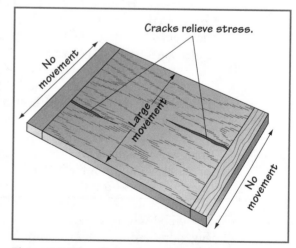

Figure 1-2. The effects of wood movement

that will receive rough use, it may soon be scratched and dented beyond repair. Fortunately, most of the species commonly used for furniture are relatively hard. These include woods like birch, ash, oak, walnut, cherry, maple, and mahogany. In terms of durability, they are all pretty much interchangeable.

There are many other characteristics to look at if you have a specific application in mind. Black walnut, for example, is easy to turn on a lathe. Mahogany resists splitting and doesn't expand and contract as much as some other species do. Chestnut—if you can find it—is very resistant to decay. As you plan your work, take the time to think out the uses (and abuses) it will be up against, and you'll have a much easier time choosing what wood to use.

There is one final consideration you should be aware of, especially if you work with some of the imported species: toxicity. In my shop it can be comical to see everyone start sneezing when we sand mahogany or walnut, but it's no laughing matter when you have a more severe reaction. In my case, the effect of someone sawing a piece of zebra wood is instantaneous: one cut and I can't breathe. Be *very* careful the first time you work with a species new to you.

Sizes. Hardwood is sold by the board foot. A board foot is equal to 144 cubic inches of wood, or a piece of wood 1 inch thick and 12 inches square. It comes in random widths and lengths, with a premium charged for the wider and longer boards. It is usually cut into one of several standard thicknesses measured by quarters of an inch: 4/4 (four-quarter) is 1 inch thick; 5/4 (five-quarter) is 1¼ inches thick, 6/4 (six-quarter) is 1½ inches thick, and 8/4 (eight-quarter) is 2 inches thick. You can sometimes find a place that carries extra-thick stock like 10/4 (ten-quarter; 2½ inches thick), or even 16/4 (sixteen-quarter; 4 inches thick), but these places are rare.

If you buy wood rough (as it comes from the mill), a board will measure its nominal thickness, but you'll lose some of that thickness as you plane it smooth. A 4/4 board will usually yield a piece ¾ to ¹³⁄₁₆ inch thick after you plane it.

Drying methods. Most commercially available hardwood has been *kiln-dried*. Wood, as cut from a tree, is considered wet (or green) and must be dried before it can be used. Drying is done in a large oven called a kiln, where the moisture is cooked out of the wood. Wood can also be *air-dried*. Air drying is stacking the wood in a covered location and allowing the moisture to gradually evaporate. Air-dried lumber is not usually available commercially, although it is commonly sold through the classified ads.

Sources. The best place to get hardwood is from a large lumberyard that specializes in handling hardwood. Unfortunately, most of these yards are not retail oriented. They're wholesalers who generally deal with manufacturers. Their minimum sale is often several hundred board feet. It may take some fast talking to get your foot in the door of such an establishment. Sometimes you can piggyback your order on top of one for a local cabinet shop.

A good hardwood lumberyard can be a real asset. It will mill boards for you, planing them to a required thickness. It can straighten edges and even cut up pieces to specific widths and lengths. Of course, you'll be charged for all of this, but it's a tremendous service if you can't do the work yourself.

Sawmills are another possible source for wood. Buying wood from the operator of a small mill can be a real pleasure, especially if he can tell you about the history of a particular tree. Make sure you're buying dry wood, however. Wet (or green) lumber is unsuitable for cabinet work.

If the mill owner dries his own wood, try to find out how well he knows his trade before parting with too much of your hard-earned money. Drying wood is an art. Improperly done, it can turn a stack of expensive hardwood into firewood. It can be done too quickly, which can cause wood to check internally, a defect known as honeycombing. Or if not dried enough, wood may warp and crack considerably when you bring it into your shop. And, even if wood was initially dried properly, it can be spoiled by improper storage, like being exposed to bad weather. Any or all of these problems can adversely affect the quality of your project.

If you find a mill that sells air-dried lumber, look it over carefully before you buy. Varmints that will be killed by the high heat in a kiln will not be affected by air drying. Find out before you invest your money and labor in a lovely project that may have a short life because of some bug.

Softwood

Much of the general information about hardwood applies to softwood as well. There are some differences, though. Softwood is often preplaned and is sometimes sold by the linear foot rather than the board foot. Many of the lumberyards that sell hardwoods often sell softwoods as well. Along with pine and fir, you may find some less common species that have a lot to offer. Redwood, cypress, several types of cedar, and sugar pine are some of the species my local supplier carries. I tell you this because there are times when I like to use softwood in my work. I have a particular fondness for pine, although I don't like the way it gums up my saw blades and cutters. Perhaps if it weren't so pretty, I'd have an easier time keeping my tools clean.

PLYWOOD

Tip

If your blades get gummed up from cutting resinous woods, clean them with oven cleaner. Just spray it on, wait a few minutes, then rinse it off. For really stubborn deposits, try scrubbing with a brass wire brush.

When I speak of using plywood for cabinet work, I'm talking about hardwood plywood, not the softwood plywood commonly available from lumberyards and home centers. Softwood plywood is a great construction material, but it really has no place in fine woodwork. Hardwood plywood, on the other hand, combines the strength and beauty of solid hardwood with the relative uniformity of machine production.

Plywood was invented in answer to a problem inherent in solid wood: dimensional instability. It provides wide panels with the look, feel, and workability of solid wood without solid wood's expansion and contraction problems.

These stable panels are made up of many thin layers of wood called *veneers*. The veneers are laminated together, with the grain of each successive sheet turned 90 degrees to the previous sheet, as shown in *Figure 1-3*. The resulting sandwich is much more stable than any of the individual layers.

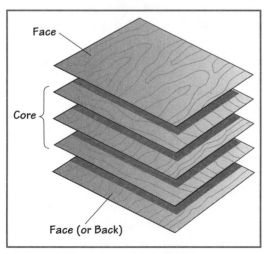

Face

Core

Face (or Back)

Figure 1-3. How plywood is formed

What makes this work is that each sheet of plywood is balanced—it begins with a central layer. This is either one layer of veneer or two veneers laminated together with their grain parallel. From this central layer, the plywood is built up to its final thickness with layers of veneer added equally to each side. As a result, each veneer on one side of the sheet has a corresponding veneer on the other side. The final veneers added are the face veneers. Everything in between them is known as the core.

Core Materials

The core material can be any species of hardwood or softwood, as shown in *Photo 1-1.* One of the most common species used is fir. Unfortunately, fir-core plywood is not a good choice for cabinet work. I avoid it whenever possible.

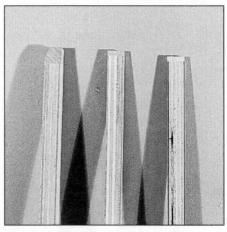

The reason fir doesn't make a very good core has to do with the way a tree grows. During a growing season, a tree will add a layer of wood all around its trunk. If you look at the end of a tree trunk, you can see these layers, called the annual rings. Usually, each ring will have a wider, light band and a darker, narrow band. The light band is spring-wood, grown during the tree's growth spurt in the spring after the tree comes out of dormancy. This growth is generally less dense than the

Photo 1-1. Hardwood plywood is commonly available with either a hardwood or a softwood core. Plywood with a softwood core, *right*, is generally of a lesser quality.

darker summerwood. In fir, this difference in density is greater than in many other trees. So, as fir is worked, the softer spring-wood will compress and wear away faster than the summerwood, leaving the surface wavy. These waves will telegraph right through a face veneer, leaving it rippled as well.

Poplar and lauan, both even-grained hardwoods, are much better choices for core material. They present a smooth surface for the face veneers and are also lighter than fir. You'll appreciate this when you go to install a kitchen's worth of cabinets.

Face Materials

With hardwood plywood, the face veneers are usually different species of wood than the core veneers, and they are usually thinner, as well. The reasoning behind this is economics: The thickness of a piece of plywood is built up from a cheaper species of wood, then the visible surfaces are made from a higher-priced "show" material. These face veneers are cut thinner to get more pieces from a log. Thus, when you buy a piece of oak plywood, you're actually getting a sheet made up of poplar veneers (or some other secondary species) sandwiched between two thin layers of oak veneer.

Plywood faces are graded as to their quality. The very best

veneers are AA, followed by A, B, C, and so on. The grades are determined by the type of wood figure, width of the veneers, and other features. Most plywood has one good face and a lesser-grade back. Such a piece might be grade AB or A2.

One important factor in determining the veneer's grade is the way it was cut. The face veneer for plywood can be produced in one of two ways: rotary cut or plain sliced. With *rotary cutting,* the veneer is cut from a log much like paper towels are pulled from a roll. The log, of course doesn't have perforations; the veneer comes off as a continuous sheet and is cut to size in the process. With *plain slicing* (or flat slicing, as the process is also called), the veneer is cut from the log like very thin, individual boards. Each process yields veneer with a very distinct look.

Photo 1-2. The face of this piece of plywood was rotary cut. I use plywood like this for case interiors, but I find it unappealing for a visible surface.

Rotary cutting peels wood off the tree the way it grew, in concentric rings. It tends to exaggerate the grain, producing wild patterns, as shown in *Photo 1-2.* I find this look distracting and only use plywood with rotary-cut faces for case interiors, or not at all. For exterior surfaces, I use only plywood with plain-sliced faces. The grain pattern on a plain-sliced veneer is the same as that of a piece of solid wood, as shown in *Photo 1-3.*

Just as you can buy quarter-sawn lumber, you can get plywood with quarter-sawn veneer faces. In fact, depending on how much money you're willing to spend, you can special-order plywood with almost any type of face to suit the look you're after. One standard way to get it is with faces that are cut from the same tree. The faces will be numbered in consecutive sheets so that you can have the same appearance throughout the whole project. Some suppliers stock the plywood this way

Photo 1-3. The drawer fronts of this little cabinet are faced with plain-sliced veneer. Its appearance is similar to that of solid wood. I prefer this look for the visible surfaces of my projects.

and you can just walk in and buy a few sheets; other places may have to special-order it for you. If you're dealing in small quantities, you'll probably end up buying a segment of a larger sequential group, and your sheets may be numbered something like 36, 37, and 38.

Buying Plywood

Most plywood comes in sheets 4 feet wide × 8 feet long, with the face grain running the length of the panel. It is customary to state the size of the panel by using the cross-grain dimension first. Also available are 8 × 4-foot sheets—these have the face grain running across the width of the panel. Called *counterfront*, these panels are used where a wide expanse of vertical grain is desired.

There are a few types of plywood that are commonly available in other sizes. Baltic birch (also called Russian or Finnish birch) plywood comes in 5 × 5-foot sheets. This imported material is made up entirely of birch veneers and is a pleasure to work with. A lot of craftsmen use it to make jigs or as a core when they're gluing up their own veneered panels. Other plywoods, such as aircraft and some marine plywoods, are often stocked in 4 × 16-foot sheets. These are great if you need the extra length but are not worth the added expense for most cabinetwork.

Plywood comes in many thicknesses, ranging from $\frac{1}{16}$ inch through $1\frac{1}{4}$ inches, as well as some metric sizes. The thinner sizes are often used for bending. For the most part, I use $\frac{3}{4}$-inch plywood for case tops, bottoms, and sides, and $\frac{1}{4}$-inch plywood for case backs.

Most projects in this book use birch AB plywood with a poplar core. I try to get only plain-sliced face veneers, but rotary-cut will do for cabinet interiors. This plywood is carried by many large lumberyards and can usually be special-ordered from others. If necessary, you can use fir-core birch plywood, but I really only recommend it for cabinet interiors. As an alternative, you can use lauan-faced plywood, if you can find it. Lauan is a very even-grained imported wood (sometimes called Philippine mahogany). It used to be used extensively to make hollow-core doors, so you may already be familiar with what it looks like. Unfortunately, luaun has been over-harvested, and the supply is not as plentiful as it once was.

CASE JOINERY

2

Behind all that
beautiful woodwork

There was a time when I carefully measured for each case, laying out cut lines with a fine-point pencil and painstakingly rechecking each measurement. It would have been inconceivable then to make a case without a tape measure.

The fact of the matter is that now I rarely measure when building a cabinet case. Building cases has become so routine that it is hard to imagine that I ever chose to build them another way. The former reliance on a tape measure was, in part, a weakness. My present habits reflect confidence in a solid but simple method of work. It's so simple, in fact, that by the end of this chapter you'll be ready to build your first cabinet.

Why is it so easy? With rare exceptions, I make all of my cases the same way. True, some have face frames and others don't. But whether framed or frameless, the basic case is the same—a simple box with tongue-and-groove joints.

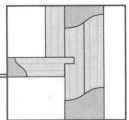

SOLID WOOD CONSTRUCTION

Building cabinets from solid wood goes back to the beginnings of woodworking, when it was the only method available. Today, with the wide availability of plywood and other sheet stock, it is not as common, particularly within the cabinet industry. But for the individual craftsman, it is still an option in many situations.

I won't kid you, however. Working in solid wood has its limitations and it is not my preferred method. Not only is it time-consuming, but you have to deal with wood's tendency to move with changes in humidity. I'd rather use plywood for the cases and save the solid wood for the doors and drawer faces, where it will really show. Still, I use solid wood casework on occasion when a project merits it. Take a look at the Pine Shelving System on page 166 and the Bookshelves in Stained Oak on page 260, and you'll see what I mean.

Should you choose to go this solid route, there are a couple of things to keep in mind. Cabinets up to about 12 inches deep can be made simply from panels of solid wood using the tongue-and-groove joint I describe later in this chapter. Once you've made the panels, they can be treated just as though they were pieces of plywood. For deeper cabinets, things get more complicated. Wide solid-wood panels just don't stay flat enough to join with a tongue and groove. So, if you want to make a deep case from solid wood, you'll have to change the way you make up the panels. See "Frame-and-Panel Construction" on the opposite page.

Stock Preparation

Tip

To flatten a board, you must first run it over a jointer. Once the board has one flat side, you can then bring it to thickness on the planer. A surface planer alone will not remove the warp from a board—it will only make the board thinner.

Before you can build anything from solid stock, it has to be prepared. First, you have to surface the lumber to flatten it and get it to the right thickness. Then, you have to edge-glue boards to make up panels wide enough for your cabinets. Finally, you have to sand all the panels to prepare them for finishing.

You can eliminate a good deal of this work if you buy your stock preplaned from the lumberyard. Make sure they run the boards over a jointer before they plane them. Simply running a board through a planer will not make it flat, it will only make it thinner. To flatten a board, it must be jointed first.

If you have the machinery, you can save a lot

FRAME-AND-PANEL CONSTRUCTION

The way old-time craftsmen built cabinets with solid wood was to make up each separate part of a case as a frame-and-panel unit. These assemblies were very strong, while accommodating any expansion or contraction in the wood. You can still do this today. Just make up the sides for your cases as frames and panels. For a complete discussion of making frames and panels, see Chapter 4. Once glued together, you can treat these assemblies just like pieces of plywood.

FRAMES FOR TOPS

I've even found a way to incorporate this technique into the way I make my standard plywood cases. I use a frame instead of plywood for the top of my base cabinet cases, as shown in the photo. This makes each case lighter and it provides access to the inside for installing drawer slides and other hardware. As an added bonus, the frame is a good handle, making it much easier to move the case around the shop. I make these frames from poplar, a light, inexpensive hardwood that comes in wide, clear boards.

Once the cabinets are installed, these top frames are under very little stress, so I don't make them the way I make my regular frames, which must be strong. Instead I use the quickest, easiest joint I know, the biscuit joint. For more information on cutting these joints, see "Biscuit Joints" on page 48.

The key to using a frame in place of the plywood top is in the way you think about

it. Make all the frames before you cut the plywood for the cases. The frames should be slightly oversize, about ¼ inch in both length and width. From this point on, treat them just like pieces of plywood, cutting and joining them with the rest of the sheet stock. One thing you should check is whether the frames are square. Should you need to square one up, see "Squaring Frames and Panels" on page 52. Another thing to keep in mind is that if the frames are not made exactly the same thickness as the plywood, you will have to reset the fence while grooving the case sides. I usually assume this and reset the saw fence for this cut. Once you make this adjustment, mark the sides for top and bottom, as there will now be a difference.

Lately, I've been using a frame instead of plywood for my case tops . The resulting case is lighter and easier to handle.

of money by buying rough-sawn wood and planing it yourself. Begin by running the face of each board over a jointer. Keep pressure on the infeed table as you start the cut. As soon as you get 8 to 10 inches of the board on the outfeed table, transfer your pressure there. The flat surface created by the cutters will sit flat on the outfeed table. This keeps the cut in the same plane as the board continues across the jointer.

Joint one face of each board you'll be using. After you've jointed the faces, send your boards through the planer. Run all the boards through at the same setting; then set the planer to cut slightly thinner and run all the boards through again. Make sure that all the boards go through the planer at the same final setting so they will all be exactly the same thickness.

Once both sides of the boards are surfaced, run one edge across the jointer to straighten it. Rip the opposite edge to make it parallel with the first. Joint the sawed edge to remove any saw marks, and you're ready to glue the boards into panels. Make the panels about ½ inch oversize in both length and width. You will trim them later.

After the glue dries, sand the panels. Start with a belt sander, running it back and forth along the board to remove all the machine marks and glue squeeze-out. Keep the sander moving. If you stop, you're likely to sand a hollow into the panel that will be difficult to fix. After belt sanding, switch to an orbital sander to finish up.

If you have a number of panels to sand, you might want to pay to have them sanded. Find a cabinet shop that has a wide belt sander. The wide belt sander is essentially a planer that has a wide sanding belt instead of blades. The wood is fed across a flat bed that can be raised or lowered in relation to the belt. As boards or panels pass under the belt, they are sanded flat and smooth, much flatter than you are likely to get them when sanding by hand.

These large machines are expensive—often prohibitively so, even for a professional shop. Because they're so expensive, shops that have them will often take in outside jobs to help pay for them. The hourly rate is high—$40 to $50 an hour—but these machines can do an awful lot of sanding in an hour. Sanding all the panels for a kitchen may not even take that long. When you consider the time, effort, and materials you'd use to sand the panels yourself, paying for an hour of sanding is a bargain.

Tip

As you make a cutting list, group similar-size parts together. Then you can make all the needed cuts with the same setup.

Once all the panels are sanded, you can start cutting them to size. Plan your work in batches so you're cutting parts with similar sizes in groups. At this point, you're working with wide, flat panels that are slightly oversize. As you're about to see, the same thing happens when you work with plywood. The tips I give you below for handling plywood work equally well for solid wood, so read on.

PLYWOOD CONSTRUCTION

Given a choice, I'll build my cases from plywood rather than solid stock. Why plywood? It's dimensionally stable and it comes in wide sheets that are already milled to thickness. So making wide case parts and countertops is a snap. As far as I'm concerned, plywood's the perfect foundation for quality work.

But plywood has some disadvantages, too. Its size makes it hard to handle. And when viewed from the edge, you can see the layers of wood that make up the sheet. I solve the first problem by cutting all the parts slightly oversize, then trimming them to size. This allows me to work with smaller pieces when making the finish cuts. It also lets me trim off the often-damaged factory edges. I solve the second problem by gluing a piece of solid wood to the edge of the plywood.

Let's say I'm cutting the sides for a set of base cabinets from standard 4 × 8 sheets of plywood. Let's also say that there's some edge banding on the front of the cabinet to hide the plies. Base cabinets are 24 inches deep, so I'll want to cut the plywood 23½ inches wide, leaving ½ inch for the back and the edge banding. First, I rip each 4 × 8 sheet of plywood in half, giving me two pieces, each roughly 24 inches wide. Until the edges are covered with either edge banding or a face frame, they are fragile, so I try to protect them. Coming off the saw, I lean the pieces against a wall with the factory edges down on the floor. If I have to support them on a freshly cut edge, I first lay down some scrap stock to keep the edge off the floor. Two 1 × 3 × 12s set perpendicular to the wall support all the stock for a large project.

After all the sheets are ripped in half, I put them through the saw again, cutting off the factory edge and taking them down to 23½ inches wide. Ideally, none of the pieces I am working with will have a factory edge when I am through cutting. Why do I go to this trouble? There are several reasons.

First, plywood is a wood product. Just like lumber, it expands and contracts with changes in humidity. It is restrained from moving because the plies are glued at a 90 degree angle to one another. Nonetheless, the wood moves, especially at the edges where the plies are exposed. The plies can't go far, but they move enough to leave an uneven edge that would ruin a seam.

Second, it would be something of a miracle if a piece of plywood left the factory and arrived at my shop undamaged. With all the handling plywood goes through, the edges are bound to be bruised somewhere along the way. Even if the damage is superficial, it still detracts from the finished piece.

Finally, I remove the factory edges to promote consistency. When a piece of plywood is sanded at the factory, the edges are left marginally thinner than the middle. This slight difference can make a joint tight at one end and sloppy at the other. I find the slight amount of plywood I waste a small price to pay for the benefits of working with freshly cut edges.

Once I have all the plywood cut to width, I then cut it to length. At this point, the pieces become much smaller and easier to handle. I lay them flat in piles to prepare for the next step.

> **Tip**
>
> Cut your plywood wider than necessary, with the factory edges against the rip fence. Cut each piece to size by trimming off the factory edge. You'll get fresh, unblemished edges for joinery and glue-ups.

CUTTING THE JOINT

I make my cabinets with a tongue-and-groove joint, as shown in *Figure 2-1*. The sides are grooved, and then the top and bottom are rabbeted to create tongues that fit in the grooves. With modern glues, the joint is also strong—especially for built-ins, which gain strength once installed. All the cuts are made on the table saw with a dado blade. Make sure the dado blade fits through the throat plate before you begin. If necessary, make up your own throat plate, as shown in "Shop-Made Throat Plates" on page 20.

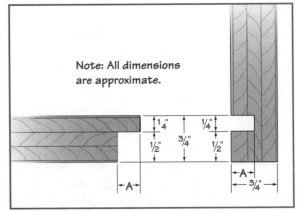

Note: All dimensions are approximate.

Figure 2-1. The tongue-and-groove joint

Setting Up to Cut the Groove

There are three settings needed to make the groove—the width of the groove, the depth of the groove, and the distance between the groove and the edge of the stock. I worry about each setting one at a time.

The width of the groove. The groove should be about ¼ inch wide. I cut it with the two outside cutters of a carbide dado head. If you use a wobble dado, set it for about ¼ inch. Whatever you do, don't take out the tape measure—just eyeball it. If it is a little wider or narrower than ¼ inch, it doesn't matter. You'll be cutting the tongue to match.

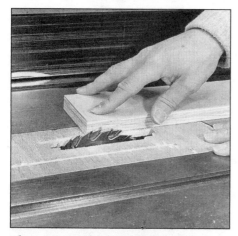

Photo 2-1. Set the dado height to cut halfway through the plywood. Don't measure, just adjust the blade until it looks right. That will be close enough.

The depth of the groove. The depth of the groove is controlled by the blade height. To set the height, simply place a piece of scrap plywood next to the blade. Plywood varies slightly in thickness from batch to batch, so select a scrap from the batch you're using. Adjust the height of the blade until the top appears to be centered in the middle ply, as shown in *Photo 2-1*. Sure, this won't be dead on, but think about it. If the blade appears to be halfway up the middle ply, and if this ply is ⅛ inch thick, chances are you won't be off by more than ¹⁄₃₂ inch. Make a trial cut in the scrap stock. If necessary, raise or lower the blade until you are satisfied with the depth of cut.

The position of the groove. In the best of all worlds, you position the groove so the top and bottom of the cabinet are flush with the cabinet sides. This, however, is the real world. No matter how carefully you make the setup, the last place these pieces will end up is dead flush.

In the real world, the sides often end up short of the top, as shown in *Figure 2-2A* on page 18. If you end up in this situation, you will have to belt sand the entire case top to make things flush. This is not one of your brighter prospects. It is much better to intentionally err on the safe side. I opt to make all the joints so the sides extend slightly beyond the top, as shown in

Figure 2-2B. Then, after the cases are assembled, I trim the edges flush with a belt sander.

Here's how I position the groove to get an overhang. The groove's location is determined by the rip fence. Unplug the saw, then move the fence over until it is about ½ inch from the blade. Take a square piece of plywood and hold it against the fence over the dado blade. For best results, use a cutoff from the plywood you'll be using. Slide it down until the plies touch the top of the blade. Then rub your index finger along the face of the scrap, as shown in *Photo 2-2.* You should feel the face of the blade sticking out slightly beyond the scrap, as shown in *Figure 2-3.* If the position isn't right, unlock the fence and shift it one way or another until you feel just a touch of blade beyond the scrap.

Once the fence is set, check the setup. First, hold a piece of scrap flat on the saw and cut a test groove. Hold the test piece against the edge of a second piece of plywood, as shown in *Figure 2-4.* If you've set the fence correctly, the groove will be just barely visible, as shown. The blade is now set and ready to cut grooves in the sides.

Cutting the Groove

Cut the groove with the stock flat on the saw. The groove goes on the inside face of the cabinet side—plan ahead and choose which face that will be. Subsequent work usually hides the outside of the cabinet, so I generally pick the

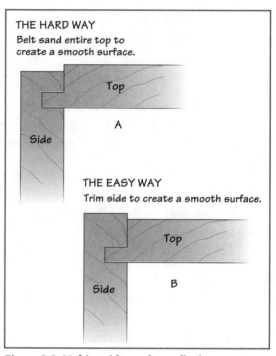

THE HARD WAY
Belt sand entire top to create a smooth surface.

Top

A

Side

THE EASY WAY
Trim side to create a smooth surface.

Top

Side

B

Figure 2-2. **Making sides and tops flush**

Photo 2-2. **Check the fence position with a piece of the actual stock you're using—and your finger. You should just barely be able to feel the blade protruding beyond the edge of the plywood. Be sure to unplug the saw while making this adjustment.**

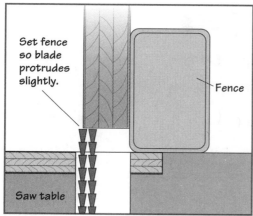

Set fence so blade protrudes slightly.

Fence

Saw table

Figure 2-3. Setting groove position

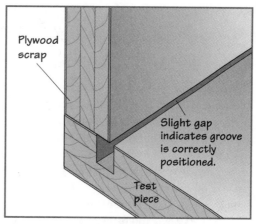

Plywood scrap

Slight gap indicates groove is correctly positioned.

Test piece

Figure 2-4. Checking finished groove

best face for the inside. If you are exposing the outside face in the finished product, then put the best face outward.

Once you've set up the fence, cut all the grooves in all the sides. Cutting them in a batch ensures that they are uniform and that all the cases will be the same height. When making the cut, don't hurry. You're cutting across the face grain of the veneer. Even with a sharp blade, you'll have some tear-out if you push too fast. Push down on the plywood so it's flat on the table while making the groove. This helps to ensure the groove is the same depth all the way across the piece.

Photo 2-3. **As you cut the pieces, stack them up in a neat pile. That way, you'll be able to tell at a glance whether you've made all the necessary cuts before you tear down a setup.**

A typical cabinet side gets two grooves: one at the top and one at the bottom. I stack the sides in a neat pile after cutting the grooves, as shown in *Photo 2-3.* This way I can see right away if there is a groove that I failed to make or if I erred making a piece. Once I've cut all the grooves, the next step is to make the matching tongues. For now, leave the table saw setup exactly as it is.

Setting Up to Cut the Tongue

In my early cabinetwork I relied on my materials being flat and uniform in thickness. I used to run plywood over a dado blade to cut a tongue. I'd lay the plywood flat on the saw; raise the blade to remove

the PROFESSIONAL view

SHOP-MADE THROAT PLATES

These days, I rarely use the throat plate that came with my saw. Instead, I prefer to make my own from ½-inch plywood. I usually make up a dozen or so at a time so I always have an extra on hand. By making my own, I can control the gap around the blade, keeping it to a minimum for splinter-free cuts.

Start by ripping the pieces to width. Use your existing plate to set the fence. Then trace the shape onto the blanks and cut them to shape on the band saw. Sand them to fit in the saw's recess.

To work perfectly, the throat plate must be adjusted until it is

perfectly level with the table surface. To adjust my wood plates, I thread allen-head set screws through them, as shown. The plates are then easily adjusted from above the table with an allen wrench.

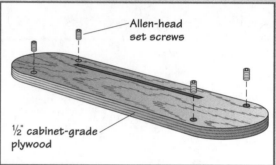

Allen-head set screws

½" cabinet-grade plywood

½ inch of stock, and make a cut, as shown in *Figure 2-5*. In theory, the resulting tongue was ¼ inch thick. In fact, I learned a painful lesson: Plywood is rarely uniform in thickness. If the plywood was thinner than ¾ inch, the resulting tongue was too thin. If the plywood was thicker than ¾ inch, the tongue was too thick. In a joint intended to be snug, either flaw is unacceptable, and too thin is fatal.

As I became increasingly frustrated with the varying thickness of plywood, I developed a better method for cutting the tongues. I now cut tongues with the stock held on edge. This way, the thickness of the tongue is determined directly by the fence setting, not by the thickness of the plywood.

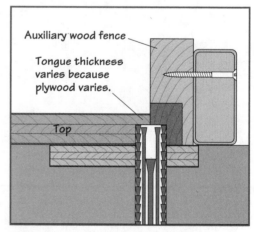

Auxiliary wood fence

Tongue thickness varies because plywood varies.

Top

Figure 2-5. **Cutting tongues horizontally**

Photo 2-4. The length of the tongue should be slightly shorter than the depth of the groove. Otherwise, imperfections in the groove may prevent you from pulling the joint closed.

There are two important measurements when cutting the tongue—length and thickness. Before you make any adjustments, however, reset the dado blade to cut a ¾-inch-wide groove. Don't change the height of the blade just yet. You'll adjust it later—but when you do, you'll need to know the exact height it was when you cut the groove.

The length of the tongue. The length of the tongue is important. If it's too long, the joint won't close properly. In fact, the joint may not close even if the groove and tongue match perfectly. Debris in the groove—or even excessive glue—can effectively make the groove shallower. I compensate by making the tongue slightly shorter than the depth of the groove, as shown in *Photo 2-4*.

Making a short tongue has a second advantage. Plywood is almost always warped. If a case side is warped and you don't press it completely flat while cutting the groove, then the groove's depth will vary. By making the tongue shorter, you can avoid this difficulty and have nice, tightly closed joints.

The length of the tongue is controlled by the height of the blade. Setting the height is a simple matter. Remember that when you changed the width of cut on the dado blade, I said to leave it at its old height. Now, if you drop the blade a trifle—about $\frac{1}{32}$ inch—the height will be perfect. Don't bother with measuring. On most saws, mine included, an eighth of a turn, more or less, will move the blade about $\frac{1}{32}$ inch.

The thickness of the tongue. When you're cutting plywood on edge, the thickness of the tongue is determined by the space between the fence and the blade, as shown in *Figure 2-6*.

Plan for mishaps. Cutting a tongue slightly too short for its mating groove can avoid problems caused by a little dust left in the groove.

Distance between blade and fence ensures uniform tongue thickness.

Top

Table saw fence

Figure 2-6. Cutting tongues vertically

Don't worry about the measurement—just make sure that the tongues fit snugly in the grooves. To achieve this, you must make what I call a "Goldilocks" cut—not too wide, and not too narrow, but ju-u-ust right. If your fence is feisty, getting it set right may be a tad tedious, but with a little patience you'll have a perfect joint. I have a Delta Unifence, which is very easy to adjust because it stays consistently parallel to the blade. It makes getting this setup right a breeze.

First, set the fence to cut slightly more than ¼ inch. Don't reach for the tape measure. You haven't used it yet and you're not going to here, either. The goal at this point—believe it or not—is to make the tongue *too big*. I set the fence for ¹⁄₃₂ inch more than ¼ inch, according to the indicator on my fence (which is pretty accurate). If your indicator isn't accurate, set the fence ⁵⁄₁₆ inch from the blade to be safe.

Next, make a trial cut with scrap stock. Try the resulting tongue in one of the grooves. If you did everything right, it won't fit—it's too big. Reset the fence to make a slightly smaller tongue. Take the same piece of stock and run it through again. Test it in the groove.

Continue with this procedure until you can just slip the tongue into the groove with light pressure. Resist the temptation to move the fence too much at one time. If you do, the tongue will be too small, and you'll have to start over again with a fresh piece of stock. Be patient and the setting will come after a few passes. It rarely takes me more than two or three settings.

Cutting the Tongue

Once you have the right setting, cut all the tongues. Run the pieces through on edge, as shown in *Photos 2-5 and 2-6*. This procedure is not as bad as you might think. Hold the piece against the fence with your left hand, while your right hand stabilizes and pushes the piece past the blade. For very long pieces, this will take getting used to. You might even want to attach a tall auxiliary fence to your rip fence for

Photo 2-5. Once you get the fence positioned, cut all the tongues by running the pieces through on edge. Press the piece tightly to the fence with your left hand as your right hand pushes it past the blade.

Photo 2-6. As you finish the cut, shift your left hand so it can still keep the piece pressed tightly to the fence.

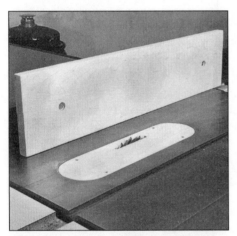

Photo 2-7. While I usually use my standard fence for this operation, you may find it easier to cut pieces on edge using a tall auxiliary fence. Just screw or bolt it in place and make sure it is square to the table.

added support, as shown in *Photo 2-7.* If you do use an auxiliary fence, be sure to make *all* the cuts using it, even those on the short pieces. This will save you from having to make two setups. For alternatives to cutting long pieces on edge, see "Casework Alternatives" on page 28.

Make the cuts with the good side of the plywood toward the fence. This way the good side will end up inside the cabinet, rather than hidden underneath it or covered by the countertop.

PUTTING IT ALL TOGETHER

Once all the parts are cut and the joints are made, sand the inside surfaces. The inside corners, in particular, will be too hard to reach after assembly.

I sand with 80- or 100-grit paper, and then 150-grit, with an orbital sander. When I'm done sanding, I blow off the sheets with high pressure air, a blessing of the system I installed in my shop. If you can add a small compressor to your shop, it is a big help. There are new, small, pancake-type compressors that aren't expensive and are adequate for most of your needs.

Once sanded, the pieces are ready to glue up. Take the pieces for one case and examine them for any splinters or debris that will prevent the joints from closing. Also look for hairs left over from cross-grain cutting with the dado blade. If these didn't come off with the initial sanding, give the piece another quick once-over with the sander. Once the case is glued up, the splinters will be in the corners and hard to reach.

Tip

An air compressor is an invaluable piece of machinery. You can use it to spray finish, dust off projects after sanding, shoot fasteners, and more. The time you'll save will quickly pay for the investment.

CASE JOINERY

The Glue-Up

Glue-ups can be stressful, with so much work on the line. But they don't have to be. With my system of building cases, clamps are not required in most instances, and the assembly can be done single-handedly. Where I assemble the cases depends mostly on their size. With a large unit like a kitchen pantry, I work right on the floor with a couple of plywood strips underneath to protect the outside of the cabinet. Small cases I put together on my bench. For medium-size cabinets, which constitute the majority of my business, I work on the Black and Decker Workmate, an adjustable-height stand.

Photo 2-8. **With a steady squeeze, run a bead of glue along each side of the groove.**

For the most part, the outsides of the cases will be hidden after installation. This allows me to use nails or screws to hold the parts together while the glue dries. Where the outside of a case will be seen, I use clamps instead. After joining the sides to the top and bottom, I attach the back, which squares the whole assembly.

Glue the first side. Start with one side of the case lying flat. Apply a bead of glue to each side of the top groove. Brace the tip of the glue bottle on one edge of the groove. Run the tip against the other edge so the groove guides you, as shown in *Photo 2-8.* Run a bead on each side of the groove. Apply a third bead on the outside flat where the shoulder of the adjoining piece will land, as shown in *Figure 2-7.* All this glue may seem like overkill, but I've never had a piece fall apart from lack of glue.

Once you've applied the glue, fit the top into its groove. Align the edges of the pieces before seating the top completely. (Alignment gets cumbersome once you've assembled the pieces.) With the pieces

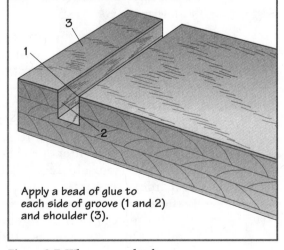

Apply a bead of glue to each side of groove (1 and 2) and shoulder (3).

Figure 2-7. **Where to apply glue**

aligned, press the top down into the groove. Repeat the process and fit the bottom into its groove.

If, despite your best efforts, the pieces are in poor alignment after they're seated, you can tap them into place with a rubber mallet. If a couple light taps don't do the trick, adjust them with a pipe clamp. When clamping, protect the edges of the plywood with wood blocks. Place one block on the side and the other on the top or bottom, as shown in *Photo 2-9.* Draw up the clamp slowly until the pieces come into

alignment. Resist the temptation to take your mallet and pound the pieces into submission. You will likely damage the edges of the plywood. Yup, I've done that.

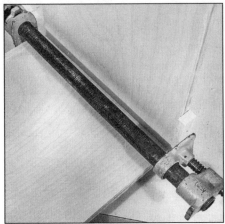

Photo 2-9. If you have to shift a side after it is seated in its groove, apply pressure with a pipe clamp. Be sure to protect the delicate edges with scrap blocks.

Glue the second side. Apply glue to both grooves on the second side. Now comes the tough part. Quickly flip the second side over and onto what you've assembled so far. Hold the piece at an angle and start the corner of the first tongue into its groove. Then get the second tongue started and flop the side down flat. This must all happen very quickly or the glue will drip and make a mess. Once the tongues are started into their grooves, they keep the glue from running.

Adjust the front-to-back alignment on one joint and use a mallet to drive the side down over the tongue. Then align and seat the second joint. Adjust the edge alignment with a pipe clamp, if necessary. If the side is a finished side that will show in the finished project, protect it with a scrap of plywood as you drive the joints home.

Fasten the unit together. Once you've assembled the top, bottom, and sides, use mechanical fasteners to hold the case together while the glue dries. Since they're so fast and convenient, I use pneumatically driven staples most of the time, as shown in *Photo 2-10* on page 26. Before I installed my compressor, I used 1½-inch-long screws—and I still consider them a very viable option. They work particularly well where the fasteners must be with-

Tip

If you are driving screws, use two drills for the job. Mount a combination drill bit and countersink in one, and a driver bit in the other. This two-drill combination is fast and efficient.

drawn before installation. A full-depth case should be fastened at four points across its width. A shallow case should be fastened at three points.

Attach the back. I use the back to square up the cabinet. I attach it immediately after screwing the case together, while the glue in the other joints is still wet. At this point, the case can still be easily squared. I cut each back from ¼-inch plywood as I assemble the case. Often, I will cut all the back plywood for a job to the proper height before I start assembling the cases. Then I just cut each one to width before installation. Once I have the back cut, I flop it in place onto the back of the case, square the case to it, and attach it with finish nails, as shown in *Photo 2-11*.

Photo 2-10. **I use mechanical fasteners in place of clamps to hold the case together while the glue dries. Base cabinets get four screws or staples across the width; wall cabinets get three.**

It's pretty much second nature to me, but if you haven't done it, I'm sure it sounds a little mysterious. Let me explain a little more. Begin by cutting the back to fit your case. Make sure the back has at least one square corner. The factory corners on most good-quality plywood are reliable. So if you are careful as you cut up the sheets, the corners will remain square. Double-check with an accurate square. Should you need to square up a piece, see "Squaring Frames and Panels" on page 52 for my sure-fire method.

Photo 2-11. **Attach the back with glue and small finish nails.**

One thing to keep in mind is that it's not necessary to make the back to the exact dimension of the case. If you make it a little too big, it'll get trimmed down when you sand the outside of the case. And even if you cut it a little short—as much as ⅛ inch—it will still be okay, as the edges of the back won't be seen in most installations.

Check the back edges of the case for debris and splinters, and brush or sand away anything that will interfere with the glue joint. Apply a bead of glue to the back edges of the case and drop

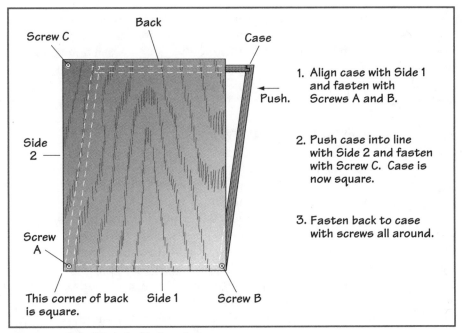

Back

Screw C

Case

Push.

Side 2

Screw A

This corner of back is square.

Side 1

Screw B

1. Align case with Side 1 and fasten with Screws A and B.

2. Push case into line with Side 2 and fasten with Screw C. Case is now square.

3. Fasten back to case with screws all around.

Figure 2-8. Attaching the back to the case

the back into position. This is where you square up the case: Align the side and top (or bottom) of the case with the known square corner of the back, as shown in *Figure 2-8*. Then fasten the three corners down as shown. By aligning adjacent sides of the case with a square corner, you've painlessly and effectively squared the whole unit. Fasten the fourth corner, then fasten the back all along the edges. Set the case aside to make room for the next one.

If I have to move a case before adding the back, I pin cross-corner braces to protect it from racking, as shown in *Photo 2-12*. With a smaller case, the braces aren't necessary as long as you handle it gingerly.

With that, you have assembled your first case using the Goldilocks method. There's more to come: You'll either trim out the front of the cabinet

Photo 2-12. **If you have to move a case before you put its back on, brace it with cross braces. These light strips will keep the case from racking as you move it around the shop.**

28

Tip

To include an adjustable shelf in your case, drill two rows of holes in each side. I use a 5mm drill bit (for 5mm shelf pins) and space the holes 1½ inches apart.

with solid wood or apply a mortise-and-tenon face frame over it. There are doors, drawers, and pulls to consider, too. But for now, you've got the case done. Let's take a break and consider how we might have solved some typical problems.

CASEWORK ALTERNATIVES

My system of building is designed for the real world, where nothing is flat, square, or exactly ¾ inch thick. It works pretty well, but reality sometimes gets the upper hand.

Take my current shop. There is a pipe about 45 inches above my table saw, so I can't cut pieces longer than this on edge. Even if I could, I'd draw the line at cutting anything more than 52 inches long on edge—it's dangerous and I won't do it. (If you choose to draw the line even sooner, go right ahead. Never make cuts that you don't feel comfortable with.)

How do I deal with these facts of life? My favorite approach is to avoid the problem. Instead of making one long cabinet, I'll make two shorter units and stack them. A 45-inch cabinet, for example, could become two 22½-inch cabinets, or a 15-inch and a 30-inch cabinet. If this option doesn't work with your plans, there are two other methods of overcoming the problem.

You can always cut the tongues with the piece held flat on the table saw. True, you may run into some of the problems I talked about earlier with inconsistent plywood thickness. But if you only have a single case to make this way, it isn't that much trouble to adjust the joint to fit.

Setting Up the Saw

This joint is cut with a dado blade and a shop-made auxiliary rabbeting fence. This fence is a useful addition to the saw, even if you never use it to make a case.

Adjust the dado. Use the dado blade set to its widest cut. Drop the blade below the table. Make sure the wide blade will fit through the throat plate before starting the saw. If necessary, make your own throat plate from ½-inch plywood. For complete directions on making your own throat plates, see "Shop-Made Throat Plates" on page 20.

Make the auxiliary fence. Next, attach a piece of straight stock to the fence, as shown in *Photo 2-13*. The fence should be

Photo 2-13. **Clamp or screw a straight length of scrap stock to your saw's fence to serve as an auxiliary rabbeting fence. Adjust it so it partially covers the blade, then raise the blade up to cut a semicircular recess. You can then adjust the fence to expose just the right amount of blade.**

about 2½ inches high, 1 inch thick, and at least as long as the saw fence. Some fences make a provision for this by providing holes to screw through. My Unifence made no such provision, so I had to drill it before I could screw the fence in place.

You'll need to notch the auxiliary fence for the blade. Move the fence so that it just barely covers the entire blade. With the saw running, raise the blade into the wood fence. Raise the blade until it is up about ¾ inch above the table, as shown in the photo. **Be careful:** Make sure your auxiliary fence is thicker than the dado blade is wide. A 1-inch-thick fence is fine for a ¹³⁄₁₆-inch-wide blade. A ¾-inch-thick fence is asking for trouble—you're bound to bring the running blade up into the metal fence.

Once you've made this initial cut, lower the blade and back off the fence. This cut is deeper than any you will have to make. When running the saw from this point on, the blade will no longer touch the wood fence.

Make the cut. Adjust the fence to expose slightly less than ⅜ inch of the dado blade. This determines the length of the tongue. (Remember, the tongue should be slightly shorter than the groove is deep.) The height of the blade should be slightly less than ½ inch. Make a test cut in a scrap and check the fit in the groove—the tongue should be too thick. Raise the blade slightly and try again. Keep cutting the same piece of stock until the tongue is the right thickness.

When the tongue just slips into the groove and does not bottom out, the saw is set correctly. You can now cut the good stock. Unlike the method of cutting on edge, this method is not flawless. Because of variations in the thickness of the stock, you may encounter a tongue that will not fit into a groove—or worse, one that is too loose.

Cut all the tongues, but leave the saw set up while you test each joint. Test fit each case. If any joint is too tight, go back to the saw and adjust the

Tip

When doweling pieces together, use grooved dowels. The grooves provide an escape route for any excess glue. Otherwise, the glue will collect in the bottom of the hole and keep the dowel from seating completely.

cut to thin the tongue. If the joint is too loose, reinforce the joint with dowels as you glue it up, as shown in *Photo 2-14*. Drill ⅜-inch holes from the outside of the case into the joint. Apply glue, then drive in a dowel that is longer than the hole is deep. A 1⅛-inch-deep hole with a 1¼-inch-long dowel will do. When the glue dries, sand the protruding dowel flush. Use three dowels for a case that is 12 inches deep and four or more for a case that is 24 inches deep.

Hiding End Grain

With my system of case making, the raw edge of the plywood is exposed on the top and bottom edges of the case sides. Most of the time, this is no problem. On base cabinets, the bottom edges face the floor and the top edges are covered by a countertop. As for upper or wall cabinets, the top edges are up near the ceiling, hidden from view. The bottom edges, however, can be seen. I like to hide these edges with edge banding whenever I can.

For edge-banding the bottom edges of case sides, I use ¼-inch-thick strips of hardwood that match the face grain of the plywood. I glue it in place before cutting the pieces to final size. This way I don't even have to think about the added ¼ inch after applying the banding. Once the edging is trimmed flush, I treat the pieces just like the other plywood parts for the case. For a detailed discussion, see "Attaching the Edging" on page 32.

Photo 2-14. If you happen to make one of the case joints too loose, don't fret. Just drill through the side and reinforce the joint with dowels.

When edge-banding adjacent edges of a piece of plywood, band the least visible edge first. Then lap it with the more visible piece, as shown. This will cover the little bit of end grain that would otherwise show.

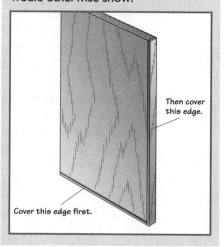

Then cover this edge.

Cover this edge first.

GOING FRAMELESS

3

The European approach
to cabinets

Now that the case is assembled, you have a choice. The traditional American cabinet has a face frame over the cabinet to hold the doors and drawers. The Europeans have devised a simpler system of hanging these things directly from the cabinet. Because it's a simpler system—and because it's the system I prefer—we'll talk about European cabinets first.

The first step in turning a basic box into a European-style cabinet is to apply ¼-inch-thick hardwood edging to cover the raw plywood edges. I use the same wood species that I am planning to use for the doors. I either miter the corners of the edging, as shown in *Photo 3-1* on page 32, or simply butt the corners. Of the two methods, the butt joint is easier and is the joint I use the most.

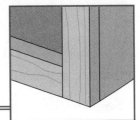

ATTACHING THE EDGING

Cut all the edging for the project at once. Choose straight-grained stock for this—the straighter the better. The strips should be wider than the plywood is thick to allow for a little bit of overhang as you glue up. For ¾-inch plywood, I use a ⅞-inch-wide strip.

Start with the sides of the case. Cut the strips slightly longer than the sides. Apply glue to the plywood, smearing it with your finger to cover the whole edge. Position the strips and nail them in place with brads, as shown in *Photo 3-2.*

Photo 3-1. For pieces that demand a little extra, I miter the corners of the edge banding.

Once you've edged the sides, move on to the top and bottom. Begin with a new piece of edging and square off one end. Hold it in place with the square end butted up against the side edging. Mark the other end for the cut. Cut strips 10 inches or longer an extra ¹⁄₃₂ inch long so you can spring them into place for a tight joint. Edge-band both the top and bottom this way, then set the case aside to dry.

> **Tip**
>
> Make your edging somewhat wider than the thickness of the stock you're applying it to. This will leave you a little margin for error as you're gluing it in place.

Trimming the Edging

Photo 3-2. Tack the edging in place with small brads and set their heads.

When the glue is dry, trim the edging flush with the case. I use a router with a 1-inch flush-trim bit. When routing, you'll find out why I recommend only straight-grained stock for edging—especially if you ignored my advice. Wild grain splits out when you're trimming the edging. Even straight pieces have a tendency to split.

Splitting can be minimized by running the router "backward" for the first cuts. Looking down at the case, run the router in a counterclockwise direction on the inside of the case and in a clockwise direction on the outside of the case. This is exactly the

the PROFESSIONAL view

FILLING WOOD

Fillers go hand in hand with my method of work. I use them to fill defects in the wood as well as brad holes and other intentional blemishes. The type of filler I use depends on the type of finish I am applying to the cabinets.

I generally like to use either an oil or a lacquer finish. When I finish with oil, I use commercial oil-based fillers. There is a set of very good fillers in a wide range of colors available from Color Putty. You can find them in paint and hardware stores. Apply these putties after the piece has been finished. When choosing a color, it is better to err to the dark side. A small, light patch is more visible than a darker one. It is even possible to mix the colors to get a better match.

When I use lacquer—or even varnish—I make my own filler. This is really quite easy. Save the sanding dust from your orbital sander. When you are ready for the filler, mix some of this dust with a little of your finish to make a thick paste, as shown. The color of this paste will match that of the finished piece almost perfectly. Also, if the wood is like cherry and darkens over time, the filler will change as well. Apply the filler before you finish. Allow it to dry, then sand it flush with fine paper.

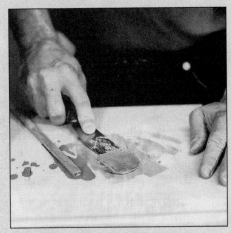

Mix the finish in with the dust until you get a nice, consistent paste.

opposite of normal practice, as this direction of feed tends to make the router race through the cut. To avoid having a runaway router, keep a tight grip on the handles and take the stock down in a series of light cuts. On your final pass, run the router in the opposite—and correct—direction.

FINISH SANDING

Use a belt sander with a 60- or 80-grit belt to sand all the surfaces of the case flush. Start with the top of the case. Sand the sides, back, and edging flush with the top. Even though you used a flush-trim bit on the edging, it won't be dead flush. A light touch with the belt sander will bring the surfaces into line. There will probably be a little bit of glue squeeze-out between the edging and the case. Use this line as a gauge to see when the two are flush. When the squeeze-out disappears, stop sanding. If there is no glue squeeze-out to watch, you're not using enough glue.

Tip

Keep a close eye on the glue lines as you sand. As soon as the squeeze-out disappears, you'll know the pieces are flush.

Try not to change the shape or round-over the corners of the case. Just bring the various surfaces flush. Once you've sanded the top, rotate the case onto its side and continue with the bottom, and finally the remaining side. When all the outside surfaces are sanded flush, roll the case onto its back and sand the front face of the edging. I use a belt sander, but it definitely requires practice. Until you're really confident in your ability to handle a belt sander, use an orbital sander for this critical task. It's safer, though not quite as fast. Sanding sometimes closes up the holes over the brads. If it doesn't, you'll have to fill them before you apply the finish. See "Filling Wood" on page 33 for information on various wood fillers.

When you finish flush-sanding the outside of the case, move on to the inside. Here, too, the edging must be flush with the plywood. Start with the corners. Flush-trimming with the router has left some stock in the corners. Trim away the excess with a sharp chisel. Then use an orbital sander to make the edging flush with the plywood. If the router didn't leave the edging close to flush, it is easier to cut away the bulk of the excess with a block plane first.

Once the edging is flush with the inside of the case, gently round all the hard corners with 100-grit sandpaper and an orbital sander. I even take the time to round those corners that will not be seen once the case is installed. This makes the case much more pleasant to handle and is well worth the few extra seconds it takes. Finally, sand the edging face with 150-grit sandpaper.

That's it. If you're making a bookcase or some open shelves, you're ready to apply a finish. And even if you're planning on doors or drawers, you're well on the way. Sound easy? It is. And that, in part, explains the popularity of European cabinets. But, as you'll see, easy doesn't mean plain. You can build frameless cabinets every bit as classy as face-framed cabinets, and I'll show you how. But first, let's take a look at face frames.

GETTING FRAMED

4

The case for face-framed cabinets

There is a certain brilliance about the face-framed cabinet. All the high-risk operations—hanging a door, squaring visible surfaces, and fitting adjoining cabinets without a gap—revolve around a frame attached to the front of the cabinet. Yet the frame is relatively easy to build.

At its simplest, you make a face-framed case by adding a face frame to a frameless case. But before you start chopping wood, there are a few more things you should know.

Unlike frameless construction, where the edging is flush with the edges of the cabinet, the frame actually overhangs the edges of face-framed cabinets. This overhang is a tremendous plus when you install cabinets. Butting a cabinet against an uneven wall? Cut the frame to fit. Having trouble getting adjoining cabinets to meet with a gap-free seam? Trim the frames.

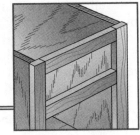

BUILDING FRAMES

All frames have common elements: stiles and rails. The stiles are the vertical pieces; the rails are horizontal. (If you have trouble remembering which is which, think of handrails on a balcony—like frame rails, they are horizontal.) In general, I build frames so the stiles run the full dimension of the frame, capturing the rails between them, as shown in *Figure 4-1.* The joint that has simplified frame construction for me is the loose tenon joint. It's strong, fast, and easy to make. As an added bonus, it doesn't require a lot of fancy machinery. In fact, you probably own the two necessary tools already—a table saw and a router.

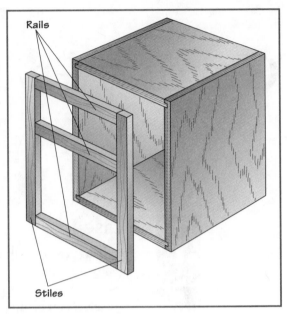

Figure 4-1. The parts of a frame

The loose tenon joint is a variation of the standard mortise-and-tenon joint. It consists of *two* mortises, one in each of the adjoining pieces. The tenon is a separate piece that bridges the mortises, as shown in *Photo 4-1.* When glued in place, a loose tenon is as strong as a traditional tenon. In fact, to call the tenon "loose" is something of a misnomer—even before glue-up, the pieces must fit together snugly. On the other hand, calling it a separate tenon joint is a mouthful. Loose tenon it is.

Cutting the Mortises

I cut the mortises with a router jig I designed myself, as shown in *Photos 4-2* and *4-3.* Because it's the heart of a system, useful for all kinds of construction, I've described building and using the jig fully in

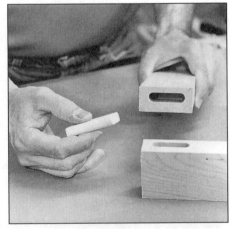

Photo 4-1. I assemble most of my frames with a loose tenon joint. The tenon slips into both mortises, creating a strong joint when the glue is dry.

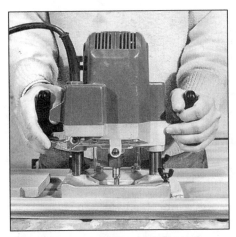

Photo 4-2. I cut mortises quickly and accurately with this simple shop-made jig. Here, I'm using the jig in conjunction with my Workmate stand. The Workmate clamps the pieces in the jig.

Photo 4-3. The jig can also be used without the Workmate. Simply hang it off the edge of your bench. Screw toggle clamps to the underside of the jig to hold the work in place.

Chapter 5. Whether you use my jig or settle on another method, the procedure is pretty much the same: Mortise each piece using the same setup. This creates consistent mortises that make for easier assembly. Once the mortises are finished, cut the tenons to fit.

Cutting the Tenons

I make the tenons in long strips, then cut them to length. These long strips are much safer to machine than the individual tenons would be. I use poplar for the tenons because it is strong, stable, and cheap. Why use expensive wood when it will be hidden inside the joint?

Tenons must fit snugly in their mortises, but not too tightly. A light tap with a mallet should be all that is necessary to drive them home. To achieve this, tenon *thickness* must be perfect. I make the *length* and *width* slightly undersize, however, to ensure that any imperfections won't ruin the joint. For example: If my mortises are each ⅜ inch wide, 1¾ inches long, and 1¹⁄₁₆ inches deep, I make the matching tenon ⅜ × 1⅝ × 2 inches.

Tip

When cutting up stock for loose tenons, use poplar or another inexpensive species. There is no sense (or cents) in cutting up your expensive primary wood to hide within the joints.

To get the tenon stock cut to the right size, start by ripping it to width. Then stand the board on edge to cut it to proper thickness. As with other Goldilocks cuts—cuts you want to fit ju-u-ust right—start by ripping the pieces a little too thick. Then nudge the fence over a bit to pare each strip down. Cut some extra tenon stock—you may need it.

The thickness and width are now right, but don't cut anything to length yet. As you look at the mortises, you'll note the router leaves the ends rounded. You'll need to rout the tenons to match. The best way to do this is with a 3/16-inch-radius roundover bit in a table-mounted router. Mount the bit in the router. Bury the bit in the fence so its guide bearing is tangent to the fence's face. Using the fence ensures that the tenon strip will have support along its full length as you rout it. Round-over the corners on the edges of the strip. Once rounded, the tenons can be cut to length from the stock.

I cut the tenons to length on the chop saw (the table saw will work, too), cutting only one frame's worth to begin with. This way, I haven't wasted a lot of stock and time if the tenons don't fit right. If these first tenons are too tight, I pick up some of my extra tenon stock and go back to my table saw, which is still set up as it was when I ripped the tenons to thickness. I bump the fence over a tad, and trim the tenons down in thickness. If the tenons are too loose, I throw the workpiece away and start over. No matter how many times you trim an undersize tenon, it will never get thicker. Once the tenon stock is cut to the right thickness, I cut tenons for all the remaining frames. **Be careful:** Only trim the tenons down if they are still in a strip. It is too dangerous to try to trim individual pieces.

If you find the tenons are too thick after you've cut them to length, you can sand one or both faces to thin them down a bit. This is tedious, so make sure the tenons fit before you cut them to length.

Gluing the Joint

To glue up this joint, apply glue to the inside of the mortises, then stir it around with a thin stick, as shown in *Photo 4-4*. Also apply glue to the end of the rail. Insert the tenon and draw the joint closed with a pipe clamp. A simple four-piece frame requires two clamps, as shown in *Photo 4-5*. For a more detailed discussion of this process, see "Clamping Frames" on page 42.

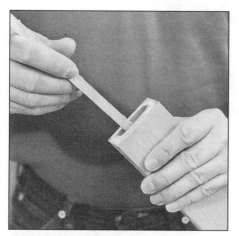

Photo 4-4. One of the secrets to a long-lasting joint is to use plenty of glue. Be sure to thoroughly coat the inside of the mortise and the shoulders of the joint.

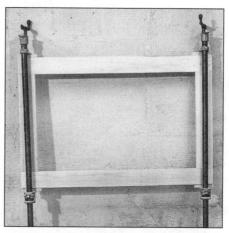

Photo 4-5. Draw the joint closed with bar clamps. Protect the wood with pieces of scrap placed between the clamp and the frame.

SANDING THE FRAMES

Once the frames are joined and glued up, they have to be sanded. No matter how carefully you made them, frame joints frequently don't align perfectly and need to be sanded flush.

In a small shop, the belt sander is often the tool of choice for this type of work. Beware! It is very difficult to make frames truly flat with a belt sander. The tool tends to hollow out areas, creating valleys with hills in between. If you form a valley, you've created a host of problems.

For instance, if you sand a valley into the back of a face frame and then join that frame to the front of a case, the valley will prevent the frame from meeting the case in a clean line. So it is imperative to keep the frames straight and flat.

The best tool I've found for flattening frames is the wide belt sander. I talked about this machine in the section on building solid wood cases. You feed the assembled frame in one end of this machine and it comes out sanded at the other end. There is bound to be a cabinet shop near you that has one of these monsters. The small amount you'll pay to have your frames sanded will be more than offset by the

Tip

Belt sanders have a tendency to dig in and leave valleys. If you're having difficulty sanding your frames flat with a belt sander, have them flattened for you by a shop equipped with a wide belt sander. Or, switch to a portable random-orbit sander, which is easier to control.

the PROFESSIONAL view

BEADED FRAMES

Currently, one of the most popular looks for cabinetwork is beaded inset construction, shown in the photo below. The bead is a part of the frame and sets off the door nicely, adding a very traditional feel to a project. It is probably the most demanding type of construction I do. The doors must be hung just right, and the cases must be installed perfectly to keep everything aligned.

Traditionally, cabinetmakers cut the bead right into the frame members. Then, as the pieces were joined, they mitered the beaded edges where they came together. Working this way is too fussy for me. Instead, I make up the bead in strips separate from the frame. Then, once the frame is glued together, I cut up the bead strips to fit inside it.

Generally, I make the strips ⁵⁄₁₆ inch thick and as wide as the frame is thick. The easiest way to do this is to start with pieces the same thickness as the frame. Set the table saw fence ⁵⁄₁₆ inch from the blade and slice the piece into strips. Make four strips for each

I round the edge of the bead with a molding head mounted on my table saw.

frame, plus a few extras. Round-over one edge of each strip, as shown in the photo above. Guide the strip along the fence as you mold it. Use featherboards to keep the strips tight along the fence. Once I've machined the strips, I sand them before installation.

Applying the bead to the frame is easy. I start by cutting the longest pieces to fit. This way, I can always cut a long piece to fit a shorter place if I make a mistake. Miter the ends of the strips at 45 degrees and fit them around the inside of each frame. I find it easiest to use a chop saw for this, but you could also do it on your table saw. Just set the miter gauge to cut a 45 degree angle. Apply glue to the inside edges of the frame and slide the strips in place, making sure they are flush with the back of the frame. Hold the strips in place with finish nails until the glue dries. Once it does, you can either pull the nails or set them, filling the holes with putty. Use a minimum of glue to keep it from squeezing out into the valley between the bead and the frame.

Here, the bead around the inside of the face frame lends a very traditional feel.

Photo 4-6. This random-orbit sander really shines when it comes to sanding frames. Unlike a belt sander, it is easy to control, and it doesn't tend to dig into the stock and leave valleys.

increased quality of your work and the time and materials saved.

Should you choose to do your own sanding, the best sander for the home shop is the random-orbit sander, shown in *Photo 4-6*. I have had workmen who couldn't keep the belt sander under control no matter how hard they tried. Switch them to the random orbit and they fly. The orbital sander I have is air-driven, but there are also electric versions of the tool on the market. If you're interested in the pneumatic model, they're often available through auto parts stores, where they sell tools and supplies for body work. These sanders require a lot of air, so be sure your compressor is up to the job before you run out and buy one.

To make sanding easier, get a piece of carpet. I have several pieces cut to cover different surfaces in the shop where I like to sand. The piece I use for major sanding is about 24 × 36 inches and covers the end of my saw outfeed table. It serves three main purposes: It keeps the stock from rattling against the bench and getting damaged during sanding, it dampens the noise of sanding, and it helps hold the pieces in place. This holds true for small pieces as well as large panels.

Start sanding with 80-grit sandpaper. This grit removes stock quickly; I use it to flush up parts. It can also modify the shape of a piece. If an edge isn't quite right after being routed, you can easily fix it by hand sanding with 80-grit paper.

Next, move to 100- or 120-grit. These grits can still remove stock, but at a slower rate. Their primary purpose is to remove the deep scratches left by sanding with 80-grit. Next comes 150- or 180-grit. These grits are not for shaping or stock removal; they're for smoothing away the marks left by the 100-grit paper. At this point, if the piece gets a lacquer finish, I'm finished sanding. If the finish is to be oil, I go on to 220-grit for a final polish. This fine paper won't remove more than the most minor scratches, so if you find some big ones now, back up a grit to get rid of them before you go any further.

Sanding a piece grit-by-grit is important. Don't rush the

(continued on page 44)

CLAMPING FRAMES

Clamping together a frame might seem like a simple matter. What could go wrong? you ask. Plenty. Unless the clamps are placed and drawn up correctly, they can cause damage to a frame that is difficult to repair. The secret is to work on a flat surface and to place the clamps so the pressure bears directly across the joint.

Ideally, you should position the clamps so that an imaginary line runs from the axis of the clamp screw through the center of the rail and into the opposing clamp jaw, as shown in illustration A. Unfortunately, it doesn't always work this way. Because the pipe or bar is only on one side of the work, it can radically bow what started as a flat glue-up.

To avoid problems, start with the frame held slightly above the pipes as you apply pressure. Snug the clamps up and sight along the top and bottom of the frame. The rails and stiles should be in the same plane. If they are, set the frame aside and glue up the next one. If they're not, the uneven pressure from the clamp is twisting the stiles out of line. If you leave them like this, the frame won't be flat and the joints aren't likely to be tight. At worst, you may have to throw the frame out and start

over. Realign the clamps before it's too late.

Before you start, note which way the stiles and rails are bowing. If the stile is being pushed *toward* the pipes, as shown in illustration B, loosen the clamps and pull the clamp away from the frame a little before you tighten things up again. If the stile is being pushed *outward,* as shown in illustration C, move the frame closer to the pipes. If the stiles are twisted in different directions, you'll have to move one side closer to the clamp and the other side farther away. Don't let the frame touch the iron pipes as you're adjusting it—the wet glue will react with the metal to form a big black stain on your work. This stain can be horrendous to sand away.

These adjustments should allow you to clamp the frame up perfectly. If you're still having problems, check a couple of other things.

Check your clamps. Look carefully at your clamps. If the pipes are bent, you'll never get things to draw up right. Do yourself a favor—toss the bent pipe and replace it with a straight one.

Change your clamp size. If you find your clamps bowing under moderate pressure,

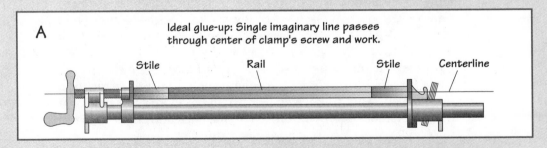

A

Ideal glue-up: Single imaginary line passes through center of clamp's screw and work.

Stile　　　Rail　　　Stile　　　Centerline

they may not be stout enough for the job. A ½-inch-diameter pipe is okay for fine work, but I prefer a ¾-inch pipe for general shop use.

Square your parts. If, after all that, you still can't get the stiles to clamp up right, check to make sure that the inside edge of each stile is square to the stile's face. If not, no amount of clamp adjustment will help. Remove the frame from the clamps, disassemble it, and wash out the glue with water. Square up the edges on the jointer or table saw, then reglue, reassemble, and clamp.

Once you get the frame to draw up the way you want it, tighten the clamps *gently*. There's no need to scrunch down on the clamp with all your might. This will only drive glue out of the joint. Believe it or not, it's possible to tighten a clamp so much that all the glue is driven out, starving the joint for adhesive. So apply pressure in moderation. If you have to force a joint to draw up, it may be a

better idea to take it apart and adjust the fit until it goes together willingly.

Once you're satisfied that the frame is flat, you can set it aside to dry and start work on the next one. Unless you're blessed with a large shop, you'll probably have to lean the frame up against a wall somewhere until you can take the clamps off. Do this with care. The weight of the clamps can still twist the frame before the glue sets up. Stand the assembly against the wall with the ends of the clamps on the floor. Make sure both clamps are in contact with both the floor and the wall and are not twisting the frame when you lean the whole mess up.

One final note about pipe clamps: When you buy the pipe, have it threaded on both ends. Protect the threads on the free end with a coupling. Then, when you need a longer clamp, you can connect two or more pipes together via the extra threads.

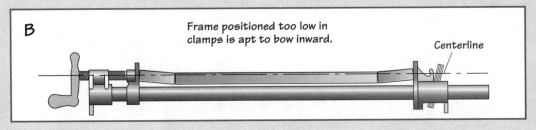

B

Frame positioned too low in clamps is apt to bow inward.

Centerline

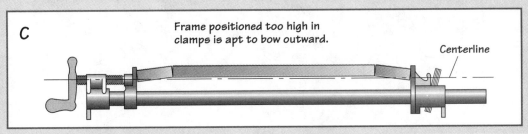

C

Frame positioned too high in clamps is apt to bow outward.

Centerline

sanding process. Take your time with the initial coarse grits and you'll find the medium and fine grits go very quickly.

FITTING THE FRAMES

Most frames overlap their cases by ¼ inch. This overlap is known as the *scribe edge*. An overlap much wider than ¼ inch wastes space inside the cabinet, as shown in *Figure 4-2A*. *Figure 4-2B* shows my typical approach.

The Scribe Edge

The scribe edge can be trimmed to fit an irregular wall or to allow the cabinet to squeeze into an undersize opening. Where two cases adjoin, the scribe edge ensures that the joint between the two will come together tightly. With no other material to get in the way, the cases butt up against each other only at the frame, as shown in *Figure 4-2B*. If the case were flush with the edge of the frame, a bowed piece of plywood or some debris could prevent the joint from closing all the way.

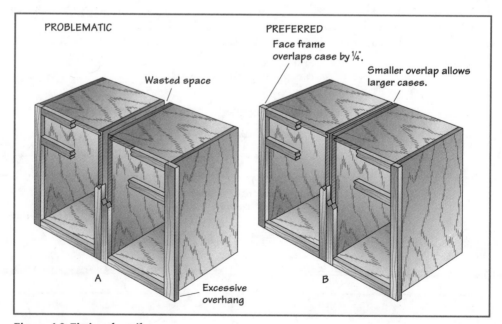

Figure 4-2. Fitting the stiles

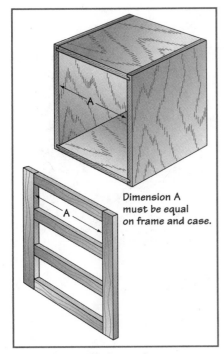

Dimension A must be equal on frame and case.

Figure 4-3. Sizing drawer frames

A scribe edge can be as small or as large as you wish. Generally ½ inch is large. The ¼ inch I use is normal for cases butting up against each other. For a case going into a corner or up against a wall, a scribe edge up to 3 inches wide is not unusual. Here, the scribe edge is also acting as a filler. The rule of thumb in custom cabinet work is to make these filler pieces as small as possible, while still allowing space for the hardware and other pieces to clear.

The exception to the rule. As always, there is an exception to the rule— base cabinets that are entirely drawers. In this case, build the frame so its inside dimension is *equal to* the inside dimension of the case, as shown in *Figure 4-3*. This way, you can screw the drawer slides directly to the case sides.

Sizing the Frames Vertically

When it comes to height, I like the case bottom flush with the inside edge of its frame and the case top flush with the outside edge, as shown in *Figure 4-4* on page 46. With the bottom flush, it is easy to get things in and out of the cabinet. It is also easy to clean the cabinet because there's no lip to trap dirt. Having the top flush is necessary because the countertop must sit flat.

That, at any rate, is the ideal. Getting this type of fit is demanding and time-consuming, so again I opt to err on the safe side. I intentionally make the case shorter than the ideal, as shown. This creates a step down from the case bottom to the inside of the frame. It still allows you to sweep the inside of the cabinet out, and it provides a stop so certain types of doors won't swing back into the case. While this stop is not necessary for all door styles, it is a nice detail.

What makes this technique so easy is that the step doesn't have to be an exact size. If it's between ⁵⁄₁₆ inch and ⁹⁄₁₆ inch, it won't take away from the interior of the case appreciably and it will look fine. There is

> *Tip*
>
> Make your scribe edges slightly more than ¼ inch wide, and build your cabinets from an inexpensive plywood like birch. If one end of the cabinet is exposed, cover it with a piece of ¼-inch plywood that matches the frame. The scribe strip will cover the edge, and it will look as if the whole project is made of the more expensive plywood.

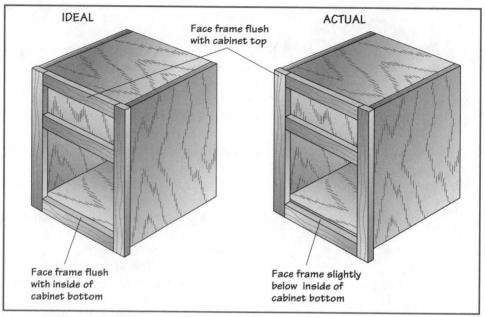

IDEAL — ACTUAL

Face frame flush
with cabinet top

Face frame flush
with inside of
cabinet bottom

Face frame slightly
below inside of
cabinet bottom

Figure 4-4. **Fitting the rails**

enough leeway within this range for a relaxed fit. The only disadvantage is that you'll have to remember to edge-band the raw front edge of the case bottom before you cut the pieces to final size.

Attaching the Frames

As always, sand the frame and the case before assembly. It's almost always easier to manipulate smaller parts. Once the frame has been glued to the case, it will probably need a little touching up to make everything flush and ready for finish.

Using screws. Spread a light coat of glue on the plywood edges of the box. Put the frame in position and clamp the two together. Drill and counterbore for the screws, then drive the screws home. For this type of hole I use a bit that drills the pilot hole and counterbore at the same time.

When I plug the holes, I like to match the color and grain of the pieces so that the plugs are nearly invisible. I have, however, seen nicely made pieces where the plugs were cut from a contrasting

> **Tip**
>
> If you want nearly invisible plugs, make them from a scrap of the actual board you are plugging. You'll get a better color match and the plugs will take finish the same way the rest of the board will.

wood. Whichever way you choose, remember to space the screws evenly and consistently on all the frames so the plugs appear consistent as well. Also orient the grain the same way on all frames (either with or against the grain of the frame).

Eliminating the screws. Most of the time I don't want the face of a cabinet dotted with plugs. Instead, I join the frame to the case with a tongue-and-groove joint. This method takes a little more effort than simply screwing the frames in place, but it is much stronger and it leaves a cleaner appearance.

The process starts when you're cutting up the plywood to make the cases. Add ⅜ inch to the width of the case sides to accommodate the tongue. Cut the tongues on the case sides with the same setup you use to cut the tongues on the case tops and bottoms. Instead of making the tongues on the inside edge of the pieces, make them on the *outside* edge, as shown in *Figure 4-5.*

Cut the grooves in the back of the frames after the cases are assembled. Turn the case onto its back. Center the frame on the case and use the tongues to mark where the grooves will go. Cut the grooves with a dado blade on the table saw. Note that the joints are only cut on the vertical parts. This allows the frame to be adjusted slightly up and down when it is being installed.

> **Tip**
>
> A face frame squares and adds considerable strength to a case, so you can leave the back off until just before installation. Leaving the back off a case makes it much easier to apply finish and install hardware.

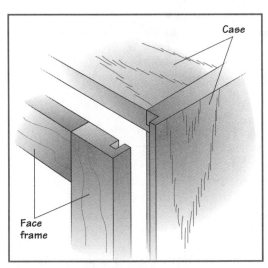

Figure 4-5. Joining the frame to the case

Attaching the frame to the case with this joint is easy. With the case on its back, apply glue to the grooves in the frame. Also run a bead of glue along the edge of the cabinet top. I only apply glue to the case bottom if the frame will cover it completely. If there is a step there, I skip the glue. Once the glue is spread, flip the frame over onto the case and insert the tongues in the grooves. Do this quickly so the glue doesn't get a chance to drip. Adjust the frame's position if necessary, then clamp the pieces together.

48

MAKING FRAMES
WITHOUT MORTISING

While I now use the loose tenon joint almost exclusively, the technique didn't dawn on me overnight. I spent a good deal of time experimenting with alternatives. I've outlined two of them here. They both work well, but they also have drawbacks that keep me from using them more often. They might work well for you, however, so let's take a look.

Biscuit Joints

The biscuit joint is perhaps the quickest and easiest of the alternatives. In comparison to the venerable mortise and

Photo 4-7. **The biscuit is a wafer of compressed wood that fits into matching slots cut in the two pieces to be joined. When it swells, it locks the pieces together.**

tenon, which has been in existence for thousands of years, the biscuit joint is a mere baby. It really has only gained popularity in this country in the past 15 years or so. The joint consists of a semicircular slot in each piece to be joined, and a small football-shaped biscuit of compressed wood that fits inside the slots, as shown in *Photo 4-7.* The biscuits come in three sizes for different-width joints. The larger the biscuit, the stronger the joint. The beauty of the joint is that the glue causes the biscuit to swell, locking the joint tight. While I don't consider biscuit joinery appropriate for heavy-duty applications like doors, I use it all the time for face frames and other low-stress constructions. It is an incredibly fast method of joining wood.

Biscuits sometimes swell from the humidity in the air to a point where they won't fit in their grooves. To prevent this, store your biscuit supply in a sealed plastic bag.

Cutting the joint. Biscuit joinery developed around a machine called a biscuit joiner. This special tool has a small, circular saw blade that makes the semicircular cuts. Unfortunately, to become a member of the biscuit joinery club, you've got to shell out at least $150. Top-of-the-line machines can run over $700. But don't skip ahead to the next section yet. I've devised a router jig that will let you in the door for the cost of a router bit. See "Router Biscuit Joinery" on page 148.

To make this joint, align the pieces you want to join. Strike a line across the seam, indicat-

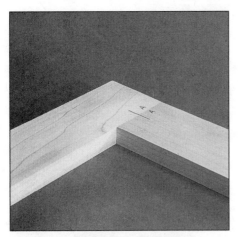

Photo 4-8. The layout for biscuit joinery couldn't be simpler. Hold the pieces together the way you want them and strike a line across the joint.

Photo 4-9. Once the pieces are marked, align the pencil mark with the indicator on the joiner. Plunge the blade into the piece to make the cut.

ing the center of the biscuit, as shown in *Photo 4-8*. Separate the pieces, then make the cuts at the marks on both pieces, as shown in *Photo 4-9*.

Gluing the joint. Once the slots are cut, the joint is ready to glue up. Apply glue to the slots, pop a biscuit in place, and clamp the pieces together. For best results, the glue should be spread on both sides of each groove. This can be done with a small paintbrush or a sliver of veneer. Unfortunately, this system gets old fast. If you have more than a few joints, it eats up a good portion of the time you saved by using biscuits in the first place.

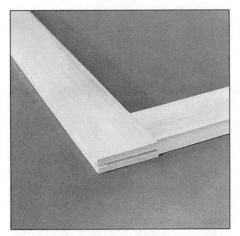

Photo 4-10. The slip joint is another good joint to have in your repertoire. It is strong enough to use for door frames and can be cut entirely on the table saw.

Luckily, there are a number of glue bottles on the market that have nozzles specially designed to fit in biscuit slots. Just slip them in the slot and squeeze. If you plan to do a lot of biscuit joinery, one of these bottles is well worth the investment.

Slip Joints

The slip joint, shown in *Photo 4-10*, is easily made on a table saw with the aid

A TABLE SAW TENONING JIG

I made up this jig for running frame pieces on end across the table saw. Used with a hand screw to keep the stock in place, the jig makes this operation a breeze. I made the parts from scraps. The only dimension that is critical is the thickness of the push block. It should be the same thickness as the material you'll be cutting with the jig.

Glue and screw the two pieces together. Then run the jig over the jointer to make the bottom surfaces flush. The hole and the diagonal cut on the backing plate make the jig easier to hold on to; make them to suit your grip. As a finishing touch, round-over all but the

bottom edges of both pieces. This keeps the plywood from splintering and makes the jig a lot nicer to use.

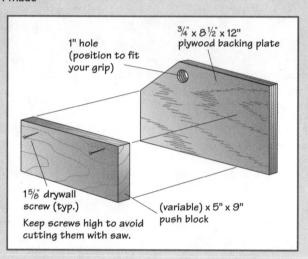

1" hole (position to fit your grip)

¾" x 8½" x 12" plywood backing plate

1⅝" drywall screw (typ.)
Keep screws high to avoid cutting them with saw.

(variable) x 5" x 9" push block

of a simple jig. It is a very strong joint and could even be used for door frames, if you are so inclined. Its major disadvantage comes into play at glue-up—it takes eight clamps to do the job properly. Still, it is a handy joint to know about. It requires cutting the mortise deep, which ensures that the door will be slightly under-size. Add an extra ⅛ inch to the overall length of your frame pieces to accommodate this.

Cutting the mortises. Cut the mortises by holding the workpieces on end and running them over the blade on the table saw. While you could do this by simply guiding the pieces along the fence, it is safer and much less stressful to use a jig. Make the jig as shown in "A Table Saw Tenoning Jig" on this page.

Let's assume you want to cut a mortise in stock ¾ inch thick. Set up a dado cutter to cut a groove that is approximately ¼ inch thick. Position the rip fence so the face of the jig is about ¼ inch from the blade.

A deep mortise ensures that the pieces will end up flush after sanding.

Figure 4-6. **The ideal slip joint**

Once the fence is set, adjust the height of the blade. Remember, you haven't used a tape measure yet when cutting a joint; don't start now. Set the height of the blade to cut about ¹⁄₁₆ inch more than the width of the rails. This ensures that the mortise will house the entire width of the rail, as shown in *Figure 4-6.*

The mortises are cut in the stiles, but don't cut your good pieces just yet. Make a test cut in a scrap the same thickness as the stiles. Hold the scrap in the jig, as shown in *Photo 4-11.* Look to see if the cut will be about centered on the stile. Don't bother to measure, just go by eye. If you think it's necessary, adjust the fence. Start the saw and make the cut. Then take the stock and turn it around so the opposite face is against the jig. Pass it through the saw again. If the fence position was perfect, you won't cut away any material. Give yourself a pat on the back and continue. You'll only have to make one pass with the rest of the mortises.

In all likelihood, however, the second pass will remove a slight bit of wood from one of the mortises. So what? The mortise is still centered on the stile; you'll just have to make two passes as you cut each piece. Welcome to the real world. Cutting the mortise in two passes centers it automatically. As long as the second cut isn't trimming away more than ¹⁄₁₆ inch, it's fine. If you find yourself cutting away more than ¹⁄₁₆ inch, discard the piece—the mortise will be too wide. Reset the fence and make a test cut in a fresh scrap. Once you are satisfied with the fence position, cut all the mortises.

Cutting the tenons. You can cut the tenons in the rails in one of two ways: with the pieces lying flat on the table, or with them standing on end. Let's start with them standing on end.

Tip

When making a two-part cut that first uses one side of a board as a reference, then the other, be careful when adjusting your setup. A small adjustment will be doubled on the work-piece because you're cutting the piece twice.

Photo 4-11. **Hold the piece against the jig's push block. Push the jig along the saw's fence to make the cut.**

SQUARING FRAMES AND PANELS

When working with a frame, a glued-up panel, or even an odd piece of plywood, play it safe and assume that it might not be square. Check the piece with an accurate square. If it's not square, here's a surefire way to square it up.

Hold your square along one edge of the workpiece and place a straight length of wood along the square's blade, as shown below. One edge of the straight piece must hang off the edge of the workpiece, as shown. Tack the straightedge in place with two nails. Don't drive the nails

Once the straightedge is attached, run the assembly through the saw to square the edge opposite the straightedge.

all the way in—the heads should be left proud so you can easily pull the nails later.

Run the piece through the table saw, guiding it with the straightedge against the fence, as shown above. Remove as little stock from the opposite edge as possible, but make sure the cut runs the full length of the piece. This will square the trimmed edge to the adjacent edge you first used as a reference. When you cut the piece to its final dimensions, cut off the edges opposite the two you've just made square to one another and you'll have squared the whole thing.

The first step toward squaring a panel is to attach a straightedge that is square to one edge of the panel.

If the stiles are the same width as the rails, leave the blade height alone. It's set perfectly from cutting the mortises. If the rails and stiles are different widths, set the blade so it's ¹⁄₁₆ inch higher than the stile width.

Next, set the fence. Position it so its face is slightly less

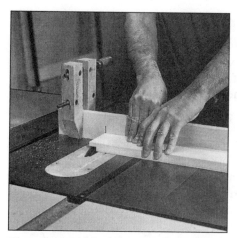

Photo 4-12. Guide the pieces with the aid of a temporary fence on the miter gauge. Notch the fence with your saw blade and use the notch to help align the cuts.

than ⅝ inch away from the blade. Hold a piece of scrap stock the same thickness as the rails in the jig and pass it by the blade, just as you did when cutting the mortise. This cuts one side of the tenon. Turn the stock around and cut the other side. By cutting from both sides, you create a centered tenon to match your centered mortise. Try the tenon in the mortise. With what you know of my work so far, you should be able to guess that the tenon won't fit—it'll be too big.

Move the fence very slightly closer to the blade. Remember: You will be cutting from both sides, so you'll remove twice the amount of the adjustment from the tenon. Be patient here—make small adjustments and you'll save time in the long run. Cut both sides of the test piece again and recheck the fit. Continue cutting and testing until the tenon is a firm fit in the mortise. Once the test piece fits, all the tenons will fit perfectly—as long as your frame stock is a consistent thickness. So start with consistent stock; otherwise you'll have to reset the saw for each joint.

You can also cut the tenons with the stock flat on the saw. First, set the dado cutter to cut its maximum width. Then lower the blade until only about ³⁄₁₆ inch is exposed. To help guide the stock, screw a temporary fence to the miter gauge. Make the fence from a straight scrap and notch it, as shown in *Photo 4-12.* The notch will show you where the blade is and help as you align your cuts.

Rather than measuring and laying out each tenon, I put a stop on the temporary fence. By putting the stock against the stop, I get exactly the same results with each cut. To position the stop, back the miter gauge away from the dado cutter. Take a stile (which you mortised earlier) and hold it on end against the temporary fence so it just covers the notch, as shown in *Figure 4-7.* Clamp a stop ¹⁄₁₆ inch away from the stile

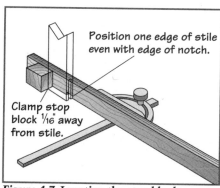

Position one edge of stile even with edge of notch.

Clamp stop block ¹⁄₁₆" away from stile.

Figure 4-7. Locating the stop block

Tip

If you're gluing up a joint that needs pressure in two or more directions, tighten the clamps a little at a time, alternating between them. This closes the joint gradually, without applying excessive pressure at any one spot.

at the side opposite the notch, as shown. This extra $\frac{1}{16}$ inch ensures that the frame members will completely overlap.

Make a test tenon on a scrap the same thickness as the rails. Start at the end of the scrap and make repeated cuts until the end butts up against the stop. Cut both sides and test the tenon in the mortise. With luck, it's too thick. Raise the blade a little bit and trim down both sides of the tenon. Check its fit again. Keep making small adjustments to the blade height until you have the desired fit. Remember that every adjustment cuts off twice that amount from the tenon.

Gluing up. Cutting slip joints goes fast, but they're a pain to glue up. You have to apply pressure in three directions to ensure a gap-free joint, as shown in *Photo 4-13*. Four pipe clamps bring the shoulders together and four hand screws squeeze the sides of the mortises against the tenons. That's a lot of clamps. And they all have blocks to keep the clamp jaws from marring the frame. That makes 28 separate pieces involved in the glue-up, counting the frame parts, the pads and the clamps. And the pipe clamps can't be positioned directly on the joints because of the $\frac{1}{16}$-inch overhang. To avoid the problem, offset the clamps, as shown in the photo.

Photo 4-13. The chief drawback to the slip joint is in the number of clamps needed to glue it up. Position them as shown for a tight joint.

The Essential Mortising Jig

Frame joinery made easy

Before I started joining frames with the loose tenon joint, I used the time-honored mortise and tenon. I started out cutting the mortises by hand—that got old fast. So I purchased a hollow chisel mortiser. While using this machine was faster than cutting the mortises by hand, I still thought I could do better. As I mused about the problem, I thought up this simple jig, but it was months before I finally broke down and built it. I'm sorry I waited.

The jig goes together quickly from scrap plywood and a few pieces of hardwood. It is designed around a plunge router and a Black and Decker Workmate, although neither of these tools is absolutely necessary. The Workmate holds the jig and clamps the stock in place. The rails on the jig guide the router as it cuts, while three stops control the position and length of the mortise. Once complete, the jig is incredibly easy to use. My teenage daughter and her friend, whom I employ part-time, routinely use it to crank out frames for my projects. They even handle setting the jig up for a run. At this rate, I may retire soon.

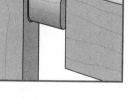

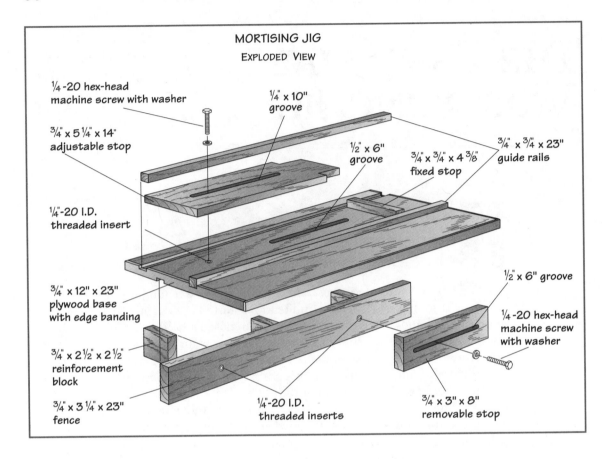

MORTISING JIG
EXPLODED VIEW

¼-20 hex-head machine screw with washer

¾" x 5 ¼" x 14" adjustable stop

¼"-20 I.D. threaded insert

¾" x 12" x 23" plywood base with edge banding

¾" x 2 ½" x 2 ½" reinforcement block

¾" x 3 ¼" x 23" fence

¼" x 10" groove

½" x 6" groove

¾" x ¾" x 4 ⅜" fixed stop

¾" x ¾" x 23" guide rails

½" x 6" groove

¼-20 hex-head machine screw with washer

¼"-20 I.D. threaded inserts

¾" x 3" x 8" removable stop

MAKING THE JIG

Begin by attaching the guide rails to the base. Make the rails from hardwood. The rails must be parallel; the fastest, easiest way I know to do this is to house them in parallel grooves. The depth and placement of these grooves isn't critical. Make them about ⅛ inch deep and space them so the router will be roughly centered across the width of the base. I cut the grooves with a regular blade on the table saw, moving the fence a little at a time until each rail just drops in. I make the space between the rails a little bit less than the width of the router base. Once the rails are glued in place, I nip away at the side of one rail on the saw until the router just drops in place, as shown in *Photo 5-1*. Run the router back and forth between the rails a few times to make sure it runs freely. It is better to have the fit a little too loose than too tight.

Photo 5-1. **When you attach the rails to the jig's base, make the distance between them slightly smaller than the width of your router base. Then open up the space by cutting away part of one rail.**

Next, put the stops on the jig. Set your router between the rails about 6 inches from one end of the jig. Position the fixed stop against the edge of the router, then glue and tack the stops to the base. Before you attach the adjustable stop, rout a ½-inch-wide × 6-inch-long groove through the base, as shown. No need to measure for this groove, just run the router between the guide rails.

Also rout a ¼-inch groove through the adjustable stop. Center this groove so it aligns with the groove you just routed in the base. Trim the adjustable stop to fit between the rails and notch its end, as shown. The notches prevent debris from building up in the corners, which could alter the jig's calibration. Place the adjustable stop between the rails and use it as a guide to drill a hole in the base for a ¼-20 inside diameter threaded insert. Place the hole near the end of the jig opposite the fixed stop for maximum adjustability. Thread the insert into the hole, then bolt the stop in place with a 1½-inch ¼-20 hex-head machine screw and washer.

On the underside of the jig, there is a fence to help position and hold the stock. It must be square to the surface of the base and parallel to the guide rails. Again, I find it easiest to groove the base to locate the fence. Be sure to guide the plywood through the saw with the same edge against the fence that you used to cut the grooves for the guide rails. This will ensure that the fence is parallel to the rails. Again, a ⅛-inch-deep groove is adequate.

Unfortunately, this limits the jig to cutting mortises a fixed distance from the fence. If you come up with an adjustable system, let me know.

Since the position of the fence determines where the mortise will go, you should consider it carefully. The frames I make are almost always one of two thicknesses, ¾ or 1 inch. I positioned the fence so the mortises would be centered on the thinner stock. Then, for the thicker frames, I put up with an off-center mortise.

> *Tip*
>
> When making jigs from plywood, edge the pieces with hardwood just as you'd do for a piece of furniture. In addition to dressing up the jig's appearance, the edging protects the plywood and makes your jig last longer.

Once you decide where the fence should go, based on the stock you plan to mortise and your router's dimensions, groove the base and glue the fence in place. Then add reinforcement blocks, as shown, for strength. Make sure the blocks are square so they'll hold the fence square to the base.

To complete the jig, add a removable stop to the fence. Rout a groove along the center of the stop, as shown, so that you can adjust it by sliding it along the bolt that holds it to the fence. You'll sometimes want to mount the stop to the right of the jig; other times you'll want it to the left. Drill the fence for two threaded inserts, placing the inserts about one-quarter of the fence length in from either end, as shown.

CALIBRATING THE JIG

Before you use the jig the first time, you'll want to calibrate it. Place the router in the jig against the fixed stop. Cut a scrap of ¼-inch plywood exactly 1⅝ inches wide and place it in the jig beside the router. Move the adjustable stop over against the piece of ¼-inch plywood. With the stop in this position, the jig will cut a 2-inch-long mortise. Mark the stop's position on the guide rails. From this mark, you can make additional marks at ¼-inch intervals, as shown in *Photo 5-2*.

To guide you in positioning your stock underneath, you'll need a reference mark on the jig's base. Place the jig on the Workmate with the fence hanging down between the jaws. Clamp a scrap of wood the same width and thickness as a typical door stile under the jig, making sure it is butted tightly to the underside of the base. Mount a ⅜-inch straight bit in your router and rout a shallow mortise.

Once the mortise is routed, set the router aside. Mark on the inside of the slot in the base to indicate where the mortise ends in relation to the fixed stop. This is your reference mark. Since the fixed stop is glued in place, the mortises will always end at this mark.

Photo 5-2. To make setting up the jig easier, lay out a rule along one of the guide rails. Either mark it in regular fractional increments or just mark the lengths of the mortises you cut most.

MARKING THE STOCK

Before you set up the jig for a run, organize the frame pieces. As you load them into the jig, you'll want to make sure that the same face of each piece—whether it's the front or the back—is against the fence. This will ensure that the joints are flush. Mark all the front surfaces with an X, then make sure that the marked face is against the fence whenever you put the piece in the jig. This is especially important if you are working with 1-inch stock because your jig is made to center the mortises on ¾-inch stock. Since the mortises will be off-center on the wider stock, mixing up the reference surfaces will result in unusable frame parts.

SETTING UP THE ROUTER

Once the stock is ready, set up the router. I mortise with a ⅜-inch straight bit, regardless of the thickness of the stock I'm mortising, so just leave the ⅜-inch bit in your router from the test cut. The depth of the mortise is determined by how far the router bit extends into the wood. Most plunge routers make some provision to set the depth of cut so that all the mortises will be equal. I usually make my mortises 1¼₆ inches deep.

SETTING UP THE JIG

Now you're ready to set up the jig. A typical frame has eight mortises: two on one edge of each stile and one at each end of both rails. To rout all these mortises, you'll have at least two separate setups on the jig: one with the removable stop toward the right side, and one with it toward the left. Lay out the mortises on the frame members. You don't need to mark the width of the mortises, just their lengths. Actually, if you're making a number of duplicate frames, you only have to lay out one frame's worth of mortises. Then use the marked pieces to set up the jig's stops. After you've used the jig several times, you may not need layout lines on the stock at all. Just make an X on the stock to mark each mortise so you won't miss any.

Start setting up the jig with a rail. I center the mortise on the end, ⅜ inch in from each edge. This means a 2½-inch-wide rail will have a 1¾-inch-long mortise. Load the marked rail in the jig so one of its layout marks aligns with the reference mark in the slot. Slide the removable stop up against the rail and lock it in position, as shown in *Photo 5-3*. The removable stop should be toward the end of the jig with the fixed stop. Then set the adjustable stop for a 1¾-inch-long mortise. With the stops in position, you can rout mortises in all the rails. Because the mortises are centered from edge to edge, both ends of each rail can be routed with this setup.

Photo 5-3. With the piece clamped in the jig, move the removable stop over to butt against it. This will allow you to load subsequent pieces in the jig with perfect alignment.

This setup will also position a mortise correctly on one end of each stile. Load each stile in the jig in turn and rout the mortise. Make sure to keep the marked face against the fence; this will tell you which end of the stile to rout. To rout the mortises in the opposite ends of the stiles, you'll have to reposition the removable stop.

To reset the removable stop quickly and accurately, clamp a rail back in the jig, then remove the stop from its original position. Switch it to the opposite side of the rail and bolt it in place, as shown in *Photo 5-4*. Then unclamp the rail and you're ready to go. If you want, you can mark the stop positions on the fence by tracing along the stop with a pencil. I've done this on my jig to make the setup easier. Since I almost always use the same size frame parts, the stop positions don't change from project to project.

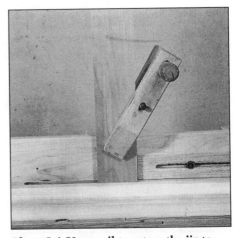

Photo 5-4. Use a rail to set up the jig to cut the mortises on the opposite ends of the stiles. Clamp a rail in the jig against the stop. Then shift the stop to the opposite side of the rail, as shown.

Rout the mortises in several shallow passes to avoid overstressing the bit. To make sure they are consistent, start with the router pushed against one fence and run it the length of the mortise. Then shift the pressure to the other fence and run it back. This will compensate for any slop in the fit between the jig and the router. You should move the router in a clockwise circle. This means moving the router to the right when pushing it up against the rear rail, and moving it to the left when pulling it tight against the front rail.

SOME FINAL NOTES

I use the jig primarily for two different thickness frames. But it is possible to give it a little more flexibility while maintaining the advantages of a fixed fence. Simply locate the fence in the right position for your thickest stock. Then, when you want to use the jig with some thinner material, attach plywood shims to the fence to position the mortises correctly.

One of the first things you'll notice about the mortises that this jig cuts is that they are rounded at the ends. Rather than trying to square them to look like traditional mortises, I find it easier to round the tenons in the table-mounted router, as explained in "Cutting the Tenons" on page 37.

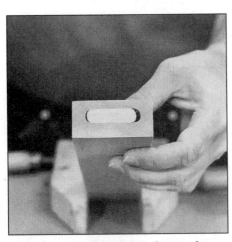

Photo 5-5. While the tenons have to be exactly the same thickness as their mating mortise, their width isn't as critical. I usually cut them a bit on the narrow side and a bit short to allow for adjustment.

Should you run into the situation where the piece you want to mortise is too long to fit under the Workmate, jack the Workmate up on blocks to give yourself some added clearance. I have several old drawers that I keep around the shop for just this purpose, but anything will work as long as it keeps the jig stable.

Don't be too concerned about the exact position of the mortise. As long as the marked face of each piece is against the fence as you rout, the face of the frame will be flush. As far as the side-to-side alignment is concerned, I make the tenons about ⅛ inch narrower than necessary, as shown in *Photo 5-5*. This gives me some room for adjustment if my setup is off a touch.

6   THE BASIC DOOR

Frame-and-panel construction

In my opinion, the best cabinet doors are made using frame-and-panel construction. This assembly consists of a strong, thin, stable frame with a wider wood or glass panel inside. The frame gives strength and stability to the assembly, and the panel fills in the opening. The panel isn't glued in place, allowing it to expand and contract freely. The result is a dimensionally stable, attractive door. When I build doors, I build the frame first, then cut the panel to fit the opening. For now, we'll talk about making the most basic of doors—the frame and flat panel. In subsequent chapters, I'll talk about alternate frame constructions and fancier panels.

There's very little difference between my door frames and my cabinet face frames. I use the loose tenon joint for both, and I follow the same construction techniques. But there are a few significant differences.

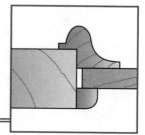

Photo 6-1. By making my cabinet door frames from 5/4 (five-quarter) stock, I end up with doors that are a full 1¹⁄₁₆ inches thick. This lets me include details like this extra-deep panel-retaining molding.

Photo 6-2. With thick frame stock, you can also cut a deep molding profile into the frame itself.

To begin with, a door frame must be stronger than a face frame. A face frame is static and fully supported by the case behind it. Its joints are under very little stress and therefore can (and should) be made the most expedient way possible. A door, on the other hand, is only supported on one side and must endure being opened and shut many times over its lifetime. As a result, I often make doors thicker than face frames, often from 5/4 (five-quarter) rather than 4/4 (four-quarter) stock.

This extra thickness makes the door stronger, as there is more stock at the joints. And the extra thickness gives me more design freedom. For example, the deep panel-retaining molding shown in *Photo 6-1* would be impossible in thinner stock. And the molded frame shown in *Photo 6-2* would lose definition if it had to be cut in thinner ¾-inch-thick material.

A door frame must also be made flat. If a face frame is slightly warped, it's really no problem since it will be fixed to the case all along its perimeter. If a door frame warps, it may be useless. This means you must make sure that the stock you are using is flat, and make sure that the frame stays flat as you glue it up. For more on my method for keeping frames flat, see "Sanding the Frames" on page 39 and "Clamping Frames" on page 42.

Finally, you shouldn't forget that a door frame will be seen on both sides; a face frame is seen on only one. This allows you to use less-than-perfect stock for the face frame. Since only one edge and one face of the frame will be seen, you can hide any defects by turning them away from the viewer. You don't have this option with doors.

Given a choice, I prefer to add the panel to the frame after

64

Tip

As you cut up stock for a project, save the best pieces for the door frames, which have two visible sides. Use the other pieces for the face frames since you can hide a bad edge or face by turning it away from the viewer.

the frame has been assembled. This method offers several advantages over the traditional approach, but it also takes more work—you have to make a separate molding to hold the panel in place. I like the look of this molding and the detail it adds to the door, so I don't mind the extra effort involved.

On the positive side, treating the panel as a separate element makes gluing up the frame easier. There is one less piece to deal with and, since the panel is not locked in the frame, it can be replaced. This is a convenience, and it's an absolute necessity on glass doors.

MAKING THE FRAME

The first step to making a door with a replaceable panel is to make the frame. But before you start to cut up wood, you'll have to calculate the overall size of the doors as well as the sizes of the individual frame members.

The overall size of the door depends on how the door is mounted. You have two choices: overlay and inset.

Overlay doors are found mostly on frameless cabinets and are so called because the door typically covers, or overlays, the edges of the case. A door that overlays most of the case edge is called full-overlay, as shown in *Figure 6-1*. A door that overlays roughly half the edge is called half-overlay, as shown.

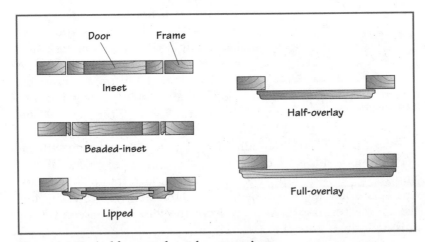

Figure 6-1. **Typical frame-and-panel constructions**

Inset doors are typically found on face-framed cabinets. The door sits inside the frame, as shown. Sometimes the frame is beaded to help disguise any discrepancy between the door and frame; this is called a beaded-inset door. Sometimes the door has a lip that partially overlays the frame; this is called a lipped door.

As you design your project, first decide what style doors to use. Then, measure the case openings and refer to *Figure 6-2* to

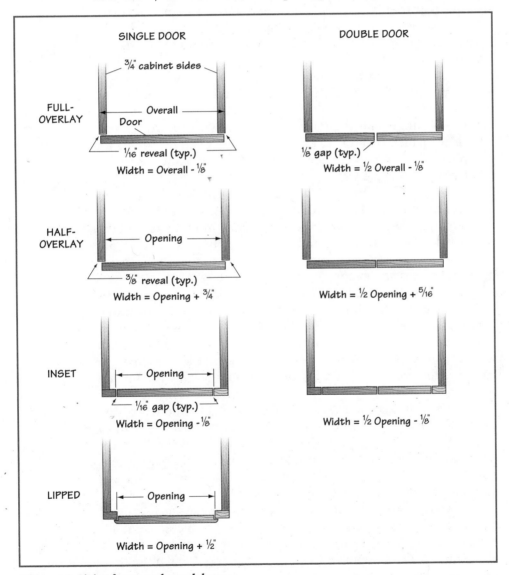

Figure 6-2. Sizing frame-and-panel doors

calculate how big the doors should be. The figure shows the various door-to-cabinet relationships in the "plan view," as if looking down from above a cabinet. This serves to calculate only the *width* of a door. The height of inset and lipped doors is determined in the same way the width is determined. But the height of an overlay door is more flexible since it can overlay the top and bottom edges totally or partially. (Note: The figure reflects the spacing required by Grass, the manufacturer of my favorite European-style hinges. If you're using another brand, the chart is only approximate. Adjust your door size according to the manufacturer's directions.)

Determining the width of the frame pieces. For a given set of cabinets, I'll make all the doors with the same width frame pieces—usually 2½ inches. I find this width is wide enough to mount the hinges and the pulls, but not so wide that the frame crowds the panel. Feel free to experiment. What you're looking for is a pleasing balance between the width of the panels and the width of the frame pieces.

This can be challenging. I ran into a problem on a project that had a handful of doors with glass panels. The rest of the doors had wood panels. The cabinets all had beaded-inset doors, and the width of the door frame members was 2¼ inches. The wood-paneled doors looked great, but when it came to the glass-paneled doors, there was a problem.

The cabinets that received glass doors were only 12 inches wide. By the time I added the widths of the door frame pieces to the widths of the face frame pieces and subtracted the total from the overall width of the cabinet, the width of the glass worked out to be 3⅞ inches. I thought it would look strange to have less than one-third of the cabinet's width be glass, so I made some changes.

On this particular job, I changed the construction of the upper cabinets. I made those with glass doors full-overlay instead of beaded-inset. This opened the glass area up to 7⅜ inches wide, which looked much better. And it allowed me to stick with a consistent width for all the door frame pieces. For more on making glass-paneled doors, see "Doors with Glass Panels" on page 69.

Determining the door thickness. As I mentioned earlier, I believe a thick door frame makes for a more durable door. As I'll explain soon, I also think it makes for a more attractive door. How thick is thick enough? Generally speaking, I make the door from 5/4 stock. This leaves me with a door frame that's 1¹⁄₁₆ inches thick after jointing and planing. In the best of all worlds, I'd make all my doors this thick. But the point I've been making all along is that this is the real world: As you look at the materials lists in my projects, you'll discover that I've occasionally used a thinner door. In any case, I would never build a door thinner than ¾ inch.

Assembling the frame. Once you know the overall size of the frame and the width of the pieces, make the frame using the same techniques I described for making a simple mortise-and-tenon face frame. Allow the glue to dry overnight, then sand the frame to make sure all the joints are flush.

ADDING THE PANEL

Once you have the frame put together and sanded, the next step is to prepare it for the panel. There are two ways to hold a removable panel in a frame. The first way is to rabbet the inside of the frame to create a ledge for the panel to sit in, then hold the panel in place with a molding, as shown in *Figure 6-3A*. The other way is to skip the rabbet and hold the panel in place with moldings on both the front and the back, as shown in *Figure 6-3B*. Generally, I choose the first method.

The molding can be on the front or back of the door. If it is on the front, it becomes a decorative element. On the back, it is there for utility and can be simpler. When I put the molding on the front of my doors, I always miter the corners. On the back, however, I use butt joints.

Rabbeting the frame. Cut the rabbet in the frame with a router and a ⅜-inch rabbeting bit. I make the rabbet deep enough so that when I hold a sample of the molding being used in place, it leaves a ¼-inch space for the panel. I find it easy to set the router this way since I usually have scraps of molding hanging around the shop. Just as with hardware, I recommend that you get the molding and have it on hand before making the rabbet. Rout the rabbet in

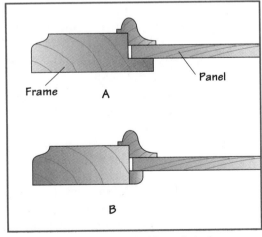

Figure 6-3. Two ways to hold panels in frames

several passes to avoid stressing the bit or damaging the work.

The router will leave the inside corners of the frame rounded, as shown in *Photo 6-3*. Once you're finished routing, cut the corners square with a chisel, as shown in *Photo 6-4*. You don't have to be exact here since the molding will cover up any slight overcuts. In fact, you may want to intentionally overcut the corners to make sure the molding will fit.

Making and fitting the molding. I use a standard molding for my projects. It's one of many available from a local supplier. Since it's a fairly standard profile, you should be able to find it—or something like it—in your area. As an alternative, you can make your own moldings. I used to do this but have since found it is simpler and cheaper to buy them.

If you decide to mill your own molding, there are several ways to go about it. One of the simplest is to outfit a table-mounted router with the appropriate bit. Run your stock along a fence and past the bit to shape it. As moldings tend to be long and narrow, be sure to use hold-downs, such as featherboards, for safety's sake. If you're making particularly narrow moldings, shape the edge of a wide board, then rip off the shaped edge on the table saw to produce your molding. If the molding requires a deep cut, make the cut in several light passes to avoid stressing the bit or the router.

Photo 6-3. Cutting a rabbet around a frame is a two-part process. First, rout the majority of the rabbet with a router.

Photo 6-4. Then, clean up the corners with a chisel.

Make the molding in long strips, then cut it to fit the frames, as shown in *Photo 6-5*. I miter the corners of molding that goes on the door fronts and rely on butt joints for the back. Since mitering is more difficult, I'll describe it here. Cutting the butt joints is simpler—just cut the ends off square and run the pieces into each other.

DOORS WITH GLASS PANELS

If you want to add a pane of glass to a door, you have several choices. The easiest is to retain the pane in a rabbet with a molding, just as you would a replaceable wood panel.

You can also use two moldings, one on either side of the glass. If you go this route, make the frame stock ⅜ inch narrower than usual—the width of the rabbet you won't need. Add the molding to the front of the door, then finish the door. Now the glass can be added from the back and held by the second molding, pinned in place.

With either method, the door and the retaining molding should be finished before installing the glass. Sand and finish all the surfaces because even those covered by the glass will be at least partially visible once the pane is installed.

When everything is ready, drop the glass in the frame and use brads or pins to hold the retaining molding in place. After setting the brads, fill the holes with a filler like Color Putty that won't mar the finish. Try to match the color as best you can, but don't worry about it too much. A slight discrepancy will go unnoticed on the inside of a door.

The fastest, most accurate way I've found to miter these moldings is with a chop saw. You could also use the miter gauge on your table saw if need be. With either method, you will have to make two setups to miter the molding.

Photo 6-5. For the moldings that go on the outside of a door, miter the corners.

As I set up to cut the 45 degree angles, I don't rely on the machine's settings. Instead, I check the setup with a small stainless steel miter square. To do this, make a test cut in a scrap. Flip one of the resulting pieces, match it up with the other angled end, and then measure the angle with a regular square.

If necessary, adjust the saw and try again. Just loosen the handle on the saw and tap it gently to change the setting. Then lock it again and make another test cut. It may take two or three cuts to get the saw set just right.

Once you get the saw set up, make all the cuts you need for that side of the cut. I usually cut a few extra pieces so I won't have to reset the saw if I make a mistake. Then miter the other end, resetting the saw as necessary.

To make things go a little faster, I line up all the frames by size. Then I start cutting the pieces to fit. I start with the longest pieces and work my way down to the shortest. I cut a part and keep checking it against a frame. As always, I start by cutting the piece too big, then keep trimming it down until it is just right. I keep a stop block clamped to the saw fence with a spring clamp. To adjust the length of the molding, I gently tap the block closer to the blade with a small hammer, as shown in *Photo 6-6*. The hammer makes it surprisingly easy to make very fine adjustments.

Photo 6-6. **To cut the molding for the doors accurately, clamp a stop block to the saw fence. For fine adjustments, tap the block gently with a hammer.**

Once you get one piece cut right, check it in all the appropriate frames. There will be minor differences. Cut enough pieces of molding to fill the places where the original fit perfectly, then adjust the stop block to cut the rest. Start with longer ones, then do those that have to be shorter than your sample. With all the pieces of that size cut, move on to cutting the next longest pieces, and so on. By cutting the longest pieces first, you'll avoid wasting stock. Should you make a mistake with a long piece, it can always be cut into smaller lengths.

Tip

Sanding molding is, at best, a tedious job. Particularly on complex profiles, it's too easy to round-over lines that should be crisp and otherwise obliterate detail. To avoid as much sanding as possible, use sharp cutters to mill the molding. The cleaner the wood is cut, the less sanding you'll have to do.

As you cut each piece, label it so you don't get mixed up as you go to assemble things. When all the pieces have been cut, gather them for sanding. The saw usually splinters the back edge of the stock slightly—sand these whiskers off gently with 220-grit sandpaper.

Shaping the frame. Doors are often shaped along the outside edge. With the frame complete, add this detail—if your design calls for it. My designs frequently do. To begin with, I like the look that a molding detail gives to the front edge of the door frame. Equally important, it helps solve a problem created by building thicker doors. The outside edge of a thick door can interfere with the the way the door closes: The hinge edge can bind against the cabinet at the end of its

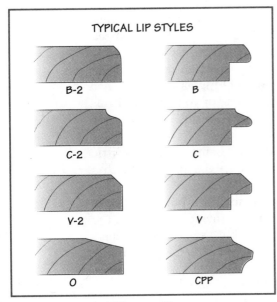

TYPICAL LIP STYLES

B-2 | B
C-2 | C
V-2 | V
O | CPP

Figure 6-4. **Typical frame profiles**

swing. Routing an edge detail removes the offending edge simply and easily.

This edge detail is called a lip. Within the industry, the lip style I like is called a C-2 lip. This means that the front edge of the door is cut to an ogee profile and the back edge is left square, as shown in *Figure 6-4.*

By simply adding this detail to the edge of my thick doors, I can hang them with my regular Grass hinges. Otherwise, I'd have to use a hinge designed to handle the extra thickness. These other hinges are okay, but they don't open as far as my ususal hinges do.

Cut the lip with either a hand-held or table-mounted router. There are many different profiles available, so you should be able to find the shape you want. Do the final sanding.

Making the panel. Before setting the frame aside, measure it from rabbet to rabbet in both directions so you'll know how big to make the panel. Then, armed with those figures, make the panel. If you're making solid wood panels, make the panel slightly narrower than necessary to allow for expansion with changes in humidity. For an average panel, ³⁄₁₆ inch is enough. If you're cutting a plywood panel, the fit can be snug or just slightly loose (¹⁄₁₆ inch or less).

The most basic panels are flat. The easiest way to come up with a flat panel is to use hardwood plywood. For frames that use my standard retaining molding, ¼-inch plywood works well. For doors with a more substantial feel, you can use ⅜-inch solid wood panels. This is how I make most of my panels. These have to be rabbeted to work with my standard molding.

If you go with plywood, use sheets with a flat-sliced face. Many commercial cabinet manufacturers use plywood with a rotary-cut face; skip back to page 9 and compare *Photo 1-2* to *Photo 1-3* and you'll see why I recommend against it.

Once you get the plywood back to your shop, another factor critical to getting good-looking panels is where you cut them from the sheets. Unless the grain is absolutely straight on your flat-sliced stock, there will be some sort of pattern on the sheet. And it will probably be bookmatched. You can use this to your advantage by selecting a specific part of the match to use as your panel. This will result in your project looking as though it had been custom veneered. You will waste some of your material this way, but the results are worth it. For more on this technique see "Selecting Bookmatches" on page 74.

If you want to minimize waste while maintaining a little control over the panels' appearance, try to get plywood with a straight-grained face.

Attaching the panel to the frame. With both the frame and the panel finally in hand, it's time to merge the two. If the panel is thicker than ¼ inch (as it is when I use solid wood panels), I rabbet the edge of the panel to fit the groove formed by the frame and the molding. I do this on the table saw with a dado cutter. Alternately, you could adjust the molding or the rabbet to accommodate the thicker panel, but I find it easier to rabbet the panel.

The next step depends on what kind of hinges you're going to use to hang the door. If you're going to use European-style hinges, you should drill the mortises for them before you install the panel. For more specifics on this process, see "European-Style Hinges" on page 123. If you're using conventional hinges, you can go ahead and install the panel.

Once the frame and the panel are both ready, drop the panel in place. Slip the molding in position and attach it to the frame with wire brads or air-driven brads. Set the fasteners with a small nail set. Then fill the indents to conceal them. I do this with putty I make myself, as described in "Filling Wood" on page 33. When the putty dries, go over the completed door one more time with 220-grit sandpaper to get it ready to finish.

AN ALTERNATE DOOR FRAME

You can also make door frames with mitered corners. Mitered corners allow frame pieces cut with a highly decorative profile to meet gracefully in the corner, the way a picture frame molding wraps around a picture. Unlike my standard doors, mitered doors have a captive panel. This makes glue-up interesting since the panel must be installed at the same time you're struggling to get the corner joints to draw up tight.

Frankly, there is no reason to make the panels in a mitered frame captive—I just do it. You could make them replaceable, as I do with my standard doors. However, a mitered frame lends itself to having fixed panels because the groove can be run all the way along the frame pieces. With my standard frames, the groove would have to stop short of the ends or it would show.

Making a frame with mitered corners is similar to making one of my regular frames. You use the same loose tenon joint cut on the same jig described in Chapter 5.

Cutting the stock to size. The first step is to mill the stock for the frame to the dimensions required. Size the door as you would any other door. For specific guidelines, see *Figure 6-2* on page 65.

With the stock prepared, you can make the miter cuts. I make these cuts on the chop saw the same way I miter the panel-retaining molding, as described on page 69. Check the saw's setup carefully—if the cuts aren't made at precisely the right angle, the joints will be open and the door won't go together square.

It is easier to cut the door parts than it is to cut retaining molding because the length of the pieces isn't as critical. If you happen to make your doors 29¹⁵⁄₁₆ inches tall rather than 29⅞ inches, it won't be noticed. Being off ¹⁄₁₆ inch with a piece of molding would be a disaster.

While you don't have to worry about the precise length of the pieces, use a stop block to make sure the lengths of similar pieces are the same. If they're not, you'll have some real problems putting the frame together. Once you have all the pieces cut (plus a few extra for tests and emergencies), it's time to mortise them on the jig.

Cutting the mortises. The only modification you'll have to make to the jig is to make a mitered stop block that attaches to the underside of the jig. This block helps hold the frame pieces at the proper angle for mortising. These must be cut at a 45 degree angle, as shown in *Photo 6-7*.

Photo 6-7. To use the mortising jig to cut the mortises in a mitered-corner door, you just have to add an angled stop block underneath. Here, the jig is shown upside down.

Always place the same surface of the frame pieces against the jig's fence. One way to do this is to keep the edge

SELECTING BOOKMATCHES

When you buy plain-sliced hardwood plywood, the veneers that make up the faces are usually bookmatched. Depending on how you cut the plywood, you may be able to take advantage of these bookmatches in your work, creating beautiful door panels, drawer fronts, and other visible parts. There is a cost to this, of course. Cutting up plywood to take advantage of the grain pattern isn't usually the most efficient way to use the material, so you end up wasting some. But I've found that the scraps can almost always be used elsewhere, so it isn't that big a problem.

To select a bookmatched pattern from a full sheet of plywood, locate the seams in the face veneer. One of these seams will be the centerline of the bookmatch, as shown. As long as you center your panel on the appropriate seam, it usually doesn't matter where you put the panel along the length of the sheet. Many times, the grain pattern will suggest what's best. On either side of the centerline, mea-

sure out one-half of your panel's width to find the edges of the panel. Then mark off the panel length to complete the layout. Cut out the panel along your layout lines.

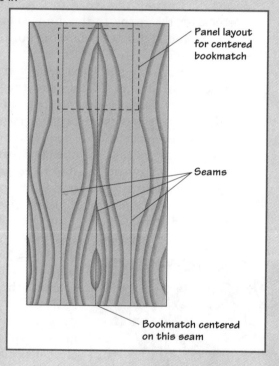

Panel layout for centered bookmatch

Seams

Bookmatch centered on this seam

---

that will get the groove against the fence, no matter which piece you're mortising. You'll discover that this means that mortising a frame requires two setups. Mortise one end of each piece first, as shown in *Photo 6-8*. Then move the mitered stop block to the other side of the jig to mortise the other end.

The placement of the mortises on a mitered frame is fairly critical. If they are started too close to the outside corner, the bit

Photo 6-8. Cutting a mortise in the end of a mitered frame piece is really no different than cutting one in a regular piece. Just be sure to position the stops so the bit doesn't come through the outside of the frame.

may cut all the way through the stock. If they start too close to the inside corner, the bit may come through the face of the stock where it has been shaped. Either way, you'll ruin the piece. You can also ruin it by cutting the mortise too deep. *Figure 6-5* shows the proper placement of a mortise on an average frame member. Use it as a guide to make your setups.

Before cutting good stock with a particular setup, make a test cut in one of the extra frame pieces to make sure you've got it right. Then, when you're ready, cut all the mortises. Save the test pieces for later.

Use the table saw to cut the groove for the panels. I use the regular blade and make two passes to make the groove fit the existing panels. The flat side of the molding rides against the fence, with the inside of the frame down toward the blade. Don't forget to cut the groove just a touch (³⁄₃₂ inch or so) deeper than the tongue on the panel is long (typically ⅜ inch).

Gluing up the doors. Gluing and clamping up mitered doors always takes a little extra effort, especially compared to my regular doors. To make this onerous task somewhat easier, I glue the doors up in two steps on a jig I made especially for the job.

As shown in *Figure 6-6*, the jig consists of a piece of ¾-inch plywood with straightedges glued and screwed along two adjacent sides. Be sure the

Mortise

1"

1¼"

¾"

|← 2½" →|
(typ.)
maximum of 2¾"

Figure 6-5.
Locating a
mortise

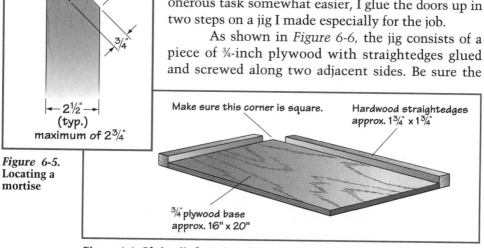

Make sure this corner is square.

Hardwood straightedges
approx. 1¾" x 1¾"

¾" plywood base
approx. 16" x 20"

Figure 6-6. Gluing jig for mitered doors

included corner is square and leave a gap between the two straightedges.

Along with the jig, you'll also need two mitered and mortised clamping blocks. These will protect the ends of the frame pieces from the clamps. Make these blocks from the pieces you used to test the mortising jig. You'll need one block from each setup. Their precise length is unimportant but make them short. I usually cut mine down to about 3 inches. Slip tenons into the mortises. These will keep the blocks aligned with the frame pieces, as shown in *Photo 6-9.*

To clamp up, take two adjacent frame members and brush glue into the mortises and on the mitered surfaces that will come together. Since the mitered surfaces are 50 percent long grain, putting glue on them will add considerably to the strength of the joint. Add a tenon to one of the pieces and fit the joint together. A rap or two with a rubber mallet may be necessary to bring the pieces together tightly.

Photo 6-9. **These short clamping blocks make it possible to put pressure along the length of the frame pieces without damaging the mitered ends. Note that the block is in line with the frame piece, rather than turning the corner as a regular miter would.**

Tip

When making a glue-up on a surface that your pieces might stick to, cover the surface with a piece of plastic food wrap to prevent mishap.

Lay a piece of plastic food wrap at the corner of the clamping jig. This will prevent the frame pieces from being glued to the jig. (No, this is one mistake I haven't made yet! Not with this jig, anyway.)

Place the half-frame in the jig with one clamping block at either end. Clamp the pieces to the jig with two pipe clamps, as shown in *Photo 6-10.* This should draw the joint closed. Keep the pieces against the straightedges to ensure that the half-frame will be square. I find it difficult to keep the frame pieces tight against the jig, so I add two hand

Photo 6-10. **Even though it involves extra time and a fair number of clamps, I prefer to glue up mitered frames one-half at a time. I find it is easier to get the joints tight this way.**

screws, as shown. That makes a total of four clamps to clamp only one-half of the door.

Clamp up the other half of the door the same way. Be sure to make the second half identical to the first. Otherwise, you'll have halves for two different doors. Once you've glued up all the pieces into half-frames, it's time to assemble the doors. If the panel is to be stained, do it now.

When making frame-and-panel doors with integral panels, finish the panels before gluing the frame up around them. The panels will be easier to handle, and no unfinished wood will be exposed should the panel shrink within its frame.

Take one of the half-frames and apply glue to its mortises and mitered surfaces, then insert the tenons. Make sure no glue runs into the groove for the panel. Put glue on the other half-frame. Put the panel into its groove in one half, then bring the two halves together. Tap the frame with the mallet to drive the joints together. With a piece of plastic under both corners, put the frame in the jig and clamp it up. You'll need four pipe clamps, as shown in *Photo 6-11.*

Photo 6-11. **Once the two half-frames are dry, you can join them to make a complete frame.**

When the glue dries, remove the door from the jig, scrape away any glue squeeze-out, and do any touch-up sanding that is necessary. The door is now ready to mortise for hinges, and then finish.

7

DECORATIVE PANELS

Raised, bookmatched, slipmatched, or herringbone

Like frames, panels come in all shapes and sizes. I divide panels into two groups: traditional and composite. You've all seen traditional panels in one form or another. The most common is the raised panel, as shown in *Photo 7-1*. This type of panel has been made for countless years. On the other hand, composite panels, as shown in *Photo 7-2*, are relatively new. They're something I developed in my work to make use of special pieces of wood that otherwise would not be suitable for cabinetwork, including pieces that have beautiful knots or unusual grain. Once you learn the technique, you'll find it limited only by your imagination.

Photo 7-1. **The time-honored raised panel lends a look of classic elegance to a cabinet.**

Photo 7-2. **This cabinet's back panels are made up of a number of smaller pieces of wood carefully selected for their unusual grain patterns. This technique opens up a whole new range of possibilities for design.**

TRADITIONAL PANELS

While I call these panels traditional, it has more to do with the method of making them than their appearance. Depending on the style you're after, you can design a traditional panel system that looks anywhere from avant garde to country antique. One form of traditional panel is the flat panel, which I discussed in Chapter 6. Another is the raised panel, which I'll get to shortly.

Even though it's easiest to use plywood for solid panels, there are drawbacks. Plywood's color usually has a different tone than that of its solid wood counterpart. Used together, the subtle contrast is generally pleasing, but it is noticeable. If you're looking for a more uniform appearance, this could be a problem. Plywood panels also have a different face on the back. The back of an A2 (A2 plywood has an A face and a #2 back) sheet will be clear (without knots or other defects), but no match for the front. Most of the time, this is not a problem since the lesser side faces the inside of the cabinet. But there are times when you want both faces to show. And, if you intend to paint the cabinets, the veneered surface of the plywood may cause the paint to crack and split.

Solid wood panels are not difficult to make. It's just a matter of edge-gluing boards to make up panels of the desired width. The panels should be at least ⅜ inch thick. To get boards this thin, resaw them from 5/4 (five-quarter) stock. For more information, see "Resawing" on page 86. Don't plane the boards until after you've glued them together. Glue up the stock. Then, when the glue is dry, plane the entire panel to the required thickness. For more information on gluing up solid stock, see "Solid Wood Construction" on page 12.

Raised Panels

These panels come in many different styles to fit different designs, but they all have certain characteristics in common, as shown in *Figure 7-1*. They are made almost exclusively of solid wood since the act of raising the field cuts into the thickness of the stock, exposing its core. There are a number of ways to create raised panels, depending on your equipment and inclination.

Raising panels on a shaper. Without question, the best tool for this job is the shaper. When set up properly and equipped with sharp knives, it can produce panels that need virtually no sanding. There are cutters available for a wide variety of profiles; should you be unable to find a suitable design, it's possible to have knives custom-made to your drawings by many cutter manufacturers or saw shops.

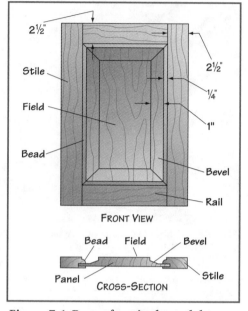

Figure 7-1. Parts of a raised-panel door

There are even systems available that allow you to grind your own profiles.

With its versatility and the quality of its work, it is easy to understand why the shaper is a mainstay in many commercial shops. In addition to making raised panels, I use mine to make moldings and to shape the edges of pieces. I've equipped it with a stock feeder, as shown in *Photo 7-3*, for safety. The feeder pushes the work through the machine for me and puts a layer of cast iron between me and the cutter. I like that.

While I think the shaper is the best tool for making raised panels, I real-

 Tip

When raising panels on a router or shaper, cut across the end grain first. Cutting across the grain is bound to produce some tear-out at the trailing edge of the cut. By making the cross-grain cuts first, you'll clean up this tear-out as you make the long-grain cuts.

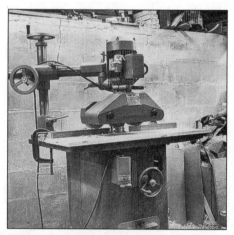

Photo 7-3. A stock feeder will hold the stock flat and tight against the shaper's fence as its wheels push the piece through the cut. This makes for safer operation and higher-quality results than feeding stock through by hand.

ize it does have some disadvantages. It is one of the most dangerous woodworking machines—and it can be intimidating, even to an experienced craftsman. The cutters are costly, especially when you consider they make only one profile. And the shaper itself is not inexpensive. Unless you are planning to do a lot of shaping, you might be better off with one of the alternative methods of panel-raising.

Raising panels with the router. In many ways, the router is like a small, hand-held shaper and often takes the place of its larger cousin in a small shop. Manufacturers have noticed this and are now producing larger routers and bigger shaper cutter–like bits to go in them. These new bits include several styles of panel-raisers.

Some of these bits look like scaled-down versions of actual shaper cutters. While they are smaller than their relations, they still seem to me to be too large to be chucked in a router. The thought of a 3½-inch-diameter bit spinning at over 15,000 rpm scares me, so I have not tried any of them. And since I have a shaper, I probably never will.

This doesn't mean you can't make raised panels with a router. On the contrary, there are panel-raising bits available that won't put too much stress on your router—or your nerves—like those big bits can.

The bits I'm referring to are called *vertical panel-raising bits.* These are mounted in a table-mounted router, and the stock is passed by them on edge, as shown in *Photo 7-4.* If you like, you can make the cuts in several light passes, either raising the router or moving the fence to expose more of the bit each time. This puts less stress on the bit and the router than making the cut in one heavy pass.

Photo 7-4. **One way to raise panels with a router is to use a vertical panel-raising bit. Mount the bit in a table-mounted router. Hold the panel on edge and guide it along a tall fence. Note that the bit is partially buried in the fence.**

Raising panels on the table saw. You can also make raised panels with a table saw. Compared to the router, the method is more labor-intensive, but the results are still first-rate. The main problem stems from the rough surface left by the dado cutter. It must be sanded vigorously to get rid of the saw marks. Sharp tools will help you to control this problem. The table saw also requires three to five separate setups to raise a panel, compared to only one for the router. Despite these shortcomings, the method is still a viable choice.

Start by cutting the panels to size. The length and width will be determined by the size of the frame; the thickness should be ¾ inch. Gather a few scraps, too, for test cuts. Their size is not critical, but just make sure they're big enough to run safely through the saw. Set up your dado cutter to cut a ¾-inch-wide swath.

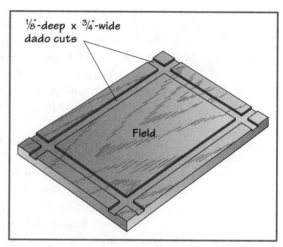

Figure 7-2. Defining the raised field

Set the depth of cut to ⅛ inch. Adjust the fence so the distance between it and the outside of the blade equals the distance from the outside edge of the panel to the edge of the raised field.

Make four passes with the panel face down on the saw, one along each side, as shown in *Figure 7-2.* Do the cross-grain cuts first. These four cuts define the raised field. Make a single cut in each scrap piece as well.

Cutting the bevel comes next. Do this with the dado cutter tilted slightly on the saw. You'll still be running the panel face down across the saw. Tilt the blade about 20 degrees from vertical. You'll probably have to play with this adjustment a little to find the angle that works just right. Set the depth of cut so the low side of the cutter is ⅛ inch above the table. Set the rip fence so the corner of the angled kerfs will coincide with the corner of the straight kerfs you just cut, as shown in *Figure 7-3.* Make a test cut to confirm your setup before cutting the good panels.

When you're sure the setup is correct, cut the good panels. As you did before, make

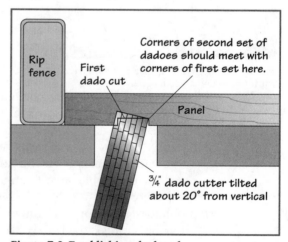

Figure 7-3. Establishing the bevel

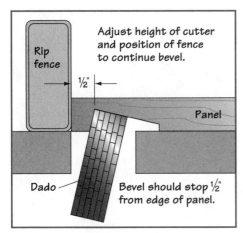

Figure 7-4. Finishing the bevel

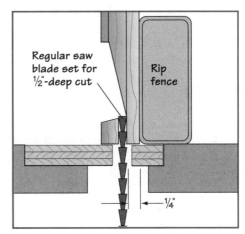

Figure 7-5. Making the tongue

the cross-grain cuts first. After making this set of cuts, move the fence closer to the blade and raise the blade slightly to set up for the next series of cuts. By trial and error on one of your scraps, you should be able to have the blade cut a smooth continuation of the bevel, as shown in *Figure 7-4.*

Continue in this fashion until the bevel stops ½ inch from the edge of the panel, as shown in *Figure 7-4.* Replace the dado cutter with a regular saw blade and reset the saw to cut vertically. Set the depth of cut to a little less (⅟₁₆ inch or so) than ½ inch and bring the fence over until it is a little more than ¼ inch from the blade. Make a test cut by running a panel along the fence vertically, as shown in *Figure 7-5.* Check the cut. The tongue should be ¼ inch thick and it should meet the beveled area cleanly. Play with the position of the fence and the depth of cut to get it right, then make the final cuts. With a little sanding (actually, quite a bit of sanding), your panel will be ready for use.

COMPOSITE PANELS

Nearly every wood shop has a pile of wood in a corner, consisting of pieces that aren't really usable but are too good to throw away. A good portion of this material is quite beautiful when used in the right way. But finding the right way can be difficult.

I've detailed the processes for making several of the different panels I've created with these scraps. I'm sure there are many more possibilities. Feel free to experiment. If you come up with something new, let me know about it.

Basic Techniques

The typical panel is made up of a number of thin, narrow slats, edge-glued together. I usually accentuate the joints by rounding the edges of each slat slightly, as shown in *Photo 7-5*. This creates a shadow line on the face of the panel. It adds detail to the panel and can help to offset minor variations in color. The joints themselves take one of two forms, either splined or shiplapped. The one you choose depends on the look you're after. (More on that later.)

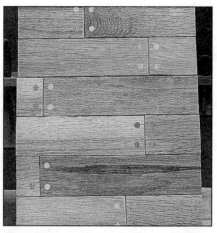

Photo 7-5. **I make no attempt to disguise the fact that these panels are made up of individual slats. In fact, I emphasize it by rounding the edges of the joints to create shadow lines across the panels.**

The slats are resawn from whatever material you're using. I generally make them about ⅜ inch thick and about 2 inches wide. At this thickness, I can usually get two slats from a 4/4 (four-quarter) board.

Sizing the slats. The size of the slats is determined by the size of the opening in the frame they're to fill. With the exception of herringbone-pattern panels, I've always oriented the grain of the slats so it runs horizontally. (This doesn't mean you can't run the grain vertically. I just never have.) So the length of the slats will be equal to the width of the opening, plus a little extra to fit in the frame's rabbets.

Determining the width of the slats is a little more involved. Measure the frame opening. This will equal the width of the exposed portion of the panel. I find that slats about 2 inches wide are the easiest to work with, so divide the opening to come out with the closest number to 2. For example, if you have a 16-inch opening, 8 slats 2 inches wide will fill it. If the opening is 15 inches high, then 8 slats 1⅞ inches wide will do the trick, and so on.

With this figure in hand, you can calculate the width of the individual slats. Here's where it gets a bit tricky because the slats are not all the same size. I like a panel to look as if it were made up of equal-width slats. To get this look, the top and bottom slats must actually be wider since they extend into the frame rabbets. So as you're cutting up the slats, you'll have to

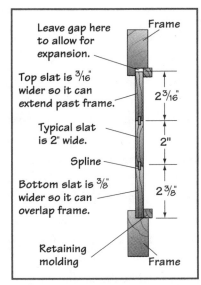

Figure 7-6. Sizing flat slats

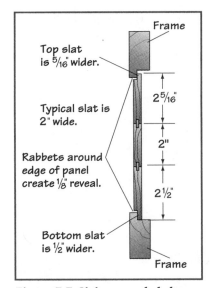

Figure 7-7. Sizing revealed slats

add ⅜ inch to the bottom slat and ³⁄₁₆ inch to the top one, as shown in *Figure 7-6*.

This all assumes that your stock lends itself to being cut up into 2-inch strips. If you have a great knot that's 5 inches wide, you'll probably want to go with wider slats to avoid cutting through it. Modify the calculations to suit the material at hand.

All of the previous calculations for slat width apply if you're making flat panels, as shown in *Figure 7-6*. Lately, however, I've taken to rabbeting the edges of my panels to create a slight reveal around the outside, as shown in *Figure 7-7*. The reveal is ⅛ inch wide. To determine the width of the slats for this type of panel, measure the inside of the frame opening and subtract ¼ inch—⅛ inch for the reveal at the top, and another ⅛ inch for the reveal at the bottom. Divide this figure by the number of slats to calculate the slat widths. This will give you the width of an average slat. The top and bottom slats are wider so they can extend into the frame rabbets. Add ½ inch to the bottom slat and ⁵⁄₁₆ inch to the top slat as you cut them.

Cutting the slats. Select the stock for your panels and cut it to length. (You may have to use two or more pieces to come up with a tall enough panel.) Then lay out the pieces so you can see the grain pattern.

Count the number of slats you can get from each board. Remember that the top and bottom slats are wider and that the saw kerf will take up about ⅛ inch of wood per cut. Sometimes, depending on the width of your boards, you may end up needing some extra stock even though your selected pieces are apparently wide enough. For example, let's say you're making a 16⁵⁄₁₆-inch-wide panel and you have two boards, one 11½ inches wide and the other 5½ inches wide. You'll need an extra piece or two even though the combined widths are greater than 16⁵⁄₁₆ inches. Of the eight

(continued on page 88)

RESAWING

Resawing is the name given to the process of cutting a board down in thickness to produce two or more thinner pieces. These cuts are parallel to the cuts made by the saw mill when the board was originally cut from the log; hence, the term resawing.

There are two machines that can be pressed into service for resawing: the table saw and the band saw. The table saw cuts faster and straighter, but its depth of cut is limited. For narrow stock, this isn't a problem—just set the fence and rip the pieces. For wider boards, however, the band saw is the machine of choice. While slower than the table saw, the band saw has a narrow blade that wastes less wood, and the operation is somewhat safer.

RESAWING ON THE BAND SAW

Before beginning any resawing, take a minute or two and make sure your saw is in top condition. Resawing, particularly if the boards are very wide, demands a lot of a saw, and a saw that is in poor adjustment can make kindling out of a valuable piece of wood in no time. So snug the guides right up to the blade and make sure the blade is ten-sioned and tracking correctly. Wide blades tend to cut straighter than narrow ones, so you may want to invest in a ½-inch or wider blade just for resawing. A skip-tooth blade with four teeth per inch does a nice job on my 14-inch saw. A bimetal blade lasts longer than a regular blade and is almost certainly worth the extra money if you plan to do a lot of resawing.

With narrow boards, such as those for

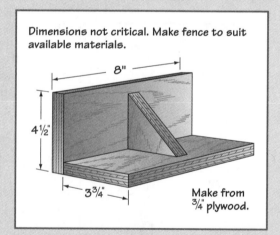

Dimensions not critical. Make fence to suit available materials.

8"

4½"

3¾"

Make from ¾ plywood.

panel slats, I simply draw a line down the center of an edge to follow as I run the board past the blade. For wider stock, I set up the fence shown above. It's made of plywood and runs from the front of the table to the back

Use a scrap to determine which way your blade leads. Then clamp the fence to the table to guide the stock along that line.

to the way the blade leads.

To determine the lead, find a scrap about 12 inches long with one straight side. Draw a line along the length of the board parallel to the straight side and in from the edge a distance equal to the thickness of the slats you want to end up with. Cut the scrap along this line, allowing the blade to find its own way. Cut in about halfway along the board and stop the saw, leaving the board in place. The straight side will be parallel to the blade's lead. Hold the fence along the edge of the scrap and clamp it in place, as shown at left.

CHOOSING YOUR STOCK

Practically any stock can be resawn. Joint one face and one edge so you'll have true surfaces to work from. Figure out how thick you want the finished pieces to be, then add ⅛ to ¼ inch for surfacing after the cut. By allowing a little extra thickness, you can plane away any warp and get rid of the saw marks at the same time. To calculate how many pieces you can get from a piece of stock, add the thickness of the individual slats plus ⅛ to ¼ inch per saw cut. This should give you an idea of how many pieces you can get from a given board.

of the blade. I don't like it extending beyond the blade because boards often will warp as they're cut and can throw the cut out of line.

The trick to setting up a fence for resawing is getting it set at the right angle in relation to the blade. You'd think this would be easy: Just set the fence up parallel to the blade and saw away. Nice thought, but it doesn't work that way. Every blade I've ever used has had a tendency to cut to one side or the other, a quirk known as leading. Some blades lead to the left, others to the right. When resawing with a fence, you have to get the fence set up parallel

88

approximately 2-inch slats you need,
you'll get only seven from your two
boards: five from the wider board, and
two from the narrower one.

With the pieces laid out on your
workbench, as shown in *Photo 7-6*, you
can play with their arrangement until
you find something that grabs your eye.
When you do, mark the top and bottom
so you'll know which slats to cut wider.
Cut the slats on the table saw. First the
top and bottom, then the narrower ones.
Reassemble the pieces in order and carefully mark them on both sides so you
don't get them mixed up.

Resawing the slats. Once you
have the slats cut to the right size, resaw
them to get them down to
the right thickness. For a
more detailed description, see "Resawing" on page 86.

Once the pieces are resawn, plane or belt sand
the freshly cut faces. A very fine pass through the
planer is best, but not if the slats are too short to feed
safely. In this case, you can sand away the saw marks.

Joining the slats. The basic joint I use is a
spline joint, as shown in
Photo 7-7. One of the main
advantages of this joint is
that none of the grain pattern is lost to the joint.

Cut the grooves in
the slats with your regular
blade on the table saw. This
will make the grooves about ⅛ inch
wide. Set up the saw with a fresh throat
plate. For more information about how
to make these saw accessories, see
"Shop-Made Throat Plates" on page 20.
Set the depth of cut to ³⁄₁₆ inch. Adjust
the fence so the cut will be approximately centered on the edge of each slat.
Don't spend too much time fussing with

Photo 7-6. Compose your panels by laying all the slats out on your bench. It's amazing how different arrangements of the same slats can yield surprisingly different results.

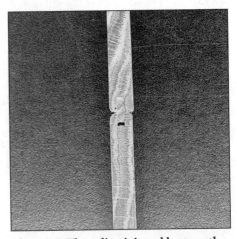
Photo 7-7. The spline joint adds strength to a panel without doing away with any of the showy grain pattern.

Tip

While I prefer to resaw slats on the band saw, I've also done it with a table saw. In fact, when working with such narrow slats, you can resaw them with a single pass on the table saw. Make sure the fence is parallel to the blade and use a push stick to keep your fingers from harm.

CABINETS AND BUILT-INS

this adjustment; close is good enough. Just be sure to cut each slat with the same face against the fence. Groove both edges of all the slats except the top and bottom ones. On these slats, the outside edges should remain ungrooved.

Make the splines next. Ordinarily in a spline joint, the grain of the spline should be perpendicular to the joint for strength. But here, since the spline is used more for alignment than for strength, I run the grain parallel to the joint. This avoids any problem with cross-grain construction.

Make the splines from a piece of the same material you used for the slats. Plane the stock to 5⁄16 inch thick to get the *width* of the spline. Then rip the splines to thickness so they slip in the grooves with a little friction. Be sure to use a push stick to keep your hands away from the blade. Planing the spline stock to thickness first ensures that the splines are slightly less than twice the groove depth wide. This will prevent the spline from holding the slats apart should there be debris in the groove when you glue up.

Sand the slats before you glue them together. I usually go over them with 220-grit paper in a pad sander. Be sure to round-over the edges with the sander to create the shadow line I mentioned earlier. Once all the slats are sanded, run a fine bead of glue along the grooves and slip in the splines. Then assemble the panel. Draw the joints closed with light clamp pressure. Allow the panels to sit overnight before going any further.

Photo 7-8. The other joint I use to make composite panels is the shiplap. It is easier to cut than the spline joint, but it requires wider slats.

The other joint I use to assemble panels is the shiplap, as shown in *Photo 7-8.* It is much easier to cut than the spline joint, but it does intrude into the grain pattern on the slats. I use this joint when I'm not worried about losing a little bit of pattern. The slats for a shiplapped panel are similar to those for a splined panel, except for their width.

Again, I like to have each slat appear to be about 2 inches wide. Start out by calculating the width just as you would for a splined panel. Once you find the visible width of the slats, add 3⁄8 inch—the width of the overlap. The total gives you the width of an average slat. As before, the top and bottom slats are different. Cut the bottom slat

Tip

When edge-gluing thin boards to make up a wide panel, hold the boards flat against the clamps with weights. This will counteract the tendency of the clamps to bow the pieces.

⅜ inch wider and the top slat 11⁄16 inch wider to allow for the part of the panel that overlaps the frame, as shown in *Figure 7-8.* This assumes that the concealed part of the tongue is on the bottom part of each slat.

Make the slats as described previously, cutting and resawing them to size. Be sure to mark the top and bottom slats to keep track of them. Once all the slats are prepared, you're ready to cut the joints. Here again, I work with a fresh throat plate for safety and to get as clean a cut as possible.

Figure 7-8. **Sizing shiplapped slats**

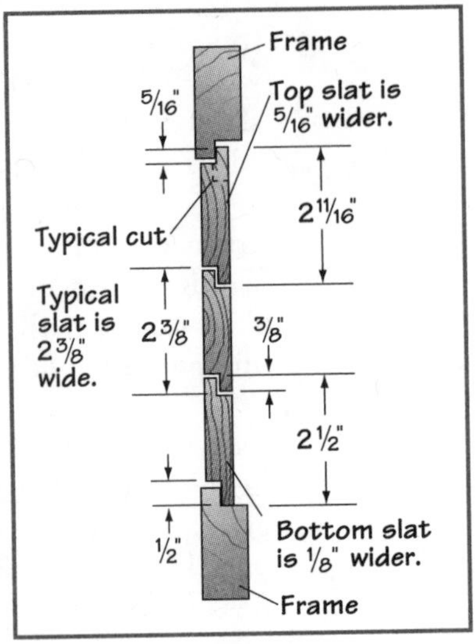

Set up a dado cutter to make a ¼-inch-wide × ⅜-inch-deep cut. Slide the rip fence over until the space between it and the blade is a little more than one-half the thickness of the slats. Run two pieces through the saw on edge to test the setup, as shown in *Photo 7-9.* Lap them to see if their surfaces are flush with one another. (By now, you should know that they won't be, at least not on the first try.) Move the fence slightly closer to the blade and try again.

When you get the setup right, cut all the slats. Each slat gets cut twice. The top edge gets a rabbet on the back, and the bottom edge gets a rabbet on the front. This holds true for all but the top and bottom slats. The bottom slat is cut just like the regular slats, except the blade should be raised to make the rabbet on the bottom edge ½ inch wide, as shown in *Figure 7-8.* The top slat is slightly different. Both of its rabbets should be cut on its front, as shown. When you're ready to cut the rabbet on the top edge, reset the blade to make the rabbet 5⁄16 inch wide.

Once the slats are machined, sand them and round-over the edges. Glue-up is easy. Starting with the top slat, apply a bead of glue to the bottom rabbet and place the slat on a flat sur-

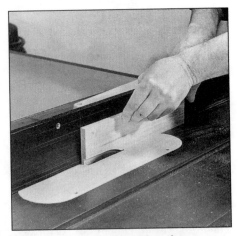

Photo 7-9. **Cutting the rabbets for a shiplap joint is similar to cutting the tongue for a tongue-and-groove joint.**

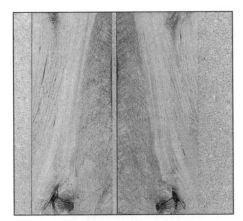

Photo 7-10. **Bookmatching allows the beauty hidden within a board to show in all its glory.**

face. Apply glue to the next slat and drop it in place. Continue adding slats until the panel is complete. Then place a flat sheet of plywood on top of the panel and weight it down. Once the glue is dry, you can fit the panel to its frame.

Bookmatched Panels

Apparent symmetry is exhibited by almost every living thing. For better or for worse, we tend to perpetuate this phenomenon in the objects we make. Often, in pursuit of this goal, potentially beautiful material is cast aside because its symmetry isn't immediately obvious. Thus, a lot of usable pieces of wood with tight knots or spectacular grain are consigned to the scrap bin because they don't have the right "look."

Try resawing these discards and opening the resulting halves like a book, as shown in *Photo 7-10.* You'll find these so-called scraps are suddenly prime candidates for use as door panels, a place ideal to display symmetrical grain patterns. Also, don't limit yourself to the wood in your shop or at your supplier when it comes time to make panels. I've had great luck using wood from less common sources, like my firewood pile. (See "Panel Materials" on page 92.)

Bookmatching works nicely when you're making up a set of composite panels for matching doors. As you're resawing the slats, make sure you label them so you can glue up identical panels. I use the spline joint to assemble the slats because I don't want to lose any of the grain pattern if I don't absolutely have to.

Be extra-careful while cutting up these odd pieces of wood. While knots and other grain "defects" will provide you with a wide palette of beautiful patterns, they also may come apart as they're sawn. As always, be sure to use adequate eye protection to reduce the risk of injury. Feed the stock with push sticks to keep your fingers clear of the blade.

Tip

When looking through your stock for panel material, use a mirror to help you spot bookmatches. Stand it vertically on a board to display the potential match. The match won't be exactly like what you see since the actual grain pattern comes from the center of the board, but it will be close.

the PROFESSIONAL view

PANEL MATERIALS

Wood for panels doesn't have to come from a lumberyard. In fact, some of the most striking panels I've made have come from boards I've cut myself, as shown below. One incident I remember in particular happened several years ago when I was out driving. I came across a crew cutting up a fallen maple tree. From what I could see of it, the wood appeared to be spalted, or in the first stages of decay. What a find! While lumber in this condition isn't great from a structural standpoint, it can be quite beautiful. The fungus that breaks down the wood often leaves a network of fine black lines throughout the grain, something like an abstract pen-and-ink drawing. Drying the wood arrests the decay, but the lines remain, adding a very delicate touch to the grain. Now if only I could get my hands on that maple.

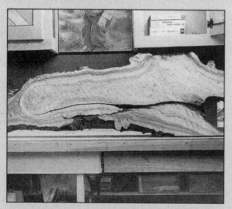

Materials for woodworking can come from anywhere. This spectacular piece almost ended up in my fireplace before I saved it for a more lasting future.

I stopped and found the foreman. I explained that I was a cabinetmaker and that I wanted the wood for cabinets. He had already cut the log to firewood lengths, but the short sections would do very nicely for panel stock. "Sure," he said with a sarcastic drawl, "you want it for making cabinets."

In spite of his skepticism, he said he would ask the owner. When I stopped back a day later, he said I could take some. Then I was faced with a problem inherent in finding one's own wood: moving it from site to shop. Despite the fact that these pieces had been cut into shorter lengths, they were still heavy.

The fates provided a friend with a truck and a strong back to save that day. Once I had the pieces back at the shop, I opened the chunks up with a chain saw, exposing some spectacular grain. With the pieces cut to a manageable size, I carried them inside and cut them into boards with my band saw. After stacking them in a corner of the shop, I had only to wait until they were dry before using them.

Drying time can vary, depending on many things—the temperature of your shop, the age of the wood, and the thickness of the pieces, to name a few. I've found that pieces cut about ½ inch thick (for herringbone panels) will dry in about three weeks if I keep them inside. Pieces I want to bookmatch I cut thicker—about 1 inch. These are usually dry enough to use in about six weeks.

Photo 7-11. This cabinet has doors with slipmatched panels. While somewhat less formal than bookmatching, the technique yields some rather dramatic results.

Herringbone Panels

Photo 7-12. The arrangement of the slats in a herringbone panel can vary to suit your tastes. Here, I put the darker slats toward the bottom to give the panel some weight. These panels were made from a spalted apple log.

Slipmatched Panels

If you have a piece of wood that simply cannot be bookmatched, or if you just don't like the look of bookmatched panels, you might try slipmatching. To slipmatch, first resaw the slats. Then, instead of opening them like a book, lay them side by side, as shown in *Photo 7-11*.

The effect is like looking at a strip of movie film. Each piece is just slightly different from its neighbor. The overall effect is very striking. For these panels, I usually use the shiplap joint because it's faster, and the loss of pattern isn't as important.

Unlike the previous two panel styles, herringbone panels do not require matching the slats at all. Herringbone is a dramatic pattern with lots of energy. It is suited for stock where bookmatches are difficult to find, or where they don't yield interesting results. Their arrangement can be totally random. Occasionally, however, I try to group the slats with the darker ones toward the bottom and the lighter ones toward the top, as shown in *Photo 7-12*. I find this adds a pleasing visual weight to a panel.

Make the slats 2⅜ inches wide and about as long as three-quarters the width of the frame opening. Join them with the shiplap joint, as described earlier. There is one extra step. The end that points toward the center of each panel must also be rabbeted, as shown in *Photo 7-13* on page 94. Make sure the end is cut square, then make this cut as

If you're making up panels with the slats arranged randomly, you can make up the herringbone pattern in long sections. When the glue dries, crosscut the sections into individual panels.

you're rabbeting the long edges of the slats. Just run the slats by the blade on end, with the front face toward the fence, as shown in *Photo 7-14*. Be extra-careful as you're making these end cuts.

Glue up the panel as you would a regular shiplapped panel. Once the glue dries, trim the panel to its final width. This can be done in three cuts. Start by laying out a centerline along the length of the panel. Then draw parallel lines on either side of the centerline to indicate the panel width. Make a final line about ¼ inch outside one of these lines. Cut along this last line on the band saw. Then guide the sawn edge along the rip fence on the table saw to the opposite side. Finally, reset the fence and trim the first edge on the table saw to cut the panel to its final width. Once you have the panel cut to the right width, crosscut it to length.

Finishing Touches

No matter which type of panel you choose to make, once the panels are glued up, there are a few things you have to do to get them ready to go in their frames. Start by double-checking their dimensions to make sure they'll fit. Remember to make the cross-grain dimension about ³⁄₁₆ inch shy of the frame dimension to allow for expansion and contraction across the width of the panel.

If you've decided to cut a rabbet around the panel's edge, as I do, now's the time to do it (or complete it if you're dealing with a shiplapped panel, since the long-grain edges have already been rabbeted). I usually use a rabbeting bit in a router, but you can also do it with a dado cutter on the table saw. The rabbet's width varies around the panel, as shown in *Figure 7-7*

Photo 7-13. All the rabbets on the slats overlap to lock the panel together.

Photo 7-14. Making the cut on the end of a slat looks worse than it is. Use a push block to back up the piece and wrap your fingers around the fence to keep them from harm. Also, make sure the opening in the throat plate is small enough to keep the slat from slipping beneath the table.

on page 85. On the sides and the bottom, it should be ½ inch wide. This will fill the rabbet in the frame and leave an ⅛-inch reveal around the edge of the panel. On the top edge, the rabbet should be ⁵⁄₁₆ inch wide to leave room for expansion. Use an edge guide to set the router up to cut the appropriate-width rabbet. Or, on the table saw, use a rabbeting fence, as shown in *Photo 2-13* on page 29.

If you have a herringbone pattern and have left very small pieces at the top corners or the center of the bottom, make sure that these are secure before beginning any cuts.

Once the rabbets are cut, sand them to clean up the machine marks. Round-over the hard edges to match the joints between the strips. It's a good idea to get these delicate panels into their frames as quickly as possible to keep them flat. However, I do take the time to finish them before installing them. This has two benefits. First, it ensures that the entire panel gets finished. So even if it shrinks after installation, no unfinished wood will be exposed. Second, it prevents the panel from getting stuck to its frame. Sometimes when a panel is finished in place, the finish acts like a glue and sticks the panel to the frame. This can prevent the panel from expanding and contracting, which can eventually cause it to crack.

8 DRAWER JOINERY

Joints for durable drawers

Of all the tasks involved in cabinetry, drawer making is among the most involved, demanding a craftsman's skill and time. There are a lot of individual pieces of wood to prepare and many joints to cut. Then, each drawer must be installed. In traditional cabinetwork, this means painstakingly adjusting each drawer to fit in its particular place. Not too tight, yet not too loose: just right. Goldilocks all over again. And even if you do fit a drawer to a case just right, some particularly humid summer afternoon it may not open despite your careful work. No, thank you.

Instead of relying on tradition, I make my drawers to a specific size, then hang them inside their cases with mechanical drawer slides. Purists may scoff at this intrusion of modern technology, but my drawers run smoothly throughout the year. They also don't require a lot of time-consuming hand fitting.

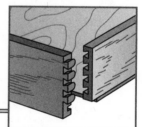

My method of drawer making has another advantage over the traditional technique. I build the entire drawer box (front, back, and sides) from a wood like birch. Then I add a good drawer face to match the doors. This separate face allows me to adjust its fit to align perfectly with the cabinets.

Regardless of how they are fitted into a cabinet, drawers must be put together with strong joints. Of all the elements of a cabinet, the drawers are under the most stress, both from constantly being opened and closed as well as from supporting a load. The joinery must be up to the job. In my mind, this means one joint: the dovetail.

DOVETAILS

I cut dovetails with a router and a commercial dovetail jig. Once you get things set up, there is no faster way to cut this joint. I use a 12-inch jig made by Porter-Cable. Relatively inexpensive, it makes excellent half-blind dovetails, the style I use for my drawers, as shown in *Photo 8-1.*

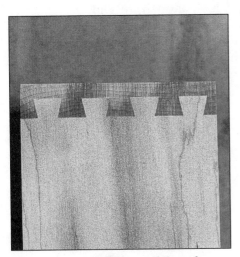

Photo 8-1. **My small dovetail jig makes cutting these half-blind dovetails very quick and easy. The dovetails are called half-blind because they're only visible from one side. Even though I cut these joints with a router, I like to contine the tradition of starting and ending on a half-pin.**

Preparing the Stock

To make drawers, your stock should be straight and flat. Warped wood will cause you nothing but grief throughout the process. If you can joint and plane the stock yourself, do it. Otherwise, try to find the straightest, flattest boards possible.

While drawer stock has to be flat, it doesn't have to be perfect. You can cut and position the pieces to deal with blemishes in the wood. The front of the drawer is covered. The back of the drawer is not seen in normal use. And the bottom inside edge of each piece is hidden by the drawer bottom. Turn the pieces so their blemishes are in these positions and the defects will practically disappear.

There are four dimensions that need to be considered when you prepare

Tip

If possible, mill all the stock for your drawers and then joint, sand, and assemble them immediately. Otherwise, your stock may warp or twist. Once together in final form, the drawers will stay straight.

the stock for drawers. These are the thickness of the stock, the height of the drawer, the length (or depth) of the drawer, and the width of the drawer. Some of these figures are standard, remaining the same drawer after drawer. Others vary from cabinet to cabinet.

Thickness. I like to make the parts for my drawer boxes ⅝ inch thick. The jig will accept stock up to ¾ inch, but I prefer the look of ⅝ inch so I plane the stock to this thickness.

Height. I make the top drawers in my cabinets 3½ inches high. For them, I allow an opening in the cabinet of 5¼ inches. This includes ½ inch of clearance under the drawer and 1¼ inches of clearance above it. The height of any lower drawers varies, but I usually make them taller. The width of the drawer stock should match the height of the drawer.

I make my drawers shorter than the cabinet opening for two reasons. The first concerns the spacing of the dovetails. Traditional hand-cut dovetails start and end with a half-pin. The pins are the part of the joint where the angle appears on the *end* of the board. The tails are cut on the mating piece—the angle appears on the *face* of the board. I like this look and with my jig it works perfectly with 3½-inch-wide stock, as shown in *Photo 8-1*. This is a small detail that not many people notice, but I enjoy including it in my work. The table below shows other widths of stock that will allow this detail when cut with the Porter-Cable jig. As you can see, I could use the next width listed, 4⅜ inches. While this height drawer would fit in the opening, I consider it too big, which brings up the second reason I make the drawers shorter.

In my experience, most people tend to overfill drawers until things run over the top. Without adequate clearance, the drawer would get stuck inside the cabinet. So I like to allow a little extra room to avoid this problem.

STOCK WIDTH	USE
1¾	
2⅝	
3½	My standard top drawer
4⅜	
5¼	
6⅛	
7	
7⅞	Lower drawers in kitchen drawer bases
8¾	
9⅝	
10½	

NOTE: Stock width allows joint to begin and end with a half-pin.

For deeper drawers, figure out the maximum space available. Then consult the table to find what width pieces will give you the proper dovetail spacing within the space allowed. Be sure to allow clearance both above and below the drawer.

Length. For a standard 24-inch-deep base cabinet, I cut the drawer sides 20 inches long. This makes the drawer about 20⅝ inches deep overall because of the way the dovetails go together. This depth drawer works well with my favorite drawer slides. The space behind the drawer can then be used to run plumbing or electrical lines if necessary.

Width. The last dimension needed is the width of the drawer. This is determined by the width of the drawer opening in the case and the space needed for the drawer slides. Most drawer slides use 1 inch overall (but check your manufacturer's instructions before you cut your stock), so an opening 13½ inches wide requires a drawer 12½ inches wide.

In fact, most slides allow for a little bit of error. I use Accuride drawer slides, which require a minimum of 1 inch of clearance and allow a maximum of 1¹⁄₁₆ inch. (This is sometimes expressed as a tolerance of +0 and −¹⁄₁₆.) What this means is that the drawer can be slightly undersize and still work properly. I use this fact to my advantage. I cut the drawer front and back to be exactly 1 inch smaller than the opening. Then, to ensure that I

Photo 8-2. **To make sure the slides have enough room, I cut the dovetails so the drawer sides are recessed slightly into the fronts and backs. After assembly, a quick belt sanding brings the slight lip flush with the side.**

have no problems with the slides, I set the dovetail jig to recess the sides slightly into the front and back, as shown in *Photo 8-2.* Then I belt sand the ends of the front and back flush to the sides, creating a slightly undersize drawer.

This adjustment is made by moving the template slightly in or out on the jig. You'll probably have to play with it a bit to get it where you want it. Remember that if you make the drawer oversize, it won't fit or it will be very stiff on its slides. On the other hand, if you make the drawer too narrow, no real harm is done. You can always shim the slide after you mount it. Just loosen the screws, slip the shim behind the slide next to a screw, and then retighten everything.

While I can't remember the last time I had to shim a drawer slide, in the past, I have had problems with drawers being too big. When I first started using the Porter-Cable jig, my drawers seemed to grow during dovetailing. It's a hard lesson to make a drawer too big. So, it's best to err on the small side.

Deliberately building an undersize drawer eliminates two potential problems. One is accidentally making an oversize drawer that won't allow room for the slides. The other is creating a joint where the drawer sides stand proud of the ends of the front and back. To make things flush, I'd have to sand down the entire drawer side. As in sanding case tops, this isn't a particularly bright prospect.

Once you've determined the sizes of the drawer components, they must be cut accurately. If one side is longer than the other or an end is out of square, you'll be in for difficulties. Even if you manage to get the drawer together, it will never fit, look, or work properly.

To cut the parts to length, attach a straight auxiliary fence to your miter gauge, as shown in *Photo 8-3*. Square the fence to the blade. Don't trust the markings on the gauge—use a square to check the setup. Cut one end of each piece of stock so that it's square. Then turn all the pieces around and mark the uncut end on one of them for length. Put the marked piece in position against the miter gauge fence. Clamp a handscrew to the fence against the square end of the piece to act as a stop. Cut all the pieces to their appropriate lengths this way.

As you're working, make a few extra pieces. You don't have to cut them to length, just make them the same width and thickness as the rest of the drawer stock. This way you'll be prepared if you should goof.

As you're cutting, make sure that the saw table is free of debris. When you clamp the handscrew to the fence, leave a little space between it and the table. This way, any sawdust will pass underneath instead of piling up and

Photo 8-3. To cut pieces accurately to length, screw an auxiliary fence to your miter gauge. I usually use a length of plywood, but any straight stock will work.

throwing off the length of your pieces. Cut all the pieces to a given length before changing the setup. Once all the pieces are cut, separate them into individual piles for each drawer. Each pile should contain two sides, one front, and one back. Save a few of the cutoffs to use as test pieces when you set up the dovetail jig. Make sure each scrap is at least 4 inches long and has at least one square end to dovetail. If none of the cutoffs are long enough, cut a few pieces from the extra drawer stock to use instead.

Tip

When you're milling a number of parts to the same dimensions, cut each one with the same setup on each machine. This will help ensure that they all end up identical. While you're cutting, you may want to make a few extra pieces—that way you'll be prepared for the inevitable mistake.

Setting Up the Router

Once the stock is ready, the next step is to set up the router and the jig. I use a 1½ horsepower Porter-Cable router with the guide bushing that came with the jig screwed to its base. You don't have to use a Porter-Cable router—any other brand will work as long as the guide bushing fits. In the router, mount a ½-inch 14-degree dovetail bit. Because the bit has a larger diameter than the guide bushing, you'll have to thread the bit through the bushing and into the router's collet to mount it.

Set the depth of cut to that recommended in the jig's instruction manual. Don't spend too much time fussing, just get it as close as possible. You're going to make a test cut before you begin cutting the actual drawers. It's a rare cabinetmaker who doesn't have to make a few adjustments after the test cut.

Making the Test Cut

With the Porter-Cable jig, and others like it, both parts of the joint are cut at once. The piece that gets the pins is clamped on top of the jig, and the piece that gets the tails is clamped on the front. Because of the rotary action of the bit, you'll notice that the pin pockets and one side of the tails are rounded. Once the joint is assembled, these curved surfaces disappear.

For the test cut, take a piece of the scrap stock and slip it in the front of the jig with its square end up. Slide it to the right side of the jig and loosely clamp it in place with its end projecting above the table surface, as shown in *Photo 8-4* on page 102. Don't worry too much about position yet; you're using this board to help locate the one you'll slip in the top of the jig.

Once you've positioned the first board, slip a second piece of scrap in the top of the jig. Its square end should butt tightly up against the first piece. Slide it all the way to the right until it touches the built-in stop, as shown in *Photo 8-5.* Double-check to be sure the pieces are still butted firmly together, then tighten the top clamp.

With the small Porter-Cable jig, this means torquing down two wing nuts, one at either end of the clamp. I tighten the wing nut directly over the stock until I can't tighten it any more. Moving to the opposite side of the jig, I tighten the other nut until the clamping bar is flat on the stock. Then I give the second nut five more turns to make sure the clamp is tight.

It is particularly important that the piece on the top of the jig be locked tightly in place. As the router cuts, it has a tendency to push this piece out of the jig. If it succeeds in doing so, the joint will be spoiled. In contrast, the router tends to push the piece on the front of the jig tight against the jig's face. This lessens the chance that the piece will slip. Therefore, you don't need to tighten the front clamp as much as you do the top one.

With the top piece locked in place, it's time to reposition the front piece. Loosen its clamp and push it up until the end is flush with the top surface of the second piece. The plastic template will act as a stop. It is flexible, however, and will bend upward with pressure from underneath. So keep one hand on the template to press it flat against the top piece as you push the front piece up. Keep the piece up against the template and slide it over until it stops against the stop at the right of the jig. Clamp it in place. Now both pieces are ready to be routed.

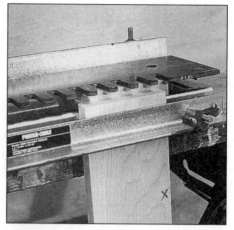

Photo 8-4. Slide the first piece roughly into position on the front of the jig. All the drawer sides will be held vertically like this as they are routed.

Photo 8-5. Next, slip the second piece into position on top of the jig. Butt it firmly against the first piece and against the side stop on the jig. The drawer fronts and backs will be cut in this horizontal top position.

Photo 8-6. Once the pieces are clamped tightly in the jig, make a light pass from right to left. By precutting along the back of the dovetails, you can virtually eliminate any tearout that might otherwise be a problem.

Set the router down on the right side of the jig. Make sure the bit is not touching the work, then flip the switch. Make a light pass from right to left, just skimming the front piece, as shown in *Photo 8-6.* This light cut will help prevent tearout as you complete the joint.

Next, start from the left and rout the joint by guiding the router in and out along the template. Be sure to rout the full depth of each slot between the fingers. When you reach the right side of the jig, slide the router back to the left and make another pass without lifting the router off the jig. On this second pass, make sure the guide bushing maintains contact with the template the entire time. When you finish, move the bit away from the stock and turn the router off. Don't lift it until the bit stops spinning. If you do, you run the risk of cutting into the template.

You may laugh at this prospect now, but don't forget—I warned you. Every time I train a new man to use the jig, I prepare myself to order a new template. And when I have to, the fellow who answers the phone at my local Porter-Cable outlet rattles off the part number from memory once I tell him what I need. I guess a few other folks have the same problem.

Inspect the joint before removing the pieces from the jig. The backs of the tails should be round and all the sockets should be the same depth, as shown in *Photo 8-7* on page 104. If they're not, trace the template again with the router. Take the parts out and try to put them together. They should fit firmly, yet you shouldn't have to bang them together.

If the joint is too loose, lower the bit. If it's too tight, raise the bit. Cut the routed ends off the scrap on the table saw and try again. Keep after it until the joint fits right.

> **Tip**
>
> Tightening the clamps on a dovetail jig is crucial to the success of the joint. But most of the simpler jigs employ small wing nuts to do the job. After a few drawers, tightening these tiny nuts can start to hurt. Rather than put up with this discomfort, replace the wing nuts with plastic knobs, such as those available from The Woodworker's Store. (See "Suppliers" on page 368 for the address and phone number.) For a few dollars, you'll be able to customize your jig, making it much easier to use.

Cutting the Drawer Joints

Once you get the router set, you can set up to cut the drawer joints. The method is exactly the same as it was for the test pieces—except that with the good stock, there are some additional concerns. You have to remember which parts get pins and which parts get tails. And you have to keep track of where the groove for the bottom goes in relation to how you load the parts in the jig.

I realize the instructions seem endless, with lots of fussy details to keep in mind. But once you've been through the process a few times, it gets much easier. It's like the old commercial for a standard transmission car, which said, "Don't worry about all the things there are to remember when trying to drive a standard; after 10,000 miles it becomes automatic."

Organizing the pieces. To help keep things straight, organize all the parts before you start routing. I find if I am organized, I don't make as many mistakes and I can get into a rhythm that makes the task go quickly. For each drawer, lay out the four parts in the positions they'll take in the assembled box, as shown in *Photo 8-8*. The outside surfaces should be face down on the bench.

Marking the pieces. Draw an X to show where the groove for the drawer bottom will go. The marks should be on the inside surface of each piece. Also mark each piece with a drawer number or letter. This will help you reorganize the pieces if they should get mixed up. Once all the parts for all the drawers are marked, you're ready to rout.

Routing the joints. As a part of the overall organizational plan, it pays to rout the joints for a drawer in the same order each time. By developing a habit like this, you are much less likely to

Photo 8-7. Before you remove the pieces from the jig, inspect them carefully. Make sure the tails are all evenly rounded and the slots are all a uniform depth.

Photo 8-8. When routing drawers, lay out the parts in order. Mark the location of the bottom groove on each piece with an X. Also, label each piece with the drawer number so you'll be able to regroup the pieces if they get mixed up.

Photo 8-9. For the right back drawer corner and the left front corner, the pieces are loaded in the jig against the left stops. The X marks should be toward the left.

make a mistake. I always start at the right front corner of the drawer and work my way around counterclockwise.

Loading drawer parts in the jig is slightly different than loading scrap pieces. With a drawer, it suddenly matters which surface faces out and which piece goes where.

The inside surfaces (marked with an X) should always face out. The fronts and backs should always go in the top of the jig, and the sides should always go in the front of the jig. Loading the pieces in this way ensures that the drawer will go together right side out. It also ensures that the pins will be cut on the front and back and the tails will be cut on the sides.

There is one final consideration. To make sure the bottom grooves align perfectly all around the drawer, the bottom edge of each drawer part should be the edge that is placed against the side stops on the jig. This means that as you work your way around the drawer, you'll cut the first joint with the pieces against the right stops, as shown in the previous photos. Then you'll cut the second joint with the pieces against the left stops, as shown in *Photo 8-9*, and so on back and forth across the jig. I find this gives the work an agreeable rhythm.

Routing all the drawers. Take a second before you rout each joint to double-check that the pieces are against the stops and the piece on the front of the jig isn't buckling the template. As you work, you needn't check every joint. Just check one joint per drawer to make sure none of the adjustments has gone astray.

Some key points to keep in mind as you work: The cut being made is a heavy one, which may pull the bit out of the collet. This will change the fit of the joint. You can do several things to avoid this problem. First, use a sharp bit. A dull bit won't cut as easily and it will vibrate more, increasing the tendency of the bit to drop.

Next, use a light touch as you feed the router into the cut. Don't ram it along the template,

Tip

If you make a lot of drawers, it may pay you to invest in an inexpensive router and leave it set up solely for dovetailing. That way you can set it up once and forget about it until it's time to replace the bit.

hoping to get through faster. The strain of too fast a feed can also cause the bit to drop. But don't cut too slowly, either. A slow rate of feed won't cause the bit to pull out, but it will burn the wood, which will result in a poor-quality glue joint. Finally, make sure the bit is good and tight to begin with. Obvious? Of course, but so is "Don't cut into the template." Just you wait.

The biggest problem with routing dovetails is setting up the router, a task I dislike. So I finally decided to leave one of my routers devoted only to making dovetails. It is set up and stays that way until the bit needs to be sharpened. I've got the stops on the jig where I like them, and I've worked out the sizes of drawers that work best for my purposes. Now, when I want a drawer, it's just a matter of cutting the stock to size.

AN ALTERNATE DRAWER JOINT

The dovetail is an excellent joint to use for drawers. It is durable and good-looking, appropriate in all situations. But there are times when you might prefer a simpler approach. While you can't beat the dovetail for strength, it does take a fair amount of time to set up and cut—time you may not want to invest in a project if it is strictly utilitarian or not intended for everyday use. Instead, you can put drawers together with the same tongue-and-groove joint used for cases, as shown in *Photo 8-10*. (Note that the dimensions of the joint in the photo are not those that I recommend.)

Preparing the Stock

Use the same ⅝-inch-thick stock used with the other joints. Cut the sides to the full depth of the drawers. Cut the front and back 1 inch shy of the full width. As shown in *Figure 8-1*, the front and back don't run the full width of the drawer, they only extend partway into the sides.

Photo 8-10. The same tongue-and-groove joint used to assemble cases can be used for drawers. While not as strong as the other interlocking drawer joints, the tongue-and-groove joint will last indefinitely as long as you don't abuse the drawer.

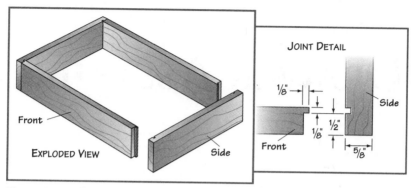

Figure 8-1. **Making tongue-and-groove drawers**

Cutting the Joint

Cut the grooves in the drawer sides with the regular blade on the table saw. They should be only ⅛ inch wide and ⅛ inch deep. Locate them as shown in the drawing. For shallow drawers, guide the pieces past the blade with the miter gauge. Use the rip fence as a stop to position the grooves.

With the grooves completed, cut tongues on the fronts and backs. As you did with the case parts, stand the pieces on end and guide them through the saw along the rip fence. Unlike the case joints, however, the tongue should completely fill the groove. Any gap would be unsightly on a completed drawer.

Assembling the Joint

Once the joinery is complete, you can treat the drawer parts just like those cut with the other joints. The next chapter describes cutting the grooves for the drawer bottom. When it comes time to glue the joint up, apply glue to the grooves and slip the tongues in place. Then drive finish nails through the sides to hold the parts together while the glue dries.

9 DRAWER ASSEMBLY

Putting together
all the pieces

With the corner joints behind you, the toughest part of making drawers is over. What remains is to put all the pieces together. This includes grooving the sides for the bottom, cutting and installing the bottom, sanding the parts, and gluing up.

While this process may seem routine, it is still critical. Drawer boxes must go together square, or you'll be faced with all sorts of troubles when you go to hang them in place.

Once the drawer boxes are assembled, I like to round the outside edges. This gives the drawer a finished look and makes it much nicer to handle.

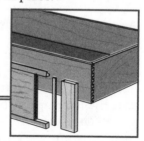

CUTTING THE GROOVE FOR THE BOTTOM

I usually use ¼-inch plywood for my drawer bottoms. (Occasionally, a client will request something more traditional. In this case, I change my technique. See "Solid Wood Drawer Bottoms" on page 110.) You'd think it would be a simple matter to set the dado cutter to ¼ inch and cut all the grooves. It's not. The plywood is rarely—if ever—exactly ¼ inch thick. So, instead of using the dado cutter, I use a regular saw blade to make the grooves for the bottom, making two or more passes as needed.

Begin by setting the blade for a ¼-inch-deep cut. Take a drawer front and place it with its inside surface (the one with an X on it from dovetailing) down on the saw table and toward the fence. Hold the front against the fence and adjust the fence so that the blade will fall into the first dovetail pocket. This will conceal the groove when the drawer is assembled.

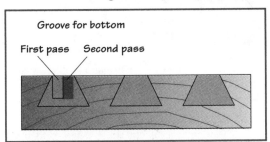

Figure 9-1. Cutting drawer bottom grooves

The groove is made by two passes of the saw. Position the fence so that both passes will fall within the pocket, as shown in *Figure 9-1*. Lock the fence in place and cut all the drawer parts plus a scrap. Be sure the Xs are down and toward the fence.

After grooving all the pieces the first time, move the fence slightly to the right to set up for the next pass. Lock it in place and make a test cut in the scrap. Check the fit of the resulting groove on the plywood for the drawer bottoms. Bump the fence over some more and cut again if necessary. The plywood should fit snugly in the groove. Make the second pass on all the pieces.

Sand the inside surfaces of the drawer parts before assembly. I use 100-grit sandpaper in the orbital sander—and a very light touch on the joint surfaces. If you want to be absolutely sure that sanding the drawer parts won't affect the fit of the joints, sand them before you cut the joints.

CUTTING THE BOTTOM

Assemble one drawer of each size to measure for the bottoms. Make sure the drawer is square, measure its inside dimensions,

(continued on page 112)

SOLID WOOD DRAWER BOTTOMS

Before plywood was commercially available, cabinetmakers used solid wood for drawer bottoms. This practice still has its place—in reproduction work, or in a piece you want to have the flavor and feel of tradition.

There are a few things to keep in mind when using solid wood. Unlike plywood, the bottom will add no strength to the drawer. It can *not* be glued in place because it must be free to expand and contract with changes in humidity. In this way, it is very much like the panel in frame-and-panel construction. And when you fit the bottom to the drawer, you have to allow for its seasonal movement. This is done by cutting down the drawer back. (More on that later.)

GLUING UP THE STOCK

Joint and plane the stock for the drawer bottom to the necessary thickness. This can be anywhere from ⅜ inch for large drawers down to ⅛ inch or so for smaller ones. Thicker stock gives you a more solid feel,

while thinner stock lends an air of delicacy. The grain should run from side to side in the drawer bottom. This will allow the bottom to expand out the back. Glue up a panel as long as the drawer is wide and as wide as the drawer is deep.

GROOVING THE SIDES AND FRONT

As with plywood-bottom drawers, the solid bottom is contained in grooves cut in the drawer parts. Only the drawer front and sides get grooved, however. As mentioned previously, the back is cut short.

Depending on the thickness of the drawer bottom, you have two choices for the grooves. You can cut them to fit the bottom exactly, or you can cut them to a standard size—¼ inch for example—then rabbet the edges of the bottom to fit.

If you choose to cut the groove to fit the bottom, set the saw blade to the appropriate height. Then make multiple passes, bumping the fence over each time, until the bottom

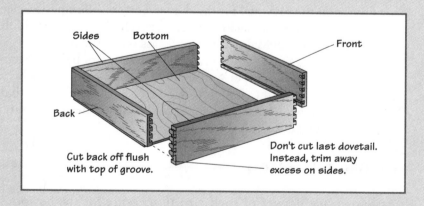

Sides   Bottom   Front

Back

Cut back off flush with top of groove.

Don't cut last dovetail. Instead, trim away excess on sides.

just slips in. If you choose to cut the groove to a standard width, set up the saw the same way, but stop moving the fence once the groove is as wide as you want. Then cut tongues on the edges of the drawer bottom as you did when making cases. For a refresher course, see "Setting Up to Cut the Tongue" on page 19.

SHORTENING THE BACK

The back must be cut flush with the top of the groove, as shown on the opposite page. The easiest time to accomplish this is right after you finish grooving the other pieces. Leave the fence in place and raise the blade high enough to cut through the back. Push the back through the saw to cut it down to size.

FITTING THE BOTTOM

Once you have the drawer parts grooved and trimmed to size, put them together without glue. Cut the bottom to length so it slides easily into the grooves in the sides. Slide the bottom in place and seat it in the front groove. Mark its width and cut it so it is flush with or slightly proud of the outside of the back of the drawer.

ASSEMBLING THE DRAWER

Glue the corner joints as you usually would and assemble the drawer without the bottom. Square it carefully, then set it aside to dry. After the drawer is dry, you can fit the bottom to the drawer. You must also make sure that there is no glue blocking the grooves. Any squeeze-out here will prevent the bottom from sliding into place. Don't attempt to glue up the bottom with the drawer. Undoubtedly some glue squeeze-out will glue the bottom in, eventually cracking the bottom.

Before you install the bottom, cut a slot in its back edge, as shown below. This will permit you to support the bottom at the back and lock it in place with a roundhead screw. Drive the screw into the bottom edge of the back at the slot. Tighten the screw down all the way, then back it off a half-turn. It should just clear the drawer bottom. This way, the bottom can expand and contract by sliding around the screw. For a wide drawer, you may want to cut two or three equally spaced slots to add more support to the bottom.

Traditionally, the only part of a drawer that was finished was the front. Today, however, this is really not acceptable and drawers are finished inside and out. When you go to finish a drawer with a solid wood bottom, take the bottom out and finish it separately. This way, should the bottom contract after reassembly, it won't have any unfinished edges to show.

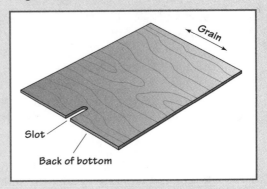

Grain

Slot

Back of bottom

then add ½ inch for the groove (¼ inch for each side). Then subtract ¹⁄₁₆ inch for insurance. Cut the bottoms to size. I run the grain from front to back, as shown in *Photo 9-1*.

ASSEMBLING THE DRAWER

Once the drawer bottoms are cut, sand them. Pay particular attention to the edges. There are always little fuzzies left from crosscutting plywood. Blow or wipe the sanding dust from the parts and you're ready to assemble.

Test Fitting

I suggest you test fit each drawer before applying glue. At this point, you've got too much time and effort invested to risk a mistake.

Photo 9-1: As an added touch, I try to select plywood with a nice-looking grain pattern for my drawer bottoms. Note that running the grain from front to back only works with plywood.

Test fit each drawer with its bottom in place. If the drawer won't go together, the bottom is probably the culprit. Remeasure; cut the bottom if needed. Also check the groove. There may be some debris in it, keeping the bottom from seating properly. Once you get the drawer to go together right, it can be glued up.

Gluing Up

Start with the parts for the drawer set out in order on a bench. Because the bottom is plywood and won't expand and contract with moisture changes, it can be glued in place. This will help stiffen the drawer, making it stronger than it would be with a solid wood bottom. Put a drop of glue into each dovetail pocket and swirl it around with a glue brush. Run a light bead of glue down the sides of each groove.

Fit the front and back into one of the sides. Spread them slightly and slide the bottom into place, as shown in *Photo 9-2*. If the bottom is warped, you may

Photo 9-2: Once the front and back are inserted in a side, spring them apart slightly and slip the bottom in place.

Photo 9-3: **Tap the second side in place with a mallet. Use a piece of scrap to protect the wood, but don't let the scrap cover the joint. Otherwise, you won't be able to seat it fully.**

have to push it flat to get it into the grooves. When the bottom is in, tap the remaining side into place with a mallet. Use a block of wood to protect the side as you drive the joints home, as shown in *Photo 9-3.* Turn the drawer over to see if the other side is fully seated. Clamps should be unnecessary once the joints are seated, unless the stock is warped and won't stay in place. If you run into this problem, leave the clamps in place until the glue dries. Should you be plagued with excess squeeze-out, wait until the glue gets gummy, then scrape it away with a chisel.

With the four corners joined, set the drawer down flat on your bench. Check it for square by holding a square in any corner. Rack the drawer into square, if necessary, by pushing on opposite corners. Then set it aside on a flat surface to dry as you assemble the next one. On a large project, I often end up with a stack of drying drawers. Leave the freshly assembled drawers to dry overnight before further machining.

SANDING THE OUTSIDE SURFACES

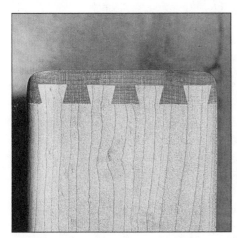

Photo 9-4: **As a finishing touch, I round-over the edges of the drawer parts. This makes them much friendlier to handle.**

Once the glue dries, sand the protruding parts of the joints flush. Then sand all the outside surfaces. I use a belt sander here, which makes fast work of the job. When you're done, the joints should have a neat, clean appearance. While you're sanding, hit both the top and bottom edges, making them flush all the way around the drawer. If you're not comfortable belt sanding the narrow edges, an orbital sander will get the job done, although not as quickly.

Next, I like to round-over the edges of the drawer to make them nicer to handle, as shown in *Photo 9-4.* I usu-

the PROFESSIONAL view

MAKING STOPPED GROOVES

Sometimes, when cutting the groove for a drawer bottom, it's necessary to stop the groove before it breaks through the end of the piece. The easiest way to do this is with a table-mounted router.

Start by mounting a straight bit in the router. Ideally, you'll have a bit that matches the piece's thickness perfectly. In reality, you'll probably have to settle for a bit that is slightly smaller. If you have to use a bit that is narrower than the plywood, make the groove in two passes.

With the bit selected, set up the fence the appropriate distance away from the cutter. Mark the location of the bit on the fence with a square. Then make marks ¼ inch outside the first marks. These will

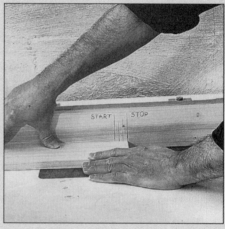

Rout until the trailing end of the piece reaches the stop mark on the fence. Then back the piece up slightly and carefully lift it off the bit.

indicate where to start and stop the cut.

Set the depth of cut as needed and make a cut in a piece of scrap to check the setup. Hold the piece against the fence with its trailing end down on the table. Tip the leading end up over the bit, aligned with the starting mark, as shown at left. Start the router and drop the piece down slowly onto the bit. Push the piece through the cut from right to left. Stop when the trailing end reaches the stop mark, as shown above. Carefully lift the piece up off the bit and check the results. If the cut starts and stops as you want it to, make the cuts in the good stock. After you cut all the pieces once, shift the fence to widen the grooves, if necessary.

Hold the piece against the fence over the bit. Its leading edge should align with the starting mark. Since you'll be routing from right to left, the starting mark is the one to the left of the bit.

Photo 9-5: **When you are rounding-over the edges of the drawer, don't rout those that will butt up to the drawer face. They look better if they're left square.**

ally do this with a hand-held router, but you may find it easier to use a table-mounted model. Mount a $5/16$-inch roundover bit in your router. This will produce a full bullnose on the $5/8$-inch-thick sides.

Round-over all four edges inside the drawer. Then round-over both outside edges of the sides and back. Don't rout the outside edge at the front. Since the drawer face is attached directly to the front, it will look better if its outside edges are left square, as shown in *Photo 9-5.*

Finally, finish sand the drawer with an orbital sander. Start with 80-grit to clean up any machine marks and irregularities from the router. Pay close attention to the corners, where the router has a tendency to burn. Then switch to 100-grit to clean up the scratches left by the 80-grit. Finish up with 150-grit to give the drawer a final polish. Dust the drawer off and it's ready to be filled and finished.

Tip

Removing excess glue is a problem every woodworker faces now and then. The best solution I've found is to allow the glue to dry partially, and then scrape the rubbery residue away with a sharp chisel. Resist the temptation to use a minimal amount of glue. It's far easier to scrape away a little excess than it is to reglue a failed joint.

10 HANGING DRAWERS

Modern hardware making a difference

The traditional way of fitting a drawer to a case involves lots of time-consuming handwork: scraping and planing each drawer to fit its individual opening. But with today's hardware, such drudgery isn't necessary. Now it is a relatively simple matter to attach hardware to a drawer and hang it in a case. As long as the drawer box is the right width and the runners are installed properly, the drawer will run in and out effortlessly for years.

I use Accuride 3017 full-extension runners (sometimes called slides). They are rated for loads up to 100 pounds and they mount to the sides of a drawer. You may be able to get them from a local commercial hardware supplier, or you can order them through the mail. I like the full-extension runners because they allow unobstructed access to the entire contents of the drawer.

Accuride runners are more expensive than most of the other brands, but their quality is worth the extra expense. The instructions that follow are fairly specific to the Accuride 3017, but the general method is adaptable to most other models.

Photo 10-1: Accuride runners include separate rails that allow the drawer to be removed from the case without having to unscrew anything. A metal tab near the rear and a plastic clip toward the front hold the rails in place.

ATTACHING THE RAILS TO THE DRAWER

Accuride runners have two parts: the *rail*, which mounts to the side of the drawer; and the *slide*, which mounts to the inside of the case. The way I mount the slides to the case varies depending on whether the case has a face frame, but the way I mount the rails on the drawers is consistent.

Work on a flat, hard surface. I use the outfeed table I built for my table saw. Brush away any accumulated debris—the drawer box and the slide must both sit flat on the surface. You'll quickly discover that a small metal tab at the back of the runner will keep it from sitting truly flat. A similar tab on the top of the runner is there to help hold the drawer in place, as shown in *Photo 10-1*. The tab on the bottom is only there to make the slide reversible. (Manufacturers don't like to make things handed.) The bottom tab serves absolutely no other purpose.

What to do? Well, you can either arrange the runner and the drawer on the table so the errant tab hangs over the edge, or you can flatten the tab out, as I do. A couple of taps with a tack hammer and you're ready to go. You can always pry the tab up again if necessary, but I've never had reason to. With the tab problem solved, you're ready to mount the rails.

Photo 10-2: With the front of the slide flush with the front of the drawer box, drill a pilot hole through one of the holes in the rail. Screw the rail to the drawer to hold its position as you drill the rest of the pilot holes.

Slip the back end of the rail under the tab on the top of the slide and clip them together, inserting the slide's clip into the rail's slot. Hold both pieces against the side of the drawer, as shown in *Photo 10-2*. Push them forward until the front end of the slide is flush with the front of the drawer. Make sure that both the drawer and the runner are sitting flat on your work surface. Drill a ⅛-inch pilot hole into the drawer side through any one of the holes in the rail, as shown in the photo. Then screw the rail in place with one of the screws supplied. This will hold things in place while you put in the other screws. I usually use three screws per rail. Predrill for them all. Be careful not to drill all the way through the drawer side as you're boring the pilot holes. I use a handy little stop with my drill to eliminate this worry entirely. See "A Precise Depth Stop" on the opposite page for further details.

Mount rails to both sides of all the drawers. Then unclip the slides so you can install them in the cases. Stack the drawers out of the way.

MOUNTING THE SLIDES IN A FRAMELESS CASE

The slides are screwed to either side of the case. They have to be installed at exactly the same level or the drawer will be askew. You might think this would involve a lot of careful measurement, but what do you know about me and tape measures?

Instead of painstakingly laying out the position of each slide, I cut plywood spacers to locate them automatically. The spacers use either the top or the bottom of the cabinet as a point of reference. Here's the process to mount the slides for a standard 3½-inch-deep drawer in a cabinet that has a drawer mounted above a door.

Referencing from the top. Lay the case on its side on your work surface. Put the appropriate slide (the little tab should point toward the top of the case) roughly in place and slip your spacer in between it and the case top. The spacer must fit between the black plastic tab and the metal tab, both on the top of the slide. You can't flatten the tab here because you will need it to hold the slide to the rail.

Push the spacer and slide tight up against the top of the case. Bring the slide forward until its front edge is flush with the front of the case, as shown in *Photo 10-3*. Two screw holes should now be

Photo 10-3: In frameless construction, the front edge of the drawer slides should be flush with the front of the case.

A PRECISE DEPTH STOP

Installing hardware like drawer slides often involves drilling a lot of pilot holes for screws. If you drill these freehand, it's too easy to drill all the way through a part. Instead of running this risk, I make one of these quick drill stops.

Make the stop from a dowel. Clamp it upright in a vise and bore into its end an inch or so with the bit you're going to use for the pilot holes.

Measure the exposed portion of the drill bit. Subtract the depth of the hole you want from that number and cut the dowel to this length. Then slip the dowel onto the bit to serve as a stop, as shown.

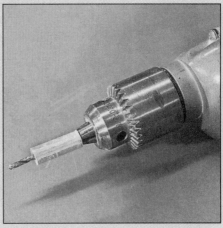

A short length of dowel makes a quick, cheap drill stop.

visible in the slide. Screw the slide to the case through these holes. The plywood is soft enough that you should be able to power drive the screws without predrilling.

Once the two screws are tight, the slide is fixed in place. Add at least one more screw, two if the drawer will be used to carry a heavy load. To find additional screw holes, slide the drawer slide out. If you need to relocate the front screw, there is an extra screw hole hidden just in front of the original. To access it, you have to move both movable elements of the slide at once.

One thing to remember: Don't let the little tab on the slide interfere with the spacer. If it does, the drawer won't run right. After the slide is fastened in place, flip the case over and do the other side. With both slides in place, the case is now ready for its drawer.

To mount the drawer, extend both slides all the way out of the case. Tip the drawer box in between the slides and catch the back end of the rails under the little tabs, as shown in *Photo 10-4* on page 120. Then push the drawer down over the black clips to lock it in place.

For my standard 3½-inch drawers, I use a spacer that is 2¾ inches wide. This provides 1¼ inches of clearance over the drawer and ½ inch underneath. If your drawers are the same size as mine and you're using the same slides, you can also use the same size spacer. If not, measure the distance from the top of the rail to the top of the drawer side and add to that number the amount of clearance you want above the drawer. Determining the clearance is discussed in detail in "Preparing the Stock" on page 97.

Photo 10-4: **These slides are designed so that the drawer just clips in place.**

Referencing from the bottom. The above method works well for a cabinet with a single drawer. But for a cabinet with a stack of drawers, I use a series of spacers that reference from the bottom of the case.

You must work from the top down, cutting the plywood spacer to size after installing all pairs of slides for that specific height. The width of the spacer is easy to find. Since it positions the bottom of the drawer slides—and the bottom of the drawer slides is level with the bottom of the drawers—all I have to know is how high the bottom of the drawers should be, and this information is always on my cabinet plans. For the bottom drawer spacer, I use a piece of ¼-inch plywood laid flat, rather than cutting the thicker spacer down any further.

MOUNTING THE SLIDES IN A FACE-FRAMED CASE

The process changes somewhat if you're mounting drawer slides in a case with a face frame. Here, you will have to shim the slides out from the case sides so they clear the frame. You'll also have to set them farther back into the case so the drawer front comes to rest at the appropriate point. The exact method depends on what style of construction you're using and what type of cabinet you're building.

Shimming the slides. On a standard face-frame cabinet that has a drawer above the door, the face frame overhangs the case opening. This isn't a problem with doors, but with drawers, the slides must be shimmed away from the sides of the case.

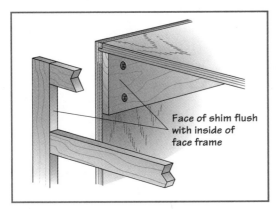

Figure 10-1. Shimming the slides

Face of shim flush with inside of face frame

Otherwise, they will run into the overhanging frame.

To shim the slides out the appropriate amount, I plane a piece of wood down until its thickness equals the distance the frame overhangs the case. Then I screw this piece right to the case side, as shown in *Figure 10-1*. Note that the shim is wide enough to cover the entire space adjacent to the drawers, from the front of the cabinet to the rear, and from the top of the cabinet down to just below the drawer.

With the shims in place on either side of the case, you can mount the slides. Use a spacer to position them properly, as described earlier. The good news is that I only use the shims in cases that have a drawer over a door. In a cabinet that is entirely drawers, I make the inside of the case flush with the inside frame opening so no shims are necessary.

Moving the slides into the case. On many cabinets, the drawer front overlays the opening. If so, the front of the slides is flush with the front of the cabinet, as described earlier. But if the drawer front is flush with the frame (an *inset* drawer) or partially recessed (a *lip offset* drawer), you'll have to set the drawer slides deeper into the case.

Photo 10-5: With inset construction, the drawers are set flush with the front of the face frame. To achieve this, the drawer slides must be mounted back slightly from the drawer opening.

For inset drawers, the front of the slides must be set in a distance equal to the thickness of the drawer face, as shown in *Photo 10-5*. Sometimes I push them back just a hair further. I like the look this creates, and it ensures that the drawers are set in deep enough. A drawer that isn't inset deep enough would really be unsightly.

With lip-offset drawers, the slides must be pushed back into the case a distance equal to the depth of the rabbet. Make a test piece as you're milling the rabbets in the drawer fronts and use it as a guide as you mount the slides.

11 HANGING DOORS

Setting things straight

Hanging a door can require up to three different kinds of hardware—hinges, pulls, and catches. On most doors, the hinges are essential, while the pull may be incorporated into the door frame itself, making a separate piece of hardware unnecessary. Likewise, some hinges have a self-closing spring, eliminating the need for a catch.

The hardware available today has taken a lot of the hassle out of this process. Some hinges allow you to adjust a door in all three needed directions (in and out, up and down, and side to side), making it a snap to align doors and keep them flat against the cabinet.

Regardless of the type of hardware you're using, there is one cardinal rule: Buy it first.

HINGES

When it comes to hinges, you have a number of choices. My favorites, the European-style cup hinges shown in *Photo 11-1*, offer the most in terms of adjustability and ease of installation. They are available in styles to suit any door, from inset to full-overlay. Make sure you buy the right model to match the style of door you're using.

The other style of hinge I use is the ball-tip hinge, shown in *Photo 11-2*. Sometimes called butt or leaf hinges, these hinges work well with inset doors. They provide a very traditional look and require real heroic craftsmanship to install. Once installed, they offer no adjustment, so they must be reset if the door needs to be moved.

Photo 11-1. **The adjustability of this hinge makes it a favorite of many cabinetmakers. By simply turning the adjustment screws, you can move a door slightly from side to side, up and down, and in and out.**

European-Style Hinges

European-style hinges fit in round mortises bored in the back of a door. These mortises are holes drilled on a drill press with a 35mm bit. Most places that sell the European hinges also carry a 35mm bit especially for this purpose. You can also use a 1⅜-inch Forstner bit. If you elect to go this route, make sure the bit doesn't have a protruding center spur. If it does, you run the risk of drilling through the face of your doors. To facilitate boring the mortises, I've made an auxiliary table with a fence on it for my drill press.

Photo 11-2. **These ball-tip hinges are very elegant, but their installation demands a lot of skill on the part of the craftsman.**

Making the jig. As shown in *Figure 11-1* on page 124, the jig consists of a ¾-inch plywood base with a 1 × 2-inch fence screwed to it along one edge. About halfway across the jig, draw a reference line perpendicular to the fence on the plywood. Continue the line up and across the fence as well. Then draw two alignment lines across the top of the fence, one 3 inches to the right of the reference line and the other 3 inches to the left. You'll align the door on the jig with these lines.

Testing the setup. Clamp the jig to the drill press with the bit centered over the original reference line. There should be about ¼ inch of space between the fence and

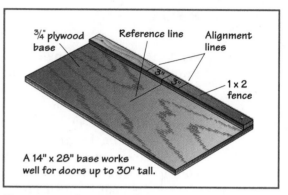

Figure 11-1. Hinge-mortising jig

the edge of the drill bit. This distance will vary with the type of hinge you're using, so check the manufacturer's specification sheet. Then, using a scrap as thick as the door stock as a guide, set the depth stop on the drill press so the mortise will be ½ inch deep.

These dimensions work with my standard hinge, the Grass 1203. If you're using a different hinge, test your setup before boring your doors. Take a length of scrap the same thickness as your door stock and hinge it to a scrap of plywood in the same orientation the actual door will be to the case. This will show you exactly how the doors will work and whether you've got the mortises placed properly. Make any adjustments necessary before moving on to mortise the actual doors.

If your doors include a routed molding detail along the edge, be sure to include this detail on your test piece. Sometimes this kind of detail can remove enough wood to interfere with the mortise. (In other words, when you drill the mortise, you also create a gaping hole in the front of the door.) This kind of mistake is more common than you might think, and it's pretty much fatal. Once a door is so drilled, it must be replaced.

Mortising the doors. As you can probably surmise from the placement of the alignment marks, I center my hinges 3 inches from either end of the door. This works well for an average door, but there are some exceptions, which I'll tell you about in a bit.

The basic procedure is simple: Place the door face down on the table and align one end with one of the alignment lines on the fence. Drill the first mortise, as shown in *Photo 11-3*. Then slide the door over, align it with the other mark, and drill the second mortise. On a door taller than 39 inches, I usually include a

Photo 11-3. This jig aligns the door on the drill press so the hinge mortises are all the same distance from the edge. The marks on the fence aid in placing the mortises a set distance from the ends of the door.

third hinge centered between the first two. To mortise for this hinge, I mark the door, then line up this mark with the reference line on the jig to drill it.

Sometimes, however, placing the hinges 3 inches from the ends of a door interferes with some cabinet detail. For example, if I've raised the bottom of a case to allow for under-cabinet lighting, the case bottom will fill the space that the hinge usually occupies. Here, I try to place the hinge 3 inches from the obstacle. This usually involves making new reference marks on the jig or on the door itself so it's easy to align as you drill the mortises. Then I drill the mortises as usual. The only real problem is that it creates a door that is *handed*.

What are handed doors? The industry calls a door by its hinge side. A *left-handed door* has the hinges on your left when you look at the closed cabinet. In many cases, a door is perfectly symmetrical and can be either a left or a right until it is hung. But sometimes you'll have doors that are specifically right- or left-handed. Adding pulls (or just drilling holes for them), installing bookmatched panels, or routing integral door pulls are all ways of creating handed doors.

If the door is handed, you must be alert to mortise for the hinges on the correct side of the door. Nothing can be so annoying as to put all that labor into a door and then mortise it wrong. Of course, the mortises can be easily patched since they're in the back of the door. Match the grain and color of the wood and a mistake will probably go unnoticed. But who wants the extra aggravation?

To avoid these potential problems, I try to make most of my doors unhanded. All this usually entails is leaving the hardware off until the door is installed on the cabinet. This keeps mistakes to a minimum. Still, at least 1 in 200 doors gets drilled incorrectly.

Mounting the hinges. After the mortises have been drilled, pop the hinges into their holes and square them to the

Tip

If you use a lot of European-style hinges, it may be worth investing in a 1⅜-inch plug cutter. This tool cuts a plug sized perfectly to fill an improperly placed hinge mortise. I keep threatening to buy one of these each time there's a screw-up—one of these days I'll follow through.

edge of the door. This is easier if you open each hinge up once it's in place. Once you have the hinges positioned, drill pilot holes for the screws and drive them home.

To hang the door, you have to screw one base plate to the inside of the case for each hinge. For the Grass 1203 hinge, I use the Grass 10186 winged base plate. If the centers of your hinges are 3 inches from the edges of the door, as mine are, measure up 3¹⁄₁₆ inches from the bottom of the case and draw a line perpendicular to the edge of the case. (Remember, the door is ⅛ inch shy of the inside case height for clearance. This translates to ¹⁄₁₆ inch top and bottom.) Otherwise, alter the dimensions to suit your hinge placement.

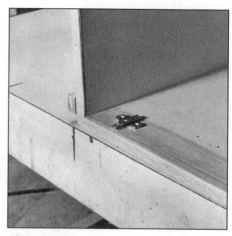

Photo 11-4. European hinges are mounted to the inside of a case via mounting plates. These are screwed to the case before the door is hung.

Make a mark on the line ⁹⁄₁₆ inch in from the edge. This is where the first screw will go for the plate. In a plywood case, you can simply drive the screw in without drilling first. In a hardwood case, however, drilling a pilot hole first is usually necessary. Mount the plate with a single screw, as shown in *Photo 11-4*. Swivel it so it is roughly square to the edge before tightening the screw. Don't put the rest of the screws in yet.

To mount the upper plate, measure the distance from the center of one hinge to the center of the other. This isn't as difficult as it might sound. Hook a tape measure onto any part of one hinge, then measure to the exact same spot on the other. This will give you the dimension between the hinges, center to center.

Make a second line on the case exactly this distance above the first line. Measure in ⁹⁄₁₆ inch and screw the upper plate in place. Once the mounting plates are installed, you can hang the door on the case.

Hanging the door. Open the hinges so the hinge arms are extended. Hold the door from the bottom and slip the hinges onto their mounts. Tighten the locking screws to hold the door in place. On the Grass hinges, the locking screw is the middle of the three screws, as shown in *Figure 11-2*. (This screw also controls the in and out adjustment.)

Once both hinges are locked in place, close the door and take a look at its position. In all likelihood, it won't be hanging

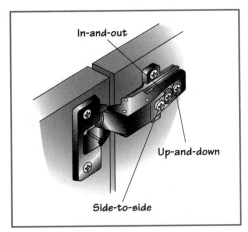

In-and-out

Up-and-down

Side-to-side

Figure 11-2. **Adjusting a Grass hinge**

straight. Don't despair. Here is where the real beauty of these hinges comes into play. (You don't really think I like them for their looks, do you?) They're adjustable in three directions: in and out, side to side, and up and down. While the cabinet is still in the shop, adjust the door so it is roughly in position. Don't spend a whole lot of time on it; you'll probably have to readjust it after installation anyway.

Start with the in-and-out adjustment. With the door closed, look at the space between the door and the case along the hinge side. The gap should be a consistent $1/16$ inch. If it's not, loosen the locking screws and slide the door in or out as needed. Once the door is aligned, tighten the screws to lock it in place.

Next, tackle the side-to-side adjustment. Close the door and check its alignment with the case. The edges of the door should be parallel to the sides of the case; the entire door should be centered from side to side. This assumes the door covers the entire width of the case. If it doesn't, align it along the hinged side only. The adjustment is made by turning one of the two other screws on the hinges in or out depending on which way you want to move the door. On the Grass hinge, the side-to-side screw is the one closest to the outside of the case.

Finally, do the up-and-down alignment. This is governed by the third screw. I generally only mess with this in the shop if the door is really off; otherwise, I just wait until after the cabinet is installed.

Once the cabinets are installed, you can make any final adjustments needed. Align each door with its case as well as with the other doors. Pay particular attention to getting the doors to line up top and bottom. This is the one adjustment my clients seem to focus on the most.

After the rough adjustments are made in the shop, you can put the rest of the screws in for the mounting plates. On the Grass plates, this can be done without removing the hinges.

As you can see, hanging doors can be time-consuming, with all the measuring and adjusting involved. The adjustments get easier with practice, but the measuring can still be a sticking point. If you have only three or four doors to hang, it's no big deal to measure for each of them. But on a larger job, like a kitchen with 10 or 20 doors, it's worth making a little jig to make the job easier. I developed a drilling guide, shown in *Figure 11-3*, to locate the screw hole for the lower mounting plate. This speeds the process considerably.

Make the guide as shown in the drawing. The dimensions are based on my standard way of working: ¾-inch plywood case and hinges centered 3 inches from the edge of the door. If you've varied the construction of your project, you'll have to alter the jig somewhat to suit.

Using the jig couldn't be easier. Hold it against the bottom of the case with the fence against the case's front edge, as shown in *Photo 11-5*. Drill the hole in the case through the hole in the guide. Just make sure there is no debris or glue squeeze-out at the juncture of the case side and bottom. This could interfere with the guide and cause the hole to be drilled wrong.

Ball-Tip Hinges

Hanging doors with ball-tip hinges is definitely for heroes. These are the most difficult and unforgiving hinges I use. They aren't adjustable and they're very difficult to move if installed wrong. Still, they lend a very distinctive look to a cabinet that can be worth the added aggravation.

To make the installation of these hinges more palatable, I've devised a router jig to aid in cutting the mortises necessary for the hinge's leaves. While the router cuts the bulk of the waste from the mortises, there is still some handwork necessary. The corners of the mortises must be squared with a chisel and, since the hinges I use are cast individually, each one can vary slightly from the next and must be custom-fit to its mortise. All this adds up to a lively time.

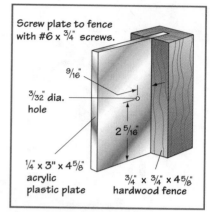

Figure 11-3. Door-hanging jig

Photo 11-5. This drilling guide makes placing the European-hinge mounting plates a snap. It's reversible so it can be used on either side of a case.

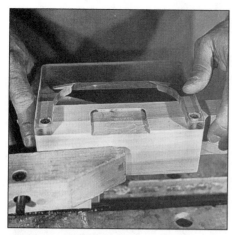

Photo 11-6. *Clamp the jig to the piece you want to mortise with the edge of the plastic aligned with the end of the piece. A hand screw is a good clamp to use since its wood jaws won't mar the workpiece.*

Photo 11-7. *Guide the router against the template to cut the mortise. The first time you use the jig you'll also cut the fence.*

Making the test cut. Build the jig, as described in "A Hinge Mortising Jig" on page 130. Once you've assembled the jig, test it on two pieces of scrap. This will give you a chance to check the fit of the hinge in the mortise and to properly set the router's depth of cut. Start with the bit protruding from the base of the router about the thickness of a single hinge leaf. Clamp the jig to one of the scraps, as shown in *Photo 11-6*. Run the router around the jig to cut the mortise, as shown in *Photo 11-7*.

To check the fit of the hinge, you'll have to square the corners of the mortise with a chisel, as shown in *Photos 11-8* and *11-9* on page 131. Once the corners are square, you can see how well the hinges fit. If the mortise is too small, disassemble the jig and recut the template with the table saw. If it's too big, a new template is in order. If the fit is close, try a few different hinges. In my experience, they vary enough that each mortise must be fine-tuned a little with a chisel to get the best fit. If the jig makes a mortise that requires just a little trimming, I'd go with it.

Once you have the jig cutting the proper-size mortise, you can concentrate on getting the bit set to the right depth. Here's where the second scrap comes into play. Cut matching mortises in both scraps and screw the hinge in place. Fold the hinge closed and check the space between the two pieces. It should be about $\frac{1}{16}$ inch.

If the gap is too wide, lower the bit slightly and recut the pieces. If the gap isn't wide enough, raise the bit and cut a second set of scraps.

Mortising the door. You're finally ready to mortise the actual door. One of the real strengths of this jig is that it practically aligns itself on a door frame, as you'll soon see. Clamp the door

A HINGE MORTISING JIG

This jig consists of a plastic template with attached fence, as shown below. The cutout in the template guides a router through the cut. I used Lexan for the template, but acrylic would work as well. Either of these plastics can be cut with regular woodworking tools.

I made the template to fit my laminate trimmer. With its small base, this little router can easily make cuts in places too tight for a regular router. You can, however, adapt the jig to work with a full-size router and a guide bushing.

As shown, the size of the cutout in the template depends on the size of the hinges, the bit you're going to use, the

Center the template over the blade. Raise the blade to make the cut. Hold the template in place carefully with a block of wood so it doesn't move. When the cut is long enough, turn the saw off and lower the blade again.

Make the cuts that form the sides of the U by standing the template on edge against a miter gauge extension and running it past the blade. Don't worry about the corners—they aren't critical to the jig's function.

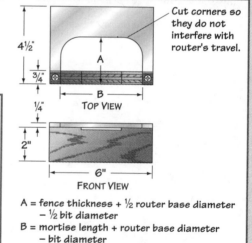

¼" plastic template

¾" x 2" x 6" fence

Cut corners so they do not interfere with router's travel.

4½"

¾"

¼"

A

B

TOP VIEW

2"

6"

FRONT VIEW

A = fence thickness + ½ router base diameter − ½ bit diameter
B = mortise length + router base diameter − bit diameter

diameter of the router base, and the thickness of the fence. I use a ⅜-inch diameter straight bit. Make your calculations according to the drawing, then lay out the opening on the template.

Make the cutout on the table saw. Start with the cut that forms the bottom of the U. Lower the blade all the way. Bring the fence over to position the template over the blade.

The fence goes on the front of the jig for two reasons: It helps prevent tearout along the door front, and it allows the jig to be used with any thickness stock. Drill and countersink the template for screws to attach the fence. Screw the fence in place. Make sure the face of the fence is parallel to the bottom of the U; otherwise, your mortises will be crooked. If necessary, enlarge the screw holes for adjustment.

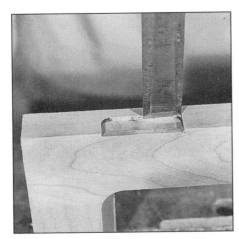

Photo 11-8. Use the routed edges of the mortise as a guide as you square the corners.

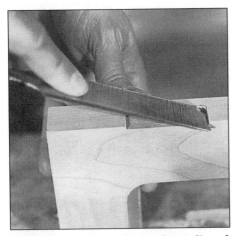

Photo 11-9. Once you've cut the outline of the square corner, use the chisel to lift out the waste.

in a Workmate. Clamp the jig to the door with its fence against the door's outside face and the edge of the jig flush with the end of the door, as you did with the test piece. Rout the mortise. Then shift the jig to the other end of the door and rout the second mortise.

With the mortises cut in the door, you can then cut their counterparts in the face frame. The first one is easy. Place a shim in the corner of the frame and butt the edge of the template up against it, as shown in *Photo 11-10* on page 132. The thickness of the shim should equal the width of the gap you want to leave around the door. Clamp the jig in place and rout the mortise.

The placement of the second hinge isn't quite as easy. You could position the jig by putting it against the second face frame corner. But it's quite likely that the door, the frame, or the hinge will be slightly off. So, if you made the cut relying on all the components being perfect, the mortise would end up in the wrong place. Instead, I hold the door in place, aligning the mortises I've already cut. Then, I scribe lines from the door directly onto the face frame to mark the position of the second mortise, as shown in *Photo 11-11* on page 132. This way, even if one of the parts isn't quite right, the mortise will still be in the right spot. Position the jig by aligning the cut in the fence with the scribe marks, then rout the mortise.

Hanging the door. Now for the moment of truth: It's time to hang the door. Drill pilot holes and mount the hinges on the door using one screw per hinge. Don't drill holes for the other screws until after you've installed the cabinets. Mount the door on the case, again with one screw per hinge.

Tip

When testing a setup on a jig you'll be using again, save the test piece with the jig. It will give you a reference to set up with the next time you have to do the same operation.

Try the door. It should pivot smoothly and close flush to the face of the frame, with an even gap all around. Hopefully, this is the case. If it isn't, you'll have to shift the door. If you have to shift it from side to side, you can either insert shims under the hinges or cut the mortises deeper, depending on which way you want to move the door. Make the shims from thin pieces of wood or veneer.

To shift the door up or down, you'll have to elongate the mortises. This can create unsightly gaps beside the hinges if you have to move the door more than $\frac{1}{16}$ inch or so. If necessary, you can fill these gaps with small pieces of scrap wood.

To move the door in or out, make the mortises wider. If you make the door mortises wider, you'll move the door out. If you make the frame mortises wider, you'll move the door in. Often, a combination of all three door adjustments is needed.

All of this takes time and skill and is generally a nuisance. This is compounded by the fact that even if you have the doors aligned perfectly in the shop, they may not stay aligned during installation.

During installation, a cabinet can get twisted or *racked*, which plays havoc with the doors. In a racked cabinet, the four corners of a surface—like the top or a side—are no longer in the same plane. Usually, a cabinet gets racked unintentionally, by either sitting on a floor that's not flat or being screwed to a wall that's not straight. The first thing you'll probably notice is that the doors no longer align. Sometimes

Photo 11-10. Since the mortises on the door were positioned using the edge of the door as a reference point, the first mortise you rout in the face frame is relatively easy to locate. Just shim the jig away from the corner a distance equal to the gap you want to leave around the door.

Photo 11-11. Scribe the location of the second face frame mortise by using the door with mounted hinges as a guide.

> ### Tip
>
> Sometimes, in the course of fitting doors, a screw hole will get worn and won't hold a screw. To fix this, cut a splinter of wood that is the same size or larger than the screw hole (sometimes a toothpick will work). Apply some glue to the hole and the splinter and insert the splinter into the hole. When the glue dries, cut it off flush with the surrounding surface and redrive the screw.

you can eliminate the racking with shims; other times you have to live with it and start shifting hinges and recutting mortises.

This is why I wait until the cabinets are installed before fastening the hinges with all the screws. It's bad enough having to reset the hinges without having to plug a bunch of screw holes first. Once everything is installed and aligned perfectly, I drive in the remaining screws.

After their initial installation, ball-tip hinges hold their alignment well and last practically forever. They are also very pretty and fit in well with the look of beaded-inset construction. Despite this, I don't go out of my way to use these hinges.

Tip

If, for some unfortunate reason, you're stuck with the task of redrilling screw holes, bore them out with a ⅜-inch bit. Then fill these larger holes with ⅜-inch plugs. After the glue dries, trim the plugs flush and you'll be able to redrill the holes without a hitch.

OTHER HARDWARE

With the doors hung, it's time to add any other hardware that might be required, like pulls and catches. Often, I'll let this step go until I get the cabinets on site and adjusted properly. This saves me from making dumb mistakes, like mounting a pull in the wrong position. Often, however, this isn't possible and the pulls have to be mounted in the shop. If this is the case, just be sure to label everything care-fully and double-check before making any cuts.

Door Pulls

In my work, I use two kinds of door pulls. On more traditional-looking designs, I usually go with a separate, commercially made pull. These are available in an incredible variety of styles from any number of different sources. Between your local hardware store and the various woodworking supply catalogs, you should be able to find a pull that suits your taste and budget.

Also, I often use pulls that I make myself from wood, especially on my original designs. The pulls can be as simple as a routed edge detail along a door's frame, or as complex as a separate piece of wood mortised into a door's face. If you choose to go this route, you're limited only by your own creativity. Almost anything is possible. For some ideas and instructions on how I go about making my own pulls, see Chapter 12.

Mounting the pull. Installing factory-made knobs and pulls is easy. You simply bore a hole through the door and screw the hardware in place. The biggest problem is spacing the holes so all the pulls line up. As mentioned earlier, I like to do this after the doors have been installed. If you wait until the doors are hung, you won't run into the possibility of boring a hole in the wrong corner.

Working like this means you'll have to drill the holes without the benefit of a drill press. To make this operation easier, I developed a jig that works with a hand drill to locate the hole and keep the bit perpendicular to the surface.

Photo 11-12. **Placing pulls on doors is a minor but important step in the cabinet-making process. Properly placed pulls add to a door's aesthetic balance.**

First, locate the pull on your door. Take a sample pull and slide it around on the door until it looks right. I usually start with the pull centered across the width of the stile and approximately in line with the bottom (or top) of the panel, as shown in *Photo 11-12*. When you have the pull where you want it, mark its location. Then take a cutoff from the door frame stiles to use as the jig body. A piece about 4 inches long will be adequate, but if you're going to use pulls that require two screws, make it 7 inches long.

Transfer the mark(s) from the door onto the jig body, measuring in from both the end and edge of the stock. Drill through the jig body with a bit slightly larger than the screw you'll be using. If your screw is ⅛ inch, use a ³⁄₁₆-inch bit. This will allow you to shift the pull if need be. Drill the jig on a drill press if possible. It's important that the hole through the jig be perpendicular to its faces so the pull will be straight when mounted.

Tack two strips of ¼-inch plywood to the jig

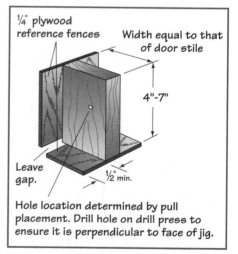

¼" plywood reference fences

Width equal to that of door stile

4"-7"

Leave gap.

½" min.

Hole location determined by pull placement. Drill hole on drill press to ensure it is perpendicular to face of jig.

Figure 11-4. **Door pull–drilling jig**

body, as shown in *Figure 11-4*. Leave a gap at the corner. The strips serve as reference fences and should overhang both sides of the body by at least ½ inch. With the overhang on both sides, you can use this jig on either right- or left-handed doors.

To use the jig, hook it on the corner of a door and hold it tightly against the door, as shown in *Photo 11-13*. The gap at the corner allows you to see if both fences are against the edges of the door as they should be. Drill the hole in the door using the jig as a guide. You should always drill from the face of the door to the back. This way, if there is any tearout where the drill exits, it will be on the back of the door where the screw head will cover it. Screw the pull in place.

As I've said, I always try to mount the pulls after the cabinets are installed, but there are exceptions to the rule. On a door with a heavily molded frame, like that shown in *Photo 11-14*, a pull won't have a flat place on which to sit. To correct this, I use a ⅜-inch Forstner bit to bore a small flat to receive the pull. Then I drill the rest of the way through the frame with a regular bit, centering the hole(s) in the flat area. Since Forstner bits don't work especially well in hand drills, I make these cuts in the shop on the drill press.

Be extra-careful to keep track of which doors are right- and left-handed. They're next to impossible to patch if you happen to drill one wrong. Yup, I've made this mistake!

Photo 11-13. The jig is located by its two plywood fences, making it a snap to position on the door.

Photo 11-14. On a shaped frame, it's sometimes necessary to create a small flat in the molding so the handle sits straight.

Catches

When I use my European-style hinges on a project, I choose one that's spring-loaded and doesn't require a catch. But with ball-tip hinges and inset construction, a catch is required. There are, of course, European hinges that can take the place of ball-tip hinges, but they just don't look right aesthetically. The only alternative to a self-closing hinge is to use a catch to keep the doors shut.

My choice is the lowly magnetic catch. You can certainly find more elegant catches, but most require more labor to install and an exacting fit to work right. Admittedly, magnetic catches are thoroughly ugly—but you don't really see them. They work well, even if slightly misaligned, and they're a breeze to install.

Installing the catch. Magnetic catches consist of two parts: the magnet and the strike plate. The magnet attaches to the case. Of course, in most situations there won't be a ready-made place in the case to mount it. You'll have to create one. I usually screw a small block of wood to the inside of the frame, as shown in *Photo 11-15*. Then I screw the magnet to it.

For the blocks, I use 1⅛-inch-thick scraps left over from making the doors. I make them about 2½ inches long and the same width as the stiles or rails they will be attached to. This way, if there are two doors with a center frame stile in between, both doors will be served by one block. If the stiles have a bead molding, the block must be as wide as the stile plus the molding.

Drill and counterbore the block for two mounting screws. Then attach the catch before screwing the block to the frame. Screw the block to the back of the frame with 1⅝-inch drywall screws. Placement is fairly arbitrary. I try to mount the catch as close as possible to the pull to keep the door from racking every time it's opened.

The strike plate mounts to the back of the door. If you have access to the inside of the cabinet with the door closed, the plate is easy to mount. Simply stick it to the magnet, close the door, then reach inside and hold the plate in place as you open the door. For cabinets that you can't reach inside, locate the strike plate by measuring. Once it's located, screw it to the back of the door.

Photo 11-15. While it probably won't win any awards for aesthetics, this magnetic catch does a good job of keeping the door closed.

CUSTOM DOOR AND DRAWER PULLS

12

When store-bought just won't do

For traditional cabinets, you can usually find a commercial pull that has the look you're after. But if your tastes run along more contemporary lines, it can be harder to find just the right manufactured hardware. I've found it often makes more sense to design a pull specifically for a project than to make do with a commercial unit that is "almost" right. In fact, some of the custom pulls I've made have become real focal points for the projects that contain them. If you're of a mind to try to make your own pulls, I've detailed some of my favorites here.

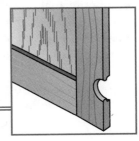

U-PULLS

Many of the pulls I've devised take shape on the drill press. One of my favorites is this U- or C-shaped pull, as shown in *Photo 12-1*. These pulls are very easy to make, but they're difficult to sand.

Shaping the Pulls

The rounded cutout is made with a drill bit. Since it's easier to drill a complete circle than it is to drill a partial one, start with a 1⅝-inch-wide × ½-inch-thick strip of hardwood. After drilling, you'll rip the pulls to width on the table saw. If you rip the strip right down the middle, you'll get two pulls per hole.

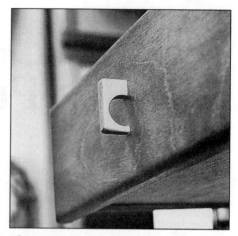

Photo 12-1: **These wood pulls come close to looking like some of their commercial counterparts, but the subtle warmth of wood puts them in a class by themselves.**

However, I prefer to cut the strips slightly off center. This yields pulls with a fuller cutout, but it wastes more stock since I only get one pull per hole.

The length of the piece depends on the number of pulls you need. Allow 2¼ inches for each pull—2 inches for the pull and ¼ inch for cutting the pulls apart. The minimum number of pulls you should make is three—any fewer and the strip will be too short to safely run through the saw. Plan to make a few extras just in case you need them. It's easier to make them now, rather than resetting all the machines if you run short or make a mistake.

Once you have the strip cut to size, drill holes along its length with a 1⅛-inch Forstner bit. Space the holes as shown in *Figure 12-1.* Clamp a fence to the drill press table to help keep the placement of the holes consistent.

After the holes are drilled, rip the strip in two on the table saw, as shown. Then separate the pulls by crosscutting them. Lay out the cuts first, then carefully guide them through the blade with the miter gauge. Sand the pieces.

Mounting the Pulls

These pulls are mounted with a single screw driven into the fatter leg. Start by locating the pull on the

Tip

When crosscutting small pieces on the table saw, screw a fresh auxiliary fence to the miter gauge. After the first cut, there will be a fresh, crisp kerf in the fence with which to line up any subsequent cuts.

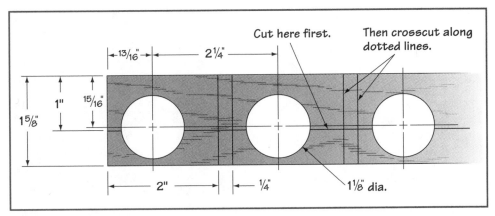

Figure 12-1. Making U-shaped drawer pulls

door or drawer face, then drill and countersink a screw hole there. This hole should let the screw just pass through. Depending on the thickness of the door or drawer face, I usually use a #6 × 1¼-inch screw.

Next, drill a pilot hole in the fatter leg of the pull. Slip a screw through the hole in the door or drawer face. Apply a dab of glue to the ends of the pull and screw it in place. Don't use too much glue—you don't want to have to clean up a lot of squeeze-out.

Photo 12-2: **The easiest of these cutout pulls to make is the circle. A quick bit of work with the drill press and router, and you've created a pull elegant in its simplicity.**

CUTOUT PULLS

Rather than being a separate piece, these pulls are cut right into the face of the door (or drawer) they serve.

You can use the method described to make any shape you can dream up. Some of the shapes I've used are shown in *Photo 12-2* and *Photo 12-3* on page 140. The idea is to create a cutout area in the door frame that you can poke your finger through to pull the door open. The front edges get rounded-over to make the opening a little friendlier, and the back is coved to make the door easier to grasp, as shown in *Figure 12-2* on page 140.

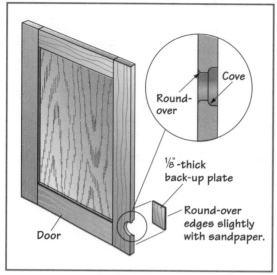

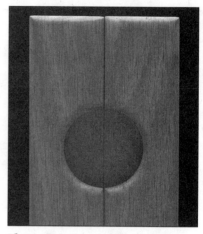

Figure 12-2. Making a cutout pull

Photo 12-3: Here, I drilled a hole in a single wide stile before ripping it in two. The amount of wood lost to the saw kerf is compensated for by the gap between the doors.

Making the Cutout

The first step toward making these pulls is to design the cutout. I'll describe the process I go through to make a circular pull. The process for creating any other shape is similar.

First, make the circular cutout with a Forstner bit of the appropriate diameter. As you're choosing the bit, remember that the cove around the inside of the hole increases the amount of space the pull requires across the width of the stile. The narrower the stile, the smaller the hole should be. On a 2¼-inch-wide stile, for example, 1 inch is the largest diameter hole I would bore. This would allow me to cut my standard ½-inch cove all the way around the hole, leaving ⅛ inch on either side of the cut. Drill all the way through the piece.

Round-over the outside lip of the hole with a ¼-inch roundover bit in a hand-held router. Then turn the piece over and cove the inside lip with a ½-inch cove bit. This size cove bit takes a big bite. To avoid straining the router, make the cut in several light passes. All these routed surfaces have to be sanded, so take your time as you make the cuts. Make the final pass for the cove a light one.

Tip

When you sit down to design a cutout, think about the shapes your tools produce—circles, lines, arcs. You'll find it's easier and more time-effective to make cutouts that incorporate these shapes rather than those that incorporate shapes that have to be made by hand.

The cove should start just about where the round-over ends. I machine all the doors at a given depth of cut. Then I lower the bit a notch and go at it again, routing each door at that depth setting. Depending on the thickness of your stock, three or four passes should do. Sanding comes next.

Drawer Pulls

Cutting a pull in a drawer face is much like cutting a pull in a door frame, with one exception. The cutout exposes the front of the drawer box, which is usually hidden.

As a solution, inlay small pieces of the face wood into the drawer box fronts where the cutouts will fall, as shown in *Figure 12-3*. When you mortise the pieces into the box front, leave them slightly proud of the surface, then sand or scrape them flush. Be very careful not to sand a hollow into the front of the box. While the process adds time to the project, it saves valuable wood.

Whichever method of backing up a cutout you choose, the surface exposed by the cutout should be sanded just as well as the inside of the pull. This adds to the pull's feel as well as its visual appeal.

On doors, you don't have to worry about backing up the pulls because they open to the inside of the cabinet. If you prefer the look you get with the drawer fronts, you can replicate it on a door. Simply cut a thin plate of wood to glue behind the cutout, as shown in *Figure 12-2*. I usually make this plate about ⅛ inch

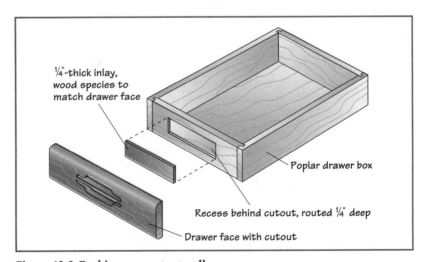

¼"-thick inlay, wood species to match drawer face

Poplar drawer box

Recess behind cutout, routed ¼" deep

Drawer face with cutout

Figure 12-3. **Backing up a cutout pull**

thick and round the corners and edges gently before gluing it in place.

TUBULAR PULLS

These pulls are similar to the cutout pulls. However, instead of being cut into the face of the door or drawer, they run along the length of an edge, as shown in *Photo 12-4.*

Photo 12-4: **This detail evolved over several years. Since I first added it to a cabinet, it has become one of my most popular pulls.**

To make this kind of pull, rout a cove in all the parts: the door, the counter, and the case. The door and counter are easy to cove. Rout them with a ½-inch cove bit and a hand-held router. Use the router's fence attachment to keep the bit from cutting too deep at the beginning and end of the cut. Increase the depth of cut gradually until you've got the desired profile.

The case presents a bigger challenge. Here you have to add a strip of hardwood edging along the case top that is wide enough for the cove, as shown in *Figure 12-4.* Unfortunately, the cove runs continuously across the front and must be added after the case is assembled. I do it by cutting off a strip of the plywood cabinet top and replacing it with a strip of solid wood.

Make up the case as usual, but keep any mechanical fasteners away from the front edge. You won't appreciate the damage a hardened screw will do to a saw blade. Run the case over the table saw to remove a ¾ × ¾-inch strip from its top front edge. Glue and clamp a piece of hardwood in its place.

I make the hardwood strip a little larger than is necessary (what a surprise!)—about ¹⁄₃₂ inch in both thickness and width and about ¹⁄₁₆ inch in length. Then when the glue dries, I sand it flush to the case. Once the strip is in place, I cut the cove with the router.

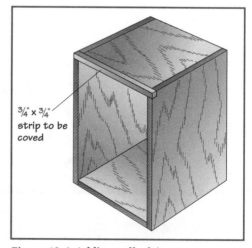

¾" × ¾" strip to be coved

Figure 12-4. **Adding pull edging**

COUNTERTOPS

13

S urfaces for every occasion

With the myriad materials available today, choosing a countertop can be almost overwhelming. To try and make some sense of this, I view these materials as belonging to one of two groups: natural or man-made. There are advantages and uses for each and, while I'm prejudiced in favor of genuine stone and wood, I've also laid my share of plastic laminate.

As you're mulling over the choices, let me warn you that stone countertops are not inexpensive. But even if your budget won't allow you to use stone throughout a project, maybe you can use it for a select part. In a kitchen, for example, you could cover only one or two cabinets with stone. Many bakers I know like a section of stone countertop for rolling out and kneading dough. That section will be well appreciated and may satisfy your desire for a natural surface.

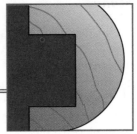

NATURAL MATERIALS

My first love when it comes to countertops is stone. Recent projects I've made have had marble, granite, limestone, and even sandstone countertops. While more expensive than most other countertop materials, stone's beauty and feel are difficult to match.

Of the stones I use, granite is the hardest. It polishes to a beautiful high gloss. Highly scratch and heat resistant, it's quite suitable for kitchen countertops. Like all stone, it is porous and either must be sealed or prestained before use.

I also use marble in kitchens, although only the harder varieties. The softer types won't hold up well under the heavy use a kitchen countertop sees. For bathroom vanity tops, where the usage is much less damaging, marble is unrivaled. Like granite, marble is usually polished to a high sheen.

Away from the mainstream are limestone and sandstone, other favorites of mine. While on the soft side, these sedimentary stones each possess a beauty that is unique. Sometimes within their structure you can even see the fossilized remains of small sea creatures that lived long ago. If you're tempted in this direction, talk over your selection carefully with your stone dealer. Only the hardest of these will hold up in a kitchen.

The other natural material I use for countertops is, of course, wood. While wood countertops in kitchens and baths are not practical, I do get an occasional request for them. For entertainment centers and other wall units, however, a wood countertop is a superior choice.

Stone

Stone, in many ways, is comparable to wood. It has grain that can impart a prominent pattern across a surface, adding to its aesthetic appeal, as shown in *Photo 13-1*. This pattern can be a problem, too, for it can vary tremendously from piece to piece. I've seen people who were very disappointed with their new stone countertops because they were unprepared for the differences they would find.

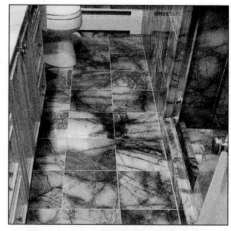

Photo 13-1: **Stone is far from being a homogeneous material. The patterns that swirl across its surface can be very striking and spectacular.**

Photo 13-2: **Selecting stone in the rough can be a challenging experience. It's hard to picture how such rough stone will look when it's polished.**

To avoid such disappointment, try to look at a complete countertop or floor made of the material you're considering before you make a commitment. Trying to picture what an expanse of stone will look like based on a small sample is just asking for trouble.

With slab material, selection is tougher, as shown in *Photo 13-2.* Looking at rough stone is a lot like looking at rough-sawn lumber—you can see the general pattern but the subtleties are hidden by the coarse surface. If you're not used to looking at raw material, picturing the final result may be a stretch. So try to look at many similar pieces of polished stone before you buy, and be prepared for surprises. That's one of the fun parts of working with a natural material.

Solid Stone

I have all my stone work done by professional stone cutters. They have the tools and expertise necessary to do the job right. Unless you're set up with the appropriate equipment, I recommend that you do the same.

First contact with the stone cutters is made during the design phase of the project. I take my clients to select the stone and find out about pricing. Then I go back to the shop to make the cabinets. About two weeks before installation, I call the stone people to let them know when I'll be ready for them. This gives them time to work me into their schedule. Then, once the cabinets are in place, they come out and make templates for the countertops.

The templates are made from sheets of foam core board, a lightweight lamination of paper and foam. Any information regarding cutouts or special features is written right on the template. All but the simplest tops have a template made for them. This way there is no question.

Back at the stone cutter's shop, the stone is cut and polished to match the template. This is all done with large machines fitted with diamond-tip cutters and abrasives—not exactly home-shop equipment. When complete, the countertops are delivered

Tip

If you make a template for a countertop or other piece that must fit precisely, include all the pertinent information right on the template. Most important, be sure to mark which side is up.

and set in place. Because stone is so heavy, there is usually no need to fasten it down.

It takes the shop I work with about two weeks to fabricate a countertop after they've made the template. During this time the cabinets are in place, but they're not very useful. My clients usually are very understanding of the delay and put up with the inconvenience. If necessary, you could cut a sheet of plywood to serve as a temporary countertop.

Solid Hardwood

For many pieces, solid wood makes a wonderful top. While it will show wear faster than some of the other materials, it still imparts a solid warmth to a piece. I try to steer my clients away from wood countertops in kitchens and baths where water damage could be a problem. But for other types of cabinetry, wood is an excellent choice.

The process is simple—just glue up a panel as wide and as thick as you need. As you're clamping the pieces together, use clamps on both sides of the panel to keep the pressure equal, as shown in *Photo 13-3*. This will help keep the panel flat.

Once the glue dries, scrape the countertop to remove any excess glue and run it through a surface planer to level out any variation between the boards. If you don't have access to a wide enough planer, glue the countertop up in narrower sections to match the machine you do have and plane them individually. Then glue them up to make your wide countertop. This way you'll only have one or two joints to fuss with by hand.

Another option is to buy a pre-glued "butcherblock" countertop. There are companies whose main business is making these solid wood laminations. They're available through many lumber-yards and come prefinished and very flat. All you have to do is screw them in place. This is a very viable option, par-

Photo 13-3: It saves a lot of aggravation when you're making a wood countertop if the glued-up panel comes out flat. Applying clamping pressure from both sides during glue-up helps ensure this.

ticularly if you don't want to go through the hassle of gluing up stock.

To fasten a wood countertop to a case, drive screws up from underneath. Drill oversize holes through the top of the case to accommodate the seasonal movement of the countertop.

MAN-MADE MATERIALS

If your budget or sense of aesthetics calls for something other than a stone or hardwood countertop, there are a number of synthetic alternatives. The four principal choices are plastic laminate, such as Wilsonart or Formica; solid-color laminate, like Colorcore; solid-surface materials, like Corian and Avonite; and hardwood plywood. Of these four, I use three: regular plastic laminate, Corian (or Avonite), and plywood.

I don't like or recommend the solid-color laminate. The idea behind it is good—having the color run all the way through the material makes any seams practically invisible. But I've found that, over time, the seams darken and show up anyway. It's disappointing to pay extra for a seamless appearance only to have dark lines creep around the edges of your countertops after a year or two. Instead, I recommend one of the solid-surface materials to my clients when they request a seamless countertop.

Solid-Surface Materials

These materials are about three times the cost of any of the laminates, but they are truly seamless. While it is sometimes possible to purchase these materials so you can fabricate your own countertops, I don't recommend it. I've seen too many Corian countertops that have cracked due to improper installation. You're better off finding a shop that has been trained and certified by the manufacturer in the use of these materials. That way you can be pretty sure the job will be done right and that the factory warranty will be good. The warranty is usually good for ten years but is void unless certified people do the work.

Plastic Laminate and Plywood

Among the less expensive choices for countertops are plastic laminate and hardwood plywood. I group these countertops together

Tip

When you use a planer to clean glued-up panels, be sure to scrape the excess glue from the boards before planing them. Otherwise you run the risk of nicking the planer's knives.

ROUTER BISCUIT JOINERY

Biscuit joints are a fast, easy way to join two pieces of wood. But finding the money for a biscuit joiner is another story. Fortunately, you don't have to. For the cost of a router bit and a little time, you can make biscuit joints with your router.

First, you need a $\frac{5}{32}$-inch wing cutter with a ball-bearing pilot. Buy one with a separate shank assembly. This way you can assemble it with the bearing on top of the cutter, rather than underneath, as is the norm. Next, make the template shown below. This guides the bit through the cut.

Once you have the bit and the template, you're ready to go. Clamp the tem-

Use the lines on the template as a guide as you set up for a cut.

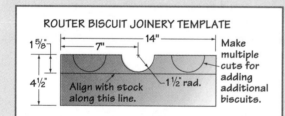

ROUTER BISCUIT JOINERY TEMPLATE

$1\frac{5}{8}$" | 14" | 7" | Make multiple cuts for adding additional biscuits.

$4\frac{1}{2}$" Align with stock along this line. $1\frac{1}{2}$" rad.

plate to the stock where you want to make the cut. Align the line on the template with the edge of the stock, as shown above. Guide the router along the template to make the cut. Repeat on the second piece of stock to make the mating part of the joint.

because they are made almost the same way. You build a plywood countertop in two steps: First, you make the horizontal surface—the *deck*. Then, you attach an edging. If you're surfacing the deck with laminate, do so before you attach the edging.

Making the deck. The finished deck should be 1½ inches thick at its edges. Build up this thickness with two layers of ¾-inch material. Unless you need an extra-stiff countertop, the bottom layer needn't run the full width of the countertop. Just run 3-inch-wide strips along the edges and 3-inch-wide strips every 24 inches across the interior, as shown in *Figure 13-1.* If you do

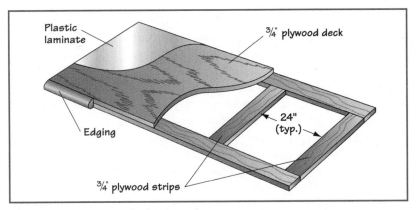

Figure 13-1. **Anatomy of a laminated countertop**

need an extra-stiff countertop (such as for a cantilevered snack bar), simply make the bottom layer solid.

Most commercial laminated countertops are laid up on particleboard. Particleboard is cheap and relatively flat. Other than that, it doesn't have much else going for it. Instead, I prefer to use hardwood plywood. Yes, it costs more. But the few extra dollars you'll spend buy quite a bit of quality, which results in a stronger, lighter-weight surface.

Rip strips for the bottom layer. Cut the top layer about ⅛ inch larger than you need—you'll trim it later. Spread glue on the strips and tack them to the top layer with small wire brads. The brads will hold the strips in place until the glue dries.

If there are any joints in the top layer, span them underneath with wider pieces of ¾-inch plywood for added reinforcement instead of the 3-inch-wide strips I mentioned earlier. If the countertop is U- or L-shaped, wait to assemble the pieces until you've trimmed the two layers even with one another.

Once the glue dries, run the built-up decks through the table saw to trim them to final size. This will make the edges of the two layers perfectly flush with each other, providing a good surface on which to glue the edging. Once the pieces are trimmed, you can put them together into the appropriate U- or L-shape.

Applying the laminate. Generally speaking, countertop fabricators glue an oversize piece of laminate to the deck with contact cement. Then they rout the laminate flush with the edges of the deck. It may seem cumbersome, but actually it's very practical. Better to waste a little material than to ruin an entire countertop.

Tip

There are special rollers available for spreading contact cement, but I find a decent-quality paint roller works just as well at a lower cost. Don't go overboard saving money, though. The adhesive pulls the nap right off the cheaper rollers. This can give your countertop a real case of the lumps.

If possible, cover the countertop with a single sheet of laminate to avoid seams. Laminate comes in sheets up to 5 × 12 feet. If your countertop is smaller than this, you're in good shape. If not, see "Creating Perfect Seams" on page 152 for my method of making surface seams. Cut the laminate ½ inch or so oversize in all directions to allow yourself a little leeway.

As I said, plastic laminate is glued in place with contact cement. I use the solvent-based cement rather than the water-based because I think the bond is superior. Be careful as you're working with this noxious stuff. Work in a well-ventilated area and wear a respirator to cut down on the amount of bad air you have to breathe.

Spread the adhesive on both the laminate and the deck with a roller. Try to apply an even coat. Both surfaces should be completely covered, but avoid leaving puddles of cement. Be patient and wait for both surfaces to dry. This usually takes 10 to 20 minutes. You'll know the glue is dry when it loses its sheen and is no longer tacky to the touch.

Once two surfaces coated with cement come into contact, they won't budge—regardless of whether they're properly positioned. As a result, the big trick in laminate work is to position the laminate as accurately as possible *before* the surfaces touch. I do this with the help of dowels.

When you're ready to apply the laminate, lay a ⅜-inch dowel across the deck every foot or so. The ends of the dowel should hang over the edges of the deck, as shown in *Photo 13-4*. Put the laminate on top of the dowels and position it precisely. The dowels will keep the two glue-covered surfaces apart until you're ready to stick them together.

When you have the laminate in the right position, slip a dowel out from near the center. Press the laminate down to make contact with the deck and smooth it out with your hand. Move out toward the ends, removing

Photo 13-4: **One of the secrets to laying laminate is keeping the plastic off the deck until you're ready to stick it down for good. I use dowels to keep the surfaces apart while I position the laminate precisely.**

Photo 13-5: **While contact cement bonds with a light touch, added pressure makes the bond much stronger. Pay extra attention to the edges to help keep the laminate from lifting prematurely.**

dowels and securing the plastic as you go. Then go over the entire top with a J-roller (made especially for use with plastic laminate) or a smooth, soft block of pine, pressing down hard to bring the laminate into firm contact with the deck, as shown in *Photo 13-5.* If anything goes wrong—and it sometimes does—you can usually separate the two surfaces with lacquer thinner.

With the laminate stuck down, cut it flush to the edges of the deck with a flush-trim bit in a router. You'll be able to trim all but the inside corners this way. Those you can finish with a sharp chisel.

Adding the edging. To complete the countertop, I glue a hardwood edging to all the exposed edges. I mill this edging somewhat thicker than necessary—about ¹⁄₁₆ inch. This leaves a little room for adjustment as I'm gluing the edging in place. Glue the edging with regular wood glue. Miter the corners as necessary.

When the glue dries, rout the edging flush with the countertop with a flush-trim bit. Make sure the bearing on the bit spins freely so you don't burn the surface of the plastic. Then rout the edging to its finished shape. Any of the profiles in *Figure 13-2* will work here as well. Sand and finish the edge to complete the countertop, as shown in *Photo 13-6* on page 153. Take care not to scratch the plastic laminate as you sand.

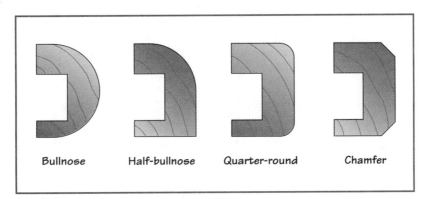

Bullnose   Half-bullnose   Quarter-round   Chamfer

Figure 13-2. **Typical edging profiles**

CREATING PERFECT SEAMS

Ideally, a laminated countertop has no seams. But this limits the size of the countertop you can make. As a compromise, I try to keep seams to a minimum.

The first step is to make the two adjoining edges absolutely straight. Do this with a straight length of scrap and a flush-trim bit in a router. Clamp the straightedge about 1/16 inch away from the edge of the plastic. Flip the work over so the straightedge is underneath. Guide the router along the scrap to trim the laminate, as shown at right. Repeat with the other piece of plastic.

Next, apply adhesive and lay the two pieces on dowels. There should be a dowel about 12 inches on either side of the seam.

Start pressing one piece in place at the seam. Work your way away from the joint, removing dowels and smoothing the plastic into place until it is adhered. Butt the second piece to the first and press it down along the seam. Then move 24 to 30 inches from the seam and press the laminate down in a second place. Leave a dowel in place, as shown below.

When you clamp the straightedge to the laminate, make sure the clamps won't interfere with the router.

Once the laminate is stuck in two places, remove the intervening dowel. The laminate will be slightly bowed up. Work from the stuck area farthest from the seam, smoothing the laminate into place. This will put a little bit of pressure on the seam, keeping it tight. Once this initial area of laminate is stuck down, adhere the rest of the piece in the same manner.

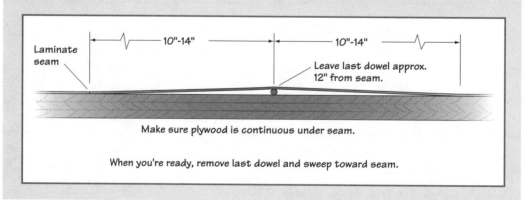

Photo 13-6: **As a finishing touch, I apply a strip of hardwood to the front edge of the counter. This hides the edge of the laminate and provides a visual tie-in with the rest of the wood cabinetry.**

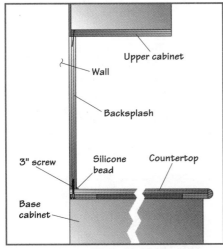

Figure 13-3. **Installing a backsplash**

BACKSPLASHES

A backsplash extends up the wall behind a countertop and protects the wall from all manner of spills and splatters. It should be made of a durable, washable material. The logical choice is to make the backsplash from the same material as the countertop.

On many commercial cabinets, the backsplash only rises 6 inches or so above the countertop. This offers a minimum of protection to the wall. I only use a low backsplash like this on vanities and other projects that don't have upper cabinets. In almost all other situations, I make the backsplash rise all the way to the underside of the upper cabinets. This method offers two advantages: It provides great protection for the wall and it creates a perch for the upper cabinets to rest on, as shown in *Figure 13-3*.

Stone and Corian backsplashes are installed after the countertop is in place on the cabinets. A plastic laminate backsplash, however, is installed before the countertop is screwed in place. Laminate the backsplash first. Then screw it to the countertop from underneath, as shown. I run a bead of silicone caulk between the two pieces to help waterproof the joint. Clean up squeeze-out with a wet rag.

14 INSTALLATION

Out of the shop and into the home

The final stage of a cabinet project is installation. This usually involves attaching the pieces to a house's floor, walls, and/or ceiling. There are two important aspects here. One is to put the cabinets in so they are plumb and level. The other is to make sure the intersections between the cabinets and the architecture look good. The problem is that houses are usually crooked, which means your nice, square cabinets won't sit right unless you adapt them to fit. So, by the time you've coaxed the cabinets into sitting plumb and level, there are apt to be odd gaps to hide to make them look right.

The gaps can usually be taken care of with moldings and other filler strips. It's the initial leveling that can be tough. I eventually developed a simple method of building and installing cabinets that overcame many of the problems that I seemed to keep running into on the job site.

BASE CABINETS

One of the key differences between my base cabinets and those of many commercial manufacturers is that mine have a separate base. This allows me to set the base in place first, level it, then set the cabinets on top. Making the base separate from the cabinet involves slightly more work in the shop, but it makes installation a breeze.

The sides of a typical commercial cabinet run all the way down to the floor. The lower front corner of each is notched to form a kick space along the front of the cabinet. The back of this space is sealed with a toekick. The two sides plus the toekick form a three-sided base for the cabinet to sit on. This is great if the floor the cabinet is to rest on is flat and level. However, this is rarely the case. To make the cabinet sit right, shims have to be added underneath to raise the low areas. Here's where the fun starts.

Shims are wedge-shaped pieces of wood, 12 to 15 inches long, that taper from nothing at one end to about ½ inch at the other. Many professional installers, as well as carpenters, use narrow wooden shingles for this purpose. They're available at most lumberyards.

Shims are driven between a cabinet and the floor to raise the cabinet as needed. Once the cabinet is positioned correctly and anchored, the shim can be trimmed flush with the cabinet. So what's the big deal about shimming a cabinet with an integral base? Access. Most of the time you can't get to the back of the cabinet to insert the shims.

To get the shims in place, you have to move the cabinet, set the shims on the floor, then set the cabinet back in place. This becomes a trial-and-error process as you try to guess how much to raise each cabinet. It's not uncommon to have to repeat the process two or three times until you get it right. This has never impressed me as being a very efficient way of working.

With my system, I bring the base in from the truck, plop it in place, level it with shims, and screw it to the floor. The entire process takes hardly more than 5 minutes. With the base installed, I have a level surface on which to place the rest of the cabinet.

Making the Bases

I make my bases from ¾-inch plywood. There always seem to be scraps of the stuff lying around the shop. Rip the pieces to about

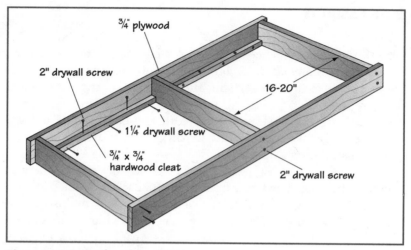

Figure 14-1. Parts of a cabinet base

4½ inches wide, then screw them together with 2-inch drywall screws into a ladderlike assembly, as shown in *Figure 14-1.* Screw ¾-inch-square hardwood cleats (I usually use poplar) between the crosspieces with 1¼-inch drywall screws, as shown. The length of each base varies. Generally, I try to make a single base for each run of cabinets. Sometimes, however, I have to make up a base in two or more sections to accommodate an appliance or some architectural feature. The width of the ladder is not critical. I usually make them about 4 inches narrower than the overall depth of the cabinet. This allows 3 inches of depth for a toespace and 1 inch at the rear of the cabinet for wiring or other utilities. Don't worry about the screws showing on the front of the base. They'll be covered with a facing later.

Installing the Bases

The first thing to do is to find the highest point on the floor. To do this, set a level on the floor parallel to the wall and push it up against the baseboard. The longer a level you use, the better. If the floor isn't level (most aren't) the bubble will show you which side is higher. Slide the level along the floor toward the high side until you locate the highest point. (After this point the bubble will shift to the other side of the vial.)

Once you have the high point, set the base section that goes over this point on the floor. The front of the base should be 21 inches from the wall (assuming your cabinets are 24 inches deep). Shim the base until it reads level both side to side and front

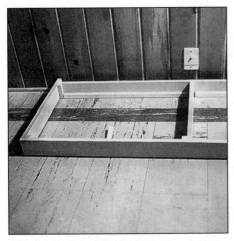

Photo 14-1: **Once the bases are level, they can be screwed in place. Drive the screws through the shims to help keep them secure. This photo shows additional glue blocks in the corners for added strength.**

to back. Once the base is level, screw it to the floor through both the cleats and shims with 2-inch drywall screws, as shown in *Photo 14-1.* As long as the screws are going into wood or plywood, it's not necessary for them to hit the floor joists. With a ceramic floor, drill through the tile first so the screws can find the subfloor underneath.

After the first base is screwed down, put the adjacent bases in place and repeat the process, leveling them even with the first. Continue until all the bases are fastened in place.

Once the bases are screwed in place, you'll have a flat, level surface on which to rest your base cabinets. You won't have to fuss getting each one to line up. And you'll have a good reference to work from if you have upper cabinets to hang.

Installing the Base Cabinets

The next step is to install the base cabinets. If there is a corner included in the project, start there. Otherwise, just start at one end. Put the cabinets on the base and slide them into position. Keep adding cabinets until they are all on the base. This is easiest to do without the drawers and doors in place.

Next, fasten the cases to each other. With frameless construction, align the front edges of the cases and clamp them together. Then join them with screws driven right through the case sides. Four 1¼-inch drywall screws will do the trick: two near the top front and back and two toward the bottom front and back, as shown in *Figure 14-2* on page 158. I align the screws near the bottom with the holes for the adjustable shelf brackets, as shown. This keeps them from being too obvious. The screws near the top will be hidden by the drawer.

Cabinets with face frames are dealt with differently. Screw these together through their frames,

Occasionally, you may need to use a screw to draw two pieces together during installation. In this case, drill a hole in the first piece that is big enough to allow the screw to pass through without threading. Then drill a regular pilot hole in the second piece. The threads will catch in this second hole and the head of the screw will pull the first piece in tight.

as shown in *Figure 14-3*. Align the cases so the faces of the frames are flush. Predrill the screw holes to avoid spoiling the frames and counterbore for the screw heads. I use two 2½-inch drywall screws per joint.

How can you hide screws? Well, if you put the screws in from the hinge side of a door frame, the screws will usually be out of sight. On drawer bases, if you keep the screws low in an opening, they will be less visible. Yet another way is to place them underneath the hinges.

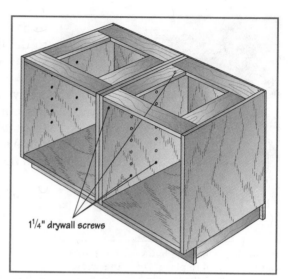

Figure 14-2. Fastening frameless cabinets

The cabinets are now fixed to each other, but not to anything else. You can still slide them around on the base. Make any final adjustments to their position, then lock them in place with 2-inch drywall screws driven down into the base rails. These screws will be visible inside the cabinets, which may or may not be a problem depending on how fussy you (or your clients) are.

Since the cabinets are joined together, not every cabinet needs to be screwed down. So you may be able to hide the screws in the bottoms of the drawer bases. Or, if necessary, you can countersink the screws and putty over them if they're objectionable.

Why don't I screw my base cabinets to the wall as other installers do? Walls, like floors, are rarely flat. So unless you shim the cabinets out from the wall, any mounting screws are apt to pull the cabinets out of line. Plus, you have to find the studs in the wall to screw into. They're rarely where you want them. If your

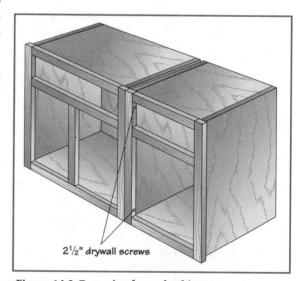

Figure 14-3. Fastening framed cabinets

project involves upper cabinets, you'll have to do this later anyway. But for a project that only involves base cabinets, it's nicer to be free of this chore. Finally, cabinets that are screwed to a wall require a mounting strip to be fixed across the back of the case, a piece that I'd rather not have to deal with.

My method of installation sidesteps all these hassles and offers another advantage. By unscrewing a few screws, you can easily pop one of my cabinets out. This can be very handy if you have to access the area behind the cases for any reason (like installing speaker or computer wires).

Facing the Bases

To finish the base cabinet installation, attach a face over the base. This takes care of two problems. First, it covers any gaps between the base and the floor. And second, it dresses the base up. Make the cover from a strip of ¼-inch plywood with the same face veneer and finish as the rest of the cabinets, as shown in *Figure 14-4*. Measure the space under the cases carefully, then cut the plywood to fit. Trim just a hair off the width to leave a gap at the top of the base—this will be hidden by the cabinet, and it makes installation much easier. Attach the face with small finish nails.

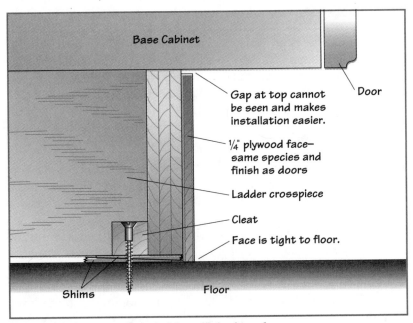

Figure 14-4. Cross-section of an installed cabinet base

COUNTERTOPS

With the base cabinets in place, you can install the countertops. Solid stone countertops are among the easiest to install. Just bring them in and set them in place. If they fit correctly, tip them up and apply a small bead of silicone caulk along the front edge of the cases. Then gently set the counters back down. That's all there is to it. Stone is so heavy it requires no further fastening.

Plastic laminate and solid wood countertops are installed alike. Position them on top of the cases and screw them in place from underneath. This lets you remove the countertop easily if it should ever be necessary. With solid wood countertops, drill oversize holes through the case tops. This will allow the counter to expand and contract with changes in humidity. Tile countertops are screwed down this way, too. Then the tile is laid once the countertop is in place.

A solid-surface countertop, like Corian, should be installed by a certified installer or its warranty will be voided. There are enough problems with these materials that an intact warranty is worth the added expense of professional installation.

WALL CABINETS

With the counters in, you can move on to the wall cabinets. Unlike base cabinets, these *must* be fastened to the wall. My system for attaching them includes a ledger at the bottom for the cabinets to rest on and a screw rail attached to the top of the cabinets to screw through into the wall.

Installing the Ledger

The ledger can be done in one of two ways. If the countertop below has an integral backsplash, the wall cabinets can rest right on its top edge. The standard splash height for these situations is 18 inches.

The other way to make the ledger is to run a molding along the wall, as shown in *Figure 14-5*. The molding is screwed to each stud in the wall with 2½-inch drywall screws, then the screw holes are plugged for appearance.

The first step toward installing this molding is to mark its location. If the project includes a tall cabinet, like a pantry or a

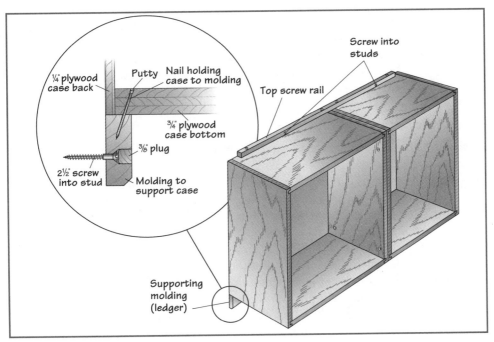

Screw into studs

Top screw rail

¼" plywood case back

Putty

Nail holding case to molding

¾" plywood case bottom

⅜" plug

2½" screw into stud

Molding to support case

Supporting molding (ledger)

Figure 14-5. **Installing wall cabinets**

linen closet, you must use it as a reference. The tops of the wall cabinets should line up with the top of the tall unit. Measure down from the top of the tall cabinet a distance equal to the height of the wall cabinets and make a mark on the wall. Here's where the top of the molding goes. If there is no tall cabinet to go by, refer to your plans and mark the wall the required distance above the countertop. Again, this is usually 18 inches.

Have a helper hold one end of a chalk line at the mark and stretch the line out along the wall where the cabinets are to go. Hold the string level (you can measure off the countertop) and snap a line on the wall to establish exactly where the cabinets are to hang. Hold the top of the molding even with the line and screw the molding to the wall.

The important part here is to make sure the screws go into the studs. So before you drill the molding for the screws, figure out where the studs are. I usually do this by rapping the wall with my knuckles. The sound and the feel change when you're over a stud. Once you think you've found one,

Tip

When you're locating studs in a wall, take a little extra time with the first one. Find and mark both edges by driving a small nail through the drywall. Then carefully mark the center. This will give you an accurate point from which to measure as you move along the wall.

INSTALLATION

drive a finish nail through the drywall to be sure. Then, from the first stud, measure to find and mark the location of the others. In most houses, you'll find a stud every 16 inches. Cut the molding to the appropriate length. Drill it for screws according to the stud spacing. Then screw it to the wall and plug the holes.

Adding the Screw Rail

Putting up the molding gets the wall ready for the cabinets—but before you hang them, you have to get the cabinets ready, too. This involves attaching a screw rail along the tops of the cabinets.

There are two approaches to this. You can add an individual rail to each cabinet, then put up the cabinets one at a time. Or you can fasten several cabinets together, span them with a single rail, and hang them as a unit. The latter approach is faster, but it requires an assistant to help lift the cabinets. It also makes shimming the cabinets a little bit more difficult.

The screw rail is simply a ¾-inch square strip of wood cut as long as necessary. Generally, I use the same species of wood as I used for the rest of the cabinetry. Screw it to the back edge of the case top, as shown in *Figure 14-5* on page 161. When the cabinets are installed, the rail will be up high enough that it won't be seen except near the ends of a run of cabinets. To keep this from being a problem, I stop the rail 3 inches short of those ends. This keeps the rail completely hidden from below. If you're fastening the cases together before you hang them, do it before attaching the rail. Join them just as you joined the base cases, as described earlier.

The last step before hanging the cabinets is to predrill the screw rail for the screws that go into the wall. Again, these screws must hit studs, so the placement of the holes is critical. If you had to find the studs to put up the molding, half the job is done. Just tranfer the measurements from the molding to the rail. If you haven't found the studs yet, go through the process described earlier.

Hanging the Cabinets

With the rails mounted and the holes drilled, the cabinets are ready to go. Hoist them up and onto the molding or the backsplash. Then drive just enough screws through the rail into the wall to hold things while you check the cabinets for plumb along their

Tip

Sometimes the space above a run of cabinets is so small that it is difficult to drive the screws through the rail and into the wall. In a situation like this, I use lag screws. I drill larger holes through the rail, then drive the lags with my ratchet via a socket at the end of a 15-inch extension.

fronts. You're apt to find that the cases tilt out at either the top or the bottom. Shim the cases as needed to make them plumb. Then drive in the rest of the screws. Finally, drive finish nails down through the case bottoms into the molding or backsplash for added security.

Photo 14-2: **Sometimes your cabinet design may provide a means of covering gaps. Here, the side panel on this cabinet was cut to match the contour of the window casing.**

FINISHING TOUCHES

Depending on how flat and plumb the walls are, there are apt to be gaps between them and the cabinets. These will have to be concealed before you can consider the job finished.

There are a couple of ways to deal with this. You can add a molding to the cabinet. Or you can add an entire panel, as shown in *Photo 14-2*. This last solution actually solves two problems, as it also dresses up the side of the end cabinet, which may not match the cabinet faces. Once these final details are taken care of, you can sit back and admire your work.

PART 2

PROJECTS

Classic Designs for Every Room in Your Home

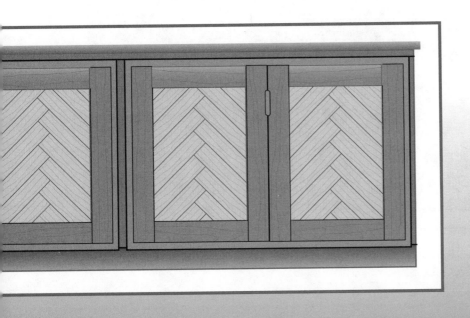

PINE SHELVING SYSTEM

Over the years, I've built quite a few of these units, each a little different from the previous one. I made the original during a slow time in the shop as utility shelving for my basement. Nothing fancy, just a place to stack the assorted odds and ends that had accumulated.

Shortly thereafter, Sally, one of my clients, asked if I would make some shelves for her sewing room. She didn't have a lot of money to spend, but she needed a place to store her sewing books and supplies. Oh, and could I incorporate a work surface where she could sit and sketch out her ideas?

I built her sewing center using the same quick, easy methods I used for my utility shelves. I installed the unit, then pretty much forgot about it. Some time later, Sally called me again and asked if I could add some drawers for her patterns and notions. I reluctantly agreed, not all that excited about adding onto a "utility" piece. However, when I went to her house to take some measurements, I was shocked. They may have been utility shelves to me, but to her they were something special. With some flowers, nice sewing books, and carefully folded stacks of colorful cloth, the unit looked like a million bucks!

Since then, I've built dozens of these units and am always surprised at how nice they look. They've become hobby centers, home offices, even budget entertainment centers. The design shown here is just one possibility. The dimensions can easily be modified to suit your specific space and purpose.

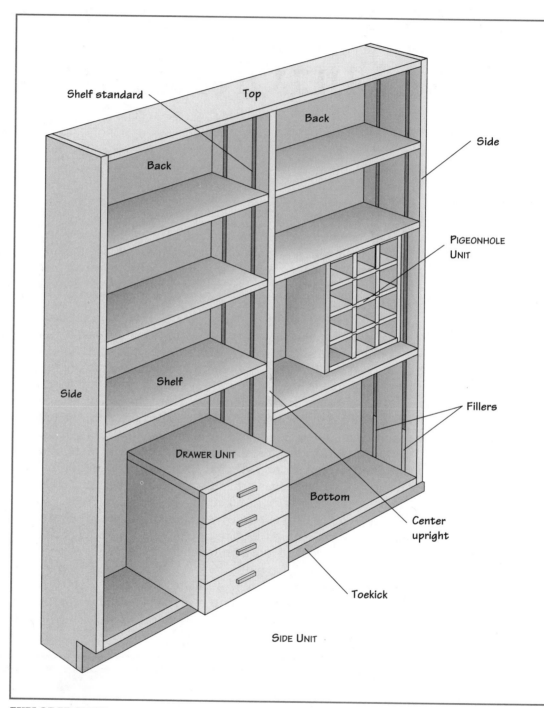

Shelf standard

Top

Back

Side

Back

PIGEONHOLE
UNIT

Side

Shelf

Fillers

DRAWER UNIT

Bottom

Center
upright

Toekick

SIDE UNIT

EXPLODED VIEW

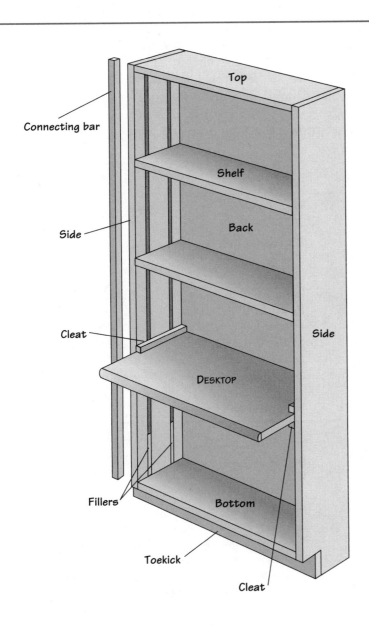

Connecting bar

Top

Shelf

Back

Side

Side

Cleat

DESKTOP

Fillers

Bottom

Toekick

Cleat

DESK UNIT

TECH <u>NOTES</u> The project pictured consists of four separate pieces: two tall cases with adjustable shelves, a small chest of drawers, and a case divided into pigeonholes. With the exception of the pigeonhole unit, the cases are joined at the corners with my standard tongue-and-groove joint, as detailed in "Cutting the Joint" on page 16. The drawers are put together with a variation of this joint, as discussed in "An Alternate Drawer Joint" on page 106. Beyond

MATERIALS LIST

PART	DIMENSION	PART	DIMENSION
Desk Unit		**Drawer Unit**	
Sides (2)	¾" × 12" × 84"	Top/Bottom (2)	¾" × 16" × 17¾"
Top/Bottom (2)	¾" × 12" × 35¼"	Sides (2)	¾" × 16" × 19½"
Back	¼" × 36" × 84"	Back	¼" × 18½" × 19½"
Fillers (4)	³⁄₁₆" × ⅝" × 6½"	Runners (8)	½" × ¾" × 16"
Toekick	¾" × 4" × 39¾"	Drawer fronts/backs (8)	⅝" × 3½" × 15⅜"
Shelves (2)	¾" × 12" × 34⅜"	Drawer sides (8)	⅝" × 3½" × 15½"
		Drawer bottoms (4)	¼" × 15⅝" × 14¾"
Side Unit		Drawer faces (4)	¾" × 4¾" × 18⅜"
Sides (2)	¾" × 12" × 84"		
Top/Bottom (2)	¾" × 12" × 70½"	**Pigeonhole Unit**	
Center upright	¾" × 12" × 79¼"	Sides (2)	½" × 7½" × 22½"
Backs (2)	¼" × 35⅝" × 84"	Shelves (5)	½" × 7½" × 16¼"
Fillers (8)	³⁄₁₆" × ⅝" × 6½"	Dividers (8)	½" × 7½" × 5¼"
Toekick	¾" × 4" × 74¼"	Back	¼" × 17" × 22½"
Shelves (6)	¾" × 12" × 34⅜"		
Connecting bar	¾" × ¾" × 80"	**Hardware**	

Desktop

Part	Dimension
Desk surface	¾" × 19¼" × 33¹⁵⁄₁₆"
Front doubler	¾" × ¾" × 34"
Side doublers (2)	¾" × ¾" × 18½"
Edging (2)	¼" × 1⅝" × 19¼"
Bullnose	¾" × 1⅝" × 34⁷⁄₁₆"
Cleats (4)	¾" × ¾" × 12"

Hardware

Shelf standards (12). Available from
   The Woodworkers' Store; part #33993
Shelf supports (32). Available from
   The Woodworkers' Store; part #33837
Plastic laminate, 19½" × 34½"
Pulls (4). Available from Forms and Surfaces;
   part #HC-208
1¼" drywall screws (as needed)
1" drywall screws (as needed)
4d finish nails (as needed)
3d finish nails (as needed)
1¼" wire brads (as needed)

that, there are a few dadoes to cut and screws to drive before you can assemble the pieces and load up the shelves.

I used solid knotty pine for everything but the case backs, drawer bottoms, and desk surface. For these I used plywood—¼-inch knotty pine for the backs, and scraps of pieces that I had for the rest. To save time and effort, I bought the solid stock in boards that were already glued up and planed. I got them slightly wider than necessary and then trimmed them to size. The only drawback with getting wood this way is that it may not be flat. Try to find a source that will let you select the actual boards you'll be getting and look them over carefully before you buy.

For simple utility shelves, you can omit the backs entirely to save money. Just attach a screw rail to the underside of the case top and screw the unit to the wall; see "Wall Cabinets" on page 160. This will make up for the rigidity you're losing by not having a back.

CONSTRUCTION STEPS

Make the Desk and Side Units

1. Cut the sides, tops, and bottoms for both units to the sizes specified in the Materials List.

2. Cut tongue-and-groove joints to join the corners, as shown in the *Side Unit Elevation/Corner Joint Detail*. See "Cutting the Joint" on page 16.

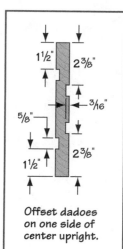

1½" 2⅜"

⅜⁶"

⅝"

1½" 2⅜"

Offset dadoes on one side of center upright.

SHELF STANDARD DADO LAYOUT

3. Notch the lower corners of the sides to accept the toe-kick, as shown in the *Side Unit Elevation* and *Desk Unit Elevation*.

4. Cut a ¾-inch-wide dado across the side unit top and bottom, as shown in the *Side Unit Elevation/Dado Detail*. Assemble the side unit without glue and cut the center upright to fit in its dadoes.

5. Disassemble everything. Cut ⅝-inch-wide grooves in the inside surfaces of the sides and the center upright for the shelf standards, as shown in the *Shelf Standard Dado Layout*. Since the center upright gets grooves in both sides, offset the dadoes on one side, as shown, to keep from weakening the piece.

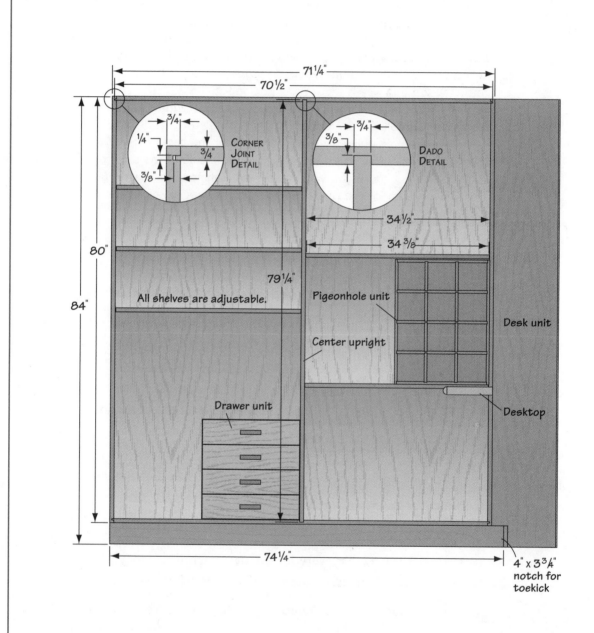

71¼"

70½"

¾"

¼"

⅜"

¾"

CORNER
JOINT
DETAIL

¾"

⅜"

DADO
DETAIL

34½"

34⅜"

80"

84"

79¼"

All shelves are adjustable.

Pigeonhole unit

Desk unit

Center upright

Drawer unit

Desktop

74¼"

4" x 3¾"
notch for
toekick

SIDE UNIT ELEVATION

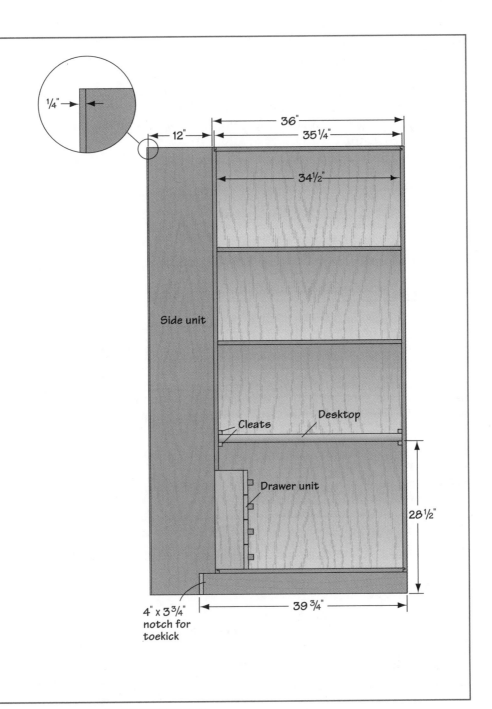

1/4"

36"

12"

35¼"

34½"

Side unit

Cleats

Desktop

Drawer unit

28½"

4" x 3¾"
notch for
toekick

39¾"

DESK UNIT ELEVATION

6. Glue the case pieces together. Use 4d finish nails to clamp and reinforce the joints as the glue dries. Set the heads and fill the holes. For more on using fillers, see "Filling Wood" on page 33.

7. Before the glue has a chance to dry, flop the units face down. Cut the backs to size, then glue and nail them in place with 1¼-inch wire brads, butting the two side unit backs tightly. If necessary, rack the cases into square using the back as a guide. For more detailed instructions, see "The Glue-Up" on page 24.

8. Slip the shelf standards into their grooves and push them up against the tops of the units. Screw or nail them in place, then cut fillers to fill the grooves underneath.

9. Cut the toekicks to the sizes listed. Glue and nail them in place with 4d finish nails in the notches you cut earlier.

Make the Desktop

1. Cut a piece of plywood to the size listed in the Materials List for the desk surface. You can use plywood with a knotty pine face veneer to match the rest of the unit, but I usually just use a scrap of whatever happens to be lying around the shop. Once I have the piece cut to size, I face it with plastic laminate, which makes for a smooth, durable work surface. For more on laying laminate, see "Plastic Laminate and Plywood" on page 147.

2. Cut the rest of the pieces for the desktop to size. Then, glue and nail the front and side doublers to the underside of the desk surface with 3d finish nails, as shown in *Desktop Assembly*. These make the surface look more substantial, and they add a little bit of stiffness. Glue them so they slightly overhang the edges of the plywood along their length (the front doubler should overhang at the ends as well). Then, after the glue dries, trim them flush with a flush-trim bit in a router.

3. Glue the edging to the sides of the surface. Trim the edging flush. Then glue the bullnose in place and trim it flush.

4. Shape the bullnose with a ¾-inch roundover bit in a table-mounted router.

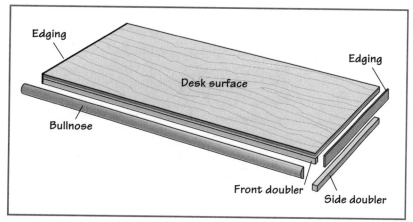

DESKTOP ASSEMBLY

5. Screw two of the cleats to the sides of the desk unit at the desired height with 1¼-inch drywall screws. Drop the desktop in place on top of them. Then screw the remaining two cleats in place on top of the desk. Drive the screws into the case sides at a slight downward angle. This will help sandwich the desk tightly between the cleats while still leaving it removable.

Make the Drawer Unit

1. Cut the top, bottom, and sides for the drawer unit to the sizes specified in the Materials List. Join them at the corners with tongue-and-groove joints as you did with the larger cases.

2. Glue and nail the pieces together with 4d finish nails. Cut the back to size and attach it with glue and 1¼-inch wire brads, squaring the case if necessary.

3. Instead of metal drawer slides, the drawers in this unit run on wooden runners that are screwed to the case sides. Cut the runners to the size specified. Drill and countersink each slide, as shown in the *Drawer Runner Detail*. Also round the front end, as shown, with a disc sander. This makes it easier to slide the drawers in place.

4. Screw the runners to the inside of the case with 1-inch drywall screws, as shown in the *Drawer Case Detail*. The easiest way to

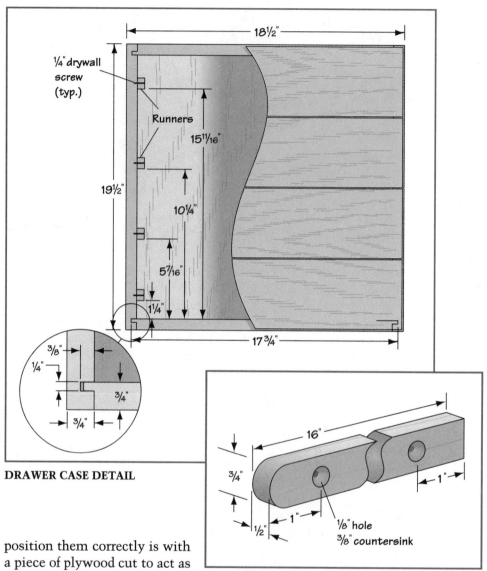

DRAWER CASE DETAIL

DRAWER RUNNER DETAIL

position them correctly is with a piece of plywood cut to act as a spacer. Cut a scrap so its width is equal to the distance you want from the underside of the top runners to the case bottom. Hold it against the case side with the runner on top of it and screw the runner in place. Repeat on the other side. Then cut the spacer down for the next pair of runners, and so on.

5. Cut the drawer fronts, backs, and sides to the sizes listed.

6. Instead of dovetails, I used a modification of my tongue-and-groove joint for the drawers, as shown in *Drawer Assembly/Joinery Detail*. Make the necessary cuts on the drawer pieces on the table saw. For more details, see "An Alternate Drawer Joint" on page 106.

7. Cut grooves for the drawer bottoms in the drawer fronts, backs, and sides. Also cut grooves for the drawer runners in the drawer sides, as shown in *Drawer Assembly*. The runner grooves should be 1 inch up from the bottom edge of the sides.

8. Cut the drawer bottoms to fit, then glue the drawers together. Measure across the diagonals to make sure each drawer is square. (If the diagonal measurements are equal, the drawer is square.)

9. Fit the drawers in the case. They should slide in and out freely. Rub a little paraffin on the runners to lubricate them if necessary.

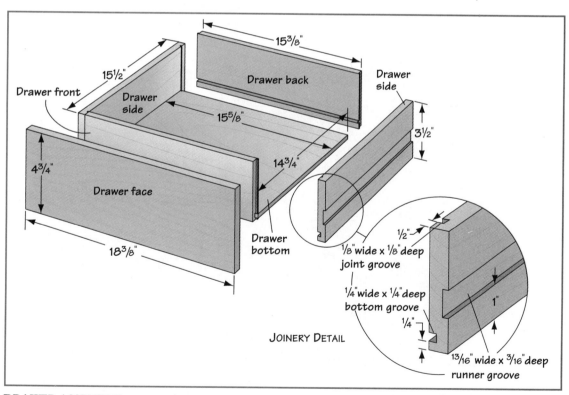

DRAWER ASSEMBLY

Cut the drawer faces to the size specified. Position them on the drawer boxes so the gaps between each drawer are equal. Use strips of double-sided carpet tape to hold things in position as you work. Once you are satisfied with their positioning, screw them in place from inside with 1-inch drywall screws. Mount the pulls on the drawer faces.

Make the Pigeonhole Unit

1. Cut the sides, shelves, and dividers to the sizes specified in the Materials List.

2. Cut the ⅛-inch-deep × ½-inch-wide dadoes and rabbets in the sides and shelves, as shown in the *Pigeonhole Detail.*

3. Glue the unit together. Before the glue dries, lay the unit face down on your bench. Cut the back to size and glue it in place, squaring the unit if necessary.

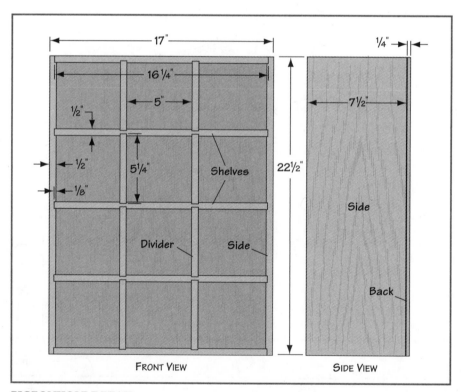

PIGEONHOLE DETAIL

Install the Unit

Set the two units up in position next to each other. Screw them together with the connecting bar, as shown in the *Installation Detail*, with 1¼-inch drywall screws. Position the drawer and pigeonhole units where you want them. You can either rest them on the shelves or screw them to the sides of the cases with 1-inch drywall screws. In the unit shown in the photo, I made a small box to raise the drawers up a little to make them more accessible. Clip the shelf supports in the standards where you want the shelves. Apply the finish of your choice according to the manufacturer's directions.

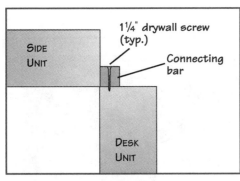

1¼" drywall screw (typ.)

Side Unit

Connecting bar

Desk Unit

INSTALLATION DETAIL

ENTERTAINMENT CENTER
IN ASH AND ASH BURL VENEER

W hen they first approached me about building an entertainment center, John and Linda had something like the Oak Breakfront (see page 230) in mind. But, by the time they finished describing what they wanted to store, I realized that a much bigger unit was in order. In the first place, their television set was something of a monster, much too big to house comfortably in a cabinet. Plus, John has a tendency to acquire new electronic gadgets as fast as they appear on the market. So, the unit would have to hold the current collection with a comfortable amount of room for expansion.

After some discussion, I arrived at a design they liked. Then it was time to discuss what kind of wood they wanted it made from. They wanted the piece to have a very distinctive look since it was to be the focal point of the room. After discussing the merits of various types of wood, I remembered some veneer I had set aside for some special project. Maybe this was the time to use it.

I dug out the veneer and showed it to John and Linda. They loved it. The swirling ash burl was even nicer than I had remembered. So nice, in fact, that I almost wished I had saved it for myself.

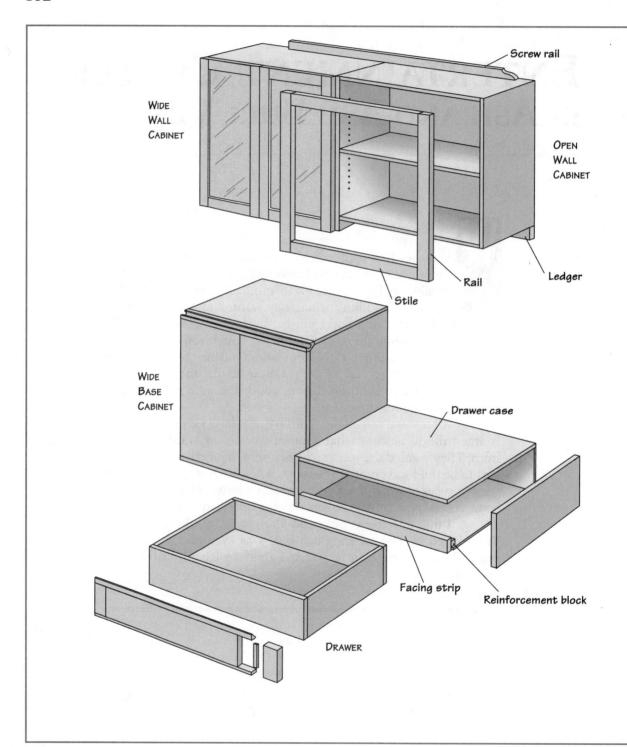

Screw rail

WIDE WALL CABINET

OPEN WALL CABINET

Ledger

Rail

Stile

WIDE BASE CABINET

Drawer case

Facing strip

Reinforcement block

DRAWER

EXPLODED VIEW

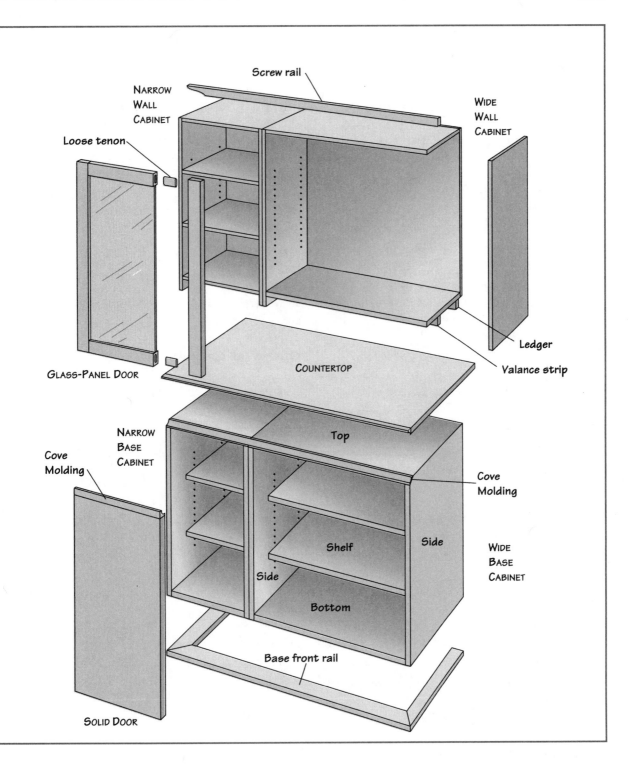

NARROW WALL CABINET

Screw rail

WIDE WALL CABINET

Loose tenon

Ledger

Valance strip

GLASS-PANEL DOOR

COUNTERTOP

Cove Molding

NARROW BASE CABINET

Top

Cove Molding

Shelf

Side

WIDE BASE CABINET

Side

Bottom

Base front rail

SOLID DOOR

MATERIALS LIST

PART	DIMENSION

Wide Base Cabinets (2)

Part	Dimension
Top/Bottom (2)	¾" × 19" × 33¼"
Sides (2)	¾" × 19¼" × 34⅜"
Edging (3)	¼" × ⅞" × 36"
Back	¼" × 33½" × 34⅜"
Cove molding	¾" × 2" × 34"
Shelves (2)	¾" × 18½" × 32⅜"
Edging (2)	¼" × ⅞" × 33"

Narrow Base Cabinet

Part	Dimension
Top/Bottom (2)	¾" × 19" × 16¼"
Sides (2)	¾" × 19¼" × 34⅜"
Back	¼" × 16½" × 34⅜"
Edging (2)	¼" × ⅞" × 36"
Edging	¼" × ⅞" × 18"
Cove molding	¾" × 2" × 17"
Shelves (2)	¾" × 18½" × 15⅜"
Edging (2)	¼" × ⅞" × 16"

Wide Wall Cabinets (2)

Part	Dimension
Top/Bottom (2)	¾" × 14" × 33¼"
Sides (2)	¾" × 14¼" × 35¾"
Edging (2)	¼" × ⅞" × 15"
Back	¼" × 33½" × 34"
Edging (4)	¼" × ⅞" × 37"
Valance strip	¾" × 2¼" × 32½"
Shelves (2)	¾" × 13½" × 32⅜"
Edging (2)	¼" × ⅞" × 33"

Narrow Wall Cabinet

Part	Dimension
Top/Bottom (2)	¾" × 14" × 16¼"
Sides (2)	¾" × 14¼" × 35¾"
Edging (2)	¼" × ⅞" × 15"
Back	¼" × 16½" × 34"
Edging (2)	¼" × ⅞" × 37"
Edging (2)	¼" × ⅞" × 18"
Valance strip	¾" × 2¼" × 15½"
Shelves (2)	¾" × 13½" × 15⅜"
Edging (2)	¼" × ⅞" × 16"

Open Wall Cabinet

Part	Dimension
Top/Bottom (2)	¾" × 14¼" × 38¼"
Sides (2)	¾" × 14⅞" × 34¾"
Edging (2)	¼" × ⅞" × 16"
Back	¼" × 38½" × 34¾"
Shelves (2)	¾" × 13½" × 37⅜"
Edging (2)	¼" × ⅞" × 38"
Face frame stiles (2)	¾" × 2" × 36"
Face frame rails (2)	¾" × 2" × 35"
Tenon stock	⅜" × 1⅛" × 12"

Drawer

Part	Dimension
Case top	¾" × 21¾" × 38¼"
Case bottom	¾" × 21¼" × 38¼"
Case sides (2)	¾" × 21¾" × 11½"
Edging (2)	¼" × ⅞" × 23"
Edging (2)	¼" × ⅞" × 13"

PART	DIMENSION
Edging	$1/4" \times 7/8" \times 40"$
Case back	$3/4" \times 10 1/2" \times 38 1/4"$
Reinforcement block	$3/4" \times 1 1/4" \times 37 1/2"$
Facing strip	$3/4" \times 3 1/4" \times 37 1/2"$
Drawer front/back (2)	$5/8" \times 6 1/8" \times 36 1/2"$
Drawer sides (2)	$5/8" \times 6 1/8" \times 19 3/8"$
Drawer bottom	$1/4" \times 19 1/4" \times 35 3/4"$
Face panel	$3/4" \times 7" \times 33 1/4"$
End caps (2)	$3/4" \times 2 1/2" \times 7"$
Moldings (2)	$3/4" \times 7/8" \times 38 1/4"$
Splines (2)	$1/4" \times 1/2" \times 7"$

Solid Doors (5)

PART	DIMENSION
Panel	$3/4" \times 16 3/8" \times 33 1/4"$
Edging	$1/4" \times 7/8" \times 18"$
Edging (2)	$1/4" \times 7/8" \times 35"$
Cove molding	$3/4" \times 7/8" \times 17"$

Glass-Panel Doors (5)

PART	DIMENSION
Stiles (2)	$3/4" \times 2" \times 35 7/8"$
Rails (2)	$3/4" \times 2" \times 12 7/8"$
Tenon stock	$3/8" \times 1 1/8" \times 12"$
Retaining strips (2)	$3/8" \times 3/8" \times 36"$
Retaining strips (2)	$3/8" \times 3/8" \times 13"$

Countertops

PART	DIMENSION
Surface	$3/4" \times 18 3/4" \times 50 1/2"$
Surface	$3/4" \times 18 3/4" \times 33 1/2"$
Cove molding	$3/4" \times 7/8" \times 51"$
Cove molding	$3/4" \times 7/8" \times 34"$
Edging (4)	$1/4" \times 7/8" \times 19"$

Installation

PART	DIMENSION
Base front rail	$7/8" \times 2 1/2" \times 51"$
Base front rail	$7/8" \times 2 1/2" \times 34"$
Base side rails (4)	$7/8" \times 2 1/2" \times 20 3/8"$
Tenon stock	$3/8" \times 1 5/8" \times 12"$
Screw rail	$3/4" \times 1 1/4" \times 118"$
Ledgers (2)	$3/4" \times 2" \times 32 1/2"$
Ledger	$3/4" \times 2" \times 15 1/2"$
Ledger	$3/4" \times 1 1/4" \times 39"$

Hardware

Grass full-overlay hinges with winged base plates (20). Available from Outwater Hardware Corp.; part #1006 and #63204

5mm pin-style shelf supports (48). Available from Outwater Hardware Corp.; part #3002

16" Little Inch cabinet lights (5). Available from most commercial lighting dealers

20" Accuride drawer slides (2). Available from Outwater Hardware Corp.; part #3017

$1/8" \times 13 1/2" \times 32 1/2"$ glass panes (5)

3" drywall screws (as needed)

$1 3/4"$ drywall screws (as needed)

$1 5/8"$ drywall screws (as needed)

$1 1/4"$ drywall screws (as needed)

1" drywall screws (as needed)

#4 $\times 5/8"$ screws (as needed)

$1 1/4"$ wire brads (as needed)

Finish nails (as needed)

186

TECH NOTES This project is made up of eight separate cases. Across the bottom are two wide base cabinets, one narrow base cabinet, and a short drawer case. The drawer case serves as a platform for the TV. Along the top are two wide wall cabinets, a narrow wall cabinet, and an open wall cabinet. Ash and ash veneer plywood were used throughout.

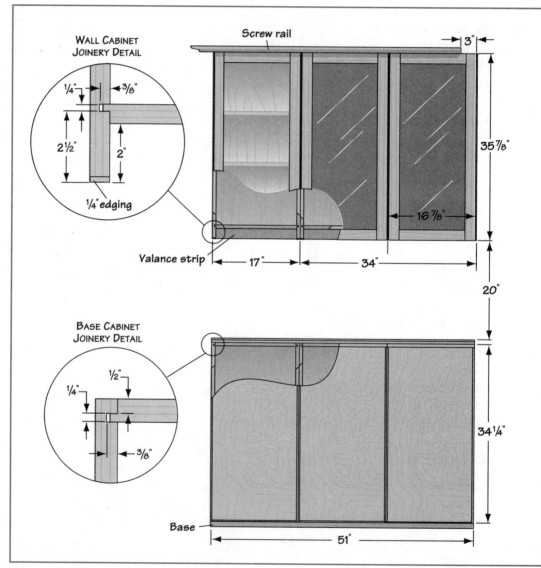

WALL CABINET
JOINERY DETAIL

Screw rail

3"

1/4"   3/8"

2½"   2"

1/4" edging

35⅞"

16⅞"

Valance strip   17"   34"

20"

BASE CABINET
JOINERY DETAIL

1/2"

1/4"

3/8"

34¼"

Base   51"

FRONT VIEW

The construction is varied, involving almost all of the techniques presented in the first part of this book, including basic cases (see Chapter 2), glass-paneled doors (see "Doors with Glass Panels" on page 69), a face frame (see Chapter 4), a dovetailed drawer (see "Dovetails" on page 97, Chapter 9, and Chapter 10), and tubular door pulls (see "Tubular Pulls" on page 142).

The doors on the base cabinets are somewhat different than any others in the book. Essentially, they're just slabs of plywood that have been drilled for hinges. What makes the doors in the picture look so nice is the special veneer I mentioned earlier. I do my own veneering, but describing the process goes beyond the scope of this book. If you want to work with veneered panels like these but lack the equipment, call Certainly Wood in East Aurora, N.Y. (see "Suppliers" on page 368 for the phone number). They've got a great selection of veneer to sell, and they'll put you in touch with someone who can glue it up for you.

You can also make the cabinets with different doors. Any of the doors detailed in Chapters 6 and 7 will work, or you could just use regular hardwood plywood. I did that on a similar piece and the results were stunning. Just select the plywood with care, and you'll be amazed at how nice it looks.

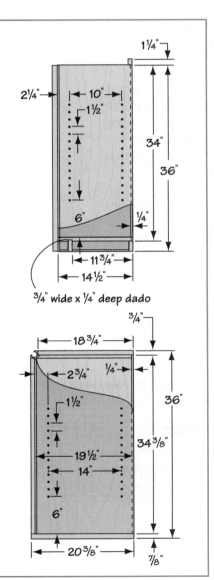

¾" wide x ¼" deep dado

SIDE VIEW

CONSTRUCTION STEPS

Build the Cases

1. Cut the tops, bottoms, and sides for all the cabinets and the drawer case to the sizes specified in the Materials List. Note that on all the cabinets except the drawer case and the open wall cabinet, the sides are ¼ inch wider than the tops and bottoms. This extra ¼ inch allows you to rabbet the sides for the back to keep it

from showing. On the open wall cabinet, the sides are ⅝ inch wider—¼ inch for the back rabbet and ⅜ inch for a tongue to join the face frame. On the drawer case, the back gets rabbeted into the top and bottom as well as the sides, so the top is the same width as the sides. The bottom, on the other hand, is ½ inch narrower to allow for the facing strip.

2. Glue edging to the bottom edges of all the wall cabinet sides and the top edges of the drawer case sides, as shown in the *Front View/Wall Cabinet Joinery Detail* and the *Base Cabinet Joinery Detail*. These edges will be exposed in the finished project, so they should be covered to hide the end grain of the plywood. Once the glue dries, trim the edging with a flush-trim bit in a router. For more information, see Chapter 3 and "Hiding End Grain" on page 30. Once this edging is in place, you can treat the pieces just like regular pieces of plywood, except that you have to remember which edge goes up or down.

3. Tilt the blade on the table saw to 45 degrees. Run the tops of the base cabinets through the saw to cut their front edges at this angle. Remove as little wood as possible while still cutting a bevel that runs from face to face. This cut creates a surface to glue the cove molding to, as shown in the *Tubular Pull Details.*

4. Join the case pieces with tongue-and-groove joints. Cut grooves in the sides and tongues on the tops and bottoms, as shown in the

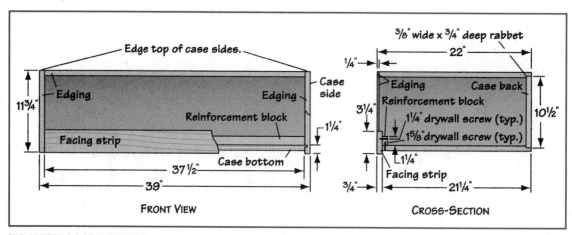

DRAWER CASE DETAILS

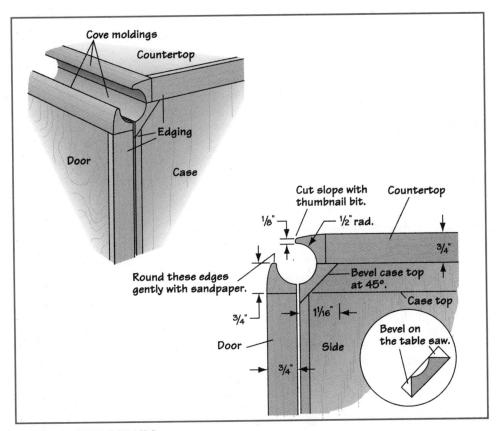

Cove moldings

Countertop

Edging

Door

Case

Cut slope with thumbnail bit.

Countertop

1/8"

1/2" rad.

3/4"

Round these edges gently with sandpaper.

Bevel case top at 45°.

Case top

3/4"

1 1/16"

Bevel on the table saw.

Door

Side

3/4"

TUBULAR PULL DETAILS

Front View/Base Cabinet Joinery Detail, *Front View/Wall Cabinet Joinery Detail*, and *Drawer Case Details/Front View*. See "Cutting the Joint" on page 16. Also cut tongues on the front edges of the open wall cabinet sides for the face frame, as shown in the *Face Frame and Back Joinery Detail*.

Note that on the drawer case and on all the wall cabinets except the open one, the case bottoms are raised. On the wall cabinets, this allows space for an under-cabinet light strip. On the drawer case, it keeps the case bottom up off the floor. If the case actually sat on its bottom, it might rock if the plywood was at all warped.

5. On the table saw, cut ¼-inch-wide × ½-inch-deep rabbets along the back edges of the sides of all but the drawer case, as shown in the *Face Frame and Back Joinery Detail*.

6. Cut ¾-inch-wide × ¼-inch-deep dadoes in the wide and narrow wall cabinet bottoms for the valance strips, as shown in the *Side View*.

7. Glue edging to the front edges of the base case sides. When the glue dries, trim the edging flush with your router. Be careful as you're routing not to let the bit dip into the grooves or you'll spoil the edging. Cut the corners of the sides off at a 45 degree angle for the cove molding, as shown in the *Tubular Pull Details*.

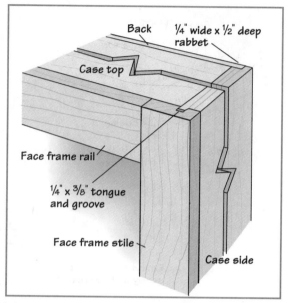

FACE FRAME AND BACK JOINERY DETAIL

8. Test fit the base case tops in the grooves in the sides. Slide the tops forward until the beveled front edges are flush with the angled cuts on the sides. Check the back edges of the tops. They may need to be trimmed flush with the rabbets in the sides. Trim the tops on the table saw.

9. Glue the case pieces together. Since the sides of the cases are exposed, I didn't use any mechanical fasteners but clamped the pieces together instead. Use pads under the clamp jaws to protect the plywood. Make sure the front edges of the base case tops are flush with the sides, as mentioned in the previous step.

10. While the glue is drying, flop each case (except the drawer case) face down and measure for its back. Cut the back to size, then glue and nail it in place with 1¼-inch wire brads. Be sure at least one corner of the back is square so you can use it to square the case, as described in "The Glue-Up" on page 24.

On the drawer case, you'll have to cut a rabbet around the back edges first. With a rabbeting bit in a router, cut a ¾-inch-deep × ⅜-inch-wide rabbet, as shown in the *Drawer Case Details/Cross-Section*, and square the corners with a chisel. Leave the back off the drawer case for now. You'll find it much easier to install the drawer slides if you have access to the inside of the case from both the front and the back. Just check the case for square before leaving it to dry. Do this by measuring across the diagonals—if the diagonals are equal, the case is square.

11. Apply the rest of the edging to the fronts of the cases, except for the open wall case. All of the exposed plywood edges should now be covered except those along the top of the base cabinets and the bottom of the drawer case. For more detailed instructions on applying edging, see Chapter 3.

12. Cut the reinforcement block to fit inside the drawer case. Glue and screw it flush with the front edge of the case bottom with 1⅝-inch drywall screws, as shown in the *Drawer Case Details/Cross-Section*. Cut the facing strip to fit, then glue and screw it to the reinforcement block with 1¼-inch drywall screws, as shown. Also cut and fit the valance strips to the wide and narrow wall cabinets.

13. Cut the shelves to fit inside the cabinets. Glue edging along their front edges. Drill the sides of the cases for the adjustable shelf pins, as shown in the *Side View* on page 187 and the *Open Case Details*. The pins I use require a 5mm hole and drill bit, a

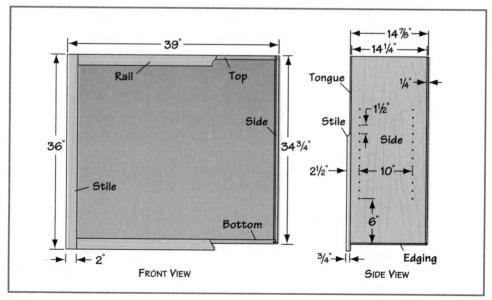

OPEN CASE DETAILS

size that is difficult to come by at most hardware stores. I've found, however, that a #8 drill works just as well.

Make the Solid Doors

1. Cut the panels for the solid doors slightly oversize (about ½ inch in both length and width). Veneer them (or have them veneered). Trim the veneer so it is flush with the edges.

2. Glue edging along the bottom edges. Trim it flush. Then trim the panels to width. This will cut the ends of the bottom edging dead flush with the sides of the panels. Glue edging to the sides, then cut the panel to length, trimming the side edging in the process.

3. Cut the cove moldings to the size specified in the Materials List. Glue the cove moldings to the doors. When the glue dries, trim the molding flush with a flush-trim bit in a table-mounted router.

Make the Glass-Panel Doors and the Face Frame

1. Cut the stiles and rails for both the doors and the face frame to the dimensions specified in the Materials List. On the front face of each piece, round-over all four edges with a ³⁄₁₆-inch roundover bit in a table-mounted router, as shown in the *Frame Details*. This detail softens the frames and creates a nice shadow line at the joints.

2. Join the frame pieces at the corners with loose tenon joints, as shown in the *Frame Details*. For more information, see Chapter 4.

3. Glue the frames up flat and square. See "Clamping Frames" on page 42.

4. Cut two grooves in the back of the face frame stiles to match the tongues on the sides of the open wall cabinet, as shown in the *Face Frame and Back Joinery Detail* and the *Frame Details*. Glue the frame to the front of the cabinet.

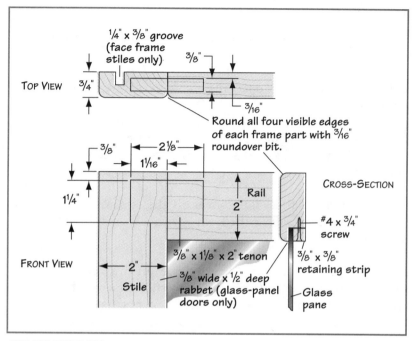

FRAME DETAILS

Make sure the top edge of the frame's bottom rail is flush with the top of the case bottom.

5. Cut rabbets around the insides of the glass-panel door frames, as shown in the *Frame Details*. Use a rabbeting bit in a hand-held router. Carefully square the rounded corners with a sharp chisel. Take your time here—any mistakes will show.

6. Cut the glass retaining strips to fit around the inside of the rabbets. Miter the corners on the table saw (or chop saw). Drill and countersink them for #4 × ⅝-inch screws, one screw every 6 inches or so. (Wait to get the glass until just after you install the unit. You'll probably need to replace fewer panes that way.)

7. Drill all the doors for European-style cup hinges. Hang the doors on the cases. For more information, see "European-Style Hinges" on page 123. Once you have the hinges mounted and the doors roughly adjusted, remove them until after installation.

Make the Drawer

1. Cut the drawer front, back, and sides to the sizes specified in the Materials List.

2. Join the pieces with dovetails cut with a router jig. For more specifics, see Chapter 8.

3. Rout a ¼-inch × ¼-inch groove for the bottom in all four pieces. Cut the bottom to size and glue up the drawer. See Chapter 9 for more details.

4. After the glue dries, round-over all the square edges—except those along the outside of the front—with a ¼-inch roundover bit in a router.

5. Mount the drawer inside the case on drawer slides. See Chapter 10 for further details. Add the back to the drawer case. I used ¾-inch plywood instead of my usual ¼-inch to strengthen the case.

Make the Drawer Face

1. Cut the panel slightly larger than specified, about ½ inch in each direction. Veneer it (or have it veneered) to match the solid doors. Trim the veneer flush with the panel edges.

2. Cut the panel to length, but leave it wider than necessary for now. Cut the end caps to width and about ¼ inch longer than needed. Rout ¼-inch-wide × ¼-inch-deep grooves in both ends of the panel and along one edge of each end cap, as shown in the *Drawer Details/Exploded View*. Use a ¼-inch straight bit in a table-mounted router and center the groove from front to back. Cut splines to fit the grooves and glue the end caps to the panels, centering them from side to side. When the glue dries, sand the end caps flush with the face of the panel.

3. Trim the panel to width. Cut one side to establish a clean, straight edge. Then cut the panel to width along the second side, running the first along the table saw fence. These cuts will trim the ends of the end caps perfectly flush with the edges of the panel.

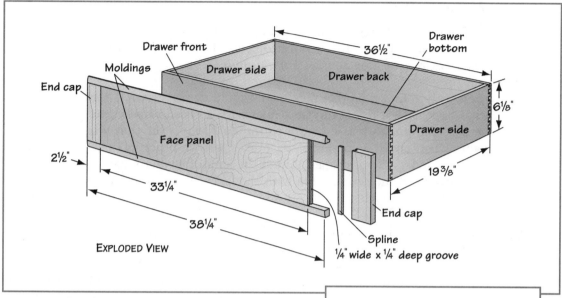

EXPLODED VIEW

DRAWER DETAILS

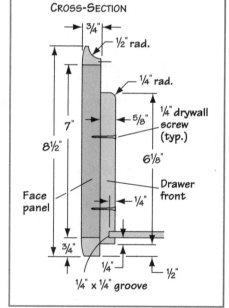

CROSS-SECTION

4. Cut the moldings to the size specified. Glue them to the edges of the panel. When the glue dries, trim them flush with the faces of the panel. Screw the drawer face to the front of the drawer from inside the drawer with 1-inch drywall screws.

Make the Countertops

1. Cut the two surfaces to the sizes specified in the Materials List. Glue edging to the ends and trim it with a flush-trim bit in a router.

2. Cut the cove moldings to the sizes specified. Glue them to the front edges of the countertops. Trim them flush with the countertop surfaces with your router.

Make the Pulls

1. Rout a ½-inch cove in the molding attached to the solid doors, the drawer face, and the countertops, as shown in the *Drawer Details/Cross-Section* and the *Tubular Pull Details.*

2. Gently round the other side of the molding, as shown. I find this slope easiest to cut on the shaper with a raised panel cutter; you could probably also find a thumbnail router bit that will work. You could also shape the pieces with a block plane, a scraper, and some sandpaper. Round the small flat that separates the cove from the gentle slope with sandpaper to make the pulls friendly to the touch.

3. Next, add the molding to the top edge of the base cabinets where you made the beveled cuts earlier. Bevel the edges of the cove molding, as shown in the *Tubular Pull Details.* Make the molding ¹⁄₁₆ inch wider than necessary so you can be sure it will fit. Glue the molding to the cabinets. Position it so any extra width overlaps the case top, not the front. Use masking tape to hold it in place as the glue dries.

4. When the glue dries, sand the molding flush with the top of the case. Rout a cove the length of the molding to match the coves you routed in the doors and countertops.

Install the Cabinets

1. Cut the base front and side rails to the sizes listed. Miter the corners and join them with loose tenon joints, as shown in the *Base Joinery Detail.* For more on the miter joint, see "An Alternate Door Frame" on page 72. Glue the pieces together. When the glue dries, round the outside edges slightly. This will create a shadow line between the base and the cases.

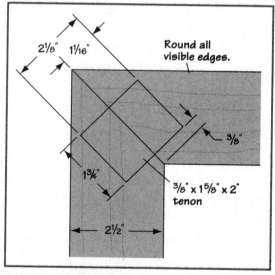

BASE JOINERY DETAIL

2. Finish the cabinet. The cabinet shown was finished with several coats of Watco Danish oil.

3. Move all the components to the site. Screw the narrow base cabinet to one of the wide base cabinets with 1¼-inch drywall screws. Make sure they are flush along their front and top edges. Then screw the wider base to the underside of this assembly and the narrower base to the other wide base cabinet with 1¼-inch drywall screws.

4. Strike a level line on the wall to indicate the top of the wall cabinets. Mark the position of the cabinets laterally along this line. Find the studs and mark their locations.

5. Screw the wall cases together with 1¼-inch drywall screws so their tops and front edges are flush. Cut the screw rail to size and fasten it in place with 1¾-inch drywall screws. It should span all four cases. Have some helpers hold the cases in position against the wall. Drive 3-inch drywall screws through the rail into the studs. Three or four screws should be enough to hold everything in place. For more details, see Chapter 14.

6. Cut the ledgers to size, then screw them to the wall beneath the cases with 3-inch drywall screws. Drive finish nails through the case bottoms to attach the cases to the ledgers. Add more 3-inch screws to the screw rail above, one screw per stud.

7. Slide the base cabinets and the drawer cabinet into place and screw them all together with 1¼-inch drywall screws. Set the countertops in place and screw them to the cases from underneath with more 1¼-inch drywall screws.

8. Rehang the doors and adjust them so they hang straight. Fit the glass in the rabbets and hold it in place with the retaining strips. Add the shelves on the shelf pins and load them up.

9. Screw the lighting units to the underside of the wall cabinets and wire them according to the manufacturer's instructions. Install the television, tune to your favorite station, and enjoy.

DINING ROOM CABINETS

Many years ago, upon completing a project for a customer, I was offered an apple tree that he just had taken down. I accepted gratefully. The tree men put the trunk into my truck, and I drove off imagining what I would build. I dropped the apple trunk off at the sawmill, and a few days later I got a call from Bob Davis, the owner of the mill. "It's half rotted away," he said of the apple trunk. "Do you want me to cut off the rotted half and saw up the rest?" I said yes, but returned to my work a little disappointed. I had been thinking of building apple cabinets for my dining area, but half the log wouldn't yield enough lumber for the project.

An hour later I received another call from Bob. "The other half is punky and has started to rot." I drove over to the mill to have a look. When I stepped up on the saw platform, the log was mounted in the saw with one board already sawn off. The two open faces stared at me in a classic bookmatch. It was beautiful. Delicate spalt line patterns permeated the whole piece.

"Saw it up," I said as I hopped back in my truck. I headed home, all the way designing my spalted apple panel dining room cabinets.

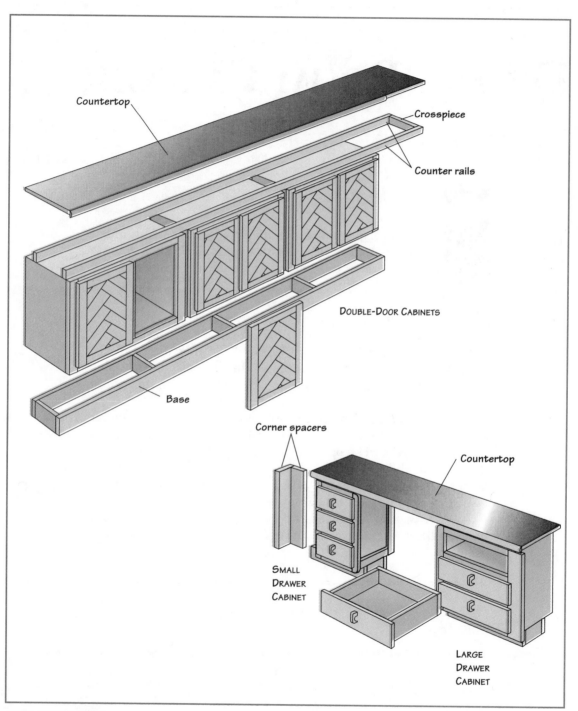

Countertop

Crosspiece

Counter rails

DOUBLE-DOOR CABINETS

Base

Corner spacers

Countertop

SMALL
DRAWER
CABINET

LARGE
DRAWER
CABINET

EXPLODED VIEW

MATERIALS LIST

PART	DIMENSION
Double-Door Cabinets(3)	
Case top/bottom (2)	$\frac{3}{4}$" × $16\frac{3}{4}$" × 33"
Case sides (2)	$\frac{3}{4}$" × $16\frac{3}{4}$" × 22"
Case backs (1)	$\frac{1}{4}$" × 22" × $33\frac{3}{4}$"
Frame stiles (2)	$\frac{13}{16}$" × $1\frac{1}{2}$" × 23"
Frame rails (2)	$\frac{13}{16}$" × $1\frac{1}{2}$" × $32\frac{1}{4}$"
Center stile	$\frac{13}{16}$" × 2" × 20"
Tenon stock	$\frac{3}{8}$" × $\frac{5}{8}$" × 12"
Door stiles (12)	$\frac{13}{16}$" × $2\frac{1}{2}$" × 21"
Door top rails (6)	$\frac{13}{16}$" × $2\frac{1}{2}$" × $11\frac{1}{8}$"
Door bottom rails (6)	$\frac{13}{16}$" × $3\frac{1}{2}$" × $11\frac{1}{8}$"
Door tenon stock	$\frac{3}{8}$" × $1\frac{3}{8}$" × 48"
Panel stock (102)	$\frac{3}{8}$" × $2\frac{3}{8}$" × $10\frac{1}{2}$"
Batten stock (6)	$\frac{3}{8}$" × $1\frac{1}{4}$" × 60"
Small Drawer Cabinet	
Case top/bottom (2)	$\frac{3}{4}$" × $15\frac{7}{8}$" × $12\frac{7}{8}$"
Case sides (2)	$\frac{3}{4}$" × $15\frac{7}{8}$" × 22"
Case back	$\frac{1}{4}$" × $13\frac{5}{8}$" × 22"
Frame stiles (2)	$\frac{13}{16}$" × $1\frac{1}{2}$" × 23"
Frame top/bottom rails (2)	$\frac{13}{16}$" × $1\frac{1}{2}$" × $12\frac{1}{8}$"
Frame mid rails (2)	$\frac{13}{16}$" × 2" × $12\frac{1}{8}$"
Tenon stock	$\frac{3}{8}$" × $\frac{5}{8}$" × 15"
Drawer sides (6)	$\frac{5}{8}$" × $4\frac{3}{8}$" × 16"
Drawer front/back (6)	$\frac{5}{8}$" × $4\frac{3}{8}$" × $11\frac{1}{16}$"
Drawer bottoms (3)	$\frac{1}{4}$" × $10\frac{5}{16}$" × $15\frac{7}{8}$"
Drawer faces (3)	$\frac{13}{16}$" × $5\frac{3}{4}$" × $13\frac{1}{8}$"
Drawer pulls (3)	$\frac{1}{2}$" × 1" × 2"
Large Drawer Cabinet	
Case top/bottom (2)	$\frac{3}{4}$" × $15\frac{7}{8}$" × $18\frac{3}{4}$"
Case sides (2)	$\frac{3}{4}$" × $15\frac{7}{8}$" × 22"
Case back	$\frac{1}{4}$" × $19\frac{1}{2}$" × 22"
Frame stiles (2)	$\frac{13}{16}$" × $1\frac{1}{2}$" × 23"
Frame top/bottom rails (2)	$\frac{13}{16}$" × $1\frac{1}{2}$" × 18"
Frame mid rails (2)	$\frac{13}{16}$" × 2" × 18"
Tenon stock	$\frac{3}{8}$" × $\frac{5}{8}$" × 15"
Drawer sides (6)	$\frac{5}{8}$" × $4\frac{3}{8}$" × 16"
Drawer front/back (6)	$\frac{5}{8}$" × $4\frac{3}{8}$" × $16\frac{15}{16}$"
Drawer bottoms (3)	$\frac{1}{4}$" × $16\frac{3}{16}$" × $15\frac{7}{8}$"
Drawer faces (3)	$\frac{13}{16}$" × $5\frac{3}{4}$" × 19"
Drawer pulls (3)	$\frac{1}{2}$" × 1" × 2"

PART	DIMENSION
Drawer Cabinet Side Frames (2)	
Side frame stiles (2)	$\frac{3}{4}$" × $2\frac{1}{2}$" × 23"
Side frame top rail	$\frac{3}{4}$" × $2\frac{1}{2}$" × $11\frac{1}{8}$"
Side frame bottom rail	$\frac{3}{4}$" × $3\frac{1}{2}$" × $11\frac{1}{8}$"
Tenon stock	$\frac{3}{8}$" × $1\frac{7}{8}$" × 4"
Panel	$\frac{3}{4}$" × $11\frac{3}{4}$" × $17\frac{5}{8}$"
Installation	
Base rail stock (2)	$\frac{3}{4}$" × $4\frac{1}{4}$" × $113\frac{1}{4}$"
Base rail stock (2)	$\frac{3}{4}$" × $4\frac{1}{4}$" × $14\frac{5}{8}$"
Base rail stock (2)	$\frac{3}{4}$" × $4\frac{1}{4}$" × 18"
Crosspieces (6)	$\frac{3}{4}$" × $4\frac{1}{4}$" × 12"
Crosspieces (4)	$\frac{3}{4}$" × $4\frac{1}{4}$" × $11\frac{1}{8}$"
Facing	$\frac{1}{4}$" × 4" × 96"
Facing	$\frac{1}{4}$" × 4" × 12"
Facing	$\frac{1}{4}$" × 4" × 18"
Cleats	$\frac{3}{4}$" × $\frac{3}{4}$" × (as needed)
Spacers (3)	$\frac{3}{4}$" × $2\frac{1}{2}$" × 23"
Wide corner spacer	$\frac{3}{4}$" × $3\frac{1}{2}$" × 23"
Narrow corner spacer	$\frac{3}{4}$" × $2\frac{3}{4}$" × 23"
Counter rail stock (2)	$\frac{3}{4}$" × $1\frac{1}{2}$" × 125"
Counter rail stock (2)	$\frac{3}{4}$" × $1\frac{1}{2}$" × $41\frac{7}{8}$"
Crosspiece	$\frac{3}{4}$" × 2" × $12\frac{1}{8}$"
Counter edge stock	$\frac{3}{4}$" × $1\frac{1}{2}$" × 42"
Counter edge stock	$\frac{3}{4}$" × $1\frac{1}{2}$" × 109"
Countertop	$\frac{3}{4}$" × $16\frac{15}{16}$" × $41\frac{7}{8}$"
Countertop	$\frac{3}{4}$" × $17\frac{3}{4}$" × 125"

Hardware

Grass full-overlay hinges with winged base plates (12). Available from Outwater Hardware Corp.; part #1006 and #63204

20" Accuride full-extension drawer slides (6 pair). Available from Outwater Hardware Corp.; part #3017

3" drywall screws (as needed)

2" drywall screws (as needed)

$1\frac{5}{8}$" drywall screws (as needed)

$1\frac{1}{4}$" drywall screws (as needed)

1" drywall screws (as needed)

4d finish nails (as needed)

1" wire brads (as needed)

18" × 125" piece of plastic laminate

17" × 43" piece of plastic laminate

$\frac{3}{8}$"-diameter wood plugs (as needed)

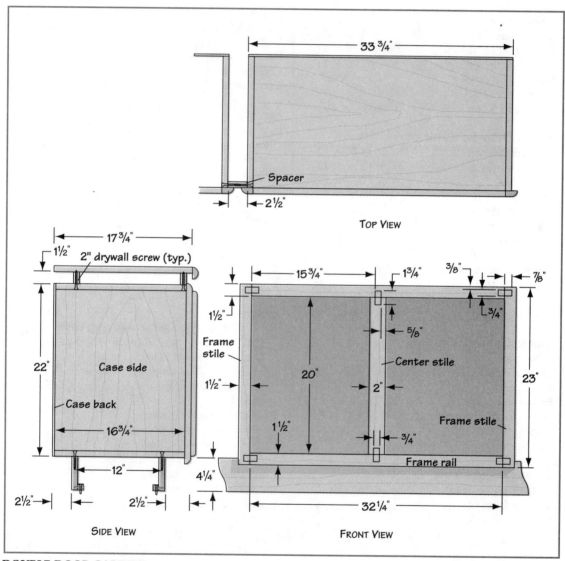

33 ³/₄"

Spacer

2¹/₂"

TOP VIEW

17 ³/₄"

1¹/₂"

2" drywall screw (typ.)

22"

Case side

Case back

16 ³/₄"

12"

2¹/₂"

2¹/₂"

SIDE VIEW

15 ³/₄"

1 ³/₄"

³/₈"

⁷/₈"

1¹/₂"

Frame stile

1¹/₂"

20"

³/₄"

⁵/₈"

Center stile

2"

23"

Frame stile

1¹/₂"

³/₄"

Frame rail

4¹/₄"

32 ¹/₄"

FRONT VIEW

DOUBLE-DOOR CABINET

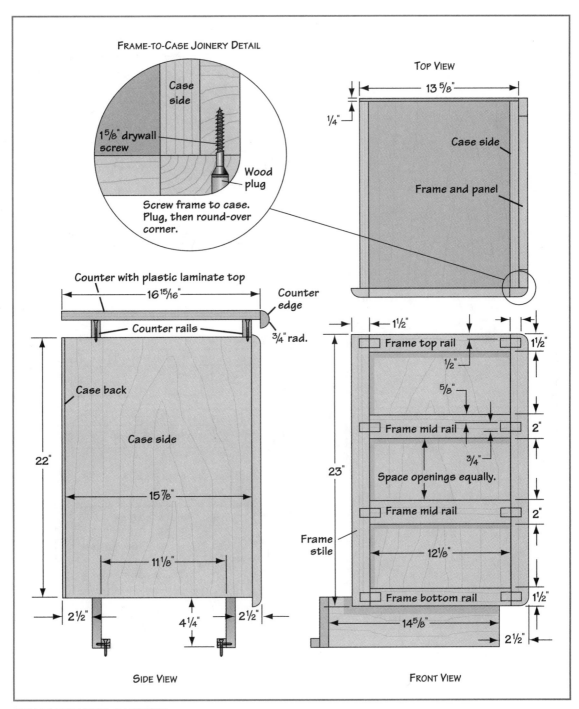

FRAME-TO-CASE JOINERY DETAIL

Case side

1⅝" drywall screw

Wood plug

Screw frame to case. Plug, then round-over corner.

TOP VIEW

13⅝"

¼"

Case side

Frame and panel

Counter with plastic laminate top

16¹⁵⁄₁₆"

Counter edge

¾" rad.

Counter rails

Case back

Case side

22"

15⅞"

11⅛"

2½"

4¼"

2½"

SIDE VIEW

1½"

Frame top rail

1½"

½"

⅝"

Frame mid rail

2"

¾"

Space openings equally.

23"

Frame mid rail

2"

Frame stile

12⅛"

Frame bottom rail

1½"

14⅝"

2½"

FRONT VIEW

SMALL DRAWER CABINET

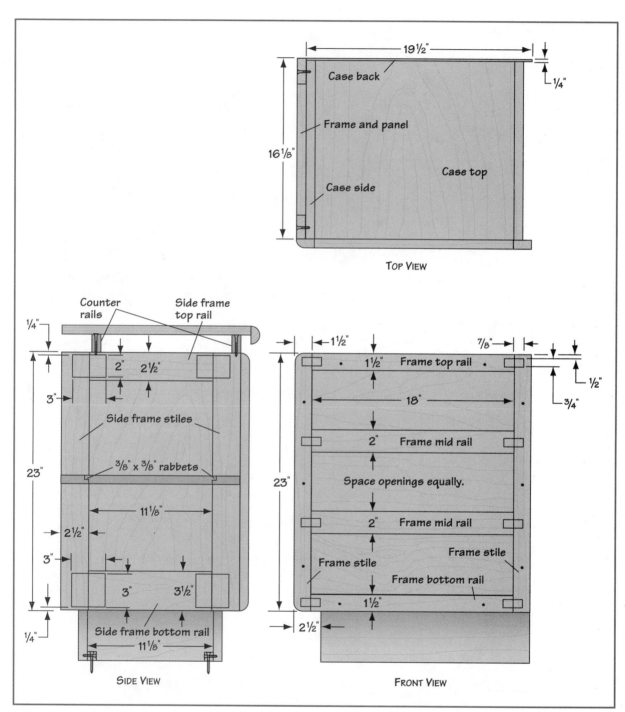

Top View

Case back

Frame and panel

Case top

Case side

19½"

16⅛"

¼"

Counter rails

Side frame top rail

¼"

2" 2½"

3"

Side frame stiles

⅜" x ⅜" rabbets

23"

11⅛"

2½"

3"

3" 3½"

Side frame bottom rail

11⅛"

¼"

Side View

1½"

1½" Frame top rail

7/8"

½"

18"

¾"

2" Frame mid rail

23"

Space openings equally.

2" Frame mid rail

Frame stile

Frame stile

Frame bottom rail

1½"

2½"

Front View

LARGE DRAWER CABINET

TECH <u>NOTES</u> As shown, this project is a gathering of three double-door cabinets and two drawer cabinets. The cabinets sit on a system of base rails and are topped with a separate counter. The combination of the drawer cabinets and the counter creates a desk-like area, and the exposed sides of the drawer cabinets under the desk are finished off with framed panels. These cabinets may not exactly fit your dining room, so adjust the dimensions and cabinet combinations as needed.

Each cabinet by itself consists of a basic case with a face frame. The doors are frames with composite panels. The drawers are dove-tailed together and have a separate applied face. For more in-depth information on building these components, see "Plywood Construction" on page 15, "Building Frames" on page 36, Chapter 7, Chapter 8, and Chapter 14.

CONSTRUCTION <u>STEPS</u>

Build the Cases

1. Cut all the case tops, bottoms, and sides to the sizes specified in the Materials List.

2. Cut grooves in the case sides for the case tops and bottoms, as shown in the *Plywood Case Joinery Detail.* See "Cutting the Joint" on page 16.

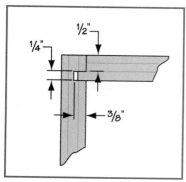

PLYWOOD CASE JOINERY DETAIL

3. Cut matching tongues on the case tops and bottoms to fit the grooves in the case sides.

4. Glue and screw the case sides to the case tops and bottoms with 1¼-inch drywall screws.

5. Cut the case backs to size, lay the cases on their faces, and attach the backs with glue and 1-inch wire brads. Square the cabinets with the backs, if necessary, as discussed in "The Glue-Up" on page 24.

Build the Face Frames

1. Cut all the frame rails and stiles to the dimensions specified in the Materials List.

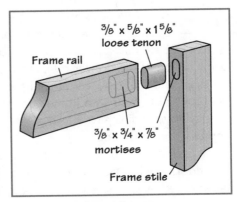

FRAME JOINERY DETAIL

2. Join the stiles and rails with loose tenon joints, as shown in the *Double-Door Cabinet/Front View, Small Drawer Cabinet/Front View, Large Drawer Cabinet/Front View,* and *Frame Joinery Detail.* See "Building Frames" on page 36. In the photo on page 198, you'll see that the stile on the extreme right-hand side of the desk is about 10 inches wide. This was to fill in an odd corner in my house. Unless you have a similar space to fill, this stile should be identical to the others.

3. Glue the frames up, making sure to keep them flat and square. See "Clamping Frames" on page 42 for further details.

4. Attach the frames to the cases. One at a time, spread glue on the front edges of each case and position the appropriate frame over it. The frames should be centered from side to side, and the top edge of the bottom rail should be flush with the top surface of the case bottom. Drill pilot holes for 1⅝-inch drywall screws and counterbore holes for ⅜-inch-diameter wood plugs through the frames and into the case sides. Counterbore about halfway through the stock so the screws will be well out of the way when the edges of the frame are rounded-over. Space three screws along each rail and two on each stile. Drive the screws and tap plugs into the holes. Try to match the color and grain direction of the plugs with that of the frame.

5. Lay the cases on their backs and round-over the outside edges of the face frames with a ¾-inch-radius roundover bit in a handheld router. Clamp a piece of stock along the back edge of the frame stiles and rails to give the pilot bearing a surface on which to ride. This guide stock should be flush with the outside edge of the frame.

Build the Side Frames

1. Each drawer cabinet has a finished side frame with a rabbeted panel, as shown in the *Side Frame Assembly*. Cut the side frame parts to the dimensions specified in the Materials List. The panels are slightly narrower than necessary to allow room for expansion.

2. Join the stiles and rails with loose tenon joints, as shown in *Large Drawer Cabinet/Side View*. The side frames on each drawer cabinet share identical dimensions.

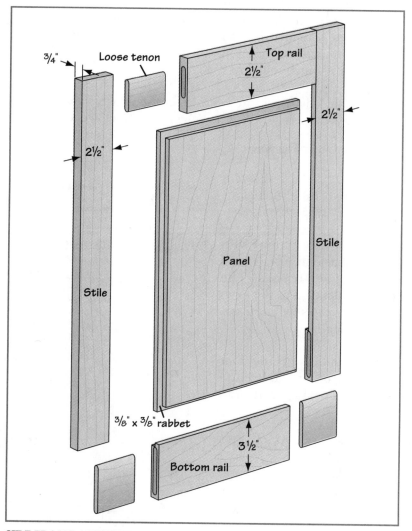

SIDE FRAME ASSEMBLY

3. Glue the side frames together, being careful to keep them square and flat.

4. When the glue is dry, rout a ⅜-inch-deep × ⅜-inch-wide rabbet around the inside back of each side frame and around the front edges of each panel, as shown in *Large Drawer Cabinet/Side View* and *Side Frame Assembly.*

5. Fit each panel into the back of its frame. Drill and counterbore the frames as you did for the face frames. Then glue and screw each side frame to the side of its drawer case with 1¼-inch drywall screws, trapping the panels in place. Plug the screw holes. When the frames have been installed, round their top and bottom edges with a ¾-inch roundover bit.

6. Screw the side frames to the sides of the drawer cabinets with 1¼-inch drywall screws. Plug the holes with ⅜-inch wood plugs.

Build the Door Frames

1. Cut the rails and stiles for the doors to the dimensions specified in the Materials List.

2. Join the door frames with loose tenon joints as you did with the face frames. The joints are detailed in the *Door Details/Front View* and *Door Joinery Detail.*

3. Glue and clamp the door frames together. Make sure the frames stay flat and square.

4. Let the door frames dry overnight, then rout a ³⁄₁₆-inch-deep × ⅜-inch-wide panel rabbet around the back of each door frame, as shown in the *Door Details/Cross-*

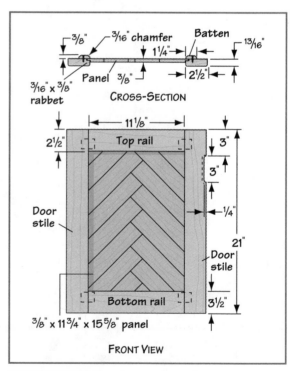

DOOR DETAILS

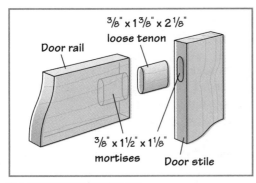

3/8" x 1 3/8" x 2 1/8"
loose tenon

Door rail

3/8" x 1 1/2" x 1 1/8"
mortises

Door stile

DOOR JOINERY DETAIL

Section. Square the rabbets at the inside corners of the frame with a sharp chisel.

5. Drill holes in the backs of the door frames for European-style hinges. As described in "European-Style Hinges" on page 123, these holes should be spaced in ¼ inch from the edge of the stile and centered 3 inches in from either end.

Build the Door Panels

1. The door panels are composed of narrow slats arranged in a herringbone pattern. Cut the panel stock to the dimensions specified in the Materials List.

2. Rout a ³⁄₁₆-inch-deep × ⅜-inch-wide rabbet in both long edges and one end of each slat, as shown in *Composite Panel Assembly Process*. When the rabbets have been cut, sand away any machine

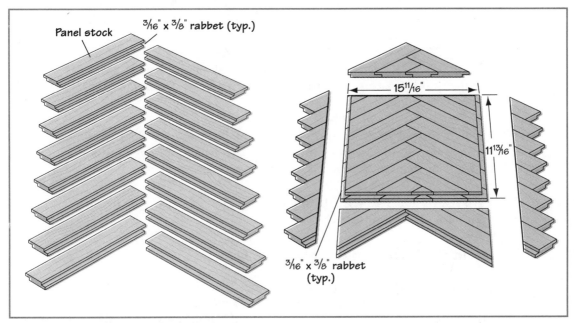

Panel stock

³⁄₁₆" x ⅜" rabbet (typ.)

15¹¹⁄₁₆"

11¹³⁄₁₆"

³⁄₁₆" x ⅜" rabbet
(typ.)

COMPOSITE PANEL ASSEMBLY PROCESS

marks and round-over the sharp edges of each slat slightly with sandpaper. See "Herringbone Panels" on page 93.

3. Glue the slats together on top of a flat surface. Put some newspaper underneath to keep any squeeze-out off the table. When they have all been glued together, lay a piece of plywood on top of the slats to weigh them down until the glue dries.

4. When the glue is dry, lay out the finished size of the panel ($11^{13}/_{16}$ inches $\times$ $15^{11}/_{16}$ inches) on the assembled slats. Cut along one of the long edges of the panel with a jigsaw or on the band saw. Once you have one straight edge, you can cut the other edges on the table saw.

5. Cut a $^{3}/_{16}$-inch-deep $\times$ $^{3}/_{8}$-inch-wide rabbet around the front edge of each panel.

Fit the Panels

1. Fit the rabbeted composite door panels into the rabbets in the backs of the door frames.

2. Cut the batten stock to the dimensions specified in the Materials List.

3. Rout a $^{3}/_{16}$-inch chamfer along the edges of the batten stock with a table-mounted router, as shown in the *Door Details/ Cross-Section*.

4. Cut the batten stock to fit around the back of each door with simple butt joints at the corners. The battens should overlap the rabbets by $^{3}/_{8}$ inch.

5. Predrill and screw the battens to the back of each door frame with 1-inch drywall screws.

Rout the Door Pulls and Hang the Doors

1. Rout a handle notch in the adjoining stiles of each pair of door frames, as shown in the *Door Details/Front View*. First, lay out the notches on the backs of each pair of adjoining stiles. Make sure you end up with three matched sets of doors. Rout a cove within the layout lines on the back of the door stiles with a ½-inch-radius cove bit in a hand-held router.

2. When the coves have been cut, round the front edges of each door to within about 1 inch of either side of the cove with a ⅜-inch roundover bit in your router. (If you rout through the coved area, the roundover bit's bearing will fall into the cove and ruin the stile.)

3. Clamp a straightedge to the door to guide the router along this edge. To do this, turn off the router and hold it in position above the cove on one of the door fronts as if you were routing the roundover. Mark the outer edge of the router base on the face of the door. Then, position the router below the cove and again mark the outer edge of the router base. Make new marks ¼ inch toward the center of the door from the router base edge marks and clamp a straightedge along these new marks.

Turn the router on and guide the ⅜-inch-radius roundover bit across the coved portion of the stiles. The bit's bearing will drop into the cove, but only until the router base hits the straightedge. As a result, you'll create a ¼-inch reveal along the cove.

4. Hang the doors on their cases with European-style hinges. See "European-Style Hinges" on page 123.

Build the Drawers

1. Cut the drawer parts for both drawer cabinets to the dimensions specified in the Materials List.

2. Rout the dovetails and pins in the drawer sides, backs, and fronts. Position the parts in the jig to produce the layout shown in the *Small Drawer Details/Side View*. See "Dovetails" on page 97.

3. Cut the ¼-inch-wide × ¼-inch-deep grooves for the bottoms in the sides, fronts, and backs, as shown in the *Small Drawer Details/Side View*. Cut the grooves in two passes on the table saw.

4. Glue the drawers together, trapping the drawer bottoms in their grooves as you assemble the parts.

5. Round-over the top edges of the drawer sides and drawer backs with a ⁵⁄₁₆-inch-radius roundover bit. Also round-over the inside

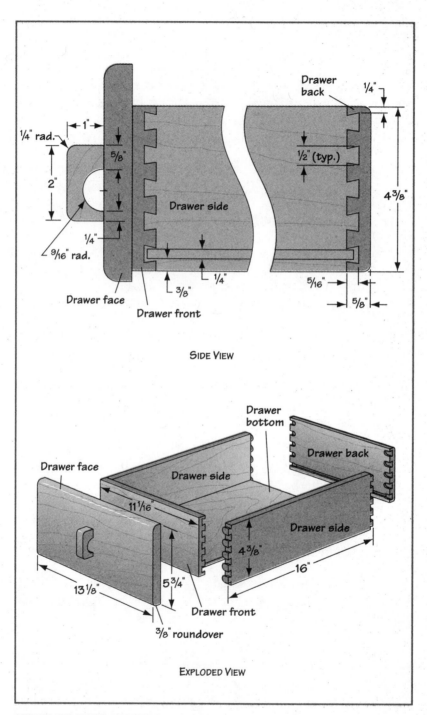

1" rad.

5/8"

2"

1/4"

9/16" rad.

Drawer face

1"

Drawer front

3/8"

1/4"

Drawer side

Drawer back

1/4"

1/2" (typ.)

4 3/8"

5/16"

5/8"

SIDE VIEW

Drawer face

Drawer bottom

Drawer side

11 1/16"

Drawer back

Drawer side

4 3/8"

16"

Drawer front

5 3/4"

13 1/8"

3/8" roundover

EXPLODED VIEW

SMALL DRAWER DETAILS

top edge of the drawer front, but leave the drawer front square where it meets the drawer face. When the top edges have been rounded-over, turn the drawer upside down and round-over the outside bottom edges of the drawer sides and drawer back.

6. Hang the drawers in their cases on full-extension drawer slides, as explained in Chapter 10.

7. Round the front edges of the drawer faces with a $\frac{1}{4}$-inch-roundover bit in a table-mounted router.

8. Shape the drawer pulls, as shown in the *Small Drawer Details/Side View*. Attach the pulls to the center of the drawer faces with glue and one $1\frac{1}{4}$-inch drywall screw each. Drill pilot holes for the screws to avoid splitting.

9. Make sure the drawer slides are adjusted properly, then attach the drawer faces to the drawer assemblies with $1\frac{1}{4}$-inch drywall screws. The faces should be centered on the frame openings.

Install the Cabinets

1. The cabinets rest on my standard ladder-style base, as shown in the *Exploded View*. Cut the base parts (rails, crosspieces, and cleats) to size and screw them together with $1\frac{5}{8}$-inch drywall screws. See "Making the Bases" on page 155 for further details.

2. At the site, position the bases $2\frac{1}{4}$ inches away from the walls. Level them and screw them to the floor through the cleats with 2-inch drywall screws, as described in "Installing the Bases" on page 156.

3. Set the double-door cabinets on top of the base and fit spacers between the cabinets, as shown in *Double-Door Cabinet/Top View*. Also, fit a spacer between the first cabinet and the wall. Screw the cabinets to the spacers with $1\frac{5}{8}$-inch drywall screws, as shown.

4. Set the drawer cabinets in place and fit spacers between the small drawer cabinet and the double-door cabinet at the corner, as shown in the *Corner Detail Top View*. Screw the corner spacer in place with $1\frac{5}{8}$-inch drywall screws, as shown.

5. Screw the cabinets to the base with 2-inch drywall screws.

6. Fit spacers between the cabinets and the walls.

7. Position the counter rails on top of the double-door cabinets, as shown in the *Double-Door Cabinet/Side View*. Fasten them to the cabinet tops with 2-inch drywall screws driven from inside the cabinets.

In the corner between the double-door cabinets and small drawer cabinet, the countertop will need some extra support. Make sure the counter rails extend all the way to the wall in this corner. Screw the crosspiece between them with 2-inch drywall screws, as shown in the *Exploded View*. Then screw the crosspiece to the wall with 3-inch drywall screws.

Position the counter rails on the drawer cabinets, as shown in the *Large Drawer Cabinet/Side View* and *Small Drawer Cabinet/Side View*. They should bridge the gap that forms the desk between the two cabinets. Screw the rails to the cabinets as you did with the rails on the other cabinets.

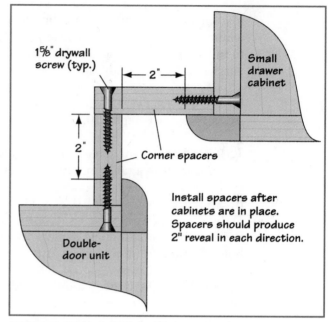

CORNER DETAIL TOP VIEW

Make and Install the Countertop

1. Make the countertop from ¾-inch plywood and plastic laminate. Cut the plywood counters to the sizes listed. The counter for the double-door cabinets runs all the way into the corner. It will have to be made of two pieces butted together. The counter over the drawer units simply butts to the others.

2. Run a bead of silicone along the top of the rails. Set the counters in place. The silicone will hold the counter in place, but will also allow you to easily remove it if necessary.

3. Cut the plastic laminate oversize and glue it down with contact adhesive. Trim it flush with the edges of the plywood with a flush-trim bit in a router. See "Plastic Laminate and Plywood" on page 147 for further details.

4. Cut the counter edge stock to the sizes specified. Fit the pieces along the front of the counters, mitering the ends where they meet in the corner.

5. Cut biscuit joints between the counter and the edging. The biscuits should keep the top edge of the edge stock flush with the surface of the laminate. If you don't have a biscuit joiner, cut the joints with a router, as discussed in "Router Biscuit Joinery" on page 148.

6. Round-over the two front edges of the edge stock with a ¾-inch roundover bit in a table-mounted router.

7. Glue the edge stock to the front of the counter. Use 4d finish nails to hold the edge stock in place as the glue dries. Set the nail heads and fill the holes.

8. Cut the facings to fit along the fronts of the base rails and tack them in place with 1-inch wire brads.

9. Apply the finish of your choice according to the manufacturer's directions. The piece shown is finished with several coats of Watco Danish oil.

CHERRY WINDOW SEAT AND SHELVES

When Sue and Ed had me over to discuss building them a window seat, fond memories of my youth came flooding back. I grew up on Riverside Drive in Manhattan, where our windows looked out over the Hudson River. I used to love to sit on the warm radiator during snowstorms and gaze across the water. I hoped I could create for them a similar kind of perch—a special place to curl up with a hot cup of coffee and watch the world go by.

The place Sue and Ed had in mind for their window seat couldn't have been better. They had one blank wall in their living room where they wanted to cut in a new window to overlook their beautiful backyard. Their requirements were few: a seat, plus some cabinets for storage and shelves for display. (Ed's a golfer and has quite a few trophies to his credit.)

I worked with them to match the size of the window to that of the room and the seat I had in mind. While the dimensions listed here are for the window seat shown, there is no reason why you can't adapt things to suit your own situation.

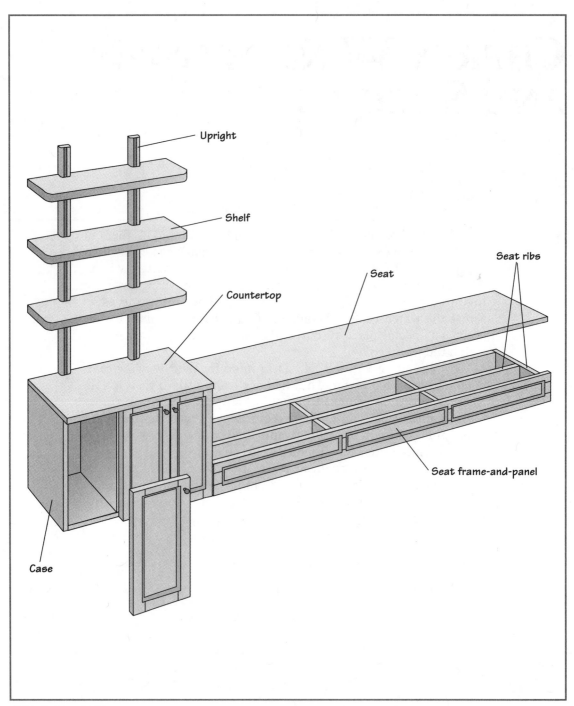

Upright

Shelf

Seat

Seat ribs

Countertop

Seat frame-and-panel

Case

EXPLODED VIEW

MATERIALS LIST

PART	DIMENSION	PART	DIMENSION
Cases (2)		Inside ribs (10)	¾" × 5" × 6⅛"
Top/bottom (2)	¾" × 14" × 35¼"	Top	½" × 14½" × 96"
Sides (2)	¾" × 14¼" × 24"	Bottom	¼" × 14½" × 96"
Back	¼" × 24" × 35½"		
Divider	¾" × 14" × 22½"	**Shelves (6)**	
Short screw rail	¾" × 1½" × 11¼"	Long ribs (2)	¾" × 1" × 31½"
Long screw rail	¾" × 1½" × 22½"	Side ribs (2)	¾" × 1" × 9½"
Edging stock (3)	¼" × ⅞" × 25"	Short ribs (2)	¾" × 1" × 6½"
Edging stock (3)	¼" × ⅞" × 37"	Top/bottom (2)	¼" × 9½" × 33"
Narrow shelf	¾" × 13" × 11⅛"	Long edging	½" × 1⅝" × 34"
Wide shelf	¾" × 13" × 22⅜"	Short edging (2)	½" × 1⅝" × 9½"
Granite countertop	1" × 15¾" × 36¼"	Diagonal edging (2)	⅞" × 1⅝" × 4⅞"
		Uprights (4)	1¼" × 2½" × 54"
Doors (6)			
Stiles (2)	1" × 2½" × 23⅞"	**Hardware**	
Rails (2)	1" × 2½" × 6⅞"	Grass full-overlay hinges with winged base	
Tenon stock	⅜" × 1⅝" × 10"	plates (12). Available from Outwater	
Long moldings (2)	¹³⁄₁₆" × ⅞" × 21"	Hardware Corp.; part #1006 and #63204	
Short moldings (2)	¹³⁄₁₆" × ⅞" × 9"	Shelf standards (4). Available from Fixture	
Panel	⅜" × 7⁷⁄₁₆" × 19½"	Hardware Mfg. Corp.; part #538	
		Shelf brackets (12). Available from Fixture	
Seat Frame-and-Panel		Hardware Mfg. Corp.; part #512	
Long moldings (6)	¹³⁄₁₆" × ⅞" × 30"	5mm pin-style shelf supports (16). Available	
Short moldings (6)	¹³⁄₁₆" × ⅞" × 4"	from Outwater Hardware Corp.; part #3002	
Rails (2)	1" × 1¾" × 96"	1½" × 13'6" steel angle iron	
End stiles (2)	1" × 2½" × 2½"	Oval brass pulls (6). Available from Cliffside	
Center stiles (2)	1" × 3⅛" × 2½"	Industries; part #101PB	
Panels (3)	⅜" × 3⅛" × 29"	¼ × 2½" lag screws (as needed)	
Tenon stock	⅜" × 2¼" × 10"	2½" drywall screws (as needed)	
Tenon stock	⅜" × 1⅝" × 10"	1⅝" drywall screws (as needed)	
		1¼" drywall screws (as needed)	
Seat		¾" drywall screws (as needed)	
Long ribs (3)	¾" × 5" × 94½"	1" wire brads (as needed)	
End ribs (2)	¾" × 5" × 14½"	⅜" staples (as needed)	

TECH NOTES The project, as shown, consists of two basic cases with granite countertops and full-overlay frame-and-panel doors. For a more detailed look at making these components, see Chapters 2 and 6.

The seat spanning the distance between the two cases is a torsion box, as are the shelves. Torsion boxes are similar in construction to hollow-core doors or corrugated cardboard—a lightweight core separating two thin skins. In a torsion box, the central core is made of a grid of fairly thin pieces of wood and the skins are plywood. This kind of construction is quite strong, light, and stable.

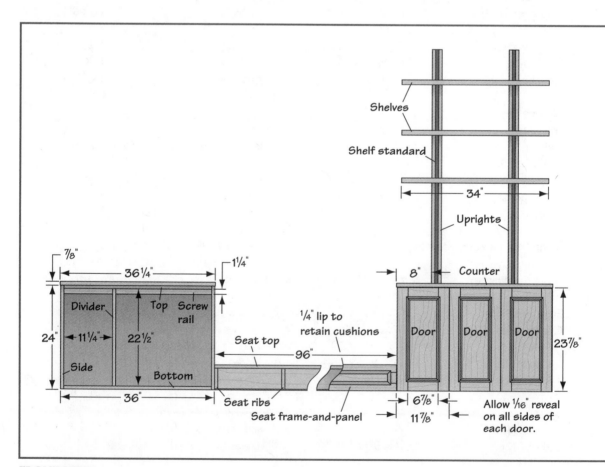

FRONT VIEW

CONSTRUCTION STEPS

Make the Cases

1. Cut the tops, bottoms, and sides for the cases to the sizes specified in the Materials List. Since the cases are exposed in this project, you may want to match the face veneer of the plywood with the wood you're using for the doors and shelves. The unit pictured is done in cherry and cherry plywood

2. Join the case pieces with tongue-and-groove joints. Cut grooves in the case sides and tongues on the tops and bottoms, as shown in the *Case Joinery Detail.* See "Cutting the Joint" on page 16. Also cut ¼-inch-wide × ½-inch-deep rabbets along the back edges of the sides. The backs will sit in these so their edges won't show.

3. Glue and clamp the case pieces together. Since the sides of the cases are exposed, I didn't use any mechanical fasteners. Use pads under the clamp jaws to protect the plywood.

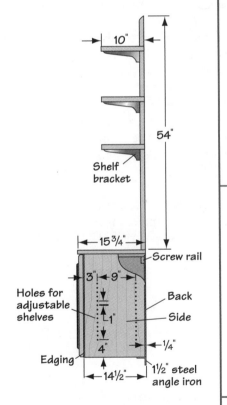

SIDE VIEW

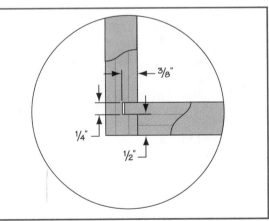

CASE JOINERY DETAIL

4. Lay the assembled cases face down and measure for the backs.

5. Cut the backs to drop inside the rabbets. The fit should be reasonably tight so the back can square the case. Glue and nail the backs in place with 1-inch wire brads.

6. In addition to the usual pieces, these cases also include a vertical divider and two screw rails each. The divider is where the hinges for the middle door get attached. Cut the dividers to fit inside the cases, as shown in the *Front View.* They should butt against the back of the case and be flush with the front edges of the top and bottom. Attach them, as shown, with 1⅝-inch drywall screws driven through the top and bottom. Then screw the screw rails in place through the top of the cases with 1⅝-inch drywall screws, as shown in the *Front View* and *Side View.*

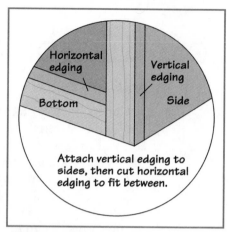

EDGING DETAIL

7. When each case has been assembled, apply the edging, as shown in the *Edging Detail,* and as described in "Attaching the Edging" on page 32. At the same time, apply edging to the front edges of the dividers. Also, cut the interior shelves to size and edge their front edges.

8. Next, drill 5mm-diameter adjustable shelf holes in the case sides and dividers, as shown in the *Side View.* I usually make up a quick drilling guide to help with this step. Simply drill a series of holes, spaced the proper distance apart, in a strip of hardwood. Then hold the strip in place in the cabinet to use as a guide as you're drilling the holes.

Make the Doors

1. Cut the door stiles and rails to the dimensions specified in the Materials List.

2. Lay out and cut the mortises in the door rails and stiles, as shown in the *Door Frame Joinery Details* and *Door Assembly.* See "Building Frames" on page 36.

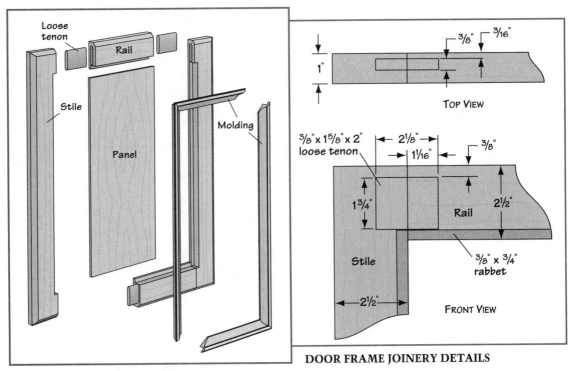

DOOR ASSEMBLY

DOOR FRAME JOINERY DETAILS

3. Cut tenons from the tenon stock to fit the mortises.

4. Glue and clamp the door frames together with the tenons in their mortises. Be sure to keep the frames from twisting while they're in the clamps.

5. Let the frames dry overnight. Sand them flat. Then rout a ¾-inch-deep × ⅜-inch-wide rabbet around the inside front edge of each frame. Square the rounded corners with a sharp chisel.

6. After cutting the rabbets, bore the mortises for the hinges, as described in Chapter 11. The holes should be in about ¼ inch from the edge and centered 3 inches in from the ends of the stile.

7. Shape the outside edges of each frame with an ogee profile, as shown in the *Frame-and-Panel Cross-Section*. This detail provides relief so the doors won't bind as they open.

CHERRY WINDOW SEAT AND SHELVES

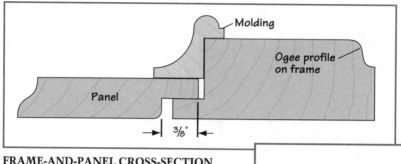

FRAME-AND-PANEL CROSS-SECTION

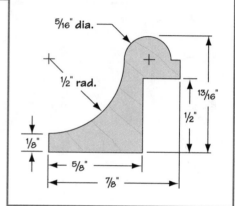

MOLDING PROFILE

8. Make the moldings that hold the door panels in place. While you're at it, make the moldings for the seat front, too. Delta makes a shaper cutter (#43-958) that will produce the shape shown in the *Molding Profile*. Or you can closely reproduce this molding with a router, as shown in the *Molding Routing Sequence* on page 283.

9. Cut the panels to the sizes specified in the Materials List. Rabbet the back edges of each panel to fit the gap left by the molding. The rabbet should be ⅜ inch wide and as deep as necessary to make the panel fit.

10. Miter the corners of the molding to fit inside the frame. Sand all the pieces, then assemble the doors. For more information, see Chapter 6.

11. Mount the doors on the cases, as described in Chapter 11.

Make the Seat

1. Make the frame-and-panel unit for the seat just as you did for the doors. The only real difference is that here, the stiles are sandwiched between the rails rather than the other way around. This assembly is detailed in the *Seat Frame Joinery Detail*, *Seat Frame Detail*, and *Seat Frame-and-Panel Assembly*.

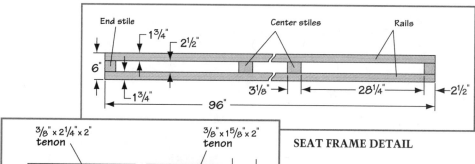

SEAT FRAME DETAIL

SEAT FRAME JOINERY DETAIL

2. Cut the seat ribs to the sizes specified in the Materials List. Lay them out on a flat surface, as shown in *Seat Rib Layout* and *Seat Torsion Box Detail*. Butt the pieces together tightly and fasten them with ⅜-inch staples across the joints. Once you have the whole assembly stapled, flip it over and staple the joints on the opposite side. Don't worry if it seems flimsy—the real strength comes after you glue the top and bottom in place.

3. Cut the top and bottom slightly wider than the dimensions specified, then get ready to glue them to the ribs. The key to gluing up a torsion box is to find a flat surface to work on—the flatter the better. If necessary, use a sheet of plywood with several

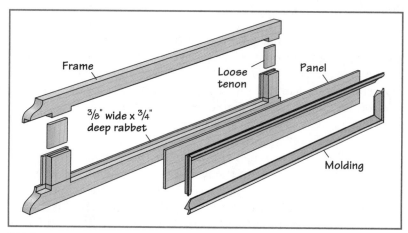

SEAT FRAME-AND-PANEL ASSEMBLY

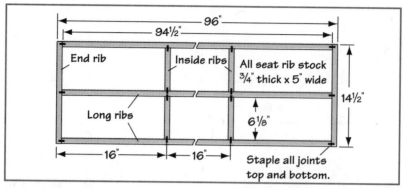

SEAT RIB LAYOUT

sawhorses underneath. Just make sure this temporary table doesn't sag in the middle.

Lay the bottom down, then apply glue to the edges of the ribs. Set the structure in place on top of the bottom and check to be sure it's square. Follow with the top and an extra piece of plywood to protect the good plywood from being scratched or marred. Add cinder blocks, bricks, or sandbags to clamp the pieces together.

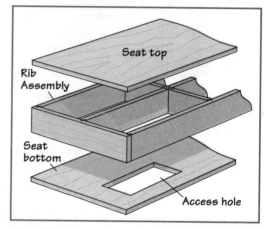

SEAT TORSION BOX DETAIL

4. When the glue dries, trim the top and bottom flush with the ribs with a flush-trim bit in a router.

5. Cut access holes in the bottom of the seat box so you can drive screws through the front rib to attach the frame-and-panel unit. The unit is attached with two screws driven into each stile; place the access holes accordingly. Cut the holes with a flush-trim bit in a router. Drill a ¾-inch diameter hole first, then use the ribs to guide your router to create the hole.

6. Drill pilot holes through the rib from the outside, then mark the frame with an awl from the inside. Attach the frame with 1⅝-inch drywall screws. You may have to drive them with a stubby screwdriver, as the space in the box is tight. The frame should project beyond the top of the box by ¼ inch. This little lip keeps the cushions from slipping off.

Make the Shelves

1. The shelves are torsion boxes, too. Cut the ribs, top, and bottom to size (the top and bottom should be slightly oversize) and assemble the boxes just as you did the seat. Trim the top and bottom flush after the glue dries. The layout and assembly are detailed in *Shelf Rib Layout* and *Shelf Torsion Box Detail.*

2. Cut the shelf edging to the size specified and glue the pieces to the edges of the shelves, as shown in the *Shelf Edging Detail*. Don't worry too much about the corner joints—you'll be cutting them off shortly. You can either clamp the edging in place until it dries or fasten it with 1-inch wire brads to hasten the process. If you use brads, keep them away from the corners where you'll be cutting.

3. Once the edging is secure, trim it flush with the surfaces of the top and bottom with a flush-trim bit in a router.

4. Cut the corners off the shelves, as shown in the *Shelf Edging Detail*. Make the cuts on the table saw, guiding the pieces past the blade with the miter gauge. A chop saw would work as well.

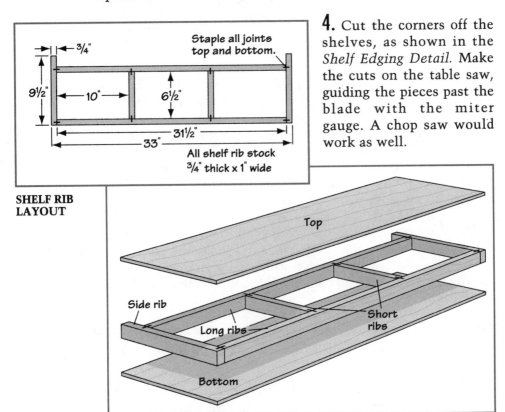

SHELF RIB LAYOUT

Staple all joints top and bottom.

3/4"

9½"

10"

6½"

31½"

33"

All shelf rib stock 3/4" thick x 1" wide

Top

Side rib

Long ribs

Short ribs

Bottom

SHELF TORSION BOX DETAIL

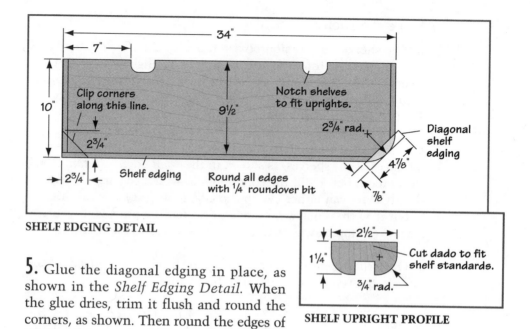

SHELF EDGING DETAIL

SHELF UPRIGHT PROFILE

5. Glue the diagonal edging in place, as shown in the *Shelf Edging Detail*. When the glue dries, trim it flush and round the corners, as shown. Then round the edges of all the edging with a ¼-inch roundover bit.

6. The backs of the shelves are notched to fit around the uprights. Make a template of the notch from a piece of plywood shaped like the *Shelf Upright Detail* (but without the dado). Using double-sided carpet tape, fasten it to the shelf where you want the notch. Cut the notch out roughly on the band saw. Then trim the shelf to match the template with a flush-trim bit in a table-mounted router. Make two notches in each shelf. (Be sure you know where the uprights are going to be before making any cuts.)

7. Cut the uprights to the size specified in the Materials List and dado them to accept the shelf standards. Shape the corners, as shown in the *Shelf Upright Profile*, with a ¾-inch roundover bit in a table-mounted router. Also round the top end with the same bit, as shown in the *Side View*.

8. Apply the finish of your choice according to the manufacturer's directions. The unit pictured is finished with an oil finish.

Installation

1. This unit is meant to hang on the wall, rather than sit on the floor. Its main support is an angle iron that runs the full length of the project, as shown in the *Side View*. It's easier if you get a single length of steel to run the distance, but you can use two or more pieces if necessary. I usually buy my angle iron a foot or so longer than I need. I have my supplier punch holes in one leg every 16 inches. When I get to the site and locate the studs, I simply cut the angle iron to length so the holes fall in the appropriate places. These holes should be sized for ¼-inch lag screws. I also have holes punched in the other leg so I can drive screws up into the bottom of the cabinets. Here, I use regular ¾-inch drywall screws, two to a case.

2. Snap a level line along the wall about 10 inches above the floor. Fasten the angle iron to the studs with ¼ × 2½-inch lag screws, keeping its top edge even with the line. This will locate the window seat about 16 inches off the floor, a comfortable height for sitting.

3. Set one case on the angle iron and position it laterally. Screw it to the studs through the screw rail at the top of the case with 2½-inch drywall screws. Then screw it to the angle iron from underneath with ¾-inch drywall screws. Next, position the seat box on the angle iron. Screw it to the first case with 1¼-inch drywall screws driven from inside the case. Finally, add the second case and screw it home.

4. Set the countertops in place. Position the uprights and screw them to the walls. For fairly light use, you can attach them with hollow wall anchors. However, for heavier loads like books, you should either screw them to the studs with 2½-inch drywall screws or install special blocking inside the walls to screw into. This will require opening up the wall and nailing short lengths of 2 × 4 between the studs where you need them.

Drive the screws through the bottom of the dado so they'll be hidden by the shelf standards. Once the uprights are in place, screw the standards in their grooves with the screws supplied.

5. Rehang the doors and adjust them. Drill the doors for the pulls. For more information on locating pulls, see Chapter 12.

OAK BREAKFRONT

This is one of my most popular designs, so I have had a lot of practice building it. I am always amazed at the ways people use a cabinet like this. The one shown in the photo ended up in a dining room as a china cabinet. With glass doors, the upper cabinets make very nice showcases, and the lower cabinets offer ample storage space. I've also had clients who use their breakfront as an entertainment center. With some slight modifications, a television can sit right on the countertop, while the lower cabinets house stereo equipment. Modify the drawer sizes as needed to fit videotapes, cassettes, or compact discs.

Each breakfront I build is a little different than the last because I get bored so easily doing the same thing. The breakfront shown here has a unique pull design that's not difficult to make—simply bore a hole and make a couple of router cuts. Plus, all the solid oak stock I chose has holes from insects. At first I thought I would use this wood only where it was out of sight. However, like many pieces of wood that have natural defects, it became a special part of the piece's look.

232

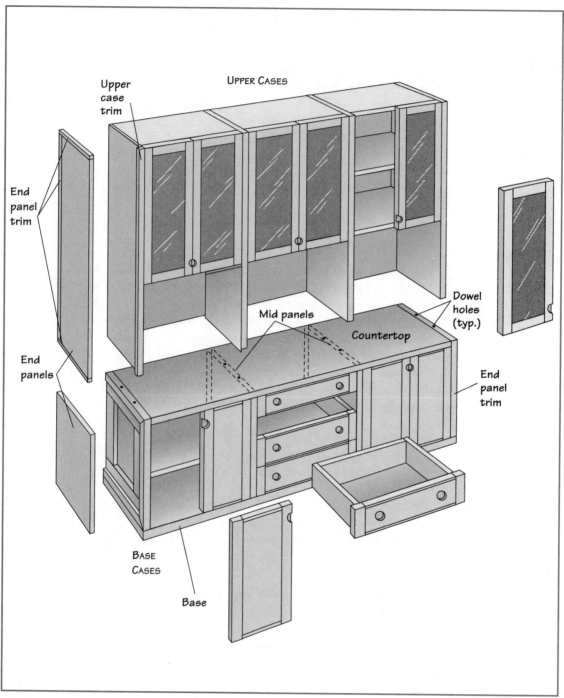

Upper case trim

UPPER CASES

End panel trim

End panels

Mid panels

Countertop

Dowel holes (typ.)

End panel trim

BASE CASES

Base

EXPLODED VIEW

TECH NOTES The freestanding cabinet shown in the photo is made up of six individual cases: three basic cases on the bottom and three slightly modified cases on top. End panels finish off the cabinets, and mid panels separate the three bottom case units. This cabinet is frameless, but the vertical edging on the cabinet's front serves as a partial frame—the doors and drawer faces are inset between the vertical edging. The glass doors use my typical loose tenon frame construction, and the lower doors and drawer faces consist of edged plywood with solid wood "stiles" attached to their outer edges. The drawer boxes are assembled with machine-cut dovetails. The pulls are routed directly into the solid wood parts. For more in-depth information on building these components, see Chapters 2, 9, and 12.

CONSTRUCTION STEPS

Build the Base Cases

1. Cut the tops, bottoms, and sides for all the base cases to the sizes specified in the Materials List.

2. Cut grooves in the lower case sides for the case tops and bottoms, as shown in the *Breakfront/Lower Case Joinery Detail.* Cut tongues on the case tops and bottoms to fit the grooves in the case sides. See "Cutting the Joint" on page 16.

3. Glue and screw the case sides to the case tops and bottoms with 1⅝-inch drywall screws.

4. Lay the assembled cases face down. Cut the backs to size and attach them with glue and 1½-inch wire brads as you square up the cabinets, as discussed in "The Glue-Up" on page 24.

5. When each case has been assembled, apply the edging, as shown in the *Breakfront/Lower Case Joinery Detail,* and as described in "Attaching the Edging" on page 32.

MATERIALS LIST

PART	DIMENSION
Base Cases (3)	
Tops/Bottoms (2)	$\frac{3}{4}$" × $20\frac{5}{8}$" × $29\frac{1}{4}$"
Sides (2)	$\frac{3}{4}$" × $20\frac{5}{8}$" × 27"
Back	$\frac{1}{4}$" × 30" × 27"
Edging (4)	$\frac{1}{4}$" × $\frac{13}{16}$" × 30"
Base Case Panel Assemblies	
End panels (2)	$\frac{3}{4}$" × $20\frac{1}{2}$" × 27"
Upper/lower spacers (4)	$\frac{3}{4}$" × 3" × $20\frac{1}{2}$"
Outside spacers (4)	$\frac{3}{4}$" × 3" × 21"
End panel trim (8)	$\frac{3}{4}$" × $1\frac{9}{16}$" × 29"
Mid panels (2)	$\frac{3}{4}$" × $21\frac{1}{4}$" × 27"
Mid panel spacers (4)	$\frac{3}{4}$" × 3" × 27"
Mid panel trim (2)	$\frac{3}{4}$" × $1\frac{1}{2}$" × 27"
Base Case Shelves (2)	
Shelf	$\frac{3}{4}$" × $20\frac{1}{2}$" × $28\frac{7}{16}$"
Edging	$\frac{1}{4}$" × $\frac{13}{16}$" × $28\frac{7}{16}$"
Counter Assembly	
Countertop	$\frac{3}{4}$" × $21\frac{1}{4}$" × $91\frac{1}{2}$"
Long core pieces (2)	$\frac{3}{4}$" × 3" × $91\frac{1}{2}$"
Short core pieces (7)	$\frac{3}{4}$" × 3" × $15\frac{1}{4}$"
Front edge stock	$\frac{3}{4}$" × $1\frac{1}{2}$" × 93"
End edge stock (2)	$\frac{3}{4}$" × $1\frac{1}{2}$" × 23"
Base Assembly	
Platform	$\frac{3}{4}$" × $21\frac{1}{4}$" × $94\frac{1}{2}$"
Long core pieces (2)	$\frac{3}{4}$" × 3" × $94\frac{1}{2}$"
Short core pieces (7)	$\frac{3}{4}$" × 3" × $15\frac{1}{4}$"
Front edge stock	$\frac{3}{4}$" × $1\frac{1}{2}$" × 96"
End edge stock (2)	$\frac{3}{4}$" × $1\frac{1}{2}$" × 23"
Upper Cases (3)	
Top/bottom (2)	$\frac{3}{4}$" × $18\frac{1}{4}$" × $30\frac{3}{4}$"
Sides (2)	$\frac{3}{4}$" × $18\frac{1}{2}$" × 60"
Top/bottom edging (6)	$\frac{1}{4}$" × $\frac{13}{16}$" × 30"
Back	$\frac{3}{4}$" × $31\frac{1}{2}$" × 60"
Hinge mounting stiles (2)	$\frac{3}{4}$" × 3" × $34\frac{1}{2}$"
Shelf	$\frac{3}{4}$" × $13\frac{3}{4}$" × $29\frac{7}{8}$"
Shelf edging	$\frac{1}{4}$" × $\frac{13}{16}$" × 30"
Upper Case Assembly	
End panels (2)	$\frac{3}{4}$" × $18\frac{1}{2}$" × $58\frac{1}{2}$"
End panel edging (4)	$\frac{3}{4}$" × $\frac{3}{4}$" × $19\frac{1}{4}$"
End panel edging (2)	$\frac{3}{4}$" × $\frac{3}{4}$" × $58\frac{1}{2}$"
Trim (4)	$\frac{3}{4}$" × $1\frac{1}{2}$" × 60"
Positioning dowels (8)	$\frac{3}{8}$"-dia. × 1"

PART	DIMENSION
Upper Case Doors (6)	
Stiles (2)	$\frac{13}{16}$" × 2" × 36"
Rails (2)	$\frac{13}{16}$" × 2" × $10\frac{7}{8}$"
Tenon stock	$\frac{3}{8}$" × $\frac{7}{8}$" × 10"
Glass retaining molding (2)	$\frac{1}{4}$" × $\frac{1}{4}$" × 36"
Glass retaining molding (2)	$\frac{1}{4}$" × $\frac{1}{4}$" × 18"
Base Case Doors (4)	
Panel	$\frac{3}{4}$" × $10\frac{3}{8}$" × $26\frac{3}{8}$"
Stiles (2)	$\frac{3}{4}$" × 2" × $26\frac{7}{8}$"
Edging (2)	$\frac{1}{4}$" × $\frac{13}{16}$" × 27"
Edging (2)	$\frac{1}{4}$" × $\frac{13}{16}$" × 12"
Splines (2)	$\frac{1}{4}$" × $\frac{15}{16}$" × 25"
Back plate	$\frac{1}{8}$" × $1\frac{3}{4}$" × 5"
Drawers	
Stiles (4)	$\frac{3}{4}$" × 2" × $5\frac{3}{8}$"
Stiles (4)	$\frac{3}{4}$" × 2" × $7\frac{7}{8}$"
Faces	$\frac{3}{4}$" × $25\frac{3}{8}$" × 25"*
Face edging (10)	$\frac{1}{4}$" × $\frac{13}{16}$" × 28"
Spline stock (2)	$\frac{1}{4}$" × $\frac{15}{16}$" × 28"
Round inserts (8)	$\frac{1}{4}$" × $2\frac{3}{4}$" dia.
Square inserts (8)	$\frac{1}{2}$" × $3\frac{1}{2}$" × $3\frac{1}{2}$"
Small sides (4)	$\frac{5}{8}$" × $4\frac{3}{8}$" × 20"
Small fronts/backs (4)	$\frac{5}{8}$" × $4\frac{3}{8}$" × $27\frac{1}{2}$"
Large sides (4)	$\frac{5}{8}$" × 6" × 20"
Large fronts/backs (4)	$\frac{5}{8}$" × 6" × $27\frac{1}{2}$"
Bottoms (4)	$\frac{1}{4}$" × $19\frac{7}{8}$" × $26\frac{3}{4}$"

Hardware

20" Accuride drawer slides (4 pair). Available from Outwater Hardware Corp.; part #3017

Grass full-overlay hinges with winged base plates (20). Available from Outwater Hardware Corp.; part #1006 and #63204

$\frac{1}{8}$" × $11\frac{1}{2}$" × $32\frac{5}{8}$" glass panes (6)

5mm pin-style shelf supports (20). Available from Outwater Hardware Corp.; part #3002

$1\frac{5}{8}$" drywall screws (as needed)

$1\frac{1}{4}$" drywall screws (as needed)

$1\frac{1}{2}$" wire brads (as needed)

$\frac{1}{2}$" wire brads (as needed)

$1\frac{1}{2}$" finish nails (as needed)

*Cut the individual faces from this piece to the sizes specified on the *Drawer Details*.

Build the Base Case End and Mid Panels

1. Cut the parts for the base case panel assemblies to the sizes specified in the Materials List. As shown in the *Panel Construction Details*, the hidden parts can be made from particleboard.

2. Assemble the panels and their spacers, as shown. Fasten the spacers to the panels with 1¼-inch drywall screws.

3. Miter the end panel trim to fit around the base case end panels, as shown. When the trim has been mitered to fit, glue and clamp it to the end panel and spacers. Make sure that the hardwood trim overhangs the edges of the end panels slightly on each side.

4. Rout the edges of the trim flush to the edges of the end panels and spacers with a router and flush-trim bit.

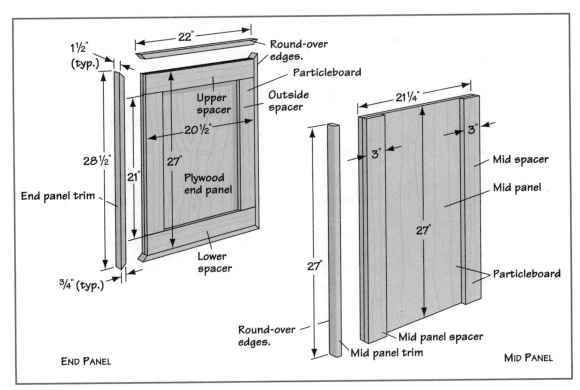

PANEL CONSTRUCTION DETAILS

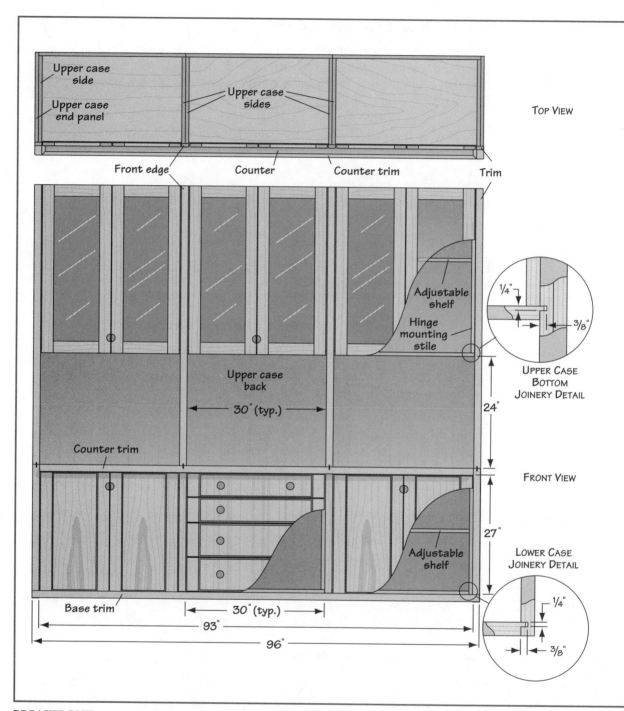

Upper case side

Upper case end panel

Upper case sides

TOP VIEW

Front edge   Counter   Counter trim   Trim

Adjustable shelf

Hinge mounting stile

¼"

⅜"

UPPER CASE BOTTOM JOINERY DETAIL

Upper case back

30" (typ.)

24"

Counter trim

FRONT VIEW

27"

Adjustable shelf

Base trim   30" (typ.)

93"

96"

LOWER CASE JOINERY DETAIL

¼"

⅜"

BREAKFRONT

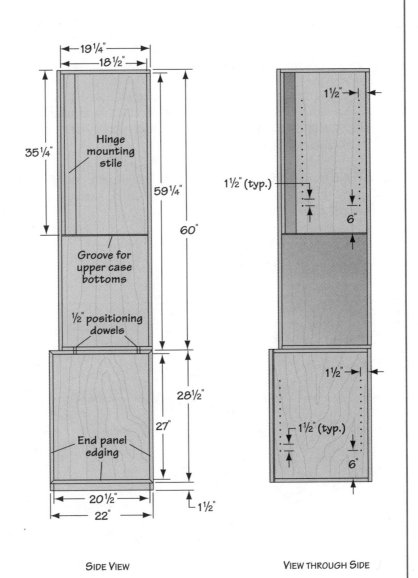

SIDE VIEW   VIEW THROUGH SIDE

5. Glue and clamp the mid panel trim to the front edge of the mid panels. Rout the edges of the trim flush to the edges of the mid panels and mid panel spacers with a router and flush-trim bit.

6. Round-over the front edges of the end panel trim and mid panel trim with a ¼-inch-radius roundover bit in a table-mounted router.

Make the Counter and Base

1. Since the counter and base have similar construction, make them at the same time. Cut the base and counter parts to the sizes specified in the Materials List. The hidden (core) parts can be made from particleboard.

2. Lay the countertop and base platform face down and glue and screw the core pieces to them with 1¼-inch drywall screws, as shown in the *Construction Details*.

3. Miter the edge stock to fit the counter and base, as shown, then glue and clamp it in place.

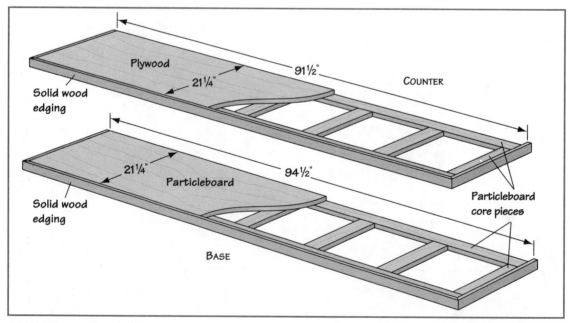

CONSTRUCTION DETAILS

Assemble the Base Cases

1. Refer to the *Exploded View* for the overall base case assembly. First, put the base flat on the floor and line up one of the outside base cases on it. Allow enough space (about 1½ inches) for the end panel, then screw the base case to the base with 1¼-inch drywall screws.

2. When the first base case has been fastened down, attach a mid panel to it with 1¼-inch drywall screws.

3. Next, align another base case with the first base case and mid panel, and screw it in place. Then, add the other mid panel and the final base case.

4. Attach the end panels. Drive 1¼-inch drywall screws through the sides of the outside base cases and into the end panels.

5. Position the counter on top of the base case assembly. It should be centered from side to side and flush with the case backs. Drive 1⅝-inch drywall screws up through the tops of the base cases and into the counter core pieces to secure the counter.

Build the Upper Cases

1. Cut the tops, bottoms, and sides for the upper cases to the sizes specified in the Materials List. Cut the bottoms a little wider at first. Glue the edging to them, then cut them to width as you cut the rest of the pieces.

2. Cut grooves in the upper case sides for the case tops and bottoms. The grooves at the top of the upper case are cut as described in "Cutting the Joint" on page 16. The grooves for the upper case bottom must be cut partway down the upper case sides, as shown in the *Breakfront/Front View* and *Breakfront/Side View*. Cut the grooves for the upper case bottoms with a router and ¼-inch-diameter straight bit. Clamp a straightedge to the sides to guide the router as you cut the grooves, as shown in *Upper Case Groove Routing Setup*. Cut tongues on the case tops and bottoms to fit the grooves in the case sides. See "Cutting the Joint" on page 16.

3. Glue and screw the case sides to the case tops and bottoms with 1⅝-inch drywall screws.

UPPER CASE GROOVE ROUTING SETUP

4. Lay the assembled cases face down. Cut the backs to size and attach them with glue and 1½-inch wire brads as you square up the cabinets, as discussed in "The Glue-Up" on page 24.

5. Cut the hinge mounting stiles to size. Position them so their front edges are flush with the front edges of the case sides, as shown in the *Breakfront/Front View* and *Side View*. Attach them to the cases with 1¼-inch drywall screws driven through the sides.

Make the Upper Case End Panels

1. Cut the upper case end panels and end panel edging to the sizes specified in the Materials List.

2. Attach the end panel edging to the end panels with glue and 1½-inch finishing nails, as shown in the *Breakfront/Side View.*

Assemble the Upper Cases

1. Align the upper cases with their front edges flush, as shown in the *Breakfront/Front View* and *Breakfront/Top View,* and screw them together with 1¼-inch drywall screws.

2. When the upper cases have been fastened together, attach the upper case end panels to the case by driving 1¼-inch drywall screws through the case sides and into the panels.

3. Cut the upper case trim to the size specified in the Materials List, and round-over its long front edges with a ¼-inch-radius roundover bit in a table-mounted router.

4. When the edges have been rounded-over, attach the upper case trim to the front edges of the upper case and to the upper case end panels with glue and 1½-inch finish nails, as shown in the *Breakfront/Front View* and *Breakfront/Top View*. Set the nails and fill the holes.

Make the Positioning Dowels and Drill Their Holes

1. Cut the positioning dowels to the size specified in the Materials List.

2. Lay the upper case assembly on its back and drill ⅜-inch-diameter × ½-inch-deep dowel holes in the bottom edge of the upper case sides, as shown in the *Breakfront/Side View*. The exact positioning of the dowels is not important, but it is important to drill the holes perpendicular to the bottom edge of the sides. Use a doweling jig to help guide the bit, if necessary.

3. When the holes have been drilled, use dowel centers to mark the dowel hole position on the base case assembly. (Dowel centers are little spiked buttons that, when fitted into a dowel hole, can mark the center of an adjoining dowel hole.)

Insert a pair of dowel centers into the first set of dowel holes in the bottom edge of the upper case assembly sides, and get a friend or two to help you carefully set the upper case assembly in position on top of the base case assembly counter. Try to get the position right the first time—moving the upper case assembly around will produce more than one set of dowel center marks.

Drill matching ½-inch-deep dowel holes centered on the dowel center marks. Take care in drilling the holes so the dowels will align perfectly.

When the holes have been drilled, round-over the ends of a pair of dowels slightly and push them into the first set of holes in the counter. Put the dowel centers in the second set of holes in the upper case assembly and reposition the upper case assembly on top of the counter. The first set of dowels will position the assembly; the dowel centers will mark the next set of holes.

Continue by drilling the next set of holes and inserting the dowels. Push the dowel centers into the next set of holes in the upper case assembly to mark the position of the matching set of dowel holes in the counter. Repeat the process to mark and drill the remaining dowel holes in the counter.

When the final dowel holes have been drilled, set the upper case assembly in place.

Make the Upper Case Doors

1. Cut the door stiles and rails to the sizes specified in the Materials List.

2. Round-over the front edges of the rails and stiles with a ¼-inch-radius roundover bit in a table-mounted router.

3. Lay out and cut the mortises in the door rails and stiles, as shown in the *Upper Door Assembly*. See "Making the Frame" on page 64.

4. Cut tenons from the tenon stock to fit the mortises.

5. Glue and clamp together the door frames.

6. Let the door frames dry overnight. Rout a ⅜-inch-deep × ⅜-inch-wide rabbet around the back of each door frame. Square the rabbets at the inside corners of the frame with a sharp chisel.

7. When the rabbet has been cut, lay the door frames face down on the drill press and bore hinge holes for European-style hinges, as described in Chapter 11.

8. To install the glass, cut the glass retaining molding to fit in the rabbet behind the glass. Predrill holes before putting the glass in place. Then tip the glass panes into their rabbets and secure the molding with ½-inch wire brads.

Make the Base Case Doors and Drawer Faces

1. Cut the door panels and stiles and the drawer stiles to the sizes

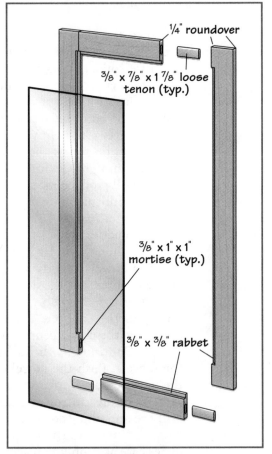

¼" roundover

⅜" x ⅞" x 1⅞" loose tenon (typ.)

⅜" x 1" x 1" mortise (typ.)

⅜" x ⅜" rabbet

UPPER DOOR ASSEMBLY

specified in the Materials List. Cut a bookmatched section of plywood to width for the drawer faces, but don't cut them to length (height) yet. For more on bookmatching, see "Selecting Bookmatches" on page 74.

2. Next, cut the door edging stock to fit around the door and drawer face panels. Glue and clamp the edging to the door panels. Edge the sides first, then the top and bottom. On the drawer face panel, glue the edging to the sides, let the glue dry, then cut the individual faces, preserving the ordered bookmatch from top drawer to bottom. When the drawer faces have been cut to the proper height, cut and glue the top and bottom edging to each drawer face.

3. Trim the edging flush to the front and back surfaces of the door panels and drawer faces with a flush-trim bit in a router. Then, round-over the front edges of the door and drawer face edging, as shown in *Lower Door/Drawer Details*. Rout the edge with a ¼-inch roundover bit in a table-mounted router. While the router is still set up, round-over the front edges of the lower door stiles and drawer stiles, as shown.

4. As shown in *Lower Door/Drawer Details*, the stiles are held to the drawer faces and door panels with a ³⁄₁₆-inch-thick spline. Cut a ½-inch-deep slot to hold the spline with a ³⁄₁₆-inch slot cutter in a table-mounted router. Center the slot on the stock thickness, as shown in *Lower Door/Drawer Details*. Although most slot cutters have a bearing guide, attach a fence to the router table to guide the cut, as shown in *Slot Routing Procedure*, just to be on the safe side. Rout the slots with the parts face up.

5. Make the splines that hold the stiles to the door panels and drawer faces from scraps of ¼-inch-thick plywood. Cut the scraps into ¹⁵⁄₁₆-inch-wide strips, then cut the strips to a thickness of ³⁄₁₆ inch on the table saw.

6. When the splines have been cut to the proper width and thickness, cut them to length—one to match each stile slot. Then curve their ends on the band saw or with a disk sander to match the ends of the slots. Don't worry about making them just the right length—a little short is okay.

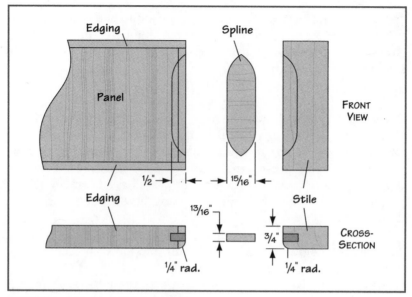

LOWER DOOR / DRAWER DETAILS

7. When all of the slots have been cut and all of the splines have been made, glue and clamp the door and drawer face parts together.

Cut the Pulls in the Doors and Drawer Faces

1. The integral pulls in the doors are produced as described in "Cutout Pulls" on page 139. Follow the *Door Pull Details* for the proper shape, size, and positioning.

2. The pulls in the drawer faces are also routed as described in "Cutout Pulls" on page 139 but, since the drawer faces are made from plywood, solid wood inserts must be glued into the pull area before they are cut. As shown in the *Drawer Pull Details*, 2¾-inch-diameter round inserts are inlaid into the front of the drawer faces. Drill holes for the round inserts with a Forstner bit or hole saw set up in a drill press. Drill the holes through the stock.

3. When the holes have been drilled, lay out the positions of the square inserts on the backs of the drawer faces, as shown in the *Drawer Pull Details*.

1. Put one corner of stock against fence and carefully pivot stock into spinning bit at first layout line.

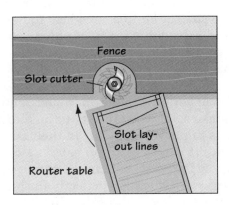

2. Push stock forward along fence.

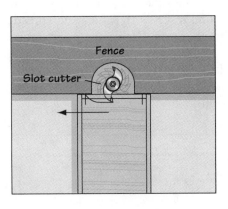

3. When slot reaches second layout line, pivot stock away from bit.

SLOT ROUTING PROCEDURE

OAK BREAKFRONT

4. Remove the stock within the layout lines to a depth of ½ inch with a straight bit in a hand-held router. Don't worry about staying perfectly within the layout lines because the back of the drawer face will be hidden. Square the corners of the square cutout with a chisel.

5. When both the round and square cutouts have been completed, make solid wood inserts to fit into the cutouts. The square inserts can have a loose fit in their cutouts, but the round ones should fit snugly with no gaps. Also, make the round inserts about ⅟₃₂ inch thicker than the cutout is deep—the excess can be sanded away later for a perfectly flush fit. Cut the square inserts on the table saw, and cut the round inserts with a circle cutter.

6. Glue the square insert into its cutout. Bevel the leading edge of the round insert with sandpaper, spread glue on its edges, and push it into its cutout. Clamp the inserts and let the glue dry.

7. Finally, drill 2-inch-diameter pull holes through the middle of the solid wood inserts and shape the pulls as you did the door pulls.

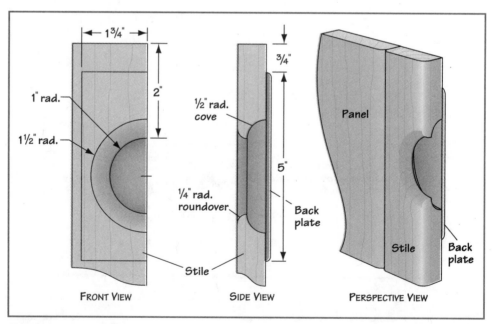

DOOR PULL DETAILS

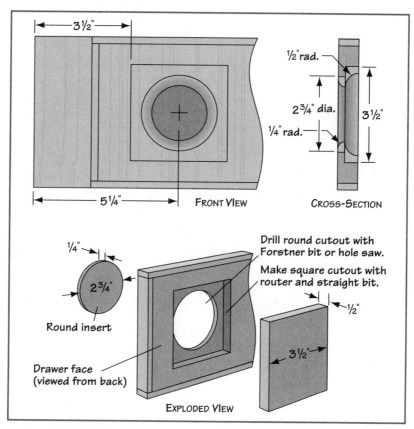

DRAWER PULL DETAILS

Make the Drawers

1. Cut the drawer parts to the dimensions specified in the Materials List.

2. Rout the dovetails and pins in the drawer sides, backs, and fronts. Position the parts in the jig to produce the layout shown in the *Drawer Details*. See "Dovetails" on page 97.

3. Cut the bottom grooves in the drawer sides, fronts, and backs, as shown. Cut the ¼-inch-wide × ¼-inch-deep grooves in two passes on the table saw.

4. Glue together the drawer sides, fronts, and backs. Trap the drawer bottoms in their grooves as you assemble the parts.

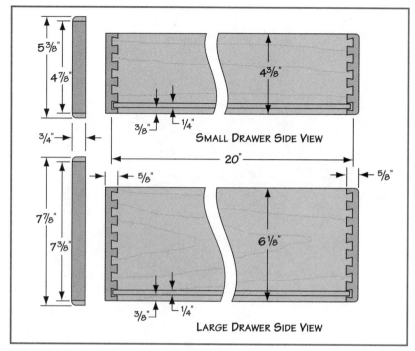

DRAWER DETAILS

5. Round-over the top edges of the drawer with a 5/16-inch-radius roundover bit. Also, round-over the inside top edge of the drawer front, but leave the drawer front square where it meets the drawer face. When the top edges have been rounded-over, turn the drawer upside down and round-over the outside bottom edges of the drawer sides and drawer back.

Drill the Shelf Peg Holes

1. The upper cases and the lower door cases have adjustable shelves held in place by shelf pegs that fit into ¼-inch-diameter × ½-inch-deep holes. To help drill the holes accurately, make the ¾-inch plywood shelf hole templates shown in the *Shelf Hole Template Layouts*. Make sure that you label one end of each template "top" and one end "bottom."

2. When the templates have been made, drill the shelf peg holes in the cases by guiding the drill bit through the holes in the template. To drill the shelf peg holes at the back of the case sides,

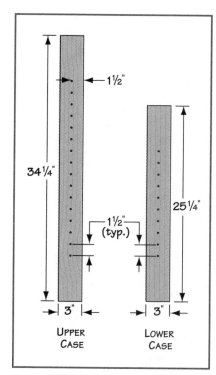

SHELF HOLE TEMPLATE LAYOUTS

hold the templates against the sides of their appropriate cases with the edge of the template against the case back. To drill the shelf peg holes at the front of the upper case sides, position the template against the side with its edge tight against the hinge mounting stile.

Drill the shelf peg holes at the front of the base case sides with the template positioned against the side and its edge aligned with the face of the edging. Remember to position the templates with the top up.

3. Cut the shelves to the size specified. Glue edging to their front edges and trim it flush.

4. Slip the shelf pins into their holes and drop the shelves in on top of them.

Hang the Lower Doors and Install the Drawers

1. Lay the doors face down on the drill press and bore hinge holes for European-style hinges. Install the doors in their cabinets, as described in Chapter 11.

2. Hang the drawer assemblies in their cases on full-extension drawer slides. See Chapter 10.

3. Make sure the drawer slides are adjusted properly, then attach the drawer faces to each drawer assembly with 1¼-inch drywall screws. Screw through the drawer front and into the drawer faces.

4. Finish the breakfront. The one shown is finished with several coats of spray lacquer.

POPLAR CLOSET

In many houses—older ones especially—storage space is at a premium. So when I redo a kitchen or other interior, I try to include as much extra storage space as possible. This often includes tall, deep cabinets or, as shown here, actual closets.

The closet in the photo is in a kitchen and is used as a pantry. It works quite well in this capacity and it fits nicely into its corner of the room. By using the dimensions given in the Materials List, you can build a similar unit. But, as is the case with most built-ins, you'll probably want to change things a bit to suit your location.

The most obvious change is to make the closet deeper. By increasing the depth by 4½ inches, you'll have a closet deep enough to hang clothing. Also, keep in mind that, as shown, the unit consists of a front with two doors and a single side. The house itself provides the back, the top, and the other side. Depending on where you want to put the closet, you may need to build one or more of these extra pieces.

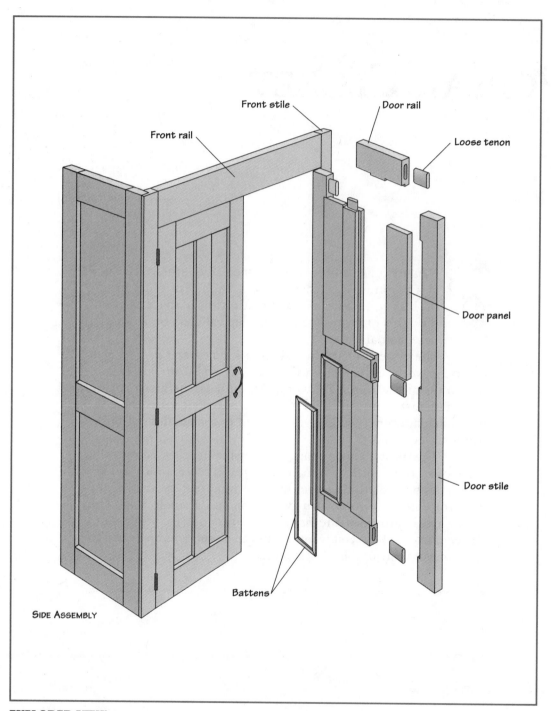

Front rail

Front stile

Door rail

Loose tenon

Door panel

Door stile

Battens

SIDE ASSEMBLY

EXPLODED VIEW

MATERIALS LIST

PART	DIMENSION	PART	DIMENSION
Front Frame		**Doors (2)**	
Stiles (2)	$1\frac{1}{2}" \times 3" \times 88"$	Stiles (2)	$1\frac{1}{2}" \times 4" \times 80"$
Rail	$1\frac{1}{2}" \times 7\frac{1}{4}" \times 49\frac{1}{2}"$	Top/bottom rails (2)	$1\frac{1}{2}" \times 5" \times 16\frac{1}{4}"$
Tenon stock	$\frac{1}{2}" \times 2\frac{3}{8}" \times 10"$	Center rail	$1\frac{1}{2}" \times 6" \times 16\frac{1}{4}"$
Beads (2)	$\frac{5}{16}" \times 1\frac{1}{2}" \times 82"$	Upper center stile	$1\frac{1}{2}" \times 4" \times 33\frac{1}{8}"$
Bead	$\frac{5}{16}" \times 1\frac{1}{2}" \times 51"$	Lower center stile	$1\frac{1}{2}" \times 4" \times 30\frac{7}{8}"$
		Tenon stock (2)	$\frac{1}{2}" \times 2\frac{3}{8}" \times 14"$
Side Assembly		Upper panels (2)	$\frac{3}{4}" \times 6\frac{3}{4}" \times 33\frac{3}{4}"$
Front stile	$1\frac{1}{2}" \times 3\frac{1}{2}" \times 88"$	Lower panels (2)	$\frac{3}{4}" \times 6\frac{3}{4}" \times 31\frac{1}{2}"$
Rear stile	$1\frac{1}{2}" \times 4" \times 88"$	Horizontal battens (8)	$\frac{3}{8}" \times 1" \times 9"$
Top/bottom rails (2)	$1\frac{1}{2}" \times 5" \times 12\frac{1}{4}"$	Upper vertical battens (4)	$\frac{3}{8}" \times 1" \times 36"$
Middle rail	$1\frac{1}{2}" \times 6" \times 12\frac{1}{4}"$	Lower vertical battens (4)	$\frac{3}{8}" \times 1" \times 34"$
Tenon stock	$\frac{1}{2}" \times 2\frac{3}{8}" \times 14"$		
Top panel	$\frac{3}{4}" \times 12\frac{13}{16}" \times 41\frac{3}{8}"$	**Hardware**	
Bottom panel	$\frac{3}{4}" \times 12\frac{13}{16}" \times 31\frac{7}{8}"$	$3" \times 3\frac{1}{2}"$ door hinges (6)	
Horizontal battens (4)	$\frac{3}{8}" \times 1" \times 15"$	Wrought-iron pulls (2)	
Upper vertical battens (2)	$\frac{3}{8}" \times 1" \times 44"$	Large magnetic catch	
Lower vertical battens (2)	$\frac{3}{8}" \times 1" \times 34"$	$2\frac{1}{2}"$ drywall screws (as needed)	
Screw rails (2)	$\frac{3}{4}" \times \frac{3}{4}" \times 88"$	$1\frac{5}{8}"$ drywall screws (as needed)	
		1" wire brads (as needed)	
		12d finish nails (as needed)	
		6d finish nails (as needed)	
		4d finish nails (as needed)	
		10d common nails (as needed)	

TECH **NOTES** In many ways, this project is a combination of cabinet-making and carpentry. The techniques are those I use for building cabinets, while the scale and look of the finished piece is more architectural. Don't be put off by the size of the project, though. I've developed a few methods that make working on a large scale fairly easy.

Chief among these methods is the jig I made for cutting mortises. It is very similar to the jig I use for mortising cabinet doors, but smaller. (See Chapter 5.) By making the jig smaller, I can move the jig to my workpiece, rather than having to lug large pieces of wood around the shop. More details on this to come.

The doors are simple frame-and-panel assemblies similar to

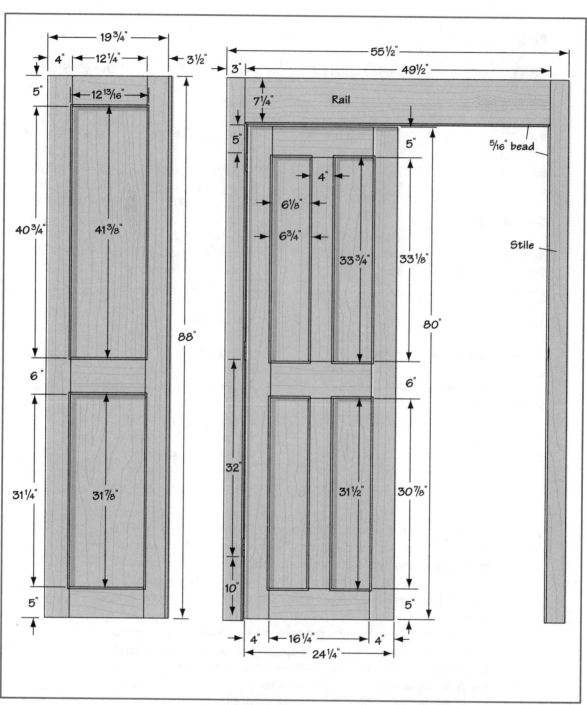

SIDE VIEW   **FRONT VIEW**

those described in Chapter 6. They're set into a surrounding frame that has an applied bead. In cabinetmaking, this is known as beaded-inset construction. For more information, see "Beaded Frames" on page 40. Most of the parts are made from heavy stock—8/4 (eight-quarter) poplar. You may have to do a little shopping to find a lumberyard that carries this.

What you do with the closet interior depends on what you have to store. The closet in the photo is used as a pantry, so it is equipped with a number of adjustable shelves. These are supported on adjustable shelf brackets attached to the wall that forms the closet back. I have made closets similar to this one that I fit with pull-out drawers, rotating shelves, and other specialized storage devices.

CONSTRUCTION STEPS

Make the Front Frame

1. Cut the stiles and rail for the front frame to the sizes specified in the Materials List.

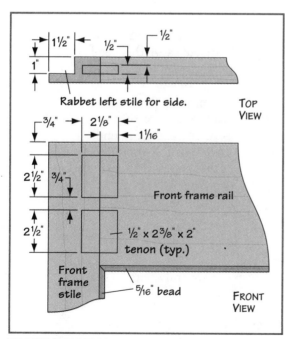

FRONT FRAME JOINERY DETAILS

2. Lay out the joints on the pieces, as shown in the *Front Frame Joinery Details*. Cut the mortises with a router equipped with a ½-inch straight bit. This task is easy if you build the mortising jig shown in the *Mortising Jig Assembly*. For more information on cutting mortises, see Chapter 4.

3. Rabbet the left-hand stile to receive the side, as shown in the *Front Frame Joinery Details*.

4. Cut tenons to fit the mortises. Insert the tenons and clamp the stiles and rail together without glue. (You won't actually glue the frame together until you have it on site.)

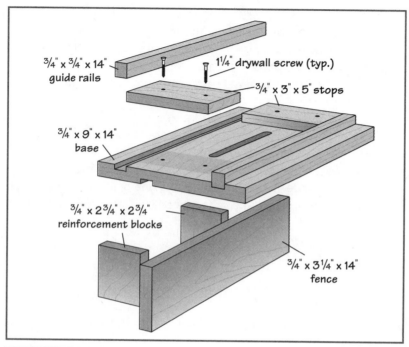

MORTISING JIG ASSEMBLY

5. Cut the bead to the sizes specified. The lengths listed allow some extra for joinery. Round-over the front edges of the bead with a ⅛-inch-diameter roundover bit in a table-mounted router.

6. You may want to cut a scrap to the same length as the rail and clamp it between the free ends of the stiles as you're fitting the bead. This will help to keep the assembly square. Miter the ends of the bead and fit the pieces around the inside of the frame, as shown in the *Front Frame Joinery Details*. Glue and nail them in place with 1½-inch finish nails. Set the heads below the surface and fill them. For more information about different fillers, see "Filling Wood" on page 33.

Make the Side and Doors

1. Cut the stiles, rails, and screw rail for the side and doors to the sizes specified.

2. Lay out the joints, as shown in the *Side and Door Joinery Detail*. Cut the mortises with a router as you did for the front frame.

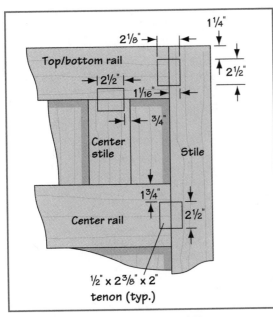

SIDE AND DOOR JOINERY DETAIL

Top/bottom rail

Center stile

Stile

Center rail

1¼"

2⅛"

2½"

2½"

1¹⁄₁₆"

¾"

1¾"

2½"

½" x 2⅜" x 2" tenon (typ.)

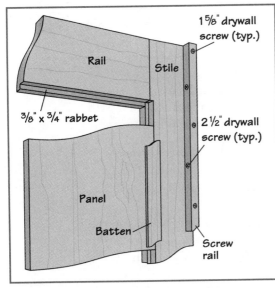

SIDE AND DOOR FRAME-AND-PANEL ASSEMBLY

Rail

Stile

⅜" x ¾" rabbet

Panel

Batten

1⅝" drywall screw (typ.)

2½" drywall screw (typ.)

Screw rail

3. Cut tenons to fit the joints, then glue the frames together. Take care to keep them square and flat. If you must lean the frames up against a wall as they dry, be sure they are adequately supported so they don't twist from the weight of the clamps. Sand the joints flat when the glue is dry.

4. Cut ⅜-inch × ¾-inch rabbets around the back of each opening in the frames to receive the panels, as shown in the *Side and Door Frame-and-Panel Assembly*. Use a rabbeting bit in a hand-held router. Square the corners with a sharp chisel.

5. Cut the panels to fit in the frames. The dimensions listed are slightly undersized to allow for a relaxed fit. If you're using solid wood, as I did, it is crucial that the panels are allowed to expand with changes in humidity. If you're using plywood panels, making them a little undersized won't hurt—and it makes installing them easier.

6. Cut the battens to the sizes specified. As with the bead, the lengths listed are long. This will give you a little leeway as you're cutting the miters.

7. Miter the corners of the battens and fit them around the panels. The battens should be centered over the gap between the panel and the frame. Glue and nail them in place with 1-inch wire brads. Take care not to get any glue on your solid panels.

8. Fit the side into the rabbet you cut in the front frame stile. Glue and nail the stile to the side with 6d finish nails. Set the nail heads below the surface and fill the holes.

9. Mortise the hinges into the edge of each door. For more information about how to make a jig that will make this job a cinch, see "A Hinge Mortising Jig" on page 130.

Installation

1. Carry the various pieces of the closet to the site unassembled. Stand the side in place and check to see if it sits plumb and level. If not, trim the edges with a plane until it does.

2. Attach the screw rail to the side with 1⅝-inch drywall screws. Then attach the entire side/front stile assembly to the wall with 2½-inch drywall screws driven through the screw rail, as shown in the *Side and Door Frame-and-Panel Assembly*. Make sure there is something solid in the wall to screw into. If necessary, add blocking between the studs inside the wall.

(Blocking is simply some extra wood added inside a wall to provide a solid anchor for screws or other fasteners. If you have to add blocking, you'll have to remove the wall board and cut 2 × 4s to fit horizontally between the studs. Nail them in place with 10d common nails. Consult a carpenter if you're uncomfortable doing this kind of work.)

3. Attach the remaining front stile to the wall with a similar screw rail. Again, blocking inside the wall may be necessary.

4. Apply glue to the joints at the top of the front frame and slip the rail into place. The side should spring enough to allow this. Clamp the joints tight. You may have unscrew the closet from the walls and move it out into the room to get the clamp in position. Check the opening for square, then allow the glue to dry overnight.

5. Toenail the side and the front stiles to the floor with 12d finish nails to steady them.

6. Shim the doors into position and use them to mark the locations of the mortises on the front frame. As shown, there is a 5/16-inch gap under the doors. Cut the mortises in the frame with the same hinge-mortising jig you used to cut the mortises in the doors. Predrill one hole in each mortise and screw the hinges in place with one screw per leaf to hang the doors. You'll probably need some help handling the doors—they're heavy. See Chapter 11 for additional information.

7. Check the way the doors swing, and look at the gap around the edges. It should be fairly consistent. If the doors come together with too little space in between, cut the mortises deeper. If there is too much space in between, add shims under the hinges to make the mortises shallower. If the doors hang crooked, you may have to shim one mortise and/or deepen another. When you get the doors installed perfectly, drive in the rest of the screws.

8. Locate the handles on the door fronts. Experiment with their position until you are happy with how they look, then screw them in place. See "Door Pulls" on page 133 for a jig that makes drilling for pulls a snap. Locate the stop/catch on the frame above the doors and screw it in place.

9. Apply the finish of your choice to the doors and any other exposed wood. The closet pictured was painted with a high-quality latex enamel.

BOOKSHELVES IN STAINED OAK

Is it possible to have too many bookshelves? I doubt it. Even if you don't have enough books to occupy all the shelf space, there is bound to be something else that needs a home, like CDs or videotapes. Everyone I've ever made a set of these shelves for has had no trouble filling them up.

I made the originals for a law office that had too many books and lawyers and not enough storage space. Those units had extra-deep shelves—about 14 inches. The extra depth allowed two rows of books to be stored on each shelf. I'm not sure how those lawyers were going to know what was stored on the inside row, but they seemed pleased with their new library after I installed it.

For your house, there is no need to make the shelves that deep—12 inches will be plenty. One of the beauties of this design is that it can easily be adapted to suit almost any space. Make it as short or tall, deep or shallow, and wide or narrow as you like. I only recommend that you don't make it much wider, or the shelves may sag under the weight of your books. If you need a wider expanse of shelves, make two or more cases.

The shelves in the photo are freestanding. If yours seem unstable, screw them to the wall and/or the floor. Since the base is separate, it should be a simple matter to level them and screw them down before installing the case.

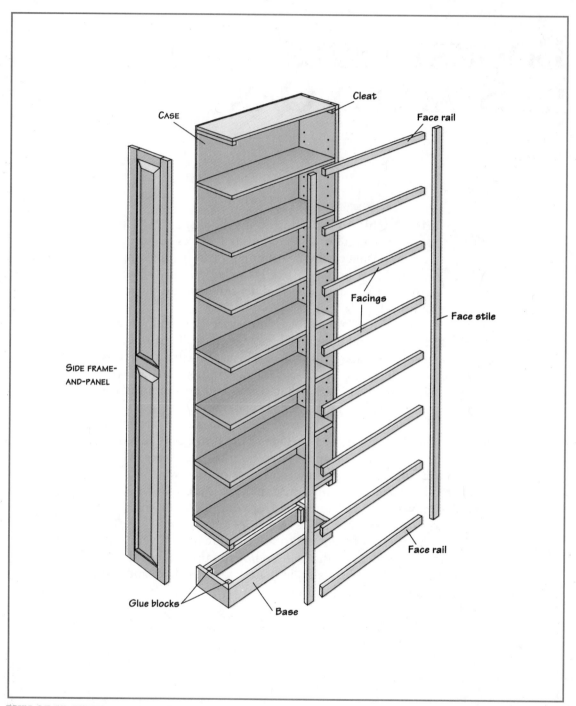

CASE

Cleat

Face rail

SIDE FRAME-
AND-PANEL

Facings

Face stile

Face rail

Glue blocks

Base

EXPLODED VIEW

MATERIALS LIST

PART	DIMENSION	PART	DIMENSION
Case		**Base**	
Side front stiles (2)	¾" × 1¾" × 90"	Front/Back (2)	¾" × 4¾" × 33"
Side back stiles (2)	¾" × 2½" × 90"	Ends (2)	¾" × 4¾" × 10½"
Side rails (6)	¾" × 2½" × 7"	Glue blocks (4)	¾" × ¾" × 4½"
Tenon stock	⅜" × 1⅝" × 20"		
Side panels (2)	¾" × 7⁹⁄₁₆" × 41⅞"	**Hardware**	
Top/Bottom (2)	¾" × 11⅜" × 35¼"	5mm pin-style shelf supports (24). Available	
Shelves (6)	¾" × 11¼" × 34⅜"	from Outwater Hardware Corp.; part #3002	
Facings (6)	¾" × 1½" × 32⅞"	2" drywall screws (as needed)	
Face stiles (2)	¾" × 1½" × 90"	1¼" drywall screws (as needed)	
Face rails (2)	¾" × 1½" × 33"		
Back	¼" × 35¼ × 90"		
Cleats (4)	¾" × ¾" × 11"		

TECH **NOTES** The construction of this project couldn't be much simpler. It is a basic case sitting on a base. The case sides are frame-and-panel units and the rest is plywood. If you're making several bookcases to sit side by side, you may want to make a common base for the whole installation. You can also make the adjoining sides from plywood since they won't show. For more information, see Chapter 2 and Chapter 14.

This case varies slightly from my standard case. Because it is so big and because it is intended to be freestanding, I added reinforcing cleats at the corners. For the top corners, this was just a matter of gluing and screwing the cleats in place. For the lower corners, I raised the bottom slightly and installed the cleats underneath. This keeps them from interfering with books sitting on the bottom surface.

Another difference is in attaching the face frame to the case. Since the frame is big and the individual pieces are relatively narrow, I don't make a joint between the rails and stiles. Instead, I just glue the frame pieces to the case individually. Since the joints are solid wood to solid wood on the side frames, I butt the two pieces; across the plywood top and bottom, I add tongue-and-groove joints for added strength. (I also use a tongue-and-groove joint on the sides if they are plywood.)

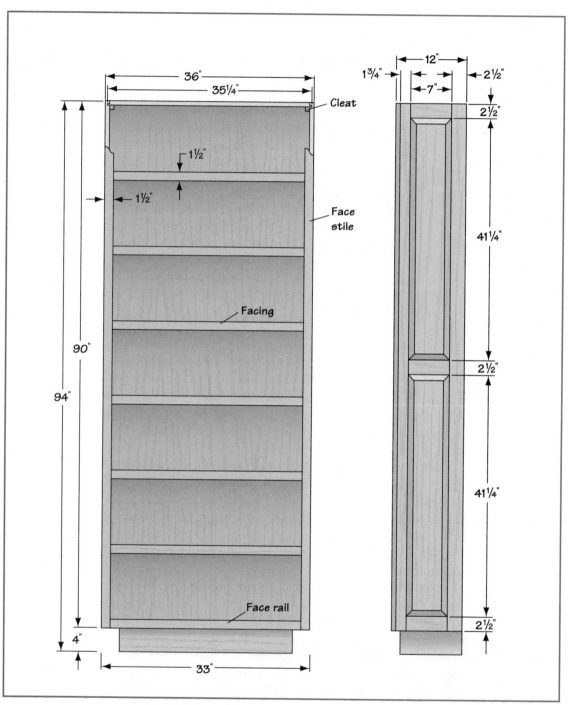

FRONT VIEW

SIDE VIEW

CONSTRUCTION STEPS

Make the Side Frames

1. Cut the stiles and rails to the sizes specified in the Materials List.

2. Join them with loose tenon joints, as shown in the *Side Frame Joinery Details.* For more information, see Chapter 4.

3. Use your dado head to cut ¼-inch-wide × ⅜-inch-deep grooves in the side frame pieces. The panel grooves in the stiles can run out the ends—you'll never see them.

4. Cut the side panels to the size specified in the Materials List. They are slightly undersized to allow for expansion. Raise the panels, as shown in the *Case Cross-Section.* For more specifics on raising panels, see "Traditional Panels" on page 79. Rabbet the backs of the panels. The rabbets should be ½ inch wide and as deep as necessary to allow the edges of the panels to slip into the grooves in the frame. If you're going to finish your shelves with stain, stain the panels now before trapping them within the frame.

5. Glue the side frames together with the panels in place. Be careful not to glue the panels to the frames so they can expand and contract. For tips on gluing up frames, see "Clamping Frames" on page 42.

6. Drill holes in the sides for the shelf pins, as shown in the *Exploded View.* Start them 8 inches from the bottom edge of the sides. Center them on the stiles and space them 1½ inches apart.

Make the Cases

1. Cut the top, bottom, shelves, face stiles, and facings to the sizes

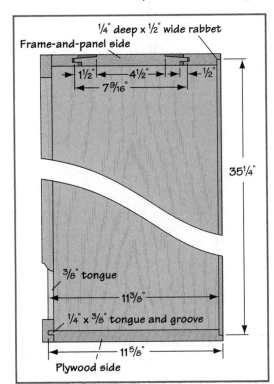

CASE CROSS-SECTION (TOP VIEW)

specified. Cut the face rails to width, but leave them ¼ inch long so you have room to trim them later. The shelves and facings are intentionally somewhat undersized since they need some clearance for adjustability.

2. Round all the front edges of the facings. This detail emphasizes the intersections while disguising the gaps. Make the cuts with a ³⁄₁₆-inch roundover bit in a table-mounted router.

3. Cut tongue-and-groove joints to join the sides to the top and bottom, the facings to the shelves, and the face rails to the top and bottom, as shown in the *Case Joinery Detail* and the *Facing Joinery Detail*. Also, cut tongues on the sides and grooves in the face stiles if you are using plywood sides, as shown in the *Case Cross-Section*. For more details, see "Cutting the Joint" on page 16. Cut ¼-inch-deep × ½-inch-wide rabbets along the back edges of the sides for the back, as shown in the *Case Cross-Section.*

4. Glue the case together. Since the sides show, don't use screws or nails. Instead, clamp the pieces together while the glue dries. Use scraps of wood to protect the sides from the clamps.

While the glue is drying, turn the case face down and attach the back. Cut the back to size first, then set it in place in the rabbets. If necessary, you can use the back to square the case; see "The Glue-Up" on page 24.

5. Glue and screw the cleats in place, as shown in the *Case Joinery Detail.* Use 1¼-inch drywall screws, three in each direction.

6. Glue the facings to the shelves. Center them from end to end. Cut away the excess tongue, as shown in the *Facing Joinery Detail.* Trim the facings flush with the top surfaces of the shelves with a flush-trim bit in a router.

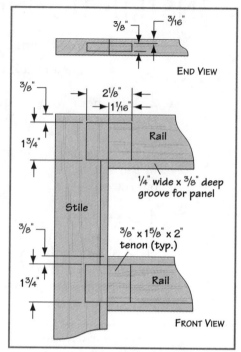

SIDE FRAME JOINERY DETAILS

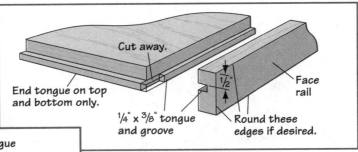

End tongue on top
and bottom only.

Cut away.

¼" x ⅜" tongue
and groove

½"

Face
rail

Round these
edges if desired.

FACING JOINERY DETAIL

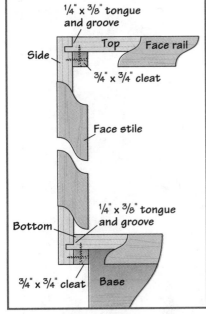

¼" x ⅜" tongue
and groove

Side

Top

Face rail

¾" x ¾" cleat

Face stile

¼" x ⅜" tongue
and groove

Bottom

¾" x ¾" cleat

Base

CASE JOINERY DETAIL

7. Trim the tongues on the top and bottom, as shown in the *Facing Joinery Detail*. Use the face stiles as a template. Glue the stiles in place to the case sides.

8. Trim the face rails to fit between the stiles. Glue them to the top and bottom.

Make the Base

1. Cut the pieces for the base to the sizes specified in the Materials List. Leave the back piece ¼ inch or so long for now.

2. Miter the front corners on the table saw, as shown in the *Exploded View*. Glue the base together.

3. Add glue blocks to reinforce the joints. Glue and screw them in place with 1¼-inch drywall screws, two in each direction.

4. Cut the back to fit between the sides. Anchor it in place about 1 inch in from the ends of the sides with a second pair of glue blocks, as shown in the *Exploded View*.

5. Set the case on the base, flush along the back and centered from side to side. Join the two with 2-inch drywall screws through the case bottom. Use 4 screws along both the front and back.

6. Finish the bookcase with your favorite finish according to the manufacturer's directions. The case in the photo is finished with walnut stain and sprayed lacquer.

MIRRORED MEDICINE CABINET

My wife complained for years that she wanted a full-length mirror. Finally, I found the time to make one for her. First, I came up with a molding for the frame. It has very simple, clean lines. Then I hit upon a neat way to mount the mirror to the wall without any visible hardware: Attach three sides of the frame to a plywood backing, screw the backing to the wall, then slip the mirror in place and cap it off with the final piece of molding. I've been making mirrors this way ever since.

Eventually, I was asked to build a medicine cabinet. In designing it, I thought I would use a smaller version of my wall mirror for the door. The result was the quick—and very useful—project you see here. Building it would be a great chance to try out my system of cabinetmaking without risking too much time or material.

You can also take this project back where I started and make a full-length mirror. Simply expand the lengths of the mirror, door trim, and backing, then mount the mirror on a closet door or wall.

TECH **NOTES** This little cabinet consists of a basic case with mitered face trim. It is designed to be set into the wall, but you could easily dress up the case sides a little and simply hang it over a sink. The face trim is flush with the inside of the case and overlaps the outside by ¼ inch. The overlap hides any gap between the case and the surrounding drywall. The mitered door trim is rabbeted to hold the mirror. The sides of the case have holes drilled for shelf supports, and the shelves are made from ¼-inch-thick plate glass. For more in-depth information on building the case, see "Plywood Construction" on page 15.

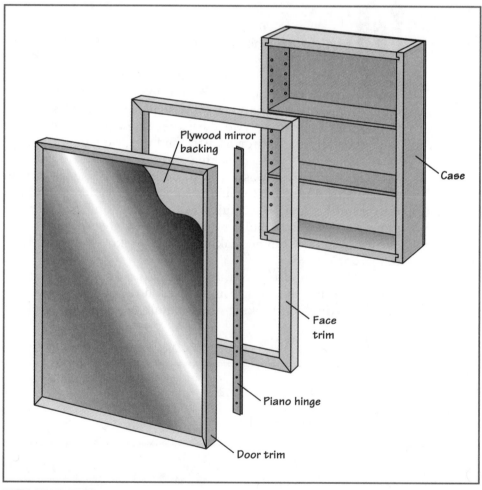

Plywood mirror backing

Case

Face trim

Piano hinge

Door trim

EXPLODED VIEW

CONSTRUCTION STEPS

Build the Case

1. Cut the case sides, top, bottom, and back to the sizes specified in the Materials List.

2. Drill the shelf support holes in the case sides, as shown in the *View through Side.*

3. Cut grooves in the case sides, then matching tongues in the case tops and bottoms, as shown in the *Front View/Joinery Detail.* See "Cutting the Joint" on page 16.

4. Attach the sides to the top and bottom with glue and 1⅝-inch drywall screws.

5. Turn the case face down on your bench and attach the back with glue and 1-inch wire brads. Square the case, if necessary, as discussed in "The Glue-Up" on page 24.

Make the Face Trim

1. Cut the face trim stock to the thickness and width specified in the Materials List.

2. Miter the trim stock on the table saw (or with a chop saw) to fit around the case opening, as shown in the *Front View.* As shown, the trim should be flush with the inside of the case.

3. Glue the trim parts to the front of the case. Hold them in place with 1-inch wire brads while the glue dries. Set the brads and fill the holes.

MATERIALS LIST

PART	DIMENSION
Case sides (2)	¾" × 3" × 23½"
Case top/bottom (2)	¾" × 3" × 16¾"
Back	¼" × 17½" × 23½"
Face trim stock (2)	½" × 1" × 26"
Face trim stock (2)	½" × 1" × 20"
Door trim stock (4)	¾" × 1½" × 24"
Mirror backing	¾" × 17" × 23"

Hardware

5mm pin-style brass shelf supports (8). Available from Outwater Hardware Corp.; part #3002
24" piano hinge
¼" × 2⅞" × 15⅞" plate glass shelves (2)
Magnetic catch
¼" × 16⅞" × 22⅞" mirror
2" drywall screws (as needed)
1⅝" drywall screws (as needed)
1" wire brads (as needed)

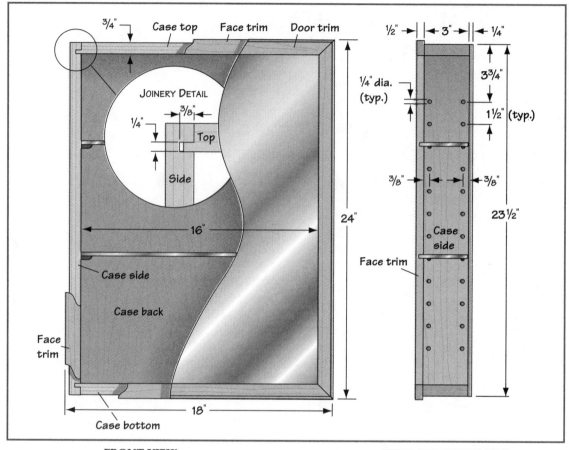

FRONT VIEW   **VIEW THROUGH SIDE**

Make and Hang the Mirror Door

1. Cut the door trim stock and mirror backing to the sizes specified in the Materials List.

2. Tilt the table saw blade 32½ degrees from vertical and position the fence so that the blade tilts away from it (on most saws this means moving the fence to the left of the blade). Position the stock as shown in the *Door Trim Bevel Setup,* and bevel the stock to produce the profile shown in the *Door Trim Profile.*

3. Return the blade to vertical and reposition the fence. Set the door trim stock on edge with the bevel facing up and cut the rabbet in the stock, as shown in the *Door Trim Profile.*

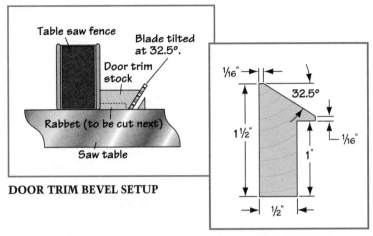

DOOR TRIM BEVEL SETUP

DOOR TRIM PROFILE

Cut the rabbet in two passes.

Check the depth of the rabbet by holding a piece of the molding in place along the side of the mirror backing. With the back edge of the molding flush with the back of the backing, the mirror should be able to just slip in place. Adjust the depth of the rabbet by raising the blade, if necessary.

4. Miter the door trim stock to fit around the mirror backing, as shown in the *Exploded View.*

5. Glue and clamp the door trim in place on the sides and bottom. When the glue is dry, slip the mirror in place and nail the top piece to the backing with three 1-inch brads, but NO glue. This will allow you to remove the molding to replace the mirror if need be.

6. Hang the door on the cabinet with a piano hinge, as shown in the *Exploded View.* The door can be hinged on either side of the cabinet. You don't have to mortise for the hinge. Just screw it in place with the screws provided, first to the cabinet and then to the door.

7. Install a magnetic catch at about the midpoint of the cabinet side opposite the hinge.

8. Finish the cabinet with the finish of your choice according to the manufacturer's instructions. I recommend a highly water-resistant finish like polyurethane if the cabinet is going in a bathroom.

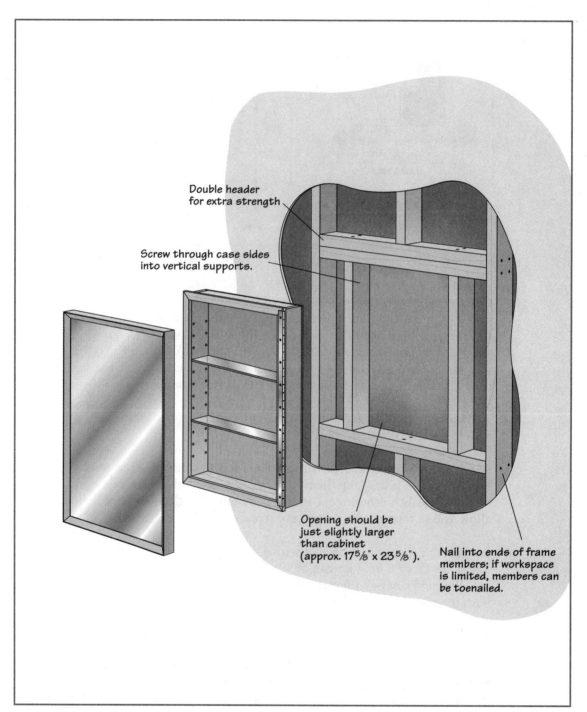

Double header
for extra strength

Screw through case sides
into vertical supports.

Opening should be
just slightly larger
than cabinet
(approx. $17\frac{5}{8}$" x $23\frac{5}{8}$").

Nail into ends of frame
members; if workspace
is limited, members can
be toenailed.

INSTALLATION OVERVIEW

Install the Cabinet

1. This cabinet is designed to be recessed into a wall, with only its face trim and door protruding. Figure out where you want to hang it (most are centered over a sink) and lay out the position on the wall. Break or cut a hole in the drywall or plaster within the layout lines to determine the position of the studs. Most modern homes have studs every 16 inches on center, but older homes may have randomly spaced studs up to 24 inches apart. Since it's unlikely that your studs will fall in exactly the right places to fit the cabinet, you'll have to cut away part of a stud and box out a space with additional 2 × 4s to support your cabinet in the wall, as shown in the *Installation Overview*.

Remove enough of the drywall or plaster so you have room to operate. Frame the cabinet opening, as shown in the *Installation Overview*, with a stacked 2 × 4 header at the top and single 2 × 4s creating the rest of the opening. Nail the 2 × 4s in place with 16d nails, as shown. In an older home, you may need to be a bit creative, since the studs you find in the walls may not match what's available from your local building supply. Consult with a carpenter if you're not sure how to proceed.

2. Replace the drywall or plaster up to the edges of the trimmed opening. Put the cabinet in place with the back of the face trim tight against the wall. Drill pilot holes through the sides of the cabinet and screw it in place with 2-inch drywall screws.

3. Insert the shelf pins into their holes and slip the shelves into place.

CHERRY/MAPLE VANITY

I made this vanity for my client Hilary's children. It has two sinks to help avoid some of the bathroom conflicts typical of youngsters. I normally make vanities 32 to 34 inches tall—it's easier on the adult back than the industry standard of 30 inches (the bare minimum, in my view). This vanity, at 32½ inches, should be anywhere from about right to too high for kids. Since kids generally grow a bit, it makes more sense to provide them with a stool rather than building cabinets that most of the rest of the population will find too short. I built a stool in on this model—you can see it at the bottom of the photo. (I didn't include it in the plans, though; I left that up to you.)

The use of a cherry base and contrasting maple molding is more playful than my usual single-wood cabinets. These colorful, warm cabinets will be enjoyed for many years. For a more subdued look, you may want to stick with a single species of wood for both the doors and the molding.

Because these cabinets are built-in, you will have to adjust their size to fit your space. If your space is really small, you may want to use just one sink base and one or two drawer bases.

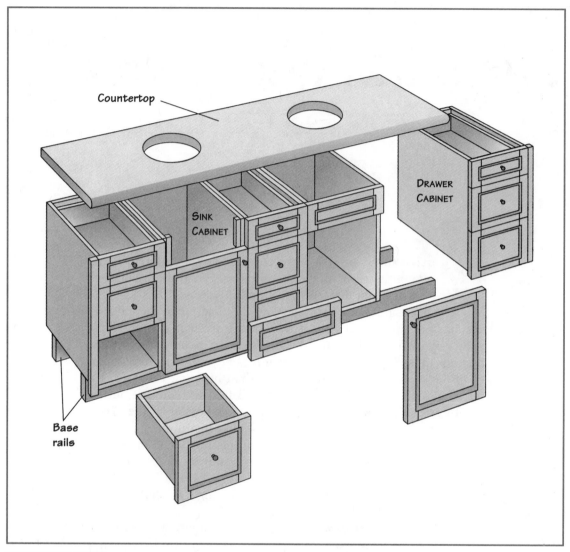

Countertop

Sink
Cabinet

Drawer
Cabinet

Base
rails

EXPLODED VIEW

TECH NOTES The vanity shown in the photo is made up of five individual cabinets: two sink units and three drawer units. These two types of cabinets include basic cases, frame-and-panel doors with inset molding, and frame-and-panel–faced drawers with inset molding. The door frames and drawer face frames are joined with loose tenon joints and the drawers are assembled with machine-cut dovetails. For more in-depth information on building these components, see Chapters 2, 6,

MATERIALS LIST

PART	DIMENSION	PART	DIMENSION
Drawer Cabinets (3)		False drawer panels	$\frac{1}{2}$" × 15$\frac{7}{16}$" × 2$\frac{1}{2}$"
Case top/bottom (2)	$\frac{3}{4}$" × 20$\frac{1}{2}$" × 14$\frac{1}{4}$"	False drawer backing	$\frac{3}{4}$" × 5$\frac{3}{16}$" × 18$\frac{1}{2}$"
Case sides (2)	$\frac{3}{4}$" × 20$\frac{1}{2}$" × 29"	Door stiles (2)	1" × 2$\frac{1}{2}$" × 22$\frac{7}{8}$"
Case back	$\frac{1}{4}$" × 15" × 29"	Door rails (2)	1" × 2$\frac{1}{2}$" × 14$\frac{7}{8}$"
Edging stock (3)	$\frac{1}{4}$" × $\frac{7}{8}$" × 32"	Tenon stock	$\frac{3}{8}$" × 1$\frac{5}{8}$" × 10"
Drawer rails (6)	1" × 2" × 9$\frac{7}{8}$"	Door panel	$\frac{1}{2}$" × 15$\frac{7}{16}$" × 18$\frac{1}{2}$"
Small drawer stiles (2)	1" × 2$\frac{1}{2}$" × 5$\frac{7}{8}$"	Molding stock (3)	$\frac{3}{4}$" × $\frac{7}{8}$" × 36"
Small drawer panel	$\frac{1}{2}$" × 10$\frac{7}{16}$" × 2$\frac{1}{2}$"	Countertop	1" × 24" × 85"
Large drawer stiles (4)	1" × 2$\frac{1}{2}$" × 11$\frac{3}{8}$"		
Large drawer panels (2)	$\frac{1}{2}$" × 10$\frac{7}{16}$" × 8$\frac{1}{16}$"	**Installation**	
Tenon stock	$\frac{3}{8}$" × 1$\frac{1}{8}$" × 32"	Base rails (2)	$\frac{3}{4}$" × 3$\frac{1}{2}$" × 85"
Molding stock	$\frac{3}{4}$" × $\frac{7}{8}$" × 36"	Crosspieces (5)	$\frac{3}{4}$" × 3$\frac{1}{2}$" × 14$\frac{1}{4}$"
Small drawer front	$\frac{5}{8}$" × 3$\frac{1}{2}$" × 12$\frac{1}{2}$"	Cleats (8)	$\frac{3}{4}$" × $\frac{3}{4}$" × 19$\frac{5}{16}$"
Small drawer sides (2)	$\frac{5}{8}$" × 3$\frac{1}{2}$" × 18"	Facing	$\frac{1}{4}$" × 3$\frac{1}{4}$" × 85"
Small drawer back	$\frac{5}{8}$" × 3$\frac{1}{2}$" × 12$\frac{1}{2}$"	Spacers (2)	$\frac{3}{4}$" × 1" × 29"
Small drawer bottom	$\frac{1}{4}$" × 11$\frac{3}{4}$" × 17$\frac{7}{8}$"		
Large drawer fronts (2)	$\frac{5}{8}$" × 7$\frac{7}{8}$" × 12$\frac{1}{2}$"	**Hardware**	
Large drawer sides (4)	$\frac{5}{8}$" × 7$\frac{7}{8}$" × 18"	Grass full-overlay hinges with winged base	
Large drawer back (2)	$\frac{5}{8}$" × 7$\frac{7}{8}$" × 12$\frac{1}{2}$"	plates (4). Available from Outwater Hardware	
Large drawer bottom (2)	$\frac{1}{4}$" × 11$\frac{3}{4}$" × 17$\frac{7}{8}$"	Corp.; part #1006 and #63204	
		20" Accuride full-extension drawer slides	
Sink Cabinets (2)		(9 pair). Available from Outwater Hardware	
Case top/bottom (2)	$\frac{3}{4}$" × 20$\frac{1}{2}$" × 19$\frac{1}{4}$"	Corp.; part #3017	
Case sides (2)	$\frac{3}{4}$" × 20$\frac{1}{2}$" × 29"	Oval brass pulls (11). Available from Cliffside	
Case back	$\frac{1}{4}$" × 20" × 29"	Industries; part #101PB	
Edging stock (4)	$\frac{1}{4}$" × $\frac{13}{16}$" × 32"	2$\frac{1}{2}$" drywall screws (as needed)	
False drawer stiles (2)	1" × 2$\frac{1}{2}$" × 5$\frac{7}{8}$"	2" drywall screws (as needed)	
False drawer rails (2)	1" × 2" × 14$\frac{7}{8}$"	1$\frac{5}{8}$" drywall screws (as needed)	
Tenon stock	$\frac{3}{8}$" × 1$\frac{1}{8}$" × 10"	1$\frac{1}{4}$" drywall screws (as needed)	
		1" wire brads (as needed)	
		$\frac{7}{8}$" wire brads (as needed)	
		$\frac{3}{4}$" wire brads (as needed)	

and 8. The cabinets are installed on a base rail system, as discussed in Chapter 14. Top off the vanity cabinets with a waterproof countertop of stone or one of the available plastic counter products. See Chapter 13 for several options.

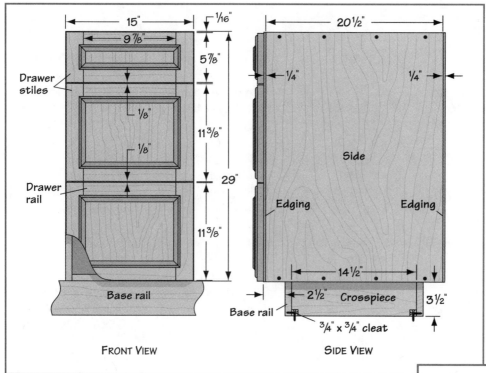

FRONT VIEW

SIDE VIEW

DRAWER BASE

CONSTRUCTION <u>STEPS</u>

Build the Cases

1. Cut the case tops, bottoms, and sides for the drawer and sink cabinets to the dimensions specified in the Materials List.

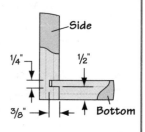

JOINERY DETAIL

2. Cut grooves in the case sides for the case tops and bottoms, as shown in the *Joinery Detail*. Cut matching tongues on the case tops and bottoms. See "Cutting the Joint" on page 16.

3. Glue and screw the case sides to the tops and bottoms with 1⅝-inch drywall screws.

4. Cut the backs to size. Lay the cases face down and attach the backs with glue and 1-inch wire brads, using the backs to square up the cabinets. For more details, see "The Glue-Up" on page 24.

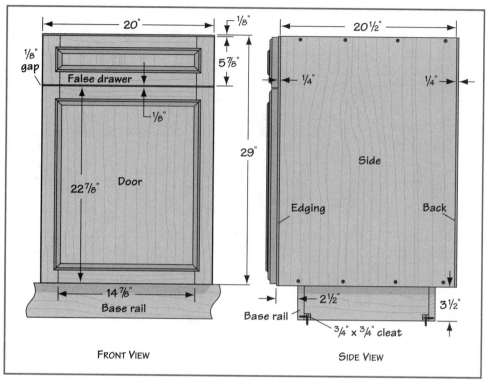

SINK BASE

5. Cut the edging to size and attach it to the front edges of the case components, as described in "Attaching the Edging" on page 32.

Make the Door Frames and Drawer Faces

1. Cut the door, drawer, and false drawer rails, stiles, and panels to the sizes specified in the Materials List.

2. Join the drawer and door rails and stiles with loose tenon joints, as shown in the *Mortise-and-Tenon Details* and the *Frame Assembly*. See "Cutting the Mortises" on page 36.

3. Glue the door frames and drawer face frames together. Allow the glue to dry overnight.

4. Rout an ogee detail around the outer edge of the frames, as shown in the *Edge Routing Detail.*

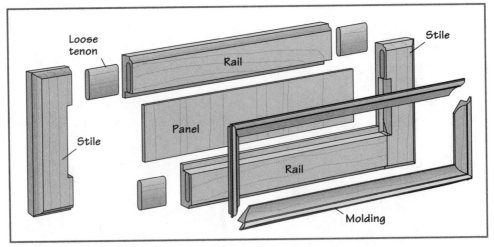

FRAME ASSEMBLY

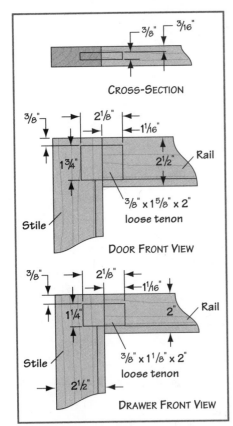

MORTISE-AND-TENON DETAILS

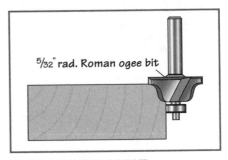

EDGE ROUTING DETAIL

5. Rabbet the inside front edges of the frames for the panels and molding with a rabbeting bit, as shown in the *Frame Cross-Section*. Square the rounded corners with a chisel when you're finished routing.

6. Lay the doors face down on the drill press and bore hinge holes for European-style hinges, as described in "European-style Hinges" on page 123.

7. Rout the door and drawer molding stock to the shape and dimensions shown in the *Molding Cross-Section*. The

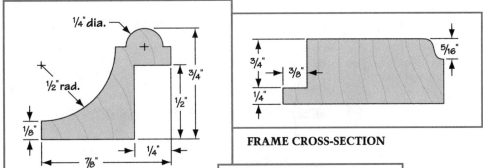

MOLDING CROSS-SECTION

FRAME CROSS-SECTION

Molding Routing Sequence shows exactly how to rout the molding stock to shape.

8. Miter the molding to fit inside each door and drawer face frame.

9. Check the fit of each panel in its particular door frame or drawer face frame. Each panel should have about ³/₁₆ inch of play across its width and about ¹/₈ inch in length. The extra space will give the panels room to expand and makes them easier to seat in their frames. Trim the panels if necessary. Drop them into the rabbet and slip the molding in place. Attach the molding to the door frames with ⅞-inch wire brads. Set the brads with a small nail set and fill the holes with putty.

MOLDING ROUTING SEQUENCE

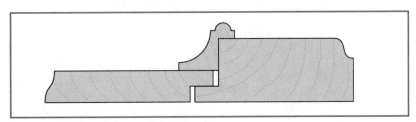

FRAME-AND-PANEL CROSS-SECTION

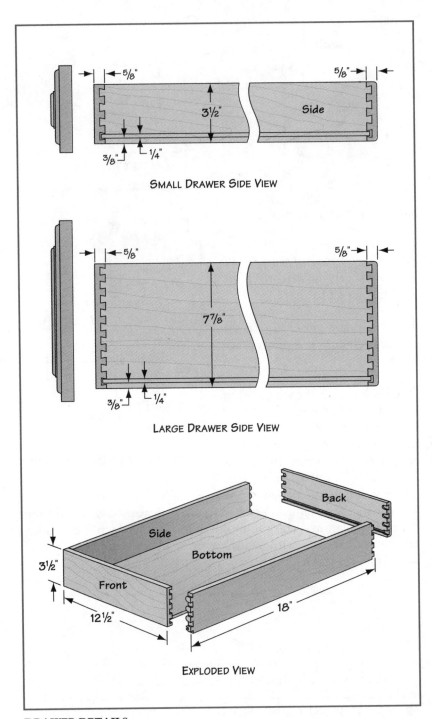

SMALL DRAWER SIDE VIEW

LARGE DRAWER SIDE VIEW

EXPLODED VIEW

DRAWER DETAILS

Make the Drawers

1. Cut the drawer fronts, sides, and backs to the dimensions specified in the Materials List.

2. Rout the dovetails and pins in the drawer sides, drawer backs, and drawer fronts. Position the parts in the jig to produce the layout shown in the *Drawer Details/Large Drawer Side View* and *Small Drawer Side View.* See "Dovetails" on page 97.

3. Cut the bottom grooves in the sides, fronts, and backs, as shown. Cut the ¼-inch-wide × ¼-inch-deep grooves in two passes on the table saw.

4. Assemble the drawer sides, fronts, and backs with glue. Trap the drawer bottoms in their grooves as you assemble the parts.

5. Round-over the top edges of the drawer sides and backs with a ⁵⁄₁₆-inch-radius roundover bit. Also, round-over the inside top edge of the drawer front, but leave the drawer front square where it meets the drawer face. When the top edges have been rounded-over, turn the drawer upside down and round-over the outside bottom edges of the drawer sides and drawer back.

6. Hang the drawer assemblies in their cases on full-extension drawer slides. See Chapter 10.

7. Make sure the drawer slides are adjusted properly, then attach the frame-and-panel drawer faces to each drawer assembly with 1¼-inch drywall screws.

8. When the drawer faces have been attached to the drawers, install ¾-inch-diameter brass pulls. Drill through the drawer face panel and drawer front, and then pass the bolt through the holes from the inside of the drawer to secure the pull.

Install the Doors and False Drawer Faces

1. Screw the false drawer backing in place on the sink base with 2-inch drywall screws driven through the sides, as shown in the *False Drawer Face Detail.* When the backing is in place, screw the frame-and-panel false drawer face to the front of it with

1⅝-inch drywall screws, as shown. Drive the screws into the frame of the false drawer face.

2. Finally, drill holes in the doors for the pulls, bolt them in place, and hang the doors.

Finish and Install the Vanity

1. Finish the vanity with your favorite wood finish according to the manufacturer's directions. The vanity in the picture has a urethane finish to protect it from the hard use it is apt to see in a children's bathroom.

2. This vanity sits on my standard ladder-style base. Cut the base rails, crosspieces, facing, and cleats to the sizes specified in the Materials List. Screw the rails to the crosspieces with 1⅝-inch drywall screws. Screw the cleats to the rails with 1¼-inch drywall screws. Details are given in Chapter 14.

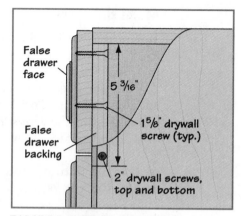

FALSE DRAWER FACE DETAIL

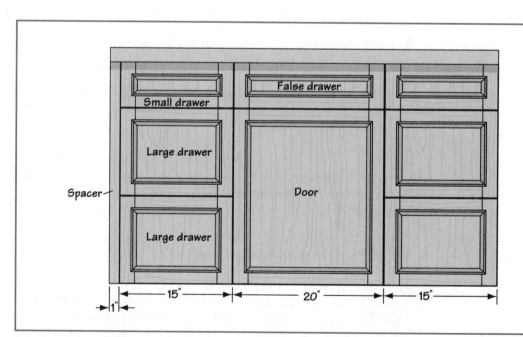

VANITY FRONT VIEW

3. On site, set the base in place and level it with shims. Then screw the base to the floor with 2½-inch drywall screws.

4. Set the cases on the rails. As shown in the *Vanity Front View,* the sink bases are installed between the drawer bases and a 1-inch-wide spacer is installed between the drawer bases and the walls. Screw the cases together, then screw the spacers to the cases, both with 1¼-inch drywall screws. The spacers can be scribed and cut to fit the wall perfectly.

5. Install the countertop of your choice from the options given in Chapter 13. The original counter was made from Corian by professional Corian fabricators.

6. Finish the facing to match the rest of the vanity. Then nail it to the front of the base with ¾-inch wire brads.

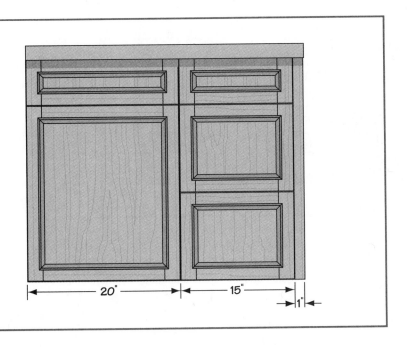

Ash Vanity with a Teak Top

When we began discussing this vanity, my client Ted pulled out a teak shoe box that his cousin had made. I could tell Ted liked the rich look of the teak, so—not to be outdone by his cousin—I suggested a solid teak top for his vanity. In this case, the teak serves more than an aesthetic purpose—teak is very practical where water is concerned. Because teak is so resinous, it will stand up to moisture for a very long time. (Teak is used for decking on sailboats for this very reason.)

When you open up fresh teak, it has a surprising light green color. The first time I sawed some open, I thought it would never darken properly; thankfully, I was wrong. Teak—even the raw green teak—darkens as it ages, turning a wonderful dark golden brown. It has one distinct disadvantage to be aware of—it has a very high mineral content that will wreak havoc on your blades. Every time I work with it, I prepare myself to send out my jointer and planer knives for resharpening. Fortunately, teak is fairly soft and cuts well with dull tools.

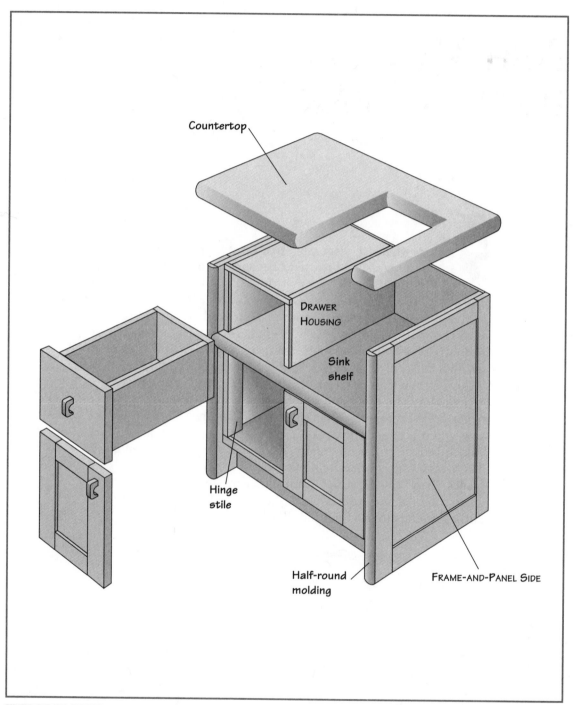

Countertop

Drawer Housing

Sink shelf

Hinge stile

Half-round molding

Frame-and-Panel Side

EXPLODED VIEW

MATERIALS LIST

PART	DIMENSION	PART	DIMENSION
Frame-and-Panel Sides (2)		Panel	$\frac{1}{4}$" × $9\frac{11}{16}$" × $12\frac{1}{8}$"
Rails (2)	$\frac{3}{4}$" × 3" × 15"	Batten stock (2)	$\frac{3}{8}$" × $1\frac{1}{4}$" × 24"
Stiles (2)	$\frac{3}{4}$" × 3" × $32\frac{1}{2}$"	Hinge stiles (2)	$\frac{3}{4}$" × 3" × $16\frac{1}{2}$"
Tenon stock	$\frac{3}{8}$" × $2\frac{1}{8}$" × 10"	Pull stock	$\frac{3}{4}$" × 1" × 12"
Panel	$\frac{3}{8}$" × $15\frac{11}{16}$" × $27\frac{3}{16}$"		
		Drawer	
Case		Front/back (2)	$\frac{5}{8}$" × $7\frac{7}{8}$" × 10"
Case sides (2)	$\frac{3}{4}$" × 21" × $32\frac{1}{2}$"	Sides (2)	$\frac{5}{8}$" × $7\frac{7}{8}$" × 16"
Sink shelf	$\frac{3}{4}$" × $20\frac{3}{4}$" × $29\frac{1}{4}$"	Bottom	$\frac{1}{4}$" × $9\frac{1}{4}$" × $15\frac{7}{8}$"
Bottom	$\frac{3}{4}$" × $19\frac{3}{4}$" × $29\frac{1}{4}$"	Face	$\frac{3}{4}$" × $9\frac{7}{8}$" × $12\frac{3}{8}$"
Back	$\frac{1}{4}$" × 30" × $32\frac{1}{2}$"		
Edging (2)	$\frac{1}{4}$" × $\frac{13}{16}$" × 35"	**Hardware**	
Drawer housing sides (2)	$\frac{3}{4}$" × 10" × $19\frac{3}{4}$"	16" Accuride drawer slides (1 pair). Available	
Drawer housing top	$\frac{3}{4}$" × $11\frac{3}{4}$" × $19\frac{3}{4}$"	from Outwater Hardware Corp.; part #3017	
Toekick	$\frac{3}{4}$" × $4\frac{1}{2}$" × $28\frac{1}{2}$"	Grass full-overlay hinges with winged base	
Cleats (2)	1" × 1" × $4\frac{1}{2}$"	plates (4). Available from Outwater	
Molding stock (3)	$1\frac{1}{2}$" × 2" × 33"	Hardware Corp.; part #1006 and #63204	
Countertop	$1\frac{1}{2}$" × $22\frac{1}{2}$" × 33"	2" drywall screws (as needed)	
		$1\frac{5}{8}$" drywall screws (as needed)	
Doors (2)		$1\frac{1}{4}$" drywall screws (as needed)	
Rails (2)	$\frac{3}{4}$" × $2\frac{1}{2}$" × $9\frac{1}{8}$"	$\frac{3}{4}$" brass wood screws (as needed)	
Stiles (2)	$\frac{3}{4}$" × $2\frac{1}{2}$" × $16\frac{1}{2}$"	1" wire brads (as needed)	
Tenon stock	$\frac{3}{8}$" × $1\frac{5}{8}$" × 10"	$\frac{1}{2}$" wire brads (as needed)	

TECH NOTES This ash vanity is similar to the other cabinets I build, but there are some important differences. Tongue-and-groove joinery is featured in the case, but the grooves are not cut at the top and bottom of the case sides, as is usual in my cabinets. Instead, the top is dropped down below the sink and becomes a sink shelf, and the bottom is moved up to make room for a toekick. I usually make my cabinets with a separate base or plinth, but moving the bottom up creates an integral base. Chapter 2 presents a thorough look at cutting the case joinery.

Just to make things interesting, I added a drawer next to the sink. The drawer housing is a separate, three-sided case joined with tongue-and-groove joints, then screwed to the sink shelf and case

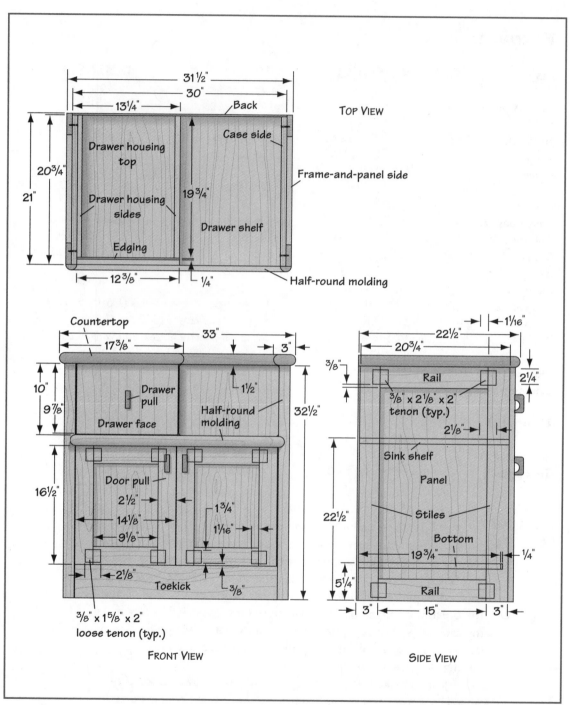

TOP VIEW

31½"

30"

13¼"

Back

Case side

Frame-and-panel side

Drawer housing top

20¾"

21"

19¾"

Drawer housing sides

Drawer shelf

Edging

12⅜"

¼"

Half-round molding

Countertop

33"

17⅜"

3"

10"

9⅞"

Drawer pull

1½"

Half-round molding

32½"

Drawer face

16½"

Door pull

2½"

14⅛"

9⅛"

1¾"

1¹⁄₁₆"

2⅛"

Toekick

⅜"

⅜" x 1⅝" x 2" loose tenon (typ.)

FRONT VIEW

22½"

20¾"

1¹⁄₁₆"

⅜"

Rail

2¼"

⅜" x 2⅛" x 2" tenon (typ.)

2⅛"

Sink shelf

Panel

Stiles

22½"

Bottom

19¾"

¼"

5¼"

Rail

3"

15"

3"

SIDE VIEW

VANITY

side. The drawer itself is dovetailed together. Chapters 8 and 9 have complete details on my methods of drawer making.

The frame-and-panel doors underneath are assembled with loose tenon joints. I cut these joints with the aid of my shop-built mortising jig. Plans for this jig are included in Chapter 5. The doors hang on European-style hinges, slick pieces of imported hardware that are fully adjustable.

The vanity is polished off with a 1½-inch-thick teak top with a sink cutout and finished side panels. I designed the cabinet to be built with either one or both sides finished. If one side of the cabinet will butt against a wall, substitute ¾-inch plywood for that side frame-and-panel assembly.

Before you even think about cutting a piece of wood, purchase the sink for your vanity. It's always better to be able to take measurements directly from a sink or other fixture rather than relying on drawings or other information. The sink shown is from an English company called Smallbone and is pretty pricey. You may want to shop around for an American-made substitute. The sink must have a finished front or apron, and should be close to the $14 \times 18 \times 10$-inch dimensions of the sink shown. On the other hand, you could install a normal drop-in sink—just cut a hole in the countertop and add a false drawer front in front of the sink.

CONSTRUCTION STEPS

Make the Frame-and-Panel Sides

1. Cut the rails, stiles, and panels to the dimensions specified in the Materials List. Use ⅜-inch plywood for the panels.

2. Lay out and cut the mortises in the stiles and rails, as shown in the *Vanity/Side View*. See "Building Frames" on page 36.

3. Cut tenons to fit the mortises. Apply glue and assemble the frames.

4. When the glue is dry, rout a ⅜-inch-deep × ⅜-inch-wide rabbet around the inside back of each side frame.

5. Glue the panels into the back of their frames and secure them with ½-inch wire brads toenailed into the frames.

Cut the Case Joinery and Assemble the Case

1. Cut the case sides, sink shelf, and bottom and the drawer housing sides and top to the sizes specified. Cut the grooves in the case sides and drawer housing sides, as shown in the *Case Joinery Detail*. Cut each groove with a dado blade on the table saw. See "Setting Up to Cut the Groove" on page 17.

2. Glue a piece of edging to the front edge of the case bottom and trim it even with a router and flush-trim bit.

3. Cut the ⅜-inch tongues on the bottom, sink shelf, and drawer housing top, as shown in the *Case Joinery Detail*. To keep the edging from splintering as the blade exits the case bottom, follow the edging through the blade with a piece of scrap. See "Setting Up to Cut the Tongue" on page 19.

4. Glue and clamp the drawer housing sides to the drawer housing top, as shown in the *Case Joinery Detail*. Glue edging to the front of the drawer housing assembly, as shown in the *Exploded View*. Trim the edging flush with a router and flush-trim bit.

5. Glue and screw the case sides to the frame-and-panel sides with 1¼-inch drywall screws, as shown in the *Case Joinery Detail*. The frames should overlap the plywood sides by ¼ inch along their back edges.

6. Assemble the case sides, sink shelf, and bottom by gluing and clamping the tongues into their grooves. The pieces should be flush along their back edges. This will leave a little bit of groove exposed on either side in front of the case bottom. Fill these grooves with a

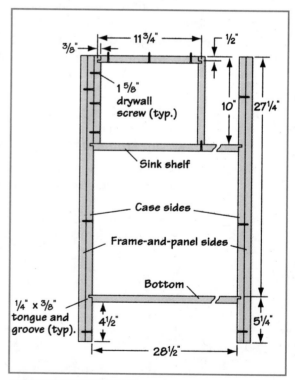

CASE JOINERY DETAIL

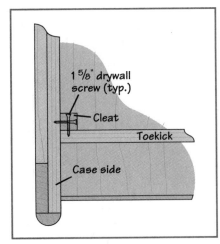

TOEKICK DETAIL

scrap of edging. While the patches will be visible, they'll be covered by the doors most of the time.

7. Lay the assembled case face down. Cut the back to fit between the frame-and-panel sides. Glue and nail the back in place with 1-inch wire brads as you square the cabinet. For more details, see "The Glue-Up" on page 24.

8. When the glue is dry, position the drawer housing on top of the sink shelf and attach it with 1⅝-inch drywall screws, as shown in the *Case Joinery Detail*. Make sure the opening remains square.

9. Finally, attach the toekick, as shown in the *Toekick Detail*. Screw the cleats to the toekick, then screw the toekick and cleat assembly to the case sides with 1⅝-inch drywall screws.

Make and Attach the Half-Round Molding

1. Round-over two corners of the molding stock with a ¾-inch-radius roundover bit in a table-mounted router.

2. When the corners have been rounded, rip the molding to its final thickness on the table saw.

3. Cut two pieces of half-round molding to the length of the case sides. Glue and clamp them in place, as shown in the *Exploded View*.

4. Cut the third piece of molding to fit on the front of the sink shelf. As shown in the *Vanity/Front View* and *Exploded View*, the sink shelf's molding should overlap the molding on the case sides halfway. The ends of the molding are then coped to fit over the ¾-inch-radius contour of the molding on the case sides. Carefully cope the ends of the drawer shelf molding on the band saw or with a coping saw, then glue it in place.

Cut Out and Attach the Countertop

1. Cut the countertop to match the shape shown in the *Countertop Top View.*

2. Round-over all except the back edges of the countertop with a ¾-inch-radius round-over bit in a table-mounted router. (If one side of the vanity fits against the wall, do not round that edge of the countertop; cut the edge flush with the cabinet side.)

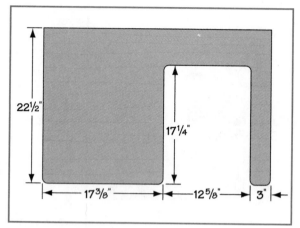

COUNTERTOP TOP VIEW

3. Position the countertop on top of the case. From underneath, drill and countersink holes up through the case side and through the top of the drawer housing, as shown in the *Case Joinery Detail* and the *Vanity/Side View.* The holes should be oversize. This will allow the screws to shift as the counter expands and contracts. The holes through the case side have to be drilled at an angle. Screw the counter in place with 1⅝-inch drywall screws.

Build the Doors

1. Cut the rails and stiles to the dimensions specified in the Materials List.

2. Lay out and cut the mortises in the door rails and stiles, as shown in the *Vanity/Front View* and *Door Assembly.* See "Building Frames" on page 36.

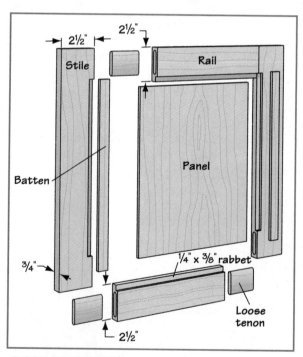

DOOR ASSEMBLY

3. Cut tenons to fit the mortises in the stiles and rails.

4. Glue and clamp the door frames together with the tenons in place.

5. Let the door frames dry overnight, then rout a ¼-inch-deep × ⅜-inch-wide panel rabbet around the back of each door frame. Square the rabbets at the inside corners of the frame with a sharp chisel.

6. Lay the door frames face down on the drill press and bore the hinge holes for European-style hinges, as described in "European-Style Hinges" on page 123.

7. Cut the panels and the batten stock to the dimensions specified in the Materials List. Drop the panels into the rabbets. Trim the battens down in length as you fit them around the frame. Butt the corners where the pieces come together. The battens should be centered on the gap between the panel and the frame, as shown in *Door-to-Case Assembly*. Screw the battens to the back of the doors with ¾-inch brass wood screws to hold the panels in place. See "Adding the Panel" on page 67.

Make the Drawer

1. Cut the drawer parts to the dimensions specified in the Materials List.

2. Rout the dovetails and pins in the drawer sides, back, and front. Position the parts in the jig to produce the layout shown in the *Drawer Details/Side View.* See "Dovetails" on page 97.

3. Cut ¼-inch-wide × ¼-inch-deep grooves in the drawer sides, drawer front, and drawer back for the bottom.

4.. Assemble the drawer sides, front, and back with glue. Trap the drawer bottom in its grooves as you assemble the parts.

5. Round-over the top edges of the drawer sides and drawer back with a ⁵⁄₁₆-inch-radius roundover bit. Round-over the inside top edge of the drawer front, but leave the drawer front square where it meets the drawer face. Turn the drawer upside down and round-over the outside bottom edges of the drawer sides and drawer back.

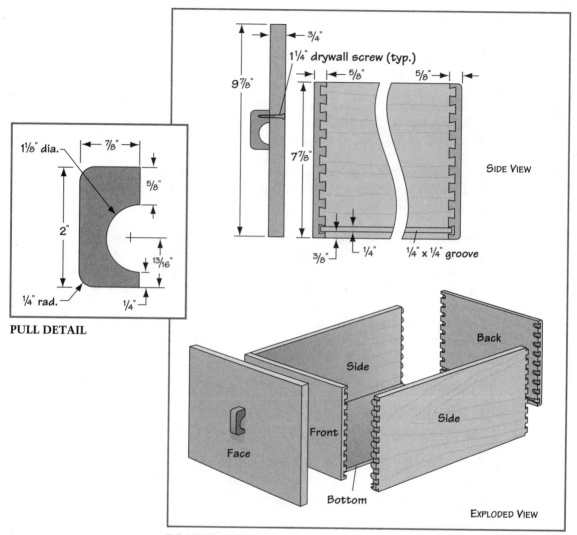

PULL DETAIL

DRAWER DETAILS

Install the Drawer and Attach the Face

1. Hang the drawer assembly in its box on full-extension drawer slides. See Chapter 10.

2. Cut the drawer and door pulls to the shape shown in the *Pull Detail*. Sand the pulls and screw one to the drawer face, as shown in the *Drawer Details/Side View*. Screw the other two pulls to the doors with 1¼-inch drywall screws.

3. Make sure the drawer slides are adjusted properly, then attach the drawer face to the drawer assembly with 1¼-inch drywall screws. Screw through the drawer front and into the drawer face.

Hang the Doors

1. Cut the hinge stiles to the size specified, then screw them to the case sides with 1¼-inch drywall screws, as shown in *Door-to-Case Assembly.*

2. Install the doors in their cabinets, as described in Chapter 11.

3. Finish the vanity with your favorite wood finish according to the manufacturer's instructions. Be aware that teak can be difficult to finish due to its oily nature. I used an oil finish that was specifically formulated for teak.

4. Set the vanity in place and screw it to the studs in the wall with 2-inch drywall screws.

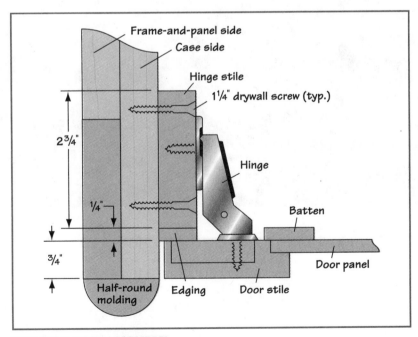

DOOR-TO-CASE ASSEMBLY

CHERRY VANITY WITH BEADED-INSET DOORS

T he ideas for the cabinets I build come from many different places. This vanity took form when Hilary, one of my best customers, showed me a magazine clipping of a vanity she liked. The style was very similar to a kitchen I had built for her, but the addition of a baseboard-type molding and reeded columns gave it a much more formal look. I adapted the magazine photo's face design—and my basic case design—and built the vanity you see here. This one was made to fit in Hilary's bathroom; chances are you'll have to do some redesigning and resizing before you can park it in yours.

When it came to making the reeding for the columns, I found I wasn't getting the results I wanted with the cutter I had. Instead of tightly defined reeds, I wound up with half-circle sections with little flats in between. To get reeding that was continuous, I cut and shaped individual ⅜-inch-thick cherry slats and glued them together side by side.

The vanity in the photo has an added detail that I didn't include in the plans—a pull-out bathroom scale drawer. It's just one example of a way to add a special touch to custom woodwork.

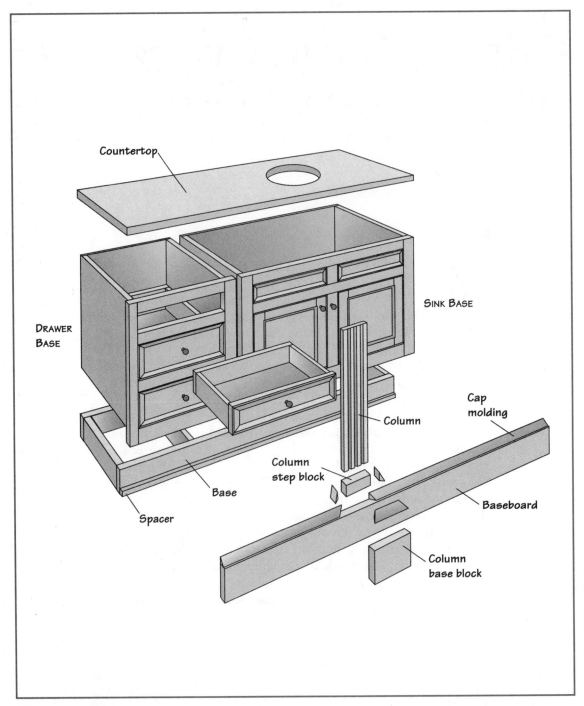

Countertop

Sink Base

Drawer Base

Column

Cap molding

Column step block

Base

Baseboard

Spacer

Column base block

EXPLODED VIEW

MATERIALS LIST

PART	DIMENSION	PART	DIMENSION
Drawer Bases (2)		Upper drawer sides (4)	$5/8" \times 3\frac{1}{2}" \times 18"$
Top	$3/4" \times 19\frac{1}{2}" \times 20\frac{1}{4}"$	Lower drawer faces (4)	$3/4" \times 18\frac{7}{8}" \times 7\frac{1}{4}"$
Bottom	$3/4" \times 19\frac{1}{2}"^* \times 20\frac{1}{4}"$	Lower drawer	
Edging	$1/4" \times {}^{13}/_{16}" \times 21"$	fronts/backs (8)	$5/8" \times 5\frac{1}{4}" \times 18\frac{1}{2}"$
Sides (2)	$3/4" \times 20\frac{1}{8}" \times 26\frac{1}{8}"$	Lower drawer sides (8)	$5/8" \times 5\frac{1}{4}" \times 18"$
Back	$1/4" \times 21" \times 26\frac{1}{8}"$	Drawer bottoms (6)	$1/4" \times 17\frac{3}{4}" \times 17\frac{7}{8}"$
Frame rails (3)	$1" \times 1\frac{1}{2}" \times 20\frac{1}{8}"$	Drawer face	
Bottom frame rail	$1" \times 2\frac{1}{2}" \times 20\frac{1}{8}"$	molding stock (11)	$3/4" \times 3{}^{1}/_{16}" \times 20"$
Frame stile	$1" \times 1\frac{1}{2}" \times 28\frac{1}{2}"$	**Trim**	
Wide stile	$1" \times 2\frac{1}{2}" \times 28\frac{1}{2}"$	Column backing (2)	$3/8" \times 3" \times 26\frac{1}{4}"$
Tenon stock	$3/8" \times 7/8" \times 18"$	Column bead stock (4)	$3/4" \times 3" \times 26\frac{1}{4}"$
Bead stock (8)	$5/16" \times 1" \times 24"$	Long base rails (2)	$3/4" \times 6\frac{3}{8}" \times 94"$
Sink Base		Crosspieces (6)	$3/4" \times 6\frac{3}{8}" \times 16\frac{1}{2}"$
Top	$3/4" \times 19\frac{1}{2}" \times 42\frac{3}{4}"$	Spacer	$1" \times 1\frac{1}{4}" \times 94"$
Bottom	$3/4" \times 19\frac{1}{2}"^* \times 42\frac{3}{4}"$	Cleats (10)	$3/4" \times 3/4" \times 17\frac{1}{8}"$
Edging	$1/4" \times {}^{13}/_{16}" \times 44"$	Baseboard	$3/4" \times 5" \times 94"$
Sides (2)	$3/4" \times 20\frac{1}{8}" \times 26\frac{1}{8}"$	Column step blocks (2)	$3/4" \times 3" \times 1\frac{1}{4}"$
Back	$1/4" \times 43\frac{1}{2}" \times 26\frac{1}{8}"$	Column base blocks (2)	$3/4" \times 5" \times 5"$
Top frame rails (2)	$1" \times 1\frac{1}{2}" \times 39"$	Cap molding stock (2)	$3/4" \times 3" \times 50"$
Bottom frame rail	$1" \times 2\frac{1}{2}" \times 39"$	Countertop	$1\frac{1}{2}" \times 21" \times 94"$
Frame stiles (2)	$1" \times 2\frac{1}{2}" \times 28\frac{1}{2}"$		
Short mid frame stile	$1" \times 1\frac{1}{2}" \times 4\frac{1}{2}"$	**Hardware**	
Long mid frame stile	$1" \times 1\frac{1}{2}" \times 18\frac{1}{2}"$	18" Accuride drawer slides (12). Available from	
Tenon stock	$3/8" \times 7/8" \times 24"$	Outwater Hardware Corp.; part #3017	
Bead stock (13)	$5/16" \times 1" \times 20"$	Solid brass cabinet hinges (4). Available from	
False drawer faces (2)	$3/4" \times 17\frac{1}{2}" \times 3\frac{1}{4}"$	Constantine's; part #VH2420	
False drawer backing	$1/4" \times 5\frac{7}{8}" \times 39"$	Oval brass pulls (8). Available from Cliffside	
False drawer cleats (2)	$9/16" \times 1" \times 39"$	Industries; part #101PB	
Doors		$1\frac{5}{8}"$ drywall screws (as needed)	
Stiles (4)	$1" \times 2\frac{1}{4}" \times 17\frac{3}{4}"$	$1\frac{1}{4}"$ drywall screws (as needed)	
Rails (4)	$1" \times 2\frac{1}{4}" \times 13\frac{1}{2}"$	1" drywall screws (as needed)	
Panels (2)	$1/4" \times 14{}^{1}/_{16}" \times 13\frac{7}{8}"$	$3/4"$ drywall screws (as needed)	
Panel retaining		1" wire brads (as needed)	
molding stock(4)	$3/4" \times 3{}^{1}/_{16}" \times 15"$	$3/4"$ wire brads (as needed)	
Tenon stock	$3/8" \times 1\frac{3}{8}" \times 10"$	4d finish nails (as needed)	
Drawers		2d finish nails (as needed)	
Upper drawer faces (2)	$3/4" \times 18\frac{7}{8}" \times 3\frac{1}{4}"$	$3/8"$ wood plugs (as needed)	
Upper drawer			
fronts/backs (4)	$5/8" \times 3\frac{1}{2}" \times 18\frac{1}{2}"$		

*Includes $1/4"$ edging.

TECH NOTES The vanity shown in the photo is made up of three individual cabinets: a central sink base and two drawer bases. These cabinets include basic cases with face frames, frame-and-panel doors with inset molding, and plywood drawer faces with mitered edge moldings. The door frames and face frames are tenoned and the drawers are assembled with machine-cut dovetails. The door panels are set in a rabbet in the front edges of the door frame, then a decorative molding is set in the rabbet to hold the panel in place. For more in-depth information on building these components, see Chapters 2, 6, and 8. The cabinets are installed on a base rail system, as discussed in Chapter 14. Top off the vanity cabinets with a waterproof countertop such as stone or one of the available plastic counter products. See Chapter 13 for several options. Beaded columns divide the cabinets visually, and several pieces of baseboard molding connect the cabinets to the floor.

CONSTRUCTION STEPS

Build the Cases

1. Cut the bottoms for the three cases ¼ inch or so larger in length and width than listed in the Materials List. Glue edging to their front edges, as described in "Attaching the Edging" on page 32. Then cut the bottoms, tops, and sides for all three cases to the sizes specified.

2. Cut grooves in the sides for the tops and bottoms, as shown in *Drawer Base/Joinery Detail*. Cut matching tongues on the tops and bottoms. See "Cutting the Joint" on page 16. Also cut tongues in the front edges of the sides to fit into the frames, as shown in the *Sink Base/Top View* and *Drawer Base/Top View*.

3. Attach the sides to the tops and bottoms with glue and 1⅝-inch drywall screws.

4. Lay the assembled cases face down. Cut the backs to size and attach them as you square up the cabinets, as discussed in "The Glue-Up" on page 24.

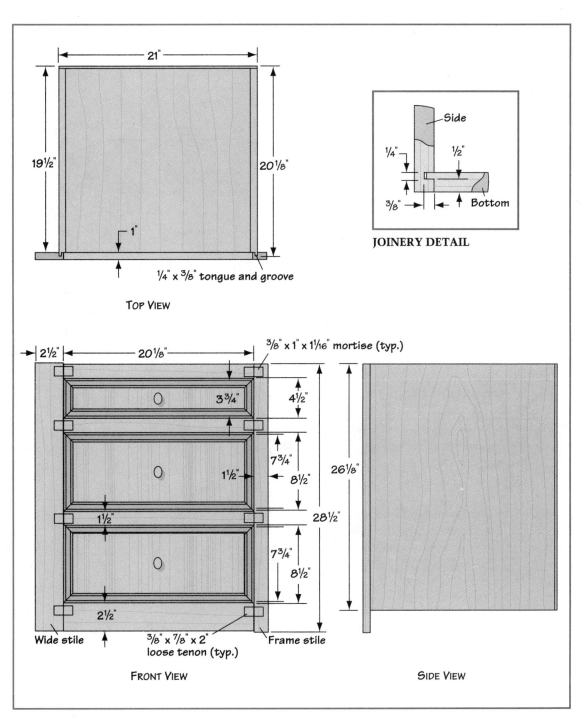

TOP VIEW

21"

19½"

20⅛"

1"

¼" x ⅜" tongue and groove

JOINERY DETAIL

Side

¼"

½"

⅜"

Bottom

FRONT VIEW

2½"

20⅛"

⅜" x 1" x 1¹⁄₁₆" mortise (typ.)

3¾"

4½"

7¾"

8½"

1½"

26⅛"

1½"

28½"

2½"

7¾"

8½"

Wide stile

⅜" x ⅞" x 2"
loose tenon (typ.)

Frame stile

SIDE VIEW

DRAWER BASE

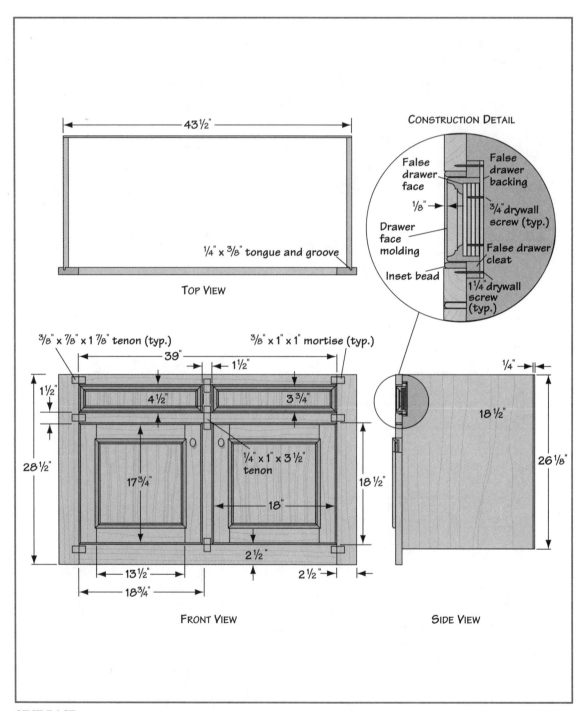

TOP VIEW

43½"

¼" x ⅜" tongue and groove

CONSTRUCTION DETAIL

False drawer face

⅛"

Drawer face molding

Inset bead

False drawer backing

¾" drywall screw (typ.)

False drawer cleat

1¼" drywall screw (typ.)

FRONT VIEW

⅜" x ⅞" x 1⅞" tenon (typ.)

⅜" x 1" x 1" mortise (typ.)

39"

1½"

1½"

4½"

3¾"

28½"

17¾"

¼" x 1" x 3½" tenon

18"

18½"

2½"

13½"

2½"

18¾"

SIDE VIEW

¼"

18½"

26⅛"

SINK BASE

Make the Face Frames and Beads

1. Cut the rails and stiles to the sizes specified in the Materials List.

2. Join the frame pieces with loose tenon joints, as shown on the *Sink Base/Front View* and *Drawer Base/Front View*. See "Cutting the Mortises" on page 36 and "Cutting the Tenons" on page 37.

3. Glue and clamp the frames together. On the sink base face frame, join the mid stiles to the rails first, then add the outer stiles.

4. While the glue is drying, cut the bead pieces to the sizes specified. Round their front edges with a ¼-inch beading cutter in a table-mounted router.

5. Miter the bead to fit inside the drawer and door openings, as shown in the *Sink Base/Front View* and *Drawer Base/Front View*. Fasten the bead in place with glue and 1-inch wire brads.

6. Groove the back of the face frame stiles to match the tongue on the sides, as shown in the *Drawer Base/Top View* and *Sink Base/Top View*. Cut each groove in two passes with the table saw blade. Do not attach the frames to the cabinet yet.

DOOR JOINERY DETAIL

Make and Hang the Doors

1. Cut the door rails, stiles, and panels to the sizes specified in the Materials List.

2. Join the frame parts with loose tenon joints, as shown in the *Door Joinery Detail*. See "Cutting the Mortises" on page 36.

3. Glue the door frames together and leave them clamped up overnight.

4. Rabbet the inside front edges of each door frame for the panel and molding with a router and

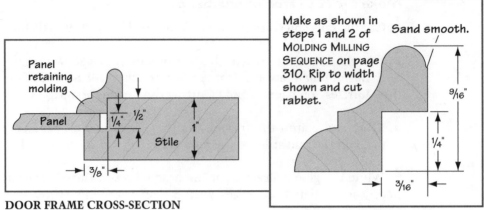

DOOR FRAME CROSS-SECTION

RETAINING MOLDING PROFILE

rabbeting bit, as shown in the *Door Frame Cross-Section.* Square the rounded corners with a chisel.

5. Rout the panel retaining molding stock to the shape and dimensions shown in the *Retaining Molding Profile.*

6. Miter the molding to fit inside each door frame.

7. Check the fit of each panel in its particular door frame. Each panel should have about ³⁄₁₆ inch play overall from side to side and ¹⁄₁₆ inch or so up and down. The extra space on the sides will give the panels room to expand, the extra space at the top and bottom just makes the panel easier to fit. Trim the panels, if necessary, then drop them into the rabbet and slip the molding in place. Attach the molding to the door frames with 1-inch wire brads. Set the brads with a small nail set and fill the holes with putty.

8. Hang the doors within the frames, as explained in "Ball-Tip Hinges" on page 128. I've developed a jig just for this purpose. You'll find plans for it in "A Hinge Mortising Jig" on page 130. Attach the face frame to the cabinets.

Make the Drawers

1. Cut the drawer fronts, backs, and sides to the dimensions specified in the Materials List.

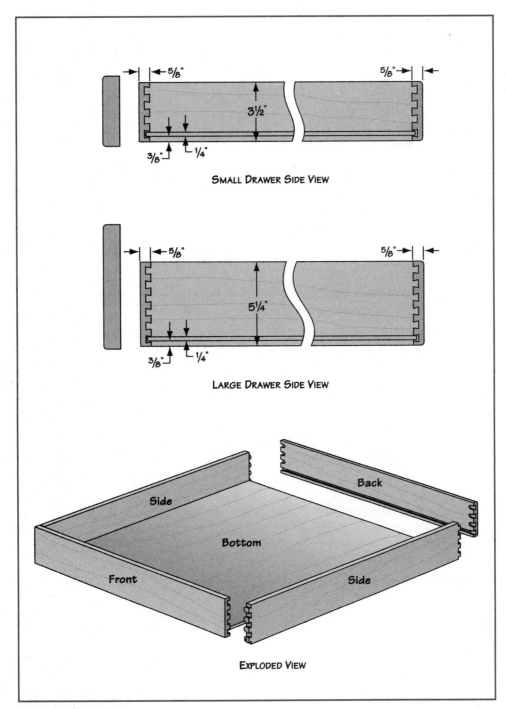

SMALL DRAWER SIDE VIEW

LARGE DRAWER SIDE VIEW

EXPLODED VIEW

DRAWER DETAILS

2. Join the pieces with dovetails, as shown in the *Drawer Details.* See "Dovetails" on page 97 for further details.

3. Cut ¼-inch-deep grooves for the drawer bottom in the sides, fronts, and backs, as shown. Cut the groove in two passes on the table saw.

4. Assemble the drawer sides, fronts, and backs with glue. Trap the bottoms in their grooves as you assemble the parts.

5. Round-over the top edges of the drawer sides and backs with a ⁵⁄₁₆-inch-radius roundover bit. Also, round-over the inside top edge of the drawer front, but leave the drawer front square where it meets the drawer face. When the top edges have been rounded-over, turn the drawer upside down and round-over the outside bottom edges of the drawer sides and back.

6. Hang the drawer assemblies in their cases on full-extension drawer slides. See Chapter 10.

Make the Drawer Faces

1. Cut the drawer faces and false drawer faces from ¾-inch-thick cherry plywood. Make sure that the grain on the drawer faces runs vertically to match the direction of grain on the door panels.

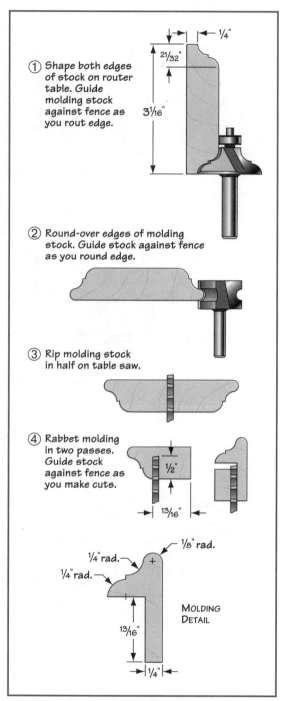

① Shape both edges of stock on router table. Guide molding stock against fence as you rout edge.

② Round-over edges of molding stock. Guide stock against fence as you round edge.

③ Rip molding stock in half on table saw.

④ Rabbet molding in two passes. Guide stock against fence as you make cuts.

MOLDING DETAIL

MOLDING MILLING SEQUENCE

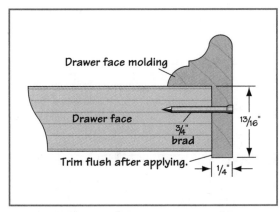

DRAWER FACE/MOLDING CROSS-SECTION

2. Prepare the drawer face molding, as shown in the *Molding Milling Sequence.*

3. Miter the molding to fit around the inside of the drawer and false drawer faces, as shown in the *Drawer Base/Front View* and *Sink Base/Front View.*

4. Attach the drawer face molding with glue and ¾-inch wire brads, as shown in the *Drawer Face/Molding Cross-Section.*

5. Attach the drawer faces to the drawer fronts with double-faced carpet tape. Center the faces in their openings.

6. Screw the drawer faces in place with 1-inch drywall screws.

7. Screw the false drawer backing to the false drawer face with ¾-inch drywall screws, as shown in the *Sink Base/Construction Detail.* Screw this assembly to the inside of the face frame with the cleats between, using 1¼-inch drywall screws. Make sure the faces are centered within their frame openings.

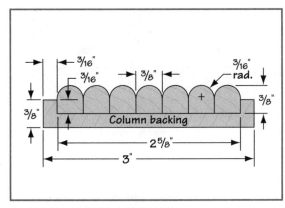

COLUMN ASSEMBLY DETAIL

Make the Beaded Columns

1. Cut the column backing stock and the column bead stock to the sizes specified in the Materials List.

2. Cut a wide groove down the middle of the column backing with a dado blade in the table saw. Size the groove as shown in the *Column Assembly Detail.*

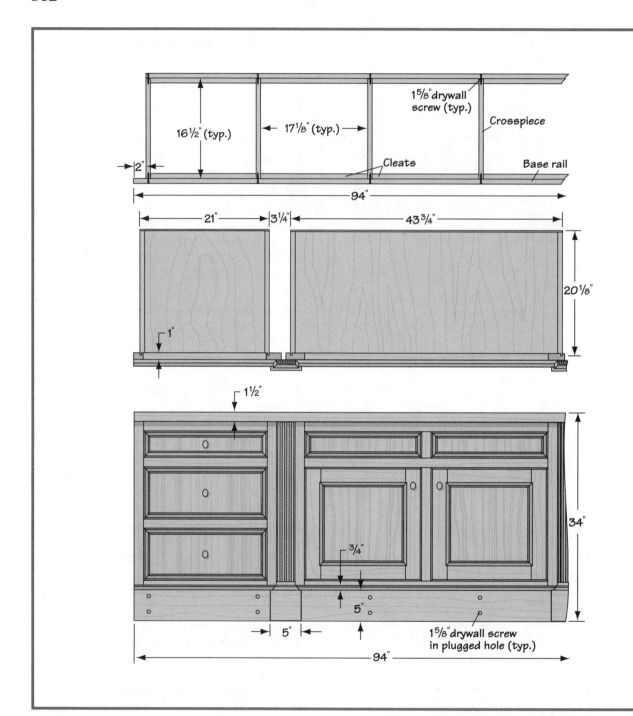

1⁵⁄₈" drywall screw (typ.)

Crosspiece

16½" (typ.)

17⅛" (typ.)

Cleats

Base rail

2"

94"

21"

3¼"

43¾"

20⅛"

1"

1½"

¾"

5"

34"

5"

1⁵⁄₈" drywall screw in plugged hole (typ.)

94"

OVERALL ASSEMBLY

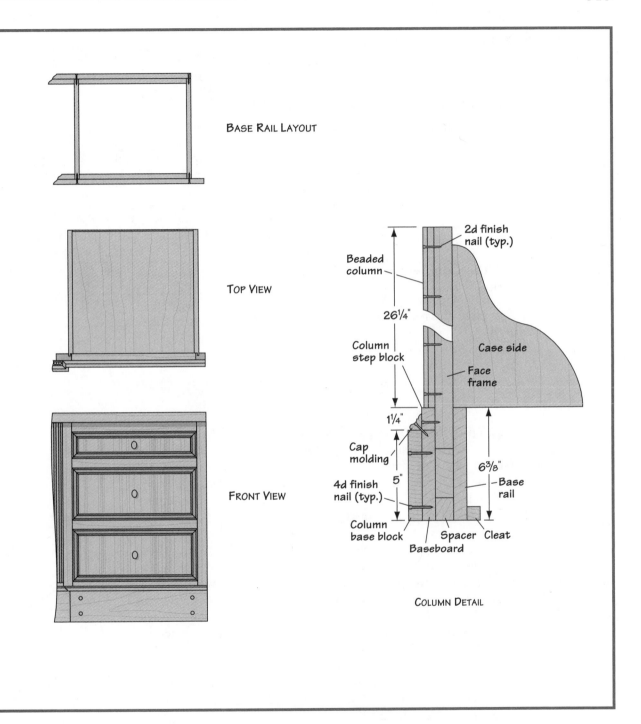

BASE RAIL LAYOUT

TOP VIEW

FRONT VIEW

Column Detail

- 2d finish nail (typ.)
- Beaded column
- 26¼"
- Column step block
- 1¼"
- Cap molding
- 5"
- 4d finish nail (typ.)
- Column base block
- Baseboard
- Spacer
- Cleat
- Case side
- Face frame
- 6³⁄₈"
- Base rail

CHERRY VANITY

3. Next, cut the individual beads from the bead stock, as shown in the *Bead Milling Sequence.* After the beads are separated from the column bead stock, rip them to their final ⅜-inch width.

4. Finally, glue and clamp seven beads side by side within the groove in the column backing, as shown in the *Column Assembly Detail.*

Install the Cabinets and Add the Trim

1. Assemble the base rails, as shown in the *Overall Assembly/Base Rail Layout,* with 1⅝-inch drywall screws. Install the base, crosspieces, and cleats, following the guidelines in Chapter 14.

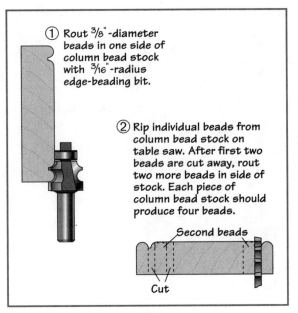

① Rout ⅜"-diameter beads in one side of column bead stock with ³⁄₁₆"-radius edge-beading bit.

② Rip individual beads from column bead stock on table saw. After first two beads are cut away, rout two more beads in side of stock. Each piece of column bead stock should produce four beads.

Second beads

Cut

BEAD MILLING SEQUENCE

2. Position the sink base and drawer bases on top of the base, as shown in *Overall Assembly/Front View.* Scribe the outside edges of the drawer base frames to follow the contour of the wall. Attach the three case assemblies to the base rail assembly by driving 1⅝-inch drywall screws through the bottoms of the drawer base cabinets into the base rails.

3. Cut the spacer, baseboard, column step blocks, column base blocks, and cap molding stock to the sizes indicated. Screw the spacer to the front of the base with 1⅝-inch drywall screws. Attach the baseboard to the front of the cases, as shown in *Overall Assembly/Front View,* with 1⅝-inch drywall screws. Countersink the screw holes and plug them when the screws are in place.

4. Center the beaded columns and column step blocks over the gaps between the cases. Secure them with 2d and 4d finish nails, as shown in *Overall Assembly/Column Detail.*

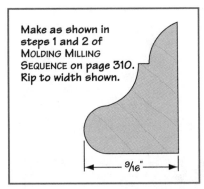

Make as shown in steps 1 and 2 of MOLDING MILLING SEQUENCE on page 310. Rip to width shown.

9/16"

BASE CAP MOLDING PROFILE

5. When the columns are in place, nail the column base blocks below each column step block with 4d finish nails, as shown in *Overall Assembly/Column Detail.*

6. Finally, cut the cap molding stock to the shape shown in *Base Cap Molding Profile* and nail it in place above the baseboard. Miter the molding to fit around the column step blocks, as shown in *Overall Assembly/Top View.*

7. Finish your vanity with your favorite wood finish according to the manufacturer's instructions. The vanity pictured is finished with several coats of Watco Danish oil.

Add a Countertop

I topped off my vanity with a plastic (Corian) top, which has the sinks molded right in place. Choose the waterproof countertop material that will best meet your needs, budget, and decor. For more information on countertops, see Chapter 13.

FRAME-AND-PANEL ASH KITCHEN

W hen I visited my client Geri prior to doing her kitchen, I noticed a downed ash tree in the backyard. So, when she selected the kitchen design and cabinet style you see here, I mentioned that we could help the tree live on. I took her tree and had it sawed into usable planks that I used for these doors. Geri not only loves her new kitchen but is happy that she didn't have to entirely lose her favorite ash tree after all.

This design makes use of some fairly traditional elements: raised-panel doors and fine brass hardware. The finish and construction techniques I used, however, are more in keeping with the contemporary home: full-overlay doors and drawers in limed ash. The combination works to create a kitchen of timeless style.

As with most of the built-in projects in this book, you will need to adjust the sizes of the cabinets to fit your space. I've presented two basic cabinets here, but there is no reason to stop with only these two designs. You can mix the components to make any type of cabinet you need or want.

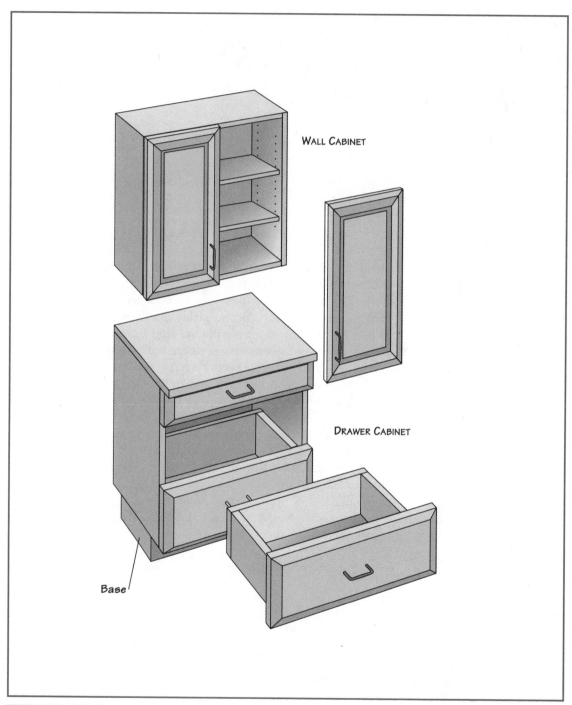

WALL CABINET

DRAWER CABINET

Base

EXPLODED VIEW

MATERIALS LIST

PART	DIMENSION	PART	DIMENSION
Wall Cabinet		**Installation**	
Sides (2)	¾" × 11½" × 30"	Base rail stock	¾" × 3½" × (as needed)
Top/bottom (2)	¾" × 11½" × 31½"	Crosspieces	¾" × 3½" × 17½"
Back	¼" × 32¼" × 30"	Cleats	¾" × ¾" × (as needed)
Edging stock (6)	¼" × ¹³⁄₁₆" × 36"	Facing	¼" × 3¼" × (as needed)
Shelves (2)	¾" × 11¼" × 30⅝"	Screw rail	¾" × 1¼" × (as needed)
Door stiles (4)	1" × 2½" × 29⅞"	Ledger	¾" × 1¾" × (as needed)
Door rails (4)	1" × 2½" × 16"	Countertop	1½" × 25½" × (as needed)
Tenon stock	⅜" × 1⅛" × 15"		
Door panels (2)	¾" × 11⁹⁄₁₆" × 25½"		

Hardware

Grass full-overlay hinges with winged base plates (4). Available from Outwater Hardware Corp.; part #1006 and #63204

Drawer Cabinet

PART	DIMENSION
Sides (2)	¾" × 23½" × 30"
Top/bottom (2)	¾" × 23½" × 28¼"
Back	¼" × 29" × 30"
Edging stock (4)	¼" × ⅞" × 31"
Small drawer stiles (2)	1" × 1½" × 5⅞"
Small drawer rails (2)	1" × 1½" × 28⅞"
Small drawer panel	¾" × 3⁷⁄₁₆" × 26½"
Large drawer stiles (4)	1" × 1½" × 11⅞"
Large drawer rails (4)	1" × 1½" × 28⅞"
Large drawer panels (2)	¾" × 9⅝" × 26⅜"
Tenon stock	⅜" × 1⅛" × 1⅝"
Small drawer sides (2)	⅝" × 3½" × 20"
Small drawer front/back (2)	⅝" × 3⅜" × 26½"
Large drawer sides (4)	⅝" × 7⅞" × 20"
Large drawer front/back (2)	⅝" × 7⅞" × 26⁹⁄₁₆"
Drawer bottoms (3)	¼" × 25¾" × 19⅞"

20" Accuride full-extension drawer slides (3 pair). Available from Outwater Hardware Corp.; part #3017

5mm pin-style shelf supports (8). Available from Outwater Hardware Corp.; part #3002

Pulls (5). Available from The Woodworkers' Store; part #26690

2½" drywall screws (as needed)
1⅝" drywall screws (as needed)
1¼" drywall screws (as needed)
1" drywall screws (as needed)
1" wire brads (as needed)
¾" wire brads (as needed)
4d finish nails (as needed)

TECH NOTES These two sample cabinets include basic cases and mitered frame-and-panel doors and drawer faces. The mitered frames are tenoned and the drawers are assembled with machine-cut dovetails. For more in-depth information on building these components, see Chapter 2, "An Alternate Door Frame" on page 72; and Chapter 8. The wall cabinets are attached to the wall and the base cabinets are installed on a base rail system, as discussed in Chapter 14.

CONSTRUCTION STEPS

Build the Cases

1. Cut the tops, bottoms, and sides for the wall cabinets and base cabinets to the dimensions specified in the Materials List.

2. Cut grooves in the case sides for the tops and bottoms, as shown in the *Wall Cabinet/Joinery Detail* and the *Drawer Cabinet/Joinery Detail.* Cut tongues on the case tops and bottoms to fit the grooves. See "Cutting the Joint" on page 16.

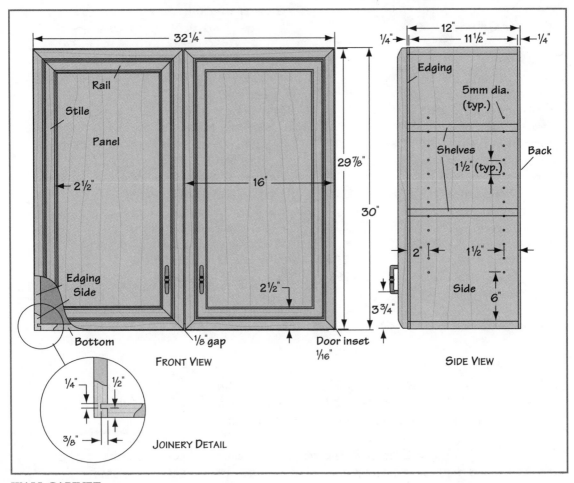

WALL CABINET

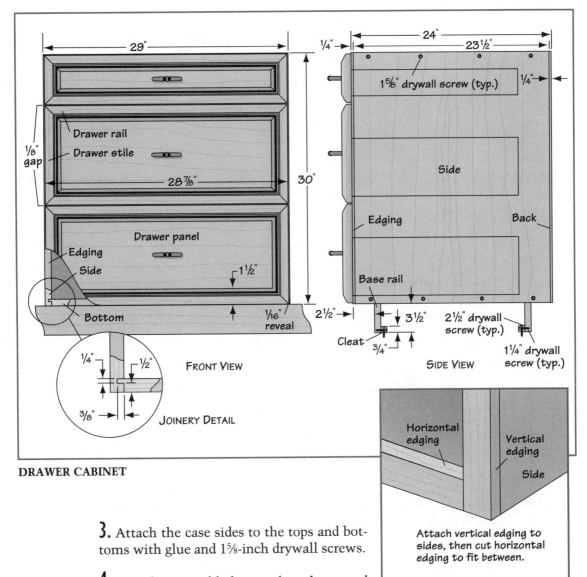

DRAWER CABINET

Labels within the diagram:

29"

Drawer rail
Drawer stile
1/8" gap
28 7/8"
Drawer panel
Edging
Side
Bottom
1 1/2"
1/16" reveal

FRONT VIEW

1/4"
1/2"
3/8"

JOINERY DETAIL

30"

1/4"
24"
23 1/2"
1 5/8" drywall screw (typ.)
1/4"
Side
Edging
Back
Base rail
2 1/2"
3 1/2"
2 1/2" drywall screw (typ.)
Cleat
3/4"
1 1/4" drywall screw (typ.)

SIDE VIEW

Horizontal edging
Vertical edging
Side

Attach vertical edging to sides, then cut horizontal edging to fit between.

EDGING DETAIL

3. Attach the case sides to the tops and bottoms with glue and 1⅝-inch drywall screws.

4. Lay the assembled cases face down and attach the backs with glue and 1-inch wire brads. If necessary, use the backs to square the cabinets, as discussed in "The Glue-Up" on page 24.

5. Apply the edging, as shown in the *Edging Detail*, and as described in "Attaching the Edging" on page 32. At the same time, apply edging to the front edge of the shelves.

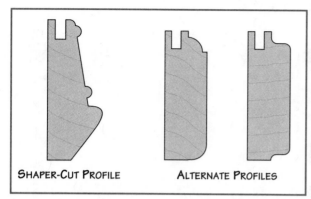

DOOR FRAME PROFILES

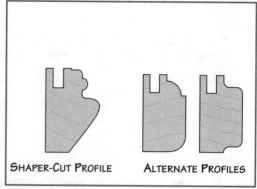

DRAWER FRAME PROFILES

6. Drill 5mm-diameter adjustable shelf holes in the wall case sides, as shown in *Wall Cabinet/Side View*.

Make the Door Frames and Drawer Faces

1. Make the doors and drawer faces at the same time. Cut the stock for both moldings to the proper thickness and width, then cut the molded profiles along their lengths.

I cut profiles in the door and drawer frame stock with custom-ground shaper cutters. If you own a shaper, you may choose to have cutters ground to my original profiles, shown in *Door Frame Profiles* and *Drawer Frame Profiles*, or you can make up your own. I have also presented a few alternate profiles that can be cut on a router table or with a table saw. Choose the profiles you like best and mill the door frame stock and drawer frame stock.

1. Cut the panel grooves in the moldings, as shown in the *Construction Details*. Make the slots in two passes on the table saw with a standard blade.

2. Miter the rails and stiles as you cut them to the lengths specified in the Materials List.

3. Join the frames at their corners with loose tenon joints, as shown in the *Construction Details*. See "An Alternate Door Frame" on page 72.

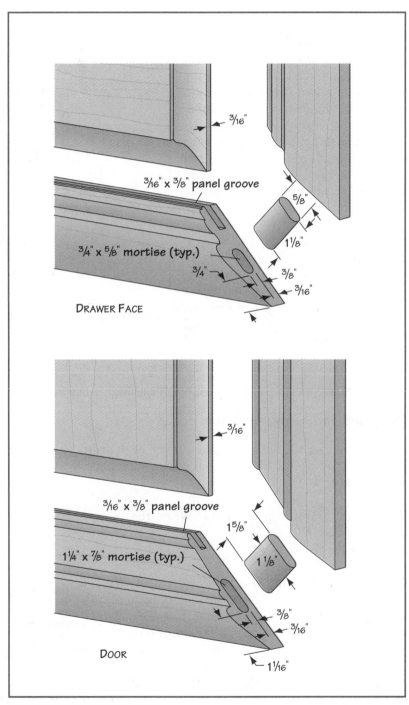

3/16"

3/16" x 3/8" panel groove

5/8"

1 1/8"

3/4" x 5/8" mortise (typ.)

3/4"

3/8"

3/16"

DRAWER FACE

3/16"

3/16" x 3/8" panel groove

1 5/8"

1 1/8"

1 1/4" x 7/8" mortise (typ.)

3/8"

3/16"

DOOR

1 1/16"

CONSTRUCTION DETAILS

Raise the Panels

1. I raised the panels for these doors and drawers with a shaper, but you can nearly duplicate the profile using a three-step router method, shown in *Raised Panel Routing Sequence*. First, rout a ⅜-inch-wide rabbet all around the fronts of the panels with a straight bit in a table-mounted router. The resulting tongues should just slip into the grooves cut in the frame members.

2. Rout a ⅜-inch-radius cove into the edge of the rabbet with a ¾-inch-diameter roundnose bit in a table-mounted router. To avoid stressing the bit, rout the cove in two passes, as shown. The second cut should just meet the bottom of the rabbet.

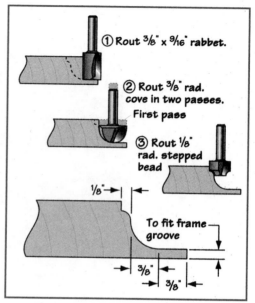

① Rout ⅜" x ⁹⁄₁₆" rabbet.

② Rout ⅜" rad. cove in two passes. First pass

③ Rout ⅛" rad. stepped bead

⅛"

To fit frame groove

⅜"

⅜"

RAISED PANEL ROUTING SEQUENCE

3. Rout the stepped bead, as shown, with a plunging bead bit.

Assemble and Hang the Doors

1. Test assemble the doors to make sure all of the parts fit together correctly. The panels should be slightly undersized to give them room to expand.

2. Glue the frames up in halves. When the glue has dried, glue the halves together with the panels in place.

3. Pin the panels from the back of the door, one pin centered from side to side in each rail, as shown in *Door Cross-Section*. The pins keep the panels from rattling around in the panel groove. Drill ⅛-inch-diameter holes for the pins, tap them in place, and cut and sand them flush with the back of the rails.

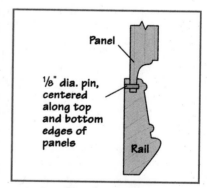

Panel

⅛" dia. pin, centered along top and bottom edges of panels

Rail

DOOR CROSS-SECTION

4. Lay the doors face down on the drill press and bore hinge holes for European-style hinges, as described in "European-Style Hinges" on page 123.

5. Drill pilot holes for the door pulls. If the door frame profile you have chosen is not flat, create a flat area for the base of the pull to sit on with a Forstner bit. Choose a bit that will match the diameter of your pull's base. Bolt the pulls in place and hang the doors on the cabinets.

Make the Drawers

1. Cut the drawer parts to the dimensions specified in the Materials List.

2. Rout the dovetails and pins in the drawer sides, backs, and fronts. Position the parts in the jig to produce the layout shown in the *Drawer Details*. See "Dovetails" on page 97.

3. Cut the bottom grooves in the drawer sides, fronts, and backs, as shown. Cut the ¼-inch-wide × ¼-inch-deep grooves in two passes on the table saw.

4. Assemble the drawer sides, fronts, and backs with glue. Trap the drawer bottoms in their grooves as you assemble the parts.

5. Round-over the top edges of the drawer sides and backs with a ⁵⁄₁₆-inch-radius roundover bit. Also, round-over the inside top edge of the drawer front, but leave the drawer front square where it meets the drawer face. When the top edges have been rounded-over, turn the drawer upside down and round-over the outside bottom edges of the drawer sides and back.

6. Hang the drawer assemblies in their cases on full-extension drawer slides. See Chapter 10.

7. Make sure the drawer slides are adjusted properly, then attach the frame-and-panel drawer faces to each drawer assembly with double-faced carpet tape. When you are satisfied with the positioning, screw through the drawer fronts at the corners and into the drawer face frame with 1-inch drywall screws.

8. Install the drawer pulls. Drill through the drawer face panel and drawer front, then pass machine screws through the holes from the inside of the drawer to secure the pulls.

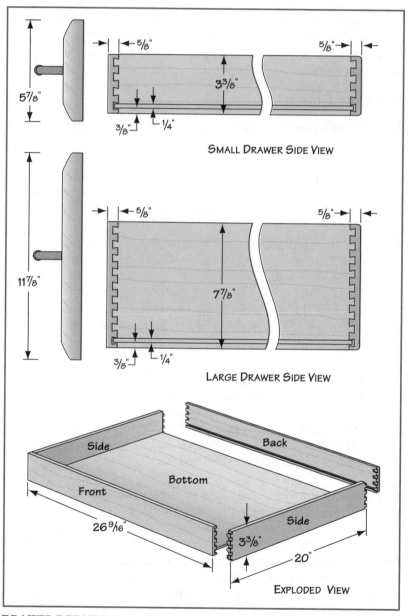

SMALL DRAWER SIDE VIEW

LARGE DRAWER SIDE VIEW

EXPLODED VIEW

DRAWER DETAILS

9. Finish the cabinets. The kitchen shown is finished with a white pickling stain and a sprayed lacquer top coat.

Installation

1. Cut the rails, crosspieces, cleats, facings, ledgers, and screw rails to the sizes specified in the Materials List. The lengths of everything but the crosspieces will depend on the layout of your kitchen. Finish the facing strip to match the rest of the kitchen.

2. Attach the rails to the crosspieces with $1\frac{5}{8}$-inch drywall screws. Attach the cleats to the rails with $1\frac{1}{4}$-inch drywall screws.

3. On site, set the base in place and level it with shims. Screw the base to the floor with $2\frac{1}{2}$-inch drywall screws driven through the cleats.

4. Set the base cabinets in place and screw them together with $1\frac{1}{4}$-inch drywall screws. Then screw everything to the base with $1\frac{5}{8}$-inch drywall screws.

5. Install the counter on top of the cabinets. Chapter 13 has detailed information about different types of counters and how to make and install them.

6. Screw the wall cabinets together with $1\frac{1}{4}$-inch drywall screws. Then screw the screw rail in place on top of them with $1\frac{5}{8}$-inch drywall screws. Three screws per case should do the trick.

7. Strike a level line on the wall to indicate the tops of the wall cabinets. Locate the studs in the wall. Hold the wall cabinets in place and screw them to the wall with $2\frac{1}{2}$-inch drywall screws driven through the the screw rail. Three or four screws are enough to hold things for now.

8. Screw the ledger to the studs under the cabinets with $2\frac{1}{2}$-inch drywall screws. Drive 4d finish nails down through the case bottom into the ledger to tie things together.

9. Drive additional $2\frac{1}{2}$-inch drywall screws through the screw rail until there is one in every stud.

10. Attach the facing to the base with $\frac{3}{4}$-inch wire brads.

PINE KITCHEN

When the parents of my daughter's schoolmate found out I was a cabinetmaker, they approached me about building them a kitchen. They were very concerned about cost, so they wanted to supply their own materials and help out with the labor. Since I usually prefer to pick my own materials and provide my own labor, I agreed only reluctantly.

My reluctance deepened when I went to pick up the materials. The wood was stored in a haphazard pile on a damp dirt floor. In the dim light, the few boards that I could see clearly were loaded with knots and suffering from water damage.

As I loaded it into my truck and drove it home, I wasn't sure if there was enough usable stock there to build a decent recipe box, let alone an entire kitchen. But as I sorted through it, I found that my first take was wrong—the wood wasn't as far gone as I had thought, and many of the knots were quite pretty. With careful planning, I made the cabinets you see in the photo. Not bad for a pile of "useless" lumber.

330

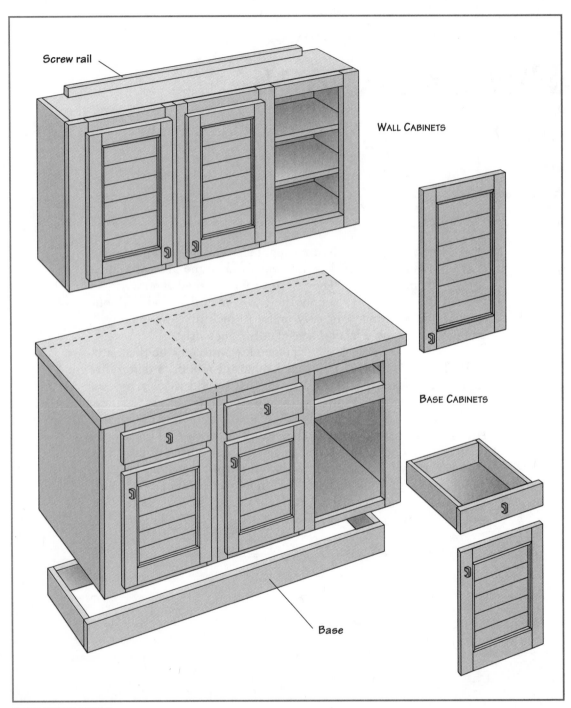

Screw rail

Wall Cabinets

Base Cabinets

Base

EXPLODED VIEW

TECH NOTES This is one of the first kitchens I made. Back then, my techniques weren't as refined as they are now. In light of that, as I was drawing up this project, I modified the way the cabinets are put together to reflect my current system. So the drawings don't match the photo exactly, but the overall look of the cabinets is pretty much the same.

The project is made up of 4 plywood cases, two upper and two base. (In the original, there were just two cases, but long cases are harder to make and install.) The cases are assembled with my standard tongue-and-groove joint; see Chapter 2. Face frames with half-overlay doors and drawer faces finish off the cabinet fronts. See Chapters 4, 6, 8, and 9.

The doors themselves are of frame-and-panel construction, with bookmatched composite panels. The composite panels made good use of some of the really knotty pieces of pine that I hauled up out of that basement. See Chapter 7. Solid mahogany countertops graced the original kitchen, although any other type of counter would work as well. See Chapter 13. The base cabinet sits on my standard ladder-style base, and the upper cabinet is hung on the wall with a ledger underneath and a screw rail across the top, as described in Chapter 14.

CONSTRUCTION STEPS

Make the Cases

1. Cut the tops, bottoms, and sides for all the cases to the sizes specified in the Materials List. Cut the base cabinet bottoms and the wall cabinet sides ¼ inch or so oversize at first.

Glue edging to the front edges of the base cabinet bottoms and the bottom edges of the wall cabinet sides. Trim the edging flush with a flush-trim bit in a router. Then cut the pieces to size as you're cutting up the rest of the parts. For more details on applying edging, see "Attaching the Edging" on page 32.

2. Join the case pieces with tongue-and-groove joints, as shown in the *Base Case Joinery Detail.* Note that the upper cabinet

(continued on page 334)

MATERIALS LIST

PART	DIMENSION	PART	DIMENSION

Narrow Base Cabinet

Part	Dimension
Top	¾" × 23" × 19¼"
Bottom	¾" × 23"* × 19¼"
Sides (2)	¾" × 23¼" × 29"
Edging	¼" × ⅞" × 24"
Back	¼" × 20" × 29"
Shelf	¾" × 16" × 18⅜"
Edging	¼" × ⅞" × 20"
Wide stile	¾" × 4" × 30"
Narrow stile	¾" × 1½" × 30"
Wide rail	¾" × 2½" × 15¾"
Medium rail	¾" × 2" × 15¾"
Narrow rail	¾" × 1½" × 15¾"
Glue block	¾" × ¾" × 20"

Wide Base Cabinet

Part	Dimension
Top	¾" × 23" × 38"
Bottom	¾" × 23"* × 38"
Sides (2)	¾" × 23¼" × 29"
Back	¼" × 38¾" × 29"
Edging	¼" × ⅞" × 39"
Shelf	¾" × 16" × 37⅛"
Edging	¼" × ⅞" × 39"
Wide stile	¾" × 4" × 30"
Medium stile	¾" × 3" × 30"
Narrow stile	¾" × 1½" × 30"
Wide rails (2)	¾" × 2½" × 15¾"
Medium rails (2)	¾" × 2" × 15¾"
Narrow rails (2)	¾" × 1½" × 15¾"
Glue block	¾" × ¾" × 38¾"

Narrow Wall Cabinet

Part	Dimension
Top/bottom (2)	¾" × 11" × 19¼"
Sides (2)	¾" × 11¼" × 29¾"*
Edging (2)	¼" × ⅞" × 12"
Back	¼" × 20" × 29¾"
Shelves (2)	¾" × 10¼" × 18⅜"
Edging (2)	¼" × ⅞" × 20"
Wide stile	¾" × 4" × 30"
Narrow stile	¾" × 1½" × 30"
Wide rails (2)	¾" × 2½" × 15¾"

Wide Wall Cabinet

Part	Dimension
Top/bottom (2)	¾" × 11" × 38"
Sides (2)	¾" × 11¼" × 29¾"*
Edging (2)	¼" × ⅞" × 12"
Back	¼" × 38¾" × 29¾"
Shelves (2)	¾" × 10¼" × 37⅛"
Edging (2)	¼" × ⅞" × 38"
Wide stile	¾" × 4" × 30"
Medium stile	¾" × 3" × 30"
Narrow stile	¾" × 1½" × 30"
Wide rails (4)	¾" × 2½" × 15¾"

Lower Doors (3)

Part	Dimension
Stiles (2)	¾" × 2½" × 21"
Upper rail	¾" × 2½" × 11¾"
Lower rail	¾" × 3½" × 11¾"
Panel	⅜" × 15⁹⁄₁₆" × 12⅜"

*Includes ¼" edging.

PART	DIMENSION
Spline stock	$1/8$" $\times$ $7/16$" $\times$ 13"
Retaining strips (2)	$3/8$" $\times$ $7/16$" $\times$ 17"
Retaining strips (2)	$3/8$" $\times$ $7/16$" $\times$ 13"
Pull	$3/4$" $\times$ 1" $\times$ 2"

Upper Doors (3)

PART	DIMENSION
Stiles (2)	$3/4$" $\times$ $2^1/2$" $\times$ 26"
Upper rail	$3/4$" $\times$ $2^1/2$" $\times$ $11^3/4$"
Lower rail	$3/4$" $\times$ $3^1/2$" $\times$ $11^3/4$"
Panel	$3/8$" $\times$ $20^9/16$" $\times$ $12^3/8$"
Spline stock (as needed)	$1/8$" $\times$ $7/16$" $\times$ 13"
Retaining strips (2)	$3/8$" $\times$ $7/16$" $\times$ 21"
Retaining strips (2)	$3/8$" $\times$ $7/16$" $\times$ 13"
Pull	$3/4$" $\times$ 1" $\times$ 2"

Loose Tenons

PART	DIMENSION
Tenon stock	$3/8$" $\times$ $5/8$" $\times$ 12"
Tenon stock	$3/8$" $\times$ $1^1/8$" $\times$ 12"
Tenon stock	$3/8$" $\times$ $1^5/8$" $\times$ 36"
Tenon stock	$3/8$" $\times$ $2^5/8$" $\times$ 24"

Drawers (3)

PART	DIMENSION
Front/back (2)	$5/8$" $\times$ 3" $\times$ $14^5/8$"
Sides (2)	$5/8$" $\times$ 3" $\times$ 20"
Bottom	$1/4$" $\times$ $14^{13}/16$" $\times$ $19^3/16$"
Square glue blocks (3)	$3/4$" $\times$ 3" $\times$ 3"
Face	$3/4$" $\times$ 5" $\times$ $16^3/4$"
Pull	$3/4$" $\times$ 1" $\times$ 2"

Installation

PART	DIMENSION
Base rails (2)	$3/4$" $\times$ $5^1/2$" $\times$ $61^1/4$"
Crosspieces (4)	$3/4$" $\times$ $5^1/2$" $\times$ $16^3/4$"
Cleats (6)	$3/4$" $\times$ $3/4$" $\times$ 18"
Screw rail	$3/4$" $\times$ $1^1/2$" $\times$ $55^1/4$"
Ledger	$3/4$" $\times$ $1^3/4$" $\times$ $18^1/2$"
Ledger	$3/4$" $\times$ $1^3/4$" $\times$ $37^1/4$"
Facing	$1/4$" $\times$ 5" $\times$ $61^1/4$"
Countertop	$1^1/2$" $\times$ 25" $\times$ $61^1/4$"

Hardware

Self-closing overlay hinges (6 pair). Available from The Woodworker's Store; part #26948

21" Accuride center-mount drawer slides (3). Available from The Woodworker's Store; part #32573

5mm pin-style shelf supports (16). Available from Outwater Hardware Corp.; part #3002

$2^1/2$" drywall screws (as needed)

2" drywall screws (as needed)

$1^5/8$" drywall screws (as needed)

1" drywall screws (as needed)

$3/4$" drywall screws (as needed)

$1^1/2$" finish nails (as needed)

1" wire brads (as needed)

$3/8$" wood plugs (as needed)

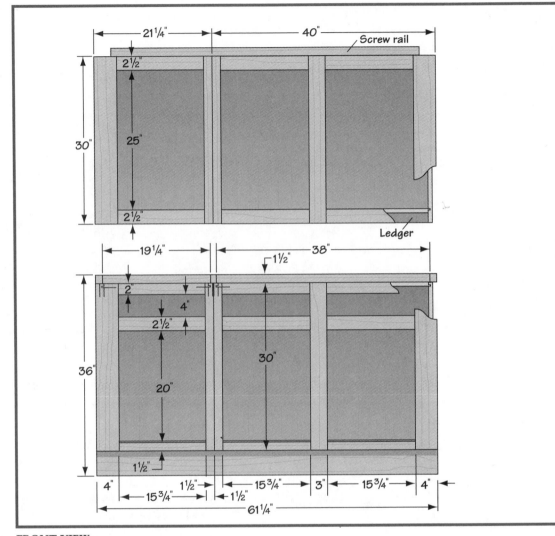

FRONT VIEW

bottoms are raised, as shown in *Upper Case Joinery Detail.* For more specifics on cutting these joints, see "Cutting the Joint" on page 16.

3. While you're set up to cut tongues and grooves, cut ¼ × ¼-inch tongues on the front edges of all the case sides for aligning and attaching the face frames, as shown in the *Joinery Details/Face Frame to Case.*

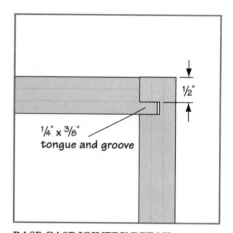

UPPER CASE JOINERY DETAIL

BASE CASE JOINERY DETAIL

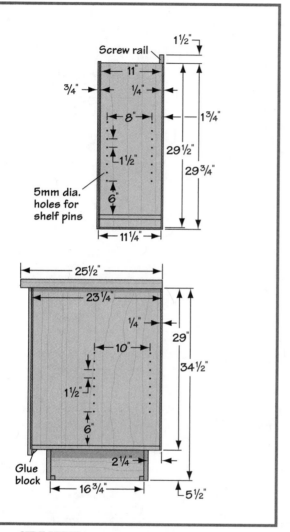

SIDE VIEW

4. Assemble the cases with glue and 1⅝-inch drywall screws. See "The Glue-Up" on page 24 for a step-by-step account of how I do this.

5. Cut the backs to size. Tip the cases face down, then glue and nail the backs in place with 1-inch wire brads. Use the backs to square the cases, if necessary, as described in "The Glue-Up" on page 24.

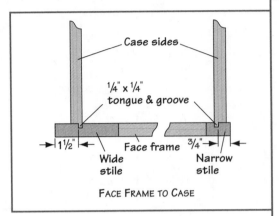

JOINERY DETAILS

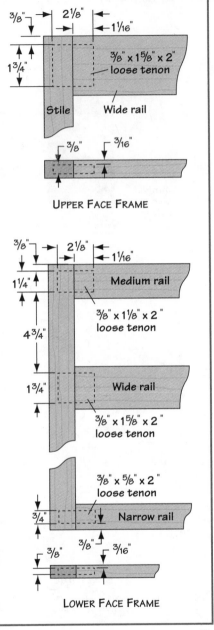

6. Drill the case sides for the shelf pins, as shown in the *Side View*. Cut the shelves to size and glue edging to their front edges.

Make the Face Frames

1. Cut the stiles and rails to the sizes specified in the Materials List.

2. Join the frame pieces together with loose tenon joints, as shown in the *Joinery Details*. For instructions detailing this process, see Chapter 4.

3. Glue up the frames, taking care to keep them flat and square. See "Clamping Frames" on page 42 for more information.

4. Cut grooves in the frame stiles to match the tongues on the case sides. The narrow stiles should overlap the cases by ¼ inch. The overlap on the other stiles will be whatever is left over. Make the cuts with a regular blade on the table saw. Set the blade height to cut the proper groove depth and position the groove with the rip fence. Make one cut, then shift the fence over to widen the groove.

5. Glue and clamp the frames to the cases. On the upper cases, the top edge of the bottom rail should be flush with the inside of the cabinet. Because the frame overhangs the top, there is plenty of room for adjustment, as shown in the *Side View.*

On the base cases, the top of the frame should be flush with the top of the case so the countertop can sit flat. This will leave about ¼ inch of the edge of the case bottom exposed, as shown in the *Front View.* (That's why you put on the edging.) Don't put glue on this bottom edge. Instead, cut a triangular glue block on the table saw and glue it in place underneath, as shown in the *Side View.*

Make the Doors

1. Cut the stiles and rails for the doors to the sizes specified in the Materials List.

2. Join the door parts at the corners with loose tenon joints, as shown in the *Door Details.*

3. Rout a ⅜-inch-wide × ½-inch-deep rabbet around the inside of the face of each frame. Square the corners with a sharp chisel. Be careful—the corners show on the finished doors.

4. Select the stock you want to use for the panels. Resaw the pieces into slats, then join them with splines to make up the panels as specified in the Materials List. This entire process in detailed in "Composite Panels" on page 83.

5. Cut the panels to fit in the frames. I usually make the panels ⅛ inch less than the frame opening in length and 3⁄16 inch less in width.

6. Cut the retaining strips to the sizes indicated. Miter the ends as you trim the strips to length. The strips should fit neatly around the inside of the frame.

7. Cut a ½-inch-wide rabbet around the back of each panel. Cut the rabbets deep enough to make the edges of the panels 3⁄16 inch thick.

8. Drop the panels in their frames and hold them in place with the retaining strips. Anchor the strips with 1-inch wire brads.

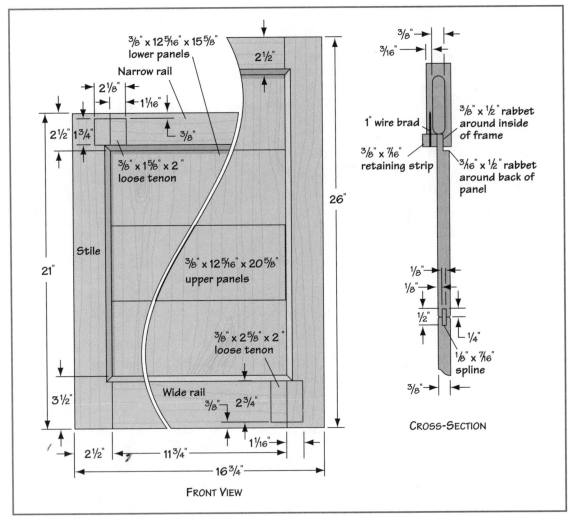

DOOR DETAILS

Cross-section labels: $\frac{3}{8}"$, $\frac{3}{16}"$, $\frac{3}{8}" \times \frac{1}{2}"$ rabbet around inside of frame, 1" wire brad, $\frac{3}{8}" \times \frac{7}{16}"$ retaining strip, $\frac{3}{16}" \times \frac{1}{2}"$ rabbet around back of panel, $\frac{1}{8}"$, $\frac{1}{8}"$, $\frac{1}{2}"$, $\frac{1}{4}"$, $\frac{1}{8}" \times \frac{7}{16}"$ spline, $\frac{3}{8}"$

CROSS-SECTION

Front view labels: $\frac{3}{8}" \times 12\frac{5}{16}" \times 15\frac{5}{8}"$ lower panels, Narrow rail, $2\frac{1}{8}"$, $1\frac{1}{16}"$, $\frac{3}{8}"$, $2\frac{1}{2}"$, $2\frac{1}{2}"$, $1\frac{3}{4}"$, 26", $\frac{3}{8}" \times 1\frac{5}{8}" \times 2"$ loose tenon, Stile, 21", $\frac{3}{8}" \times 12\frac{5}{16}" \times 20\frac{5}{8}"$ upper panels, $\frac{3}{8}" \times 2\frac{5}{8}" \times 2"$ loose tenon, Wide rail, $3\frac{1}{2}"$, $\frac{3}{8}"$, $2\frac{3}{4}"$, $1\frac{1}{16}"$, $2\frac{1}{2}"$, $11\frac{3}{4}"$, $16\frac{3}{4}"$

FRONT VIEW

9. Screw the hinges to the doors with the screws supplied. Placement is not critical; just space them in from the top and bottom edges about $\frac{1}{6}$ of the total door height.

10. To hang the doors on the cabinets, turn the cabinets onto their backs. Place the doors over the frame openings. They should overlap the frames by $\frac{1}{2}$ inch in all directions. Align the doors so they are parallel to each other and to the edges of the face frames. Screw the hinges to the frames, one screw per hinge.

Set the cases upright and check to be sure the doors are hanging straight. Add the second screw to each hinge. If a door is crooked, remove the screw from one of the hinges and make the required adjustment. Then screw the hinge in place again using the second screw hole.

Make the Drawers

1. Cut the drawer fronts, backs, sides, and square glue blocks to the sizes given.

2. Cut tongue-and-groove joints to join the drawer sides to the fronts and back, as shown in the *Drawer Details.* For specific instructions, see "An Alternate Drawer Joint" on page 106.

3. Cut a groove for the drawer bottom in all the drawer parts, as shown in *Drawer Details/Cross-Section through Side.* See "Cutting the Groove for the Bottom" on page 109 for further details.

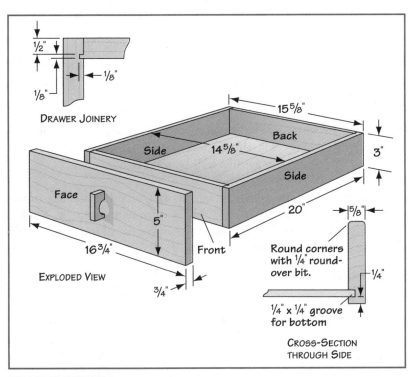

DRAWER DETAILS

4. Cut the drawer bottoms to size, then glue up the drawers. Make sure the boxes are square by measuring from corner to corner diagonally. If the measurements are equal, the drawer is square. See "Assembling the Drawer" on page 112 for more information.

5. Round all but the front edges of the drawer boxes with a ¼-inch roundover bit in a router.

6. Hang the drawers on the center-mount slides. Attach square glue blocks to the case backs with glue and ¾-inch drywall screws. Attach the slides to the glue blocks, following the manufacturer's instructions.

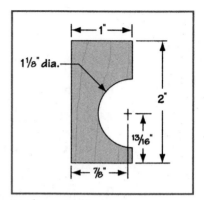

PULL DETAIL

7. Attach the drawer faces to the drawers. Hold them in place with double-faced carpet tape while you align them. Use the doors as a guide to get them on straight. Attach them permanently from inside the drawer boxes with 1-inch drywall screws.

8. The drawers and doors open via my original U-shaped pulls, shown in the *Pull Detail.* Make them as detailed in "U-Pulls" on page 138.

9. Attach the pulls to the drawers and doors with glue and 1¼-inch drywall screws. On the drawers, you'll have to counterbore the drawer fronts so the screws will be long enough.

10. Finish the cabinets with your favorite wood finish according to the manufacturer's instructions. If you're using pine, as I did, a clear water-base finish will preserve the wood's blond color while adding a great deal of protection.

Installation

1. The base cases sit on my standard ladder-style base. Cut the base parts to size and join them with 1⅝-inch drywall screws, as shown in the *Exploded View* and *Side View.* For more details on the entire installation process, see Chapter 14. Also cut the screw rail, ledgers, and facing to size before you leave the shop.

2. On site, set the base in place, level it, and screw it to the floor with 2-inch drywall screws.

3. Set the base cases on top of the base. Trim the face frames, if necessary, to get a good fit between the cases and the walls, and between the two cases themselves. Then screw the cases together through their face frames with 2-inch drywall screws. Screw the cases to the base with 1⅝-inch drywall screws.

4. Cut the countertop to size, set it in place, and anchor it with 2-inch drywall screws driven up through the case tops. Drill over-size holes in the case tops to screw through. This will give the countertop room to expand and contract.

5. The kitchen in the photo has a fascia board installed in the space between the top of the wall cabinets and the ceiling. You can either do the same or simply leave the space open.

6. Strike a level line on the wall to indicate the top of the wall cases. Screw the cases together with 2-inch drywall screws driven through the frames. Attach the screw rail to the top of both cases with 2-inch drywall screws, as shown in the *Front View* and *Side View*. Be sure the gap between the cases remains a consistent width from front to back.

7. Find the studs in the wall along the level line. Have some helpers hold the wall cases in place as you drive 2½-inch drywall screws into the studs. Three or four will be enough to hold the cases for now.

8. Hold the ledgers in place under the cases and screw them to the studs with 2½-inch drywall screws. Counterbore for the screws first and plug the holes afterward with ⅜-inch wood plugs. Nail the cases to the ledgers with 1½-inch finish nails driven at an angle through the case bottoms. Once the ledgers are in place, drive 2½-inch drywall screws through the screw rail into all the studs available.

9. Tack the facing in place on the front of the base rail with 1-inch wire brads.

CHERRY KITCHEN

I saw an article in the paper about you, and I'd like you to do my kitchen," the phone call started. Talk about the power of the press! That call resulted in this kitchen, one of my most elaborate jobs to date. While the overall look is one of grandeur, the cabinets themselves are fairly simple and straightforward. The elegant look comes from the materials (cherry and granite) and the detailing.

The look my clients and I were after was solid and traditional: beaded-inset construction, frame-and-panel doors, nice brass hinges, the works. As the design unfolded, however, it became necessary to incorporate some techniques from the other, more contemporary, end of the spectrum: full-overlay doors and concealed European-style hinges. Fortunately, these seemingly disparate styles blend well to form a spectacular kitchen.

I've included drawings for a corner cabinet here. Between this project and the other two kitchens, you should be able to mix and match cabinets to fill almost any kitchen. My modular approach to cabinetmaking makes this a breeze.

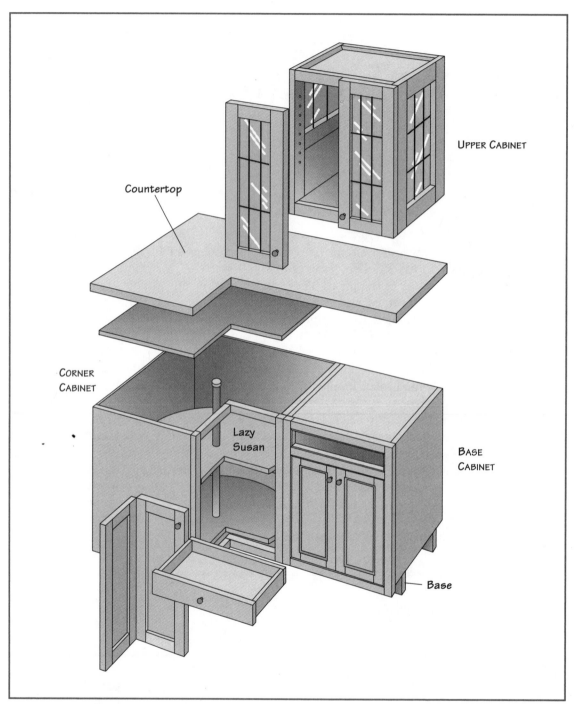

Countertop

Upper Cabinet

Corner
Cabinet

Lazy
Susan

Base
Cabinet

Base

EXPLODED VIEW

TECH NOTES You'll probably never have the opportunity to duplicate the kitchen shown in the photo—the space it was built for is too unique. But you can build a combination of these cabinets to suit your home.

This kitchen was comprised of three different cabinet styles: a drawer-over-door base cabinet, a glass-panel upper cabinet, and a corner cabinet. The construction of all the cases involves my standard tongue-and-groove joint. For more on this joint, see Chapter 2.

The two lower cases are made of plywood throughout. There are two things to be aware of here. One is that you should glue a strip of edging to the front edge of each case bottom before cutting the corner joints. This edge will be exposed and needs the edging to dress it up. The second is that the corner cabinet is designed to be 1 inch shallower than the base cabinet. In my experience, the corners of a room can cause real headaches when it comes to installing cabinets. By making the corner unit a little shallow, you'll create more clearance for it and hopefully eliminate the need for aspirin.

The upper case is twice as deep as my usual wall cabinets. Because it was meant to hang over an island, there are doors on both the front and back. Both sides are of frame-and-panel construction. On one side, the panel is entirely glass. On the other, the panel is half glass and half wood. An intermediate rail separates the two materials. You can easily modify the dimensions to suit your design. Make the case half as deep and put a back on it, and you'll have a wall cabinet. Or make both sides with full glass panels for a more symmetrical installation. The small upper cabinet in the photo is simply an 18-inch-tall version of the larger upper cabinet.

The glass panels are made up of individual panes leaded together. Look in your phone book under "Glass, Stained" for a local shop that can make these up to your specifications.

The doors on the lower cases are set into beaded face frames, a construction known as beaded-inset. A thorough discussion of this is included in "Beaded Frames" on page 40. The doors on the upper cabinets are full-overlay, meaning they lap the case edges rather than being set within them. Chapters 3 and 6 have further details. This combination of door styles is unusual, but it works well here.

The drawer is dovetailed and runs on Accuride drawer slides. See Chapters 8, 9, and 10 for complete details. The countertop in the photo is granite, but you can use any type of counter you like. See Chapter 13 for a discussion of types and installation procedures.

MATERIALS LIST

PART	DIMENSION	PART	DIMENSION
Base Cabinet		**Corner Cabinet**	
Top	$3/4" \times 22^3/4" \times 22^3/4"$	Top/bottom (2)	$3/4" \times 34^1/8" \times 34^1/8"$
Bottom	$3/4" \times 22^3/4"^* \times 22^3/4"$	Sides	$3/4" \times 21^3/4" \times 29^1/16"$
Sides (2)	$3/4" \times 23^1/8" \times 29^1/16"$	Edging (2)	$1/4" \times 7/8" \times 13"$
Edging (2)	$1/4" \times 7/8" \times 24"$	Back supports (2)	$3/4" \times 1^3/4" \times 27^9/16"$
Back	$1/4" \times 23^1/2" \times 29^1/16"$	Back (2)	$1/4" \times 24^1/8" \times 29^1/16"$
Shelf	$3/4" \times 12" \times 21^7/8"$	Back	$1/4" \times 14^1/2" \times 29^1/16"$
Stiles (2)	$1" \times 1^1/2" \times 30^1/2"$	Stiles (2)	$1" \times 1^1/2" \times 30^1/2"$
Rails (3)	$1" \times 1^1/2" \times 21"$	Long rails (2)	$1" \times 1^1/2" \times 11^1/2"$
Tenon stock	$3/8" \times 7/8" \times 16"$	Short rails (2)	$1" \times 1^1/2" \times 10^1/2"$
Beads (6)	$5/16" \times 1" \times 22"$	Tenon stock	$3/8" \times 7/8" \times 12"$
Beads (2)	$5/16" \times 1" \times 6"$	Beads (2)	$5/16" \times 1" \times 28"$
		Beads (4)	$5/16" \times 1" \times 12"$
Base Cabinet Doors (2)		Glue blocks (4)	$3/4" \times 3/4" \times 11"$
Stiles (2)	$1" \times 2^1/4" \times 20^1/2"$		
Rails (2)	$1" \times 2^1/4" \times 5^9/16"$	**Corner Cabinet Doors (2)**	
Tenon stock	$3/8" \times 1^3/8" \times 12"$	Stiles (2)	$1" \times 2^1/4" \times 26^3/4"$
Retaining molding (2)	$3/4" \times 7/8" \times 18"$	Rails (2)	$1" \times 2^1/4" \times 5^1/2"$
Retaining molding (2)	$3/4" \times 7/8" \times 7"$	Tenon stock	$3/8" \times 1^3/8" \times 12"$
Panel	$3/8" \times 6^1/8" \times 16^7/8"$	Retaining molding (2)	$3/4" \times 7/8" \times 24"$
		Retaining molding (2)	$3/4" \times 7/8" \times 8"$
Base Cabinet Drawer		Panel	$3/8" \times 6^1/16" \times 22^7/8"$
Front/back (2)	$5/8" \times 3^1/2" \times 19^3/8"$		
Sides	$5/8" \times 3^1/2" \times 19^3/8"$	**Upper Cabinet**	
Bottom	$1/4" \times 18^5/8" \times 19^1/4"$	Top/bottom (2)	$3/4" \times 20^3/4" \times 22^3/4"$
Face	$1" \times 4" \times 20^1/4"$	Side stiles (4)	$1" \times 2^1/4" \times 30"$
Spacers	$1/2" \times 6^1/2" \times 22^3/4"$	Side rails (5)	$1" \times 2^1/4" \times 17^1/2"$
		Tenon stock	$3/8" \times 1^5/8" \times 24"$

*Includes $1/4"$ edging.

CONSTRUCTION STEPS

Build the Base Cases

1. Cut the tops, bottoms, and sides for the corner cabinet and base cabinet to the sizes specified in the Materials List. Note that the base cabinet bottom is $1/4$ inch narrower than the top to allow for edging.

PART	DIMENSION
Retaining molding (2)	$\frac{3}{4}$" × $\frac{7}{8}$" × 28"
Retaining molding (2)	$\frac{3}{4}$" × $\frac{7}{8}$" × 19"
Panel	$\frac{3}{8}$" × 18$\frac{1}{16}$" × 10$\frac{3}{8}$"
Square panel molding (3)	$\frac{3}{8}$" × $\frac{3}{8}$" × 23"
Top facings (2)	1" × 1$\frac{1}{2}$" × 22$\frac{1}{4}$"
Bottom facings (2)	1" × 1$\frac{1}{2}$" × 22$\frac{1}{4}$"
Glue blocks (8)	$\frac{3}{4}$" × $\frac{3}{4}$" × 20"
Square glass molding (4)	$\frac{3}{8}$" × $\frac{7}{16}$" × 20"

Glass-Panel Doors (4)

Stiles (2)	1" × 2$\frac{1}{4}$" × 29$\frac{7}{8}$"
Rails (2)	1" × 2$\frac{1}{4}$" × 7$\frac{3}{8}$"
Tenon stock	$\frac{3}{8}$" × 1$\frac{3}{8}$" × 12"
Retaining molding (2)	$\frac{3}{4}$" × $\frac{7}{8}$" × 28"
Retaining molding (2)	$\frac{3}{4}$" × $\frac{7}{8}$" × 9"

Installation

Base rails (2)	$\frac{3}{4}$" × 5$\frac{7}{16}$" × (as needed)
Base crosspieces (as needed)	$\frac{3}{4}$" × 5$\frac{7}{16}$" × 18"
Facing	$\frac{1}{4}$" × 5$\frac{1}{4}$" × (as needed)

Hardware

2$\frac{1}{2}$" ball-tip hinges (6). Available from The Woodworkers' Store; part #26492

Grass full-overlay hinges with winged base plates (4). Available from Outwater Hardware Corp.; part #1006 and #63204

Hardware—*continued*

1$\frac{1}{2}$" × 36" piano hinge

20" Accuride drawer slides (1 pair). Available from Outwater Hardware Corp.; part #3017

5mm pin-style shelf supports (16). Available from Outwater Hardware Corp.; part #3002

7$\frac{3}{8}$" × 25$\frac{3}{8}$" leaded glass door panels (4)

18$\frac{1}{8}$" × 26$\frac{1}{8}$" leaded glass side panel

10$\frac{3}{8}$" × 18$\frac{1}{8}$" leaded glass side panel

$\frac{3}{8}$" × 21$\frac{7}{8}$" × 21$\frac{7}{8}$" glass shelves with polished edges (3)

Steel hanging bracket (see drawing)

Oval brass pulls (8). Available from Cliffside Industries; part #101PB

Rotating shelf system. Available from The Woodworkers' Store; part #83915

2$\frac{1}{2}$" drywall screws (as needed)

2" drywall screws (as needed)

1$\frac{3}{4}$" drywall screws (as needed)

1$\frac{5}{8}$" drywall screws (as needed)

1$\frac{1}{4}$" drywall screws (as needed)

#4 × $\frac{3}{4}$" screws (as needed)

$\frac{5}{16}$ × 2$\frac{1}{2}$" lag bolts (as needed)

$\frac{1}{4}$-20 × 2" machine bolts (as needed)

1$\frac{1}{4}$" wire brads (as needed)

1" wire brads (as needed)

$\frac{3}{4}$" wire brads (as needed)

2. Notch the corners of the corner cabinet top and bottom, as shown in the *Notch Detail*. The notch in the bottom should be $\frac{1}{4}$ inch bigger in both directions than the notch in the top (to allow for edging). Also cut the back corner of both pieces at an angle, as shown.

3. Glue edging to the front edge of the base cabinet bottom and along both edges of the notch in the corner cabinet bottom. Butt the edging in the corner of the notch. Allow the glue to dry, then trim the edging flush with a flush-trim bit in a router. At the corner of the notch, use a sharp chisel or block plane because the router won't fit. For more on applying edging, see Chapter 3.

4. Cut grooves in the case sides and matching tongues on the tops and bottoms to put the cases together, as shown in the *Base and Upper Cabinets/Case Joinery Detail.* Also cut tongues on the front edges of the base cabinet sides for the face frame. (Because of the geometry of the pieces, the corner cabinet face frame can't be joined this way, so don't cut tongues there.) For more information, see "Cutting the Joint" on page 16.

5. Glue the cases together. Since the sides will be concealed in the final installation, use 1⅝-inch drywall screws to clamp the pieces together as the glue dries. For further details on assembling cases, see "The Glue-Up" on page 24.

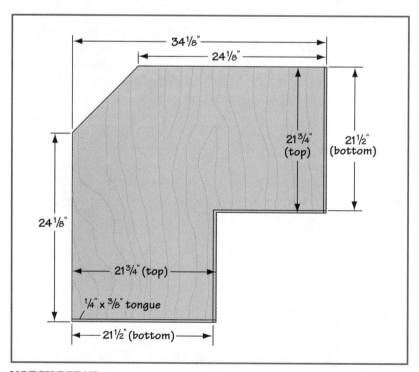

NOTCH DETAIL

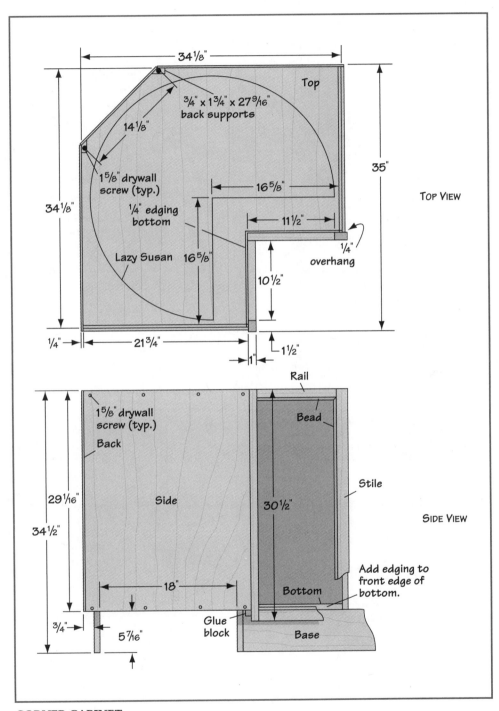

34⅛"

Top

¾" x 1¾" x 27⁹⁄₁₆"
back supports

14⅛"

35"

TOP VIEW

1⅝" drywall
screw (typ.)

16⅝"

¼" edging
bottom

11½"

¼"
overhang

Lazy Susan   16⅝"

10½"

34⅛"

¼"   21¾"   1"   1½"

Rail

1⅝" drywall
screw (typ.)

Bead

Back

Stile

Side

30½"

SIDE VIEW

29¹⁄₁₆"

34½"

Add edging to
front edge of
bottom.

18"

¾"   5⁷⁄₁₆"   Glue
block

Bottom

Base

CORNER CABINET

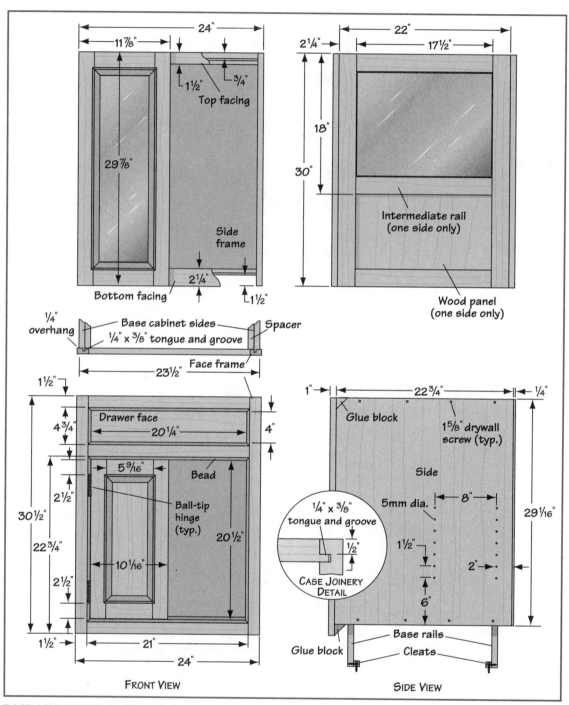

24"
11⅞"
1½"
¾"
Top facing
29⅞"
Side frame
2¼"
1½"
Bottom facing

22"
2¼"
17½"
18"
30"
Intermediate rail (one side only)
Wood panel (one side only)

¼" overhang
Base cabinet sides
¼" x ⅜" tongue and groove
Spacer
Face frame
23½"

1½"
4¾"
Drawer face
20¼"
4"
Bead
5⁹⁄₁₆"
2½"
Ball-tip hinge (typ.)
30½"
22¾"
20½"
10¹⁄₁₆"
2½"
1½"
21"
24"

FRONT VIEW

1"
22¾"
¼"
Glue block
1⅝" drywall screw (typ.)
Side
5mm dia.
8"
29¹⁄₁₆"
1½"
2"
6"
¼" x ⅜" tongue and groove
½"
CASE JOINERY DETAIL
Glue block
Base rails
Cleats

SIDE VIEW

BASE AND UPPER CABINETS

6. While the glue is drying, cut the corner cabinet back supports to the sizes specified in the Materials List. Bevel one edge at 45 degrees on the table saw, as shown in the *Corner Cabinet/Top View*. Screw the supports in place through the top and bottom with 1⅝-inch drywall screws. Turn both cases face down. Cut the backs to size, then glue and nail them in place with 1-inch wire brads. Use the back to square the base case if necessary. For more on this technique, see "The Glue-Up" on page 24.

7. Inside the base cabinet, drill 5mm holes for the shelf pins, as shown in the *Base and Upper Cabinets/Side View*.

8. Cut the base cabinet shelf to the size specified. Glue edging to the front edge and trim it flush. Set the shelf aside.

Make the Face Frames

1. Cut the stiles and rails for both the base and corner cabinet face frames to the dimensions specified in the Materials List.

2. Assemble the frames with loose tenon joints, as shown in the *Face Frame Details*. For more on cutting these joints, see Chapter 4.

3. Glue the frames together, being careful to keep them flat, as discussed in "Clamping Frames" on page 42. Glue up the corner cabinet face frame as two three-sided units. When the glue dries, join the two units at 90 degrees to one another with four 2½-inch drywall screws, two per joint, as shown in the *Exploded View*.

4. Cut grooves along the length of the stiles on the base cabinet face frame to match the tongues on the case sides. The grooves should be spaced to allow the frame to overhang the case ¼ inch on either side.

5. Cut the beads to the sizes specified in the Materials List. They are purposely listed too long so you have a little leeway to trim them to an exact fit. Round one edge of each piece with a ¼-inch beading bit in a table-mounted router. Cut the beads to fit inside the frames as you miter the ends. Make these 45 degree cuts on the table saw or with a chop saw. Glue and nail the beads around the insides of the frame with ¾-inch wire brads. For more on adding beading to a frame, see "Beaded Frames" on page 40.

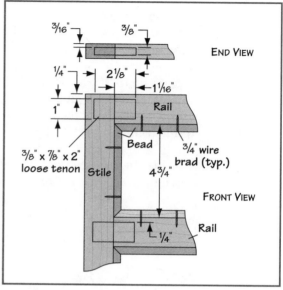

FACE FRAME DETAILS

6. Mortise the frames for the ball-tip hinges. Cut the mortises as described in "Ball-Tip Hinges" on page 128. My hinge mortising jig makes this a snap. You'll find plans for it in "A Hinge Mortising Jig" on page 130. It is much easier to cut these mortises now than after the frames are attached to the cases.

Note that only one of the doors gets hinged to the corner face frame. Which door that is depends on your particular kitchen. The second corner door is hinged to the first with a piano hinge. (More on that later.)

7. Glue and clamp the frames to the cases. Apply glue only to the sides and top (not the bottom, where it might squeeze out and show). The top edge of each frame should be flush with the top of its case. To reinforce the joint between the frame and the corner cabinet, add several glue blocks to the underside of the top and bottom, as shown in the *Side View*. For more on gluing face frames in place, see "Attaching the Frames" on page 46.

Make the Frame-and-Panel Doors

1. Cut the stiles and rails for the base and corner cabinet doors to the sizes specified in the Materials List.

2. Join the corners with loose tenon joints, as you did for the face frames. The joint layout is shown in the *Door Frame Details*. Glue the frames together.

3. When the glue dries, rout a ⅜-inch-wide × ¹¹⁄₁₆-inch-deep rabbet around the inside of each door frame to hold the panel, as shown in the *Door Cross-Sections/Frame-and-Panel Door.* Square the corners with a chisel.

4. Cut the retaining moldings to the sizes indicated. Rout them to the profile shown in *Door Cross-Sections/Molding.* The specific bits needed and the sequence of the cuts is shown in the *Molding Routing Sequence* on page 283. Rabbet the back of the molding on the table saw. The rabbet should be ¼ inch wide × ⁷⁄₁₆ inch deep. Check the fit of the molding in the frame. With the molding seated, there should be a ¼-inch gap left for the panel.

  While you're set up to cut the molding, cut the stock for the glass-panel doors and the upper cabinet side frame.

5. Miter the moldings as you fit them around the inside of the frames.

6. Cut the panels to the sizes indicated. They are specified on the narrow side to allow room for expansion. Rabbet the back side of each panel to create a tongue that will fit the gap between the molding and the frame, as shown in *Door Cross-Sections/Frame-and-Panel Door.*

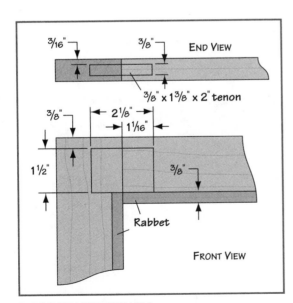

DOOR FRAME DETAILS

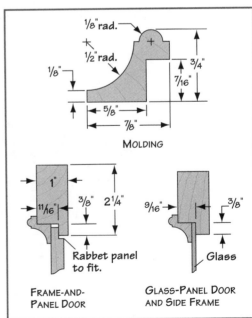

DOOR CROSS-SECTIONS

7. Finish the panels, then drop them in their frames. Nail the retaining molding to the frames with 1-inch wire brads. Set the nail heads and fill the holes. For more detailed instructions on this entire process, see Chapter 6.

8. Mortise the doors for the ball-tip hinges. On the base cabinet, both doors are hinged to the face frame, but remember the corner cabinet is a little different. Here the two doors are hinged to each other with a piano hinge. Then only one of the doors is hinged to the frame.

Screw the piano hinge between the two corner doors, then hang all the doors on the cabinets.

Make the Drawer

1. Cut the drawer front, back, and sides to the sizes specified in the Materials List.

2. Join the pieces with dovetails cut with a router jig, as shown in the *Drawer Details*. For more specifics, see Chapter 8.

3. Cut a ¼-inch wide × ¼-inch deep groove for the bottom in all four pieces. Make the cut in two passes on the table saw. Cut the bottom to size and glue up the drawer. Chapter 9 has more details.

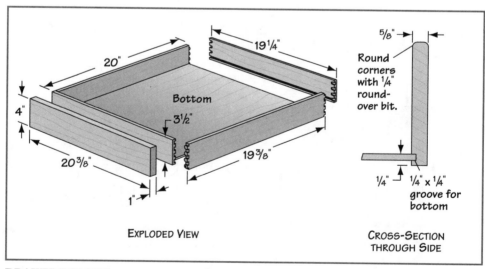

EXPLODED VIEW

CROSS-SECTION THROUGH SIDE

DRAWER DETAILS

4. After the glue dries, round-over all the square edges (except those along the outside of the front) with a ¼-inch roundover bit in a router.

5. Cut the spacers to size and screw them to the case sides, as shown in the *Base and Upper Cabinets/Front View*, with 1¼-inch drywall screws. Mount the drawer inside the case on drawer slides about ¼ inch above the frame rail. See Chapter 10 for further details.

6. Cut the drawer face to size. Position it on the drawer so it is centered within the face frame opening. Use double-sided carpet tape to hold it to the drawer front as you work. Once you have it positioned, screw it to the drawer front from inside the drawer with 1-inch drywall screws.

Make the Upper Cabinet

1. The upper cabinet is a bit different from my standard case; however, it is put together using the same techniques. Use plywood for the top and bottom. The sides are frame-and-panels. Cut the top and bottom to the sizes specified in the Materials List.

2. Cut the stiles and rails for the side frames as specified. Note that one of the two frames gets an intermediate rail, as shown in the *Upper Cabinet Cross-Sections*. The glass and the wood panels in this frame are held in place with square moldings. The glass in the other frame is held in place with retaining moldings like the ones you used on the doors.

3. Join the pieces with loose tenon joints. Glue the pieces together. Rout ⅜-inch-wide × 9/16-inch-deep rabbets around the frame openings for both the glass and wood panels, as shown in the *Upper Cabinet Cross-Sections*. On the frame with the intermediate rail, rout the rabbets on the inside face; on the other frame, rout from the outside. Check the depth of the rabbets with a piece of the retaining molding you routed earlier. The gap should be wide enough to accommodate the glass you plan to use. Square the corners with a sharp chisel.

4. Cut the panel to the size specified. Cut a ½-inch-wide rabbet around the edges to create a 3/16-inch thick tongue to fit in the frame.

5. Cut the square panel molding to the size given. Cut it to fit around the inside of the side frame to hold the wooden panel in place. Miter the corners, or simply butt the pieces together. Drop the panel in place and screw the moldings to the frame with #4 × ¾-inch screws.

6. Cut both the top and bottom facings to the thickness and width specified, but leave them about ¼ inch long to allow room for trimming them to fit.

7. Cut ¼-inch-wide × ⅜-inch-deep grooves across the top and the bottom of both the side frames, as well as along the length of the facings, as shown in the *Upper Cabinet Cross-Sections.* Cut these grooves with a ¼-inch straight bit in a table-mounted router. The grooves across the sides should stop ½ inch from either edge. For further details, see "Making Stopped Grooves" on page 114.

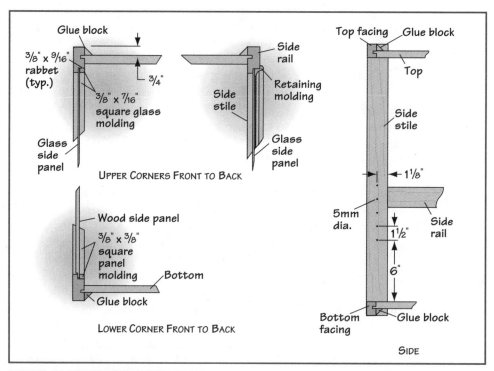

UPPER CABINET CROSS-SECTIONS

8. On all four edges of the top and bottom, cut tongues to match the grooves you just routed. The method of cutting these tongues for a perfect fit is detailed in "Cutting the Joint" on page 16.

9. Glue and clamp the top and bottom into the grooves in the sides. Make sure the pieces are centered across the width of the sides. Also be sure the case is square since there is no back to help hold things in line. Measure the diagonals—if they are equal, the case is square. Adjust the position of the clamps, if necessary. Once the glue dries, the case will stay square.

10. While the case is drying, cut the facings to fit between the sides. Glue them to the edges of the top and bottom.

11. Bevel the glue blocks on the table saw, as shown in the *Upper Cabinet Cross-Sections*. Glue them in place around the top and bottom, as shown.

12. Cut the retaining molding and the square glass molding to wrap around the inside of the side frame, but do not install it yet.

13. Drill holes inside the case for the shelf pins, as shown in the *Upper Cabinet Cross-Sections*.

Make the Glass-Panel Doors

1. Cut the stiles and rails to the sizes listed. Join them at the corners with loose tenon joints. Glue the pieces together.

2. Rout ⅜-inch-wide × approximately ⁹⁄₁₆-inch-deep rabbets around the inside of the frames, as shown in the *Door Cross-Sections/Glass-Panel Door*. Check the depth of the rabbets with a piece of the retaining molding and your glass. For regular window glass, there should be a ⅛-inch gap; for a leaded glass panel, you'll need more room.

3. Drill the backs of the doors for European-style hinges. Mount the hinges on the doors, then hang the doors on the cabinets. See Chapter 11 for complete instructions.

4. Cut the retaining molding to wrap around the inside of the frames, but do not install it yet.

Finish and Installation

1. Finish the cabinets and doors with a durable finish. I used Danish oil, but a good-quality varnish or polyurethane would also be appropriate.

2. Make up the base ladders, as described in Chapter 14.

3. Take everything to the site. Level and screw the base to the floor with 2-inch drywall screws.

4. Position the lower cabinets on the base and screw them to each other through their face frames, then to the base, with 2-inch drywall screws.

5. The upper cabinet was designed to hang from the ceiling. Have a welder or steel fabricator make up a hanger from square steel tubing and angle iron, as shown in the *Hanger Detail*. Center this

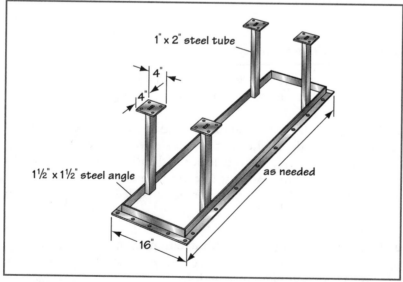

HANGER DETAIL

on top of the upper cabinet and bolt it place with ¼-20 × 2-inch machine bolts. Hold the cabinet up with the hanger against the ceiling and bolt it to the ceiling joists with ⁵⁄₁₆ × 2½-inch lag bolts.

6. Slip the glass panels in place and secure them with 1¼-inch wire brads driven through the retaining moldings and #4 × ¾-inch screws driven through the square glass moldings. Predrill holes for the brads so you won't have to pound hard to drive them home.

7. Push the shelf pins into their holes and set the shelves in place on top of them.

8. Install the revolving shelf system according to the manufacturer's instructions.

9. Add the facing to the front of the base to complete the job. Use 1-inch wire brads to hold it in place.

Appendix: Tuning Up Your Table Saw

The table saw is really the heart of a cabinetmaker's operation. All the pieces involved in a project pass by its blade at least once. It quickly rips pieces to size, cuts joints, and can even shape moldings. Because it's so essential, it should be easy to set up, its fence should lock in place quickly and accurately, and its miter gauge should fit snugly in its slots. My current saw—a Delta Unisaw equipped with a Unifence—is like this, and it's a real pleasure to use. My first saw, however, wasn't quite as nice.

I started with a 10-inch saw from Sears. While many woodworkers would disparage this saw with its diminutive 1-horsepower motor, it proved to be perfectly adequate for my system of cabinetmaking. Sure, it was finicky, but it did the job. Over time, I came to understand its shortcomings and compensated for them. By the time I could afford the Unisaw, I had my Sears saw performing like a machine that cost a lot more, so don't think you need an expensive saw to use the techniques described in this book.

No matter what saw you own, it's worth the time to make a few modifications and adjustments. They can make the difference between a tool that's merely adequate and one that you look forward to using. The following section details some of the things you can do to turn your saw into a precision cutting instrument. Some of the tips are more appropriate for lower-end machines like my original saw; others are more universal. Regardless of what tool you own, it is bound to benefit from a little fine-tuning.

Photo 1. **To set up a balky fence parallel to the blade, make two measurements. Make the first one from a tooth near the table toward the back of the saw.**

Photo 2. **Make the second measurement from the same tooth, with the tooth rotated toward the front of the saw.**

THE FENCE

One of the first stumbling blocks you'll run into with a saw is its fence. Even with the more expensive machines—like the Unisaw—I've never seen a stock fence that is truly reliable. None of them seem to automatically lock parallel to the blade. Most seem to skew in one direction or another. At best, this results in a burned cut as the wood is pinched between the blade and fence; at worst, it can cause dangerous kickback.

On my Sears saw, I never trusted the fence. If you feel the same, here's one solution: As you set up for a cut, carefully measure the distance from a tooth on the blade to the fence. First, measure at the back of the blade, as shown in *Photo 1.* Then, rotate the blade so the same tooth is now toward the front of the saw and measure again, as shown in *Photo 2.* If the two measurements are the same, the fence is parallel to the blade. (But you'll find this becomes a nuisance after a while.)

The Fixed Fence

As I looked for a better way to set the fence, I realized that many of the cuts I make are the same from job to job. For example, the first thing I do to a sheet of plywood when it comes into the shop is to rip it in half lengthwise. This cut rarely, if ever, changes. So, I devised a fixed fence and bolted it right to the saw, 24 inches from the blade and parallel to it, as shown in *Figure 1* on page 362. Now, to make this standard cut, I simply remove the rip fence from the saw and run the stock along the fixed fence. This actually solves two problems since the stock Sears saw can't make a 24-inch-wide rip and thus can't cut to the center of a piece of plywood.

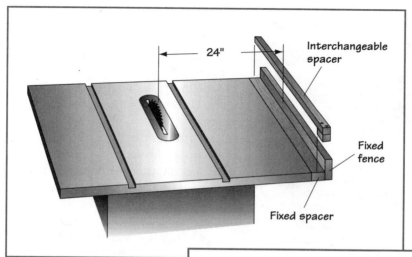

Figure 1: **Making a fixed fence**

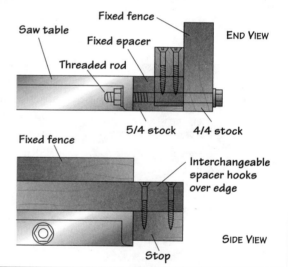

I can hear you saying, "Big Deal! If I have to make a new fence and bolt it to the saw for every cut, I'll never get any cabinets built." But do you really think I'd make you go through such a hassle? On the contrary—once you get the fixed fence in place, you can leave it there. Then all you need are interchangeable spacers to set up additional cuts. These spacers are simply straight strips of wood with a stop attached at one end that can catch on the table, as shown in *Figure 1*. I made up several to accommodate my other standard cuts. For example, the parts for my standard base cases are 23½ inches wide, so I made a ½-inch spacer to cut the half-sheets of plywood down to this size. Other spacers were used to cut pieces to 21 inches (the width I use for vanities) and 12 inches (the width I use for upper cases). I hung all my spacers on a wall near the saw so they were handy when I needed them.

Tuning the saw. To set up a fixed fence, you'll need a good reference surface on the saw that is parallel to the blade. The side of the saw table is a likely choice, but you'll have to check to make sure it is, in fact, parallel. Measure from one tooth on the saw blade to the table edge just as you would to check the rip fence (see page 361). If the edge is not parallel to the blade, you'll have to make some adjustments.

Start by checking to make sure the miter gauge slots are parallel to the blade. Since the edge of the table is usually parallel to the slots, they'll provide a good reference. If the slots are not parallel to the blade, it's time to give your saw a tune-up. If the slots are properly aligned and the table edge isn't, you'll have to shim the fixed fence to align it with the blade.

If the slots are out of alignment, you'll have to shift either the blade carriage or the tabletop. This varies from saw to saw. If the carriage bolts to the table, loosen the bolts and shift the carriage into line. Keep measuring from the tooth to the edge of one of the slots to check your progress. If the table is independent of the carriage, loosen the bolts that hold the table to the base and shift it. With either style saw, this is something of a trial-and-error process. The act of tightening the bolts again often causes the parts to shift out of alignment. Once you get the slots aligned with the blade, you should be able to forget about the adjustment for several years—it does not easily go out of true. Be careful, however, if you move your saw around a lot. If you use the tabletop or fence rails as handles, you may be shifting things out of alignment unknowingly.

Attaching the fence. On my Sears saw, I had to add a strip of wood (fixed spacer) to the right-hand extension table to extend its edge out 24 inches from the blade, as shown in *Figure 1*. Fortunately, there were holes in the edge of the extension table that I could run bolts through to attach this wooden strip. You may need to exercise your creativity if your saw has no such holes. As you attach this strip, make sure its top is level with the top of the saw table. Then, screw the fixed fence to the edge of the strip. It should project above the table about 1 inch. Once the fence is installed, check again to make sure it's parallel to the blade. If it's not, add shims to make it behave.

Make the fence, the extension strip, and the spacers from a straight-grained hardwood like maple or birch. Sand everything very smooth, give it all a coat of paste wax, and buff well. This will allow stock to slide easily across the saw.

TUNING THE MITER GAUGE

An accurate miter gauge depends on one basic adjustment: the fit of the bar in its groove. Any slop here can make crosscutting a nightmare.

Place the miter gauge in its groove and try to wiggle it from side to side. If you can feel it shift, there is too much slop. If this is the case, remove the gauge from the saw and peen the bar with a ball peen hammer, as shown in *Figure 2*. This will spread the metal. Peen the full length of the bar along both edges to keep the bar straight and to widen it uniformly. Keep trying the bar in the slot to check your progress. Don't worry about going too far; you can always thin the bar down a bit with a file. You're looking for a fit that allows the bar to run smoothly in the groove with no side-to-side play.

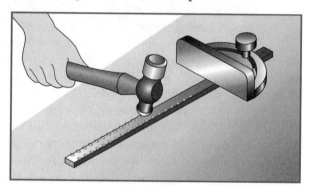

Figure 2. Peening the miter gauge

HANDLING LARGE STOCK

With a fixed fence in place, you won't have to fight to get the saw set up anymore, but you'll still find that handling large pieces—especially 4 × 8 sheets of plywood—can be nerve-racking. Short of hiring several large helpers, there is another addition to your saw you can build to make this onerous task easier.

I tried all kinds of deadmen and roller stands before finally settling on the outfeed table shown in *Photo 3*. Pieces slide over its plastic laminate–covered surface with ease since the laminate introduces less

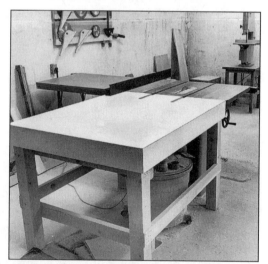

Photo 3. For supporting large pieces of plywood as you cut them, nothing beats an outfeed table. I added a layer of plastic laminate to the top of mine to help stock slide easily over it. I resurface it every so often when I get tired of the laminate color.

friction than a comparable roller stand. And because the surface is solid and butts right up to the saw table, even warped stock slides right onto it. With some of the other systems I've tried, a warped board will often knock a stand over or push it out of alignment. This can be disconcerting in the middle of a cut.

With an outfeed table, I can push the piece through the cut with ease. Then, I leave the pieces lying on the table as I calmly shut the saw off and walk around to get them out of the way. Thinking back to the days when it was just me and the saw is almost embarrassing. Then, I made a cut and held the ends of the pieces tightly against the table while the saw quit spinning. If I let one half go to grab the other, the first half would pivot and crash to the floor. This was neither professional nor good for the stock.

The outfeed table also provides another benefit. It has become one of my principal work surfaces. I often use it for sanding and assembly. For sanding, I have a piece of carpet that just fits the top to protect the freshly sanded pieces. And glue drips just pop right off the plastic laminate after assembly. This makes it easy to keep the table clean and smooth for sawing. If you go shopping for a carpet remnant, get the kind with a rubber backing to keep the carpet from sliding around as you work.

Making an Outfeed Table

I built my table as shown in *Figure 3* on page 366. The dimensions and joinery aren't critical, so just use the materials you have on hand. If you have the space, the top should be between 48 and 52 inches long. This will allow you to rip a full sheet of plywood in half with ease. Make the legs so that the height is adjustable. I countersunk a large T-nut into the bottom of each of mine and screwed in a nylon glide with a threaded shaft as the adjustment mechanism. The counterbores are deep enough to allow the feet to recess completely into the legs.

When you set the table up, adjust the glides so the table height is a hair lower than the saw table. This will keep your stock from bumping into it as it runs off the saw.

Other Adjustments

There are a few other things I've found to be useful in wringing the best performance from a table saw:
• Use a sharp, clean blade. Dull and/or dirty blades rob the saw

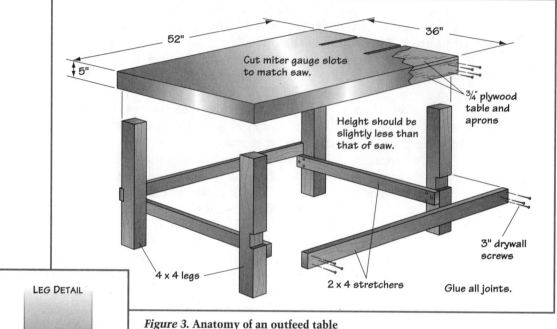

52" 36"

5"

Cut miter gauge slots
to match saw.

Height should be
slightly less than
that of saw.

3/4" plywood
table and
aprons

3" drywall
screws

4 x 4 legs

2 x 4 stretchers

Glue all joints.

LEG DETAIL

1/2"
hole

T-nut

1 1/8"
counterbore

Nylon
glide

Figure 3. Anatomy of an outfeed table

of power and have a tendency to cause materials to chip and splinter.

• Take a minute to make sure the motor and arbor pulleys are aligned. Misalignment can cause the belt to wear out faster, increase vibration, and use up valuable power. This can be easily checked with a straightedge. Hold it along the faces of the two pulleys—it should be in full contact with both of them.

• If your saw blade wobbles, use blade stabilizers to steady it. These large, heavy washers slip on the arbor on either side of the blade and help dampen vibrations. They're available from most mail-order woodworking supply houses.

• Consider replacing the motor on your saw with a larger one. A 10-inch saw really needs a 2- or 3-horsepower motor to drive it effectively. Check with the manufacturer to make sure your saw can handle the added power before upgrading.

Saw Alternatives

Not everyone has enough room around their saw to accommodate a full sheet of plywood. And sometimes it just doesn't work

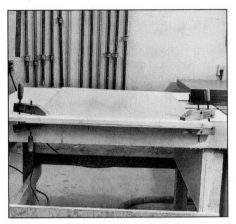

Photo 4. To straighten an edge, trim close to your layout line with a jigsaw, then clamp a straightedge along the cut and trim it with a flush-trim bit in a router.

Photo 5. To cut a piece at an odd angle on the table saw, attach a straightedge to the piece at the appropriate angle and guide it along the rip fence to make the cut.

to try to use the saw for a certain cut. There are ways of working around these difficulties.

What are these "work-arounds"? The easiest one still relies on the saw but doesn't require a lot of space. Just cut the plywood roughly to size with a hand-held jigsaw. Then true the edges on the table saw. If you do this, try to leave at least one factory edge on each piece. It's easier to square a piece up if you have one true edge to start with.

If you can't cut the pieces small enough to pass through the saw or if you end up with a piece without a true edge, all is not lost. Lay out a line on the panel to cut to. Then trim the piece down close to the line with a jigsaw. Clamp a straight length of plywood or another straightedge along this line, as shown in *Photo 4.* Turn the stock over and trim the plywood to the line with a 1-inch flush-trim bit in a router. This works well for straightening edges, squaring panels, and making angled cuts that would be difficult to accomplish on the table saw.

This trick can also be adapted to work on the table saw for cutting odd angles. Use small nails to attach a straightedge to the piece parallel to the line you wish to cut. The opposite side of the straightedge must overhang the workpiece entirely, as shown in *Photo 5.* Set the rip fence so the piece will be cut along the layout line as you run the straightedge along the fence.

Suppliers

Certainly Wood
11753 Big Tree Road
East Aurora, NY 14052
(716) 655-0206
Veneer

Cliffside Industries
P.O. Box 161
Lititz, PA 17543
(800) 873-9258
Pulls and hardware

Constantine's
2050 Eastchester Road
Bronx, NY 10461
(800) 223-8087
*Hardware, tools, veneer,
    and supplies*

Fixture Hardware Mfg. Corp.
4116 First Avenue
Brooklyn, NY 11232
(718) 499-9422
Shelf supports

Forms and Surfaces
Box 5215
Santa Barbara, CA 93150
(805) 684-8626
Pulls and hardware

**National Kitchen and
    Bath Association**
687 Willow Grove Street
Hackettstown, NJ 07840
(908) 852-0033
*Information and names
    of kitchen designers*

Outwater Hardware Corp.
11 West End Road
Totowa, NJ 07512
(201) 890-0940
Hardware and supplies

The Woodworkers' Store
21801 Industrial Boulevard
Rogers, MN 55374
(612) 428-2199
Hardware, tools, and supplies

INDEX

Note: Page references in **boldface** indicate photographs. *Italic* references indicate illustrations.